Heckler & Koch – Armorers of the Free World

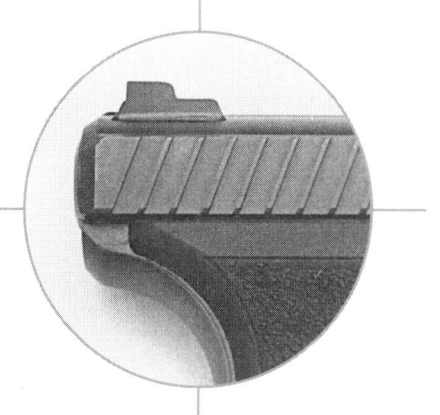

By
Gene
Gangarosa, Jr.

STOEGER PUBLISHING COMPANY

Title
Heckler & Koch – Armorers of the Free World

Staff
Project Coordinator: Studiocrafts
Design & Production Director: Dominick S. Sorrentino
Editor: William S. Jarrett
Design, Electronic Page Makeup & Photo Imaging:
   Lesley A. Notorangelo
Cover Photography: Ray Wells

Library of Congress Cataloging-in-Publication Data

Copyright 2001 by Gene Gangarosa, Jr.
All rights reserved. No part of this book may be produced or transmitted in any form or by any means, electronic or mechanical, including photocopying, recording, or by any information storage and retrieval system, without permission in writing from the Publisher.
Published by Stoeger Publishing Company
17603 Indian Head Highway
Accokeek, Maryland 20607

ISBN: 0-88317-229-1
Library of Congress Control No.: 00-135098
Manufactured in the United States of America

Distributed to the book trade and to the sporting goods trade by Stoeger Industries, 17603 Indian Head Highway, Accokeek, MD 20607

H&K

About The Author

Gene Gangarosa, Jr. is a teacher and technical writer whose four-year enlistment in the U.S. Navy (1977-1981) reinforced a lifelong interest in firearms. Since 1988, he has written hundreds of articles for most of the major gun magazines, including Combat Handguns, Gun World, Guns, Guns & Ammo and Petersen's Handguns. Gangarosa has also contributed several articles to Stoeger's annual Shooter's Bible in addition to writing several books published by Stoeger.

Books written by the author and published by Stoeger Publishing Co.:

Browning: Armorer to the World

Complete Guide to Classic Rifles

Complete Guide to Compact Handguns

Complete Guide to Modern Rifles

Complete Guide to Service Handguns

Modern Beretta Firearms

P38 Automatic Pistol

Spanish Handguns: The History of Spanish Pistols and Revolvers

The Walther Handgun Story

Gene Gangarosa, Jr.

Introduction

ARMING THE PROFESSIONALS

This book tells the story of the Heckler & Koch Company. Founded in West Germany after World War II, this firm has become world-famous for its creation of fine firearms. The company is also known for its innovative approaches, many of which have advanced the state of firearms design in significant ways. Heckler & Koch pistols, submachine guns, rifles and machine guns are in use by military and police forces throughout the world. Its sporting arms also enjoy wide distribution.

Heckler & Koch was founded in 1949 by three ex-Mauser employees—Edmund Heckler, Theodore Koch and Alex Seidel. For reasons unknown, Seidel's name was dropped from the incorporation papers. Thus the firm has always been known as Heckler & Koch. In 1949, German companies were not allowed to manufacture firearms, so the company's product line consisted initially of machine tools. The founders' interests always lay in firearms manufacture, however, and it was only a matter of time before the ban on firearms manufacture—imposed on defeated Germany in 1945 by the victorious Allies—was lifted. The term "Allies" refers to The United States, Great Britain and France. The fourth ally, the Soviet Union, was not involved in these decisions and disapproved of them. With the Cold War already underway, the three Western Allies combined their three occupation zones in Germany to create the German Federal Republic, better known as West Germany, in 1949.

When the Allied ban against West German firearms manufacture was lifted in 1955, West Germany was invited to assume its burden in the common defense—and Heckler & Koch was ready. A service rifle had already appeared on the company's drawing boards several years earlier, and would, after much development both in Spain and its native Germany, become the legendary G3 battle rifle. Using this weapon as a starting point, Heckler & Koch went on to develop the clever HK21 machine gun series, followed by the even more successful MP5 series submachine guns.

Heckler & Koch has also gained recognition as a designer of handguns. Its first pistol, the HK4, was built on prewar Mauser principles, but the later P9, P7 and USP series broke new ground. While not as successful as the G3 or MP5, H&K's pistols have gained considerable recognition. Witness the huge order for its Mark 23 pistol from the U.S. Special Operations Command.

Chapter 1 begins with the story of Heckler & Koch's pistols, from the little HK4 to the Mark 23 currently in service with U.S. Special Forces. The story continues in Chapter 2 with Heckler & Koch's military rifles, followed by separate chapters on sporting rifles and submachine guns (which became the world standard in that category). Chapter 4 ends with Heckler & Koch's efforts to remain competitive and innovative in the submachine gun arena.

Chapter 5 tells the story of Heckler & Koch's machine guns, followed by a full line of accessory products (Chapter 6). In addition to the production of miscellaneous items at their home factory in Oberndorf, Germany, Heckler & Koch has licensed production to several foreign countries (their story appears in Chapter 7). The book concludes with a complete history of H&K shotguns.

Not only are Heckler & Koch products innovative in design and construction, but their products are also remarkably durable and reliable. While some H&K guns may have their controversial points, not to mention a host of detractors, there can be no doubt that the members of elite forces in the United States and around the world owe their lives to the efficiency of Heckler & Koch weapons.

This book represents much time and effort on my part, but without the help of many other people I could not have finished it. Thanks, as always, go to my family for their patience and support. Stoeger's excellent staff and editorial team deserve praise as always. Moreover, Heckler & Koch personnel, both in the U.S. and Germany, have been most helpful, as was the staff at Benelli U.S.A. I acknowledge with gratitude all the help I received, but I take full responsibility for any errors that may have found their way into the text.

Table Of Contents

About The Author iii

Introduction iv

Chapter 1
The Handgun Story: From The HK4 To The Mark 23 7

Chapter 2
Military Rifles 63

Chapter 3
The Sporting Rifle Story 103

Chapter 4
Submachine Guns 123

Chapter 5
Farther And Faster: The H&K Machine Gun 153

Chapter 6
A Heckler & Koch Miscellany 175

Chapter 7
Worldwide Copying Of Heckler & Koch Designs 199

Chapter 8
The Shotgun Story 215

Appendix A: 50 Years of Leading Through Technology 255

Appendix B: A Sampling Of Current H&K Products 269

Index 283

The durability requirements set forth by the U.S. armed forces were daunting indeed. These included 30,000-round endurance shots, plus mud and saltwater corrosion tests run by the U.S. Army. The all-steel Colt pistol fell short. By contrast, Heckler & Koch's experimental USSOCOM model showed enough promise to pursue it further......

Chapter 1

THE HANDGUN STORY: FROM THE HK4 TO THE MARK 23

While developing the rifle that would eventually become the G3 (see Chapter 2), Heckler & Koch was also pursuing a potentially lucrative business in handguns. The company began pistol production in 1956 with the medium-frame HK4, which mirrored the Mauser HSc pistol of the 1930s in dimensions, features and even in appearance. This was a logical development, thanks to Alex Seidel, one of the Heckler & Koch founders, who led the design team responsible for developing the HSc pistol at Mauser-Werke nearly 20 years earlier. The HK4 was by no means a slavish copy of the HSc, however, primarily because Heckler & Koch had taken steps to reduce the manufacturing costs.

Based on German research during World War II, the HK4 featured a simplified slide, one of the most difficult and time-consuming elements involved in the manufacture of pistols. By making this component using a stamping process, H&K greatly reduced the time and expense involved in making this pistol. The company later applied this same technology to its rifles. While the slide may appear flimsy by comparison with one machined from a traditional steel forging, H&K compensated by including a replaceable plastic buffer in the

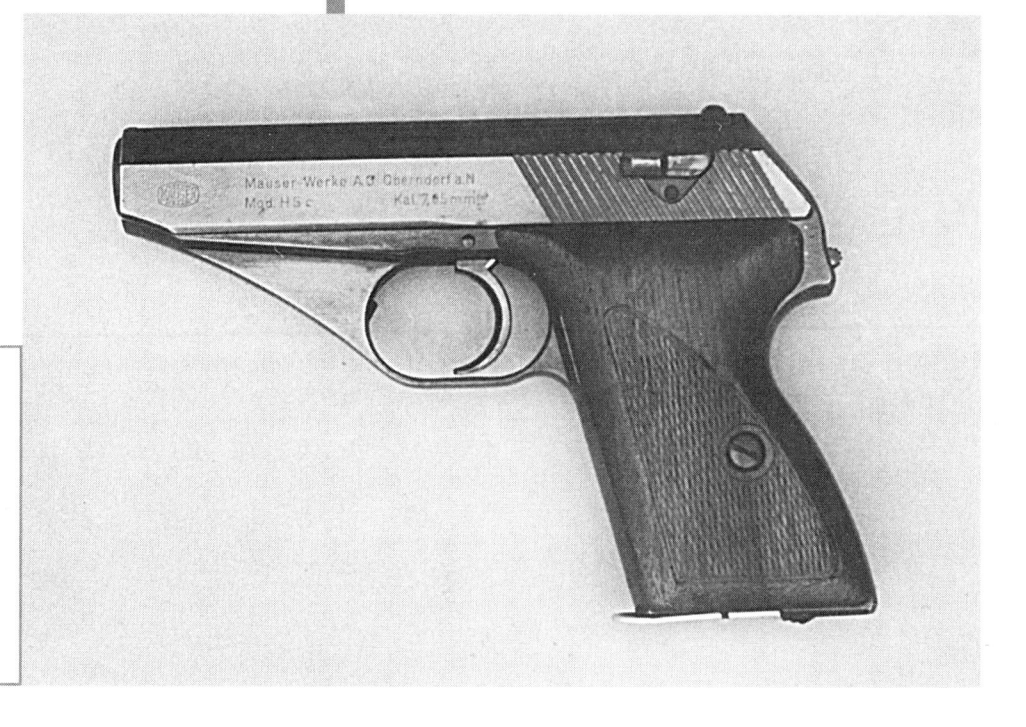

The Mauser Model HSc, introduced in 1940 and produced in modified form after World War II until the 1980s, formed the major inspiration for Heckler & Koch's first handgun, the HK4.

Chapter One 7

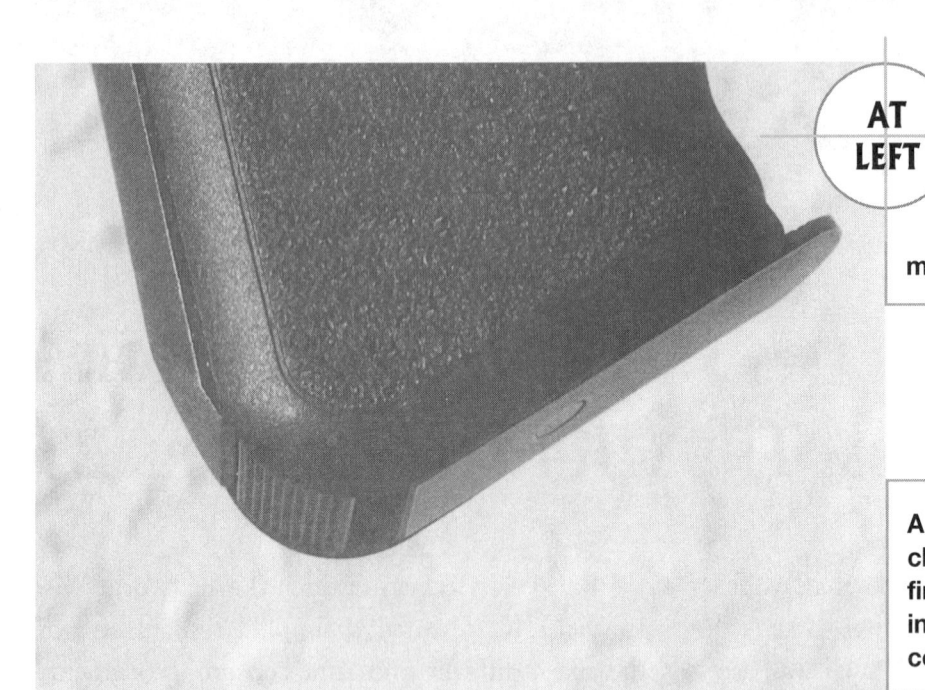

AT LEFT The P7PSP uses a bottom magazine release which pushes forward to release the magazine from the gun.

BELOW A shooter could also purchase a .22 Long Rifle rimfire conversion kit for the P7K3 in .32 ACP or .380 ACP (photo courtesy of Heckler & Koch.

AT RIGHT

The P7 uses the three-dot sights now most popular among modern "tactical" handguns, but at the time the gun first appeared this was another innovation. Painted white dots come standard, but green illuminated night sights made of radioactiv tritium are also available as an option.

BELOW

The P7's (bottom) gas-operated breech delay makes it appreciably slimmer than Walther's competing P5 (right), which relies on the comparaively bulky underbarrel locking block first introduced in the Walther P38.

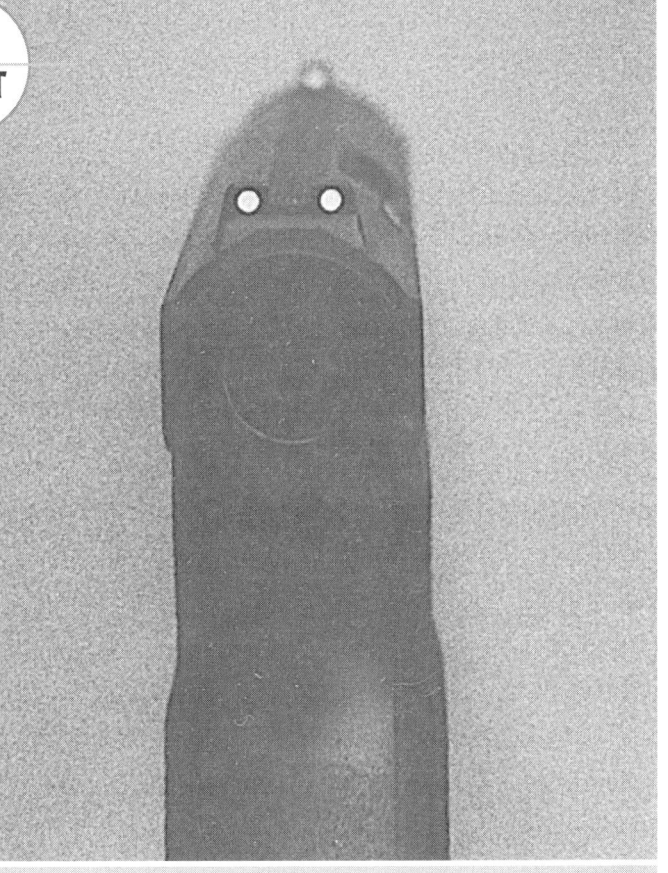

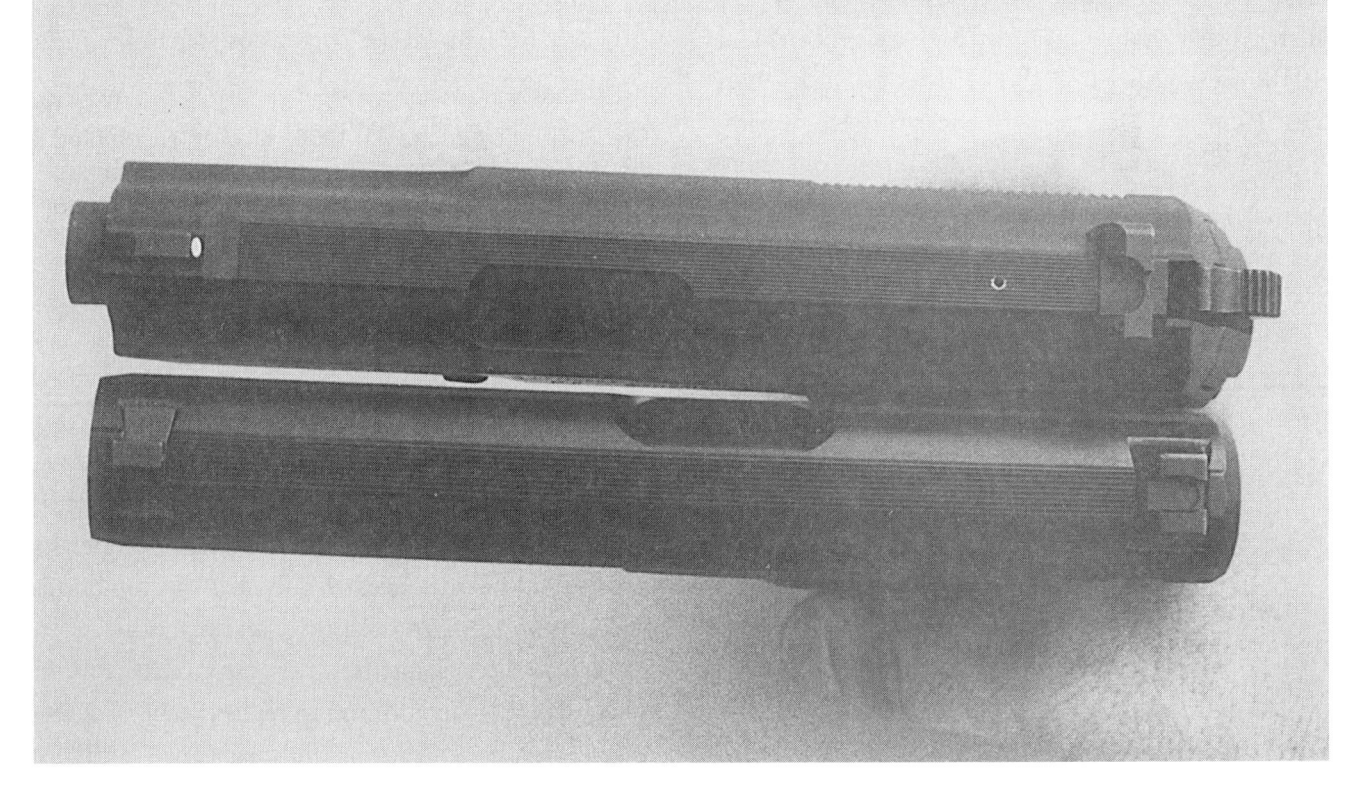

Chapter One

frame, just above the triggerguard. The result was to soften the impact of the slide against the frame during recoil. The inclusion of this buffer significantly improved slide longevity.

Like the Walther PP/PPK series, the HK4 featured a double-action trigger mechanism for the first shot, after which the slide automatically cocked the hammer for single-action shooting. The safety catch on the left rear portion of the HK4's slide operates much the same as that of a Walther PP or PPK. You push it up to the fire position and down to the safe setting. The magazine release appears in the

> **Because the slide is typically one of the most complicated parts of an automatic pistol, using a stamped steel slide significantly reduced the amount of time and expense in manufacturing the HK4.**

lower rear portion of the grip—the so-called "heel" position—and pushes back to release the magazine. This heel magazine-release position appears in many other handguns, notably the FN Model 1910, the Walther P38 and Heckler & Koch's own PSP/P7 model (see below). Though not especially favored by American shooters, this type of magazine release—in contrast to the side-mounted magazine release button featured on the German Parabellum ("Luger") and Colt Model 1911 pistols—is ambidextrous. It's unlikely to release by accident and, since the magazine can only be removed by one's hand, it's not likely to be damaged or lost.

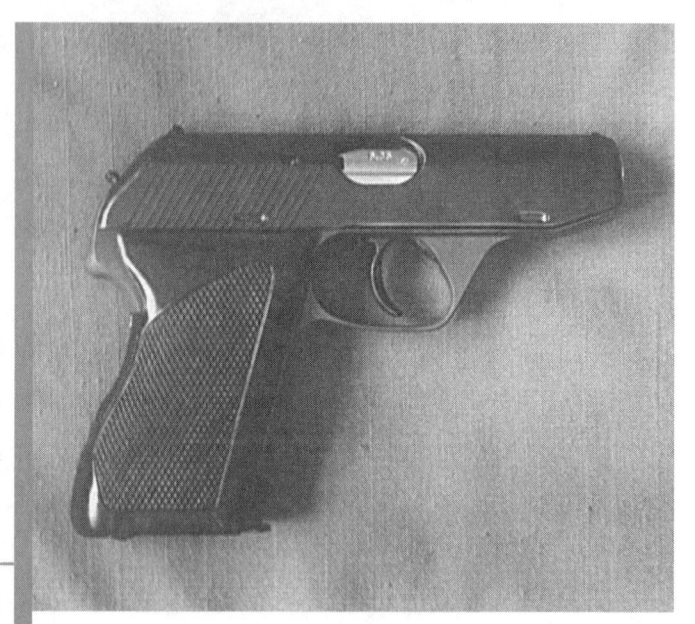

Undoubtedly the HK4's most remarkable feature was its four-caliber conversion capability. The

> **The HK4, introduced in 1956, closely resembled the Mauser HSc externally but used simplified construction techniques pioneered during World War Two but never adequately implemented until years later.**

same gun fired .22 Long Rifle, .25 ACP (6.35mm Browning), .32 ACP (7.65mm Browning) and .380 ACP (9mm Browning Short or 9mm *Kurz*) ammunition, with all but one being centerfire cartridges. To convert an HK4 from one centerfire caliber to another, the owner needed only to swap the barrel (with its attached recoil spring) and magazine.

In .22 Long Rifle, however, the caliber conversion involved—in addition to replacement with the proper barrel/recoil spring and magazine—a differ-

10 Heckler & Koch

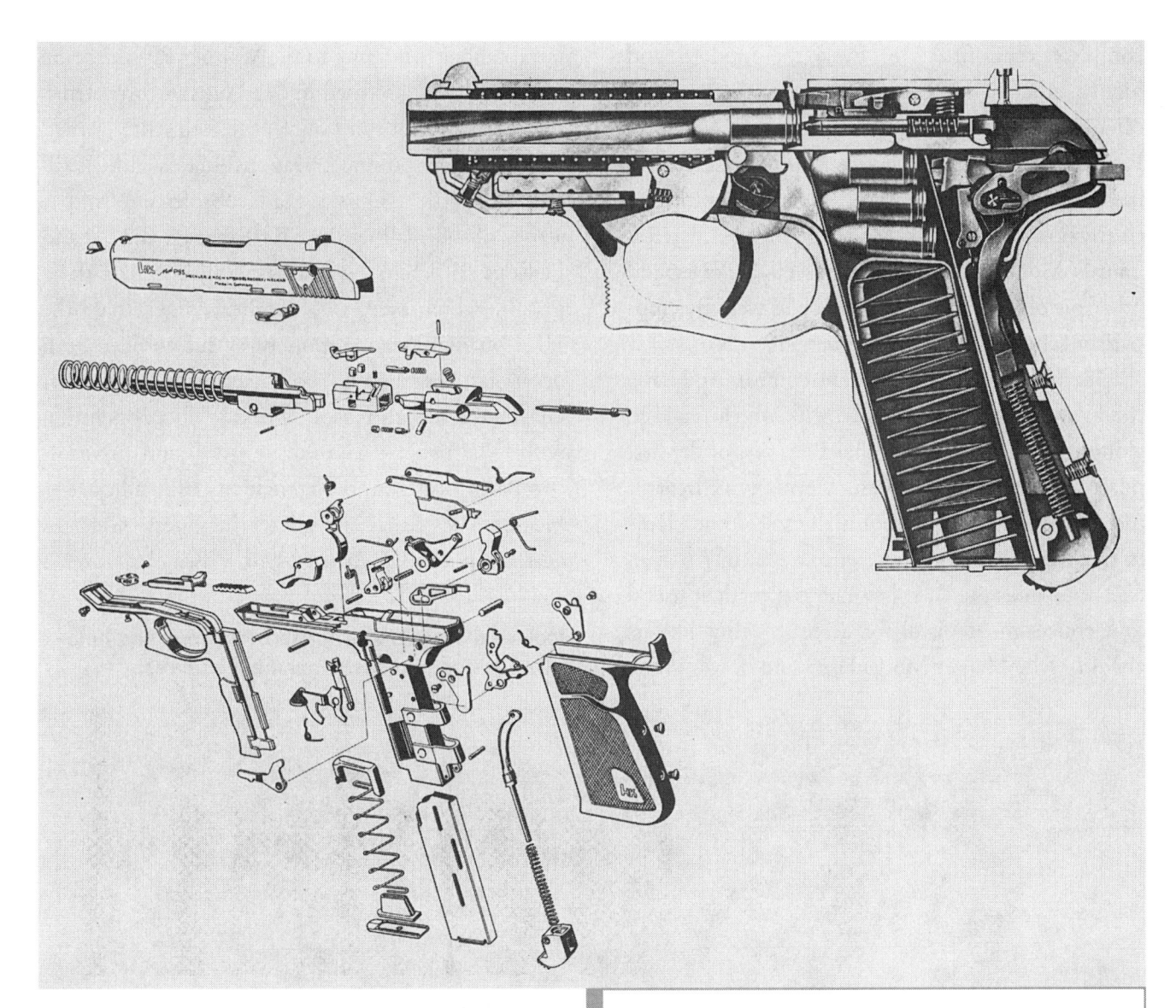

ent firing pin, one that struck the rimfire primers on the side rather than directly at the rear of the cartridge case. The recoil plate on this pistol is marked "Z" for centerfire cartridge firing and "R" for rimfire cartridge firing positions. After the extractor was pulled out and pinned in that position, the recoil plate was removed from the slide with a combination tool. When reversing the recoil plate to its "R"-marked side, the recoil plate was replaced, taking care to line up the firing pin with the matching hole in the recoil plate. The recoil plate was then screwed tightly in place. Unpinning the extractor allowed it to snap back into proper position.

> **The P9 series perpetuated the HK4's stamped sheet steel slide with separate breechblock. It did, however, add the roller-locked breech pioneered in the G3 military rifle as a way to contain the pressures of the more powerful 9mm Parabellum and .45 ACP caliber cartridges.**

As a result, the HK4 owner had, in essence, four guns in one. In these caliber conversions, it's not necessary to replace the entire slide assembly, a step that makes most caliber conversions quite expensive. For instance, in the Walther P38 series, a .22LR caliber conversion kit—a replacement slide, barrel and magazine—costs nearly as much as a

Chapter One 11

complete centerfire P38. Even the modern and highly efficient .22LR caliber conve4rsion unit offered by SIG with its legendary P210 9mm Parabellum service pistol adds $300 to the cost of the gun. And the highly regarded Ciener rimfire conversion kits for the Model 1911, the Beretta/Taurus Model 92, the Browning High Power and other pistols cost nearly that much as well. By comparison, the HK4 was quite a bargain.

Heckler & Koch wasted no time introducing the HK4. It first appeared in 1956, which made it, along with the revived Walther P38, one of the first postwar products of West Germany's firearms industry. Heckler & Koch initially sold some HK4s to the West German police, who used it in 7.65mm (.32) caliber as the P11. Its small size made it useful as a concealment pistol for detectives, but like its ancestor (the Mauser Model HSc) and pistols in the same caliber belonging to the Walther PP series, the HK4/P11 was also used in open holster carry. Until the 1970s, European police were frequently armed with such low-powered weapons. Like Walther's PP and PPK, the P11 was made obsolescent by the arrival of the Walther P5, SIG/Sauer P6 (P225) and Heckler & Koch's own P7 or PSP. The last three pistols, which were only slightly larger than the HK4 but significantly more powerful, fulfilled both open carry and concealment missions for West Germany's police forces. Working in cooperation with Manurhin—a machine tool and firearms company located in the French city of Mulhouse—Heckler & Koch supplied the West German customs police (*Zollpolizei*) with HK4s. However, a

Heckler & Koch's ads for the P9S stressed innovative design and useful handling features.

treaty signed after World War II forbade the Mulhouse police from using German-made firearms. To avoid infringing this treaty, Heckler & Koch sent unassembled HK4 parts kits to France, where Manurhin technicians assembled them into complete pistols, test-fired and proofed them (with French proofmarks, of course) and then stamped their slides with Manurhin (not Heckler & Koch) markings. About 500 of these French/German HK4s/P11s ultimately found their way into the United States.

The HK4 had an illustrious commercial history as well, beginning with Harrington & Richardson's importation of the pistol as the HK4. Upon the creation in the mid-1970s of Heckler & Koch, Inc. as the U.S. sales agent for the Heckler & Koch parent firm in Oberndorf, West Germany, importation of the HK4 shifted to this new company. Most HK4s encountered in the U.S. bear the markings of Harrington & Richardson, which imported the pistol during the years of its maximum interest in the United States, which was never great. Part of the problem was the high price. When Harrington & Richardson first began importation, it charged $99.50, but by 1978 the suggested retail price of the complete gun in the four-caliber set had increased to $310. By comparison, the Colt Government Model sold for $250, while Browning's High Power retailed for around $290. In an effort to hold down the price, H&K's American affiliate offered an HK4 model in .380 caliber for only $197 and a .380 pistol with a .22 Long Rifle conversion kit for $230. Still, there were relatively few takers—in the United States, at least—and exportation of the HK4 to the United States came to a halt in 1984. In Europe, where its versatility and quality were recognized by a more discerning market, HK4 sales were much better. The pistol remained in limited German police service until the mid-1980s before it was supplanted by more advanced compact 9mm pistols. Later, a small civilian following allowed Heckler & Koch to keep the model in production until 1990.

Despite the seeming complexity of its four-caliber mechanism, the HK4 is not a difficult handgun to handle. Its caliber conversions are relatively easy, its size is convenient, and the trigger pull, in both double and single action, is reasonably responsive and well suited to a service pistol. A logical updating of the impressive Mauser HSc design, the HK4 represented a good first step for Heckler & Koch.

SPECIFICATIONS: HK4

Overall Length: 6.2"

Barrel Length: 3.35"

Height: 4.33"

Weight: 16.9 ounces

Caliber Options/Capacity:
.22 Long Rifle/8
.25 ACP (6.35mm)/8
.32 ACP (7.65mm)/8
.380 ACP (9mmk)/7

P9 Series

While the success at the HK4 included limited police acceptance, Heckler & Koch was eager to create a full-fledged military pistol. The initial caliber choice was the 9mm Parabellum, which had been the standard of the German service since DWM created the most famous variant of the Luger pistol to fire that round.

The P9 first appeared in 1970 **(photo p. 11)**. Unlike the HK4, it was designed to use a breech locking mechanism, because of the more powerful cartridges it used. Several breech-locking designs were available, but Heckler & Koch sensibly chose a slight variation of the roller-locking design it was using with such success in its G3 military rifle (see following chapter). The P9 was not, however, the world's first mass-produced automatic pistol to feature this method of locking the breech. That honor belongs to the Czech vz. 52, the service pistol of Czechoslovakia from its introduction in 1952 until its replacement in 1983.

Compared to pistols of the World War II era still in widespread military use at the time, the P9 featured advanced construction techniques

> **At distances up to 25 feet, where most pistol combats occur, a double-action only trigger, such as the VP70's, is one of the best. Note this 1.3-inch, five-shot offhand group, with all but one within 7/10ths of an inch, all fired from 25 feet with a double-action only trigger mechanism.**

designed to reduce cost and time in the manufacturing process. As with the roller-locked breech, Heckler & Koch drew from its own experience with the G3 service rifle in adapting these nontraditional production materials and methods to the P9. The receiver or frame of this pistol consisted of heavy-gauge sheet steel stampings welded together. Guides for the slide were pressed into the upper portion of the frame. The triggerguard/front gripstrap was a single piece of plastic pinned to the frame. From 1977 on, this triggerguard evolved into a recurved shape, which was then in style. Heckler & Koch also made the slide on its P9 from heavy gauge sheet steel stamping. A separate breechblock, made of steel milled to shape in the traditional way, fit inside the slide. As with the company's own G3 service rifle, the P9 featured polygonal rifling in the barrel bore. Its hammer was fully concealed by the slide.

> **The VP70, introduced in 1972, offered several innovations that were then radical but are now quite commonplace, including a polymer frame, all double-action lockwork and a double-column, high-capacity magazine. Note the pushbutton manual safety on the triggerguard and the magazine release on the heel (bottom rear) of the frame (photo courtesy of Heckler & Koch).**

As a result, the company added a cocked-hammer indicator in the form of a signal pin. Located in the rear of the slide, this pin protruded straight back with the hammer cocked and was concealed inside the slide when the hammer was uncocked. A lever located in the front edge of the left grip, when depressed, cocked (or decocked) the hammer. This multi-purpose lever could also release the slide after

The PSP, reintroduced in 1998, harks back to the original 1970s PSP.

it locked open on the last shot. No other post-World War II handgun boasted an operating lever quite like this one. The closest was Sauer's Model 38H, an excellent .32 caliber automatic pistol used by the German police and armed forces during World War II.

A manual safety, located on the left side of the slide, pushed up to safe and down to fire. It was quite similar in appearance, location and operation to the manual safety lever found on the world-famous Walther PP and PPK models. P9-type pistols also featured a loaded-chamber indicator, but this was more like a Beretta's than a Walther's, wherein the extractor extended outward from the slide whenever a cartridge was in the firing chamber.

Once more in the time-honored European fashion, Heckler & Koch placed the magazine release on the bottom rear (or heel) portion of the frame. With this release pushed back, one could then reach up to the magazine floorplate and withdraw the magazine all the way.

The original P9 (1970-vintage) was a single action design. But in 1972 Heckler & Koch introduced the P9S with a double action trigger. It was designed to appeal to European agencies in particular because they preferred the double action capability typified in the Walther P38, which was then a highly popular pistol in military and police service. For a time, Heckler & Koch kept both P9 and P9S variants in production simultaneously, dropping the single action P9 in 1978.

The .45 caliber P9S followed the standard 9mm model. Announced in 1975, deliveries began in 1977. This pistol was slightly larger than the standard 9mm P9S, but its magazine capacity was reduced by two rounds. Oddly, the .45 caliber variant weighed slightly less than the standard 9mm model. Heckler & Koch also offered a 7.65mm Parabellum chambering for sale in countries like Italy and Brazil, which forbid private ownership of firearms in military calibers. The 7.65mm conversion was easy, since the 9mm cartridge was based on the 7.65mm cartridge case that opened up to accept a wider bullet. The 7.65mm variant was identical to the 9mm model in every dimension and performance specification except for the caliber marking on the slide.

From the beginning, the P9-series pistols boasted excellent sights, usually with white or colored highlights painted on. These generally took the form of a single white stripe that ran down the back of the front sight and white or red stripes on either side of the rear sight. The rear sight featured a square-cut notch for improved elevation control.

Chapter One 15

AT LEFT The P7K3, in this instance a .380 ACP model, is capable of good accuracy.

BELOW Heckler & Koch has parlayed the USP0's extreme ruggedness and reliability into sales to hundreds of U.S. police agencies (photo courtesy of Heckler & Koch).

16 Heckler & Koch

AT RIGHT

The P7M10 fired the .40 S&W cartridge, which from its 1990 introduction has become highly popular in U.S. police service.

BELOW

The early Mark 23 used a squarish suppressor developed in-house at Heckler & Koch, but the unit did not perform as hoped during rigorous testing (photo courtesy of Heckler & Koch).

Chapter One 17

The West German military adopted the PSP (bottom) in 1980 as its P7 to replacing the Walther P1 or P38 (top).

The P9 is important historically because it was among the first automatic pistols with truly excellent sights. Moreover, the P9s had above average trigger pulls, particularly in single action. Even

The P7's short barrel makes it difficult for an adversary to grasp and wrest away from its owner, whereas the efficient 9mm Parabellum cartridge develops most of its velocity from a short barrel, especially one equipped with low-friction polygonal rifling like the P7.

in the later P9S model, the double action trigger pull, while long, was very smooth. This combination—large sights, a good crisp trigger pull and a recoil system that kept the barrel in a straight line at all times—all added up to an extremely accurate weapon.

Disassembly was simple, always a positive feature in a firearm destined for military service. After removing the magazine, the slide is drawn back, ejecting a round that might still be in the firing chamber and cocking the hammer. Next, the barrel release latch (located inside the triggerguard) is pushed up while the slide moves forward, separating it from the frame. Finally the barrel is detached from the slide by pushing the barrel forward until it could be lifted from the slide. The breechblock could also be removed from the slide, but this was not required for normal cleaning and maintenance.

To take advantage of the excellent accuracy potential inherent in the P9's design, Heckler & Koch introduced the P9S Sport (or Target) model. It had an adjustable rear sight with a tall, matching front sight and a muzzle weight in the front. Some sport models featured a barrel measuring one inch longer than standard. Its stock consisted of an enlarged, target pistol-style hardwood grip, lending full support for a shooter's wrist

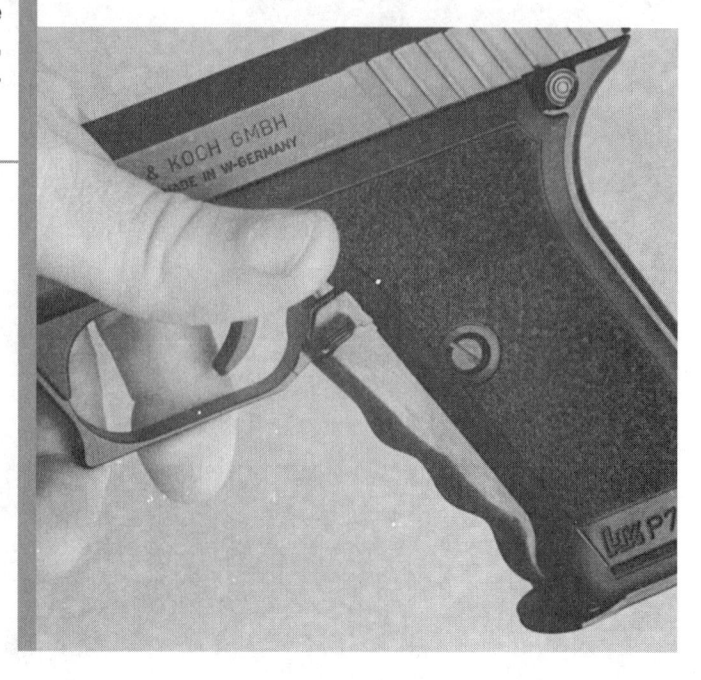

Saarland and West Germany's Federal Ministry of the Interior both issued the P9 along with special units of the *Bundesgrenschütz* (West German border police). The U.S. Navy SEALS also made limited use of a modified P9S during the 1980s, fitting the higher sights of the P9S Sport so that a sound suppressor could be installed without its bulk obscuring the shooter's view. The Navy pistols also had three-shot burst selectors, a feature of only limited utility on a pistol limited to nine rounds in its magazine.

Above. The P7 (top) is only slightly larger than a small Smith & Wesson revolver like the .38 Special Model 638 Bodyguard (below); however, the all-steel P7 weighs as much as most 9mm service pistols.

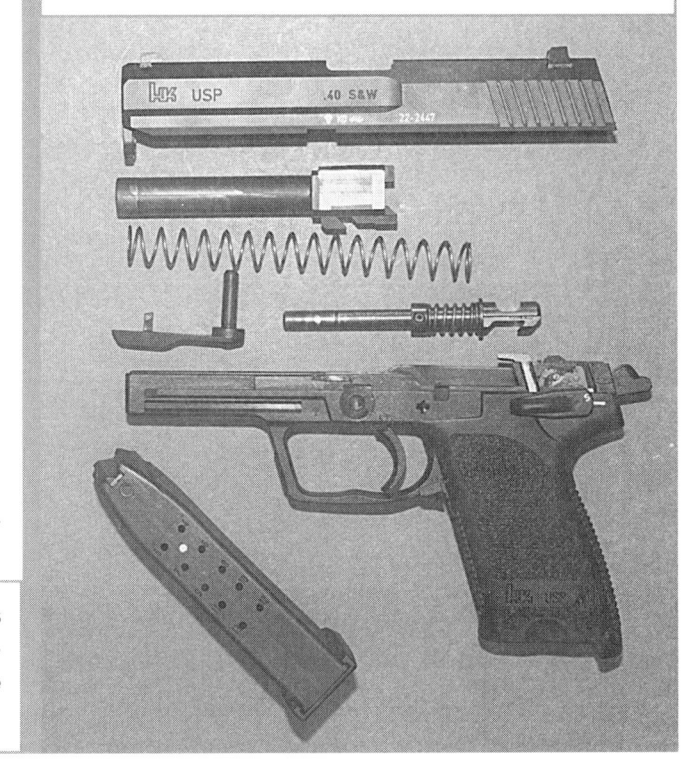

and forearm. Demand for such a specialized (and expensive) weapon was too slight and production too limited, forcing Heckler & Koch to stop production of this model in 1984. The company had made so many of these pistols, however, that its U.S. importer didn't sell out inventory until 1989, five years following the end of production. Heckler & Koch also offered a P9S Competition kit. It included an extra 5-inch barrel with muzzle weight, an enlarged walnut grip and two slides. It sold in only limited numbers and production stopped in 1984.

While the P9 never seriously threatened the well-established Colt M1911A1/Government Model, the FN/Browning High Power or the Walther P38, it did serve notice that new designs were on the horizon. The West German state of

At Right. The USP-series pistols disassemble as shown. Note the patented spring buffer mechanism at the rear of the breech mechanism above the receiver.

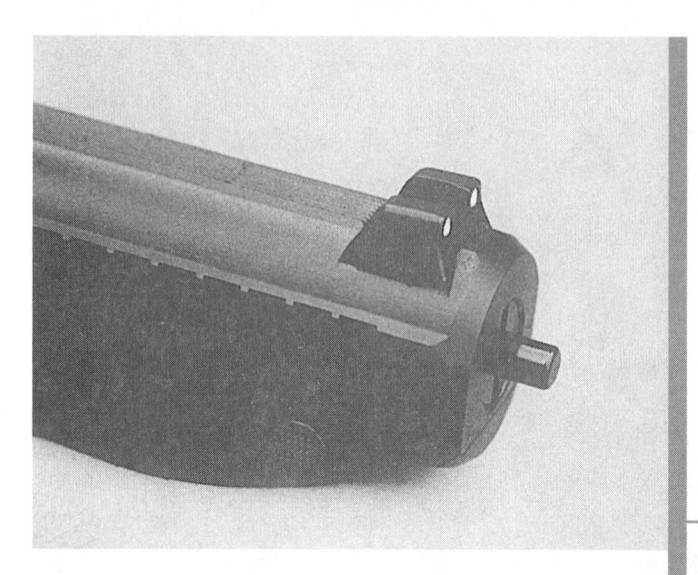

During its 20-year production run, the P9 series passed through an amazing series of price increases. In 1970, the suggested retail price for a P9 was $179, rising in 1978 to $329.95 for a standard P9S. By 1984 it had reached $1,299. Suggested retail price for the Competition Model was $369.95 in 1978, rising to $1,382 in 1984. These meteoric price increases, along with the advent of increasingly sophisticated 9mm pistols from its competitors, forced Heckler & Koch to quite production of all P9-series pistols in 1990.

Compared to modern 9mm service pistols, the P9S looks dated, but at the time of its introduction this model represented a remarkable advance. Compared to the previous trailblazer—the Walther P38, a design dating from the late 1930s—the P9 definitely advanced the state of the art in handgun design. Even today, the P9/P9S-series pistols rank high among the most accurate automatic pistol types ever made.

VP70

Always innovative, Heckler & Koch followed up its P9 Series with the equally pleasing VP70 **(photo p. 14)**. Introduced in 1972, it offered a seemingly anachronistic reversion to the machine pistol concept (i.e., an automatic pistol capable of selective fire), briefly popular in the 1890s at the birth of the automatic pistol era. The VP70 was extremely innovative and years ahead of its time. For instance, H&K made extensive use of plastic in the receiver and reinforced in critical areas by steel. This made the VP70 the first of what is now a flood of guns using similar construction.

The VP70 employed other original touches later copied by other manufacturers. Most notable was a high-capacity magazine that held up to 18 rounds of 9mm Parabellum ammunition. In common with European handgun

The P7's cocked-striker indicator protrudes once the shooter has depressed the cocking lever located at the front of the grip frame.

SPECIFICATIONS: HK P9 SERIES

	Standard	.45	Sport
Overall Length (in.)	7.55	8.01	9.0
Barrel Length (in.)	4.0	4.06	4.0/5.5
Height (in.)	5.55	5.55	5.5
Width (in.)	1.33	1.33	1.33
Weight (lbs.)	32.6 ounces	32.5 ounces	35.0 ounces
Caliber/Capacity	9mm/9 rounds	.45 ACP/7	9mm/9 rounds

At right. The P7's extractor, located just behind the ejection port, functions as a loaded-chamber indicator by standing out slightly from the slide once the shooter has introduced a cartridge into the firing chamber. Here the extractor lies flat against the slide, indicating an empty (unloaded) firing chamber.

designs at the time, Heckler & Koch placed the VP70's magazine release in the bottom rear (heel) of the grip frame. In another forward-looking step, the VP70 had a double-action only trigger mechanism, eliminating the need for a manual safety. Its front sight featured a deep vertical cut surrounded by two polished metal ramps highlighting the front sight in virtually all weather and light conditions. Obtaining a quick view of the front sight is always important for shooting.

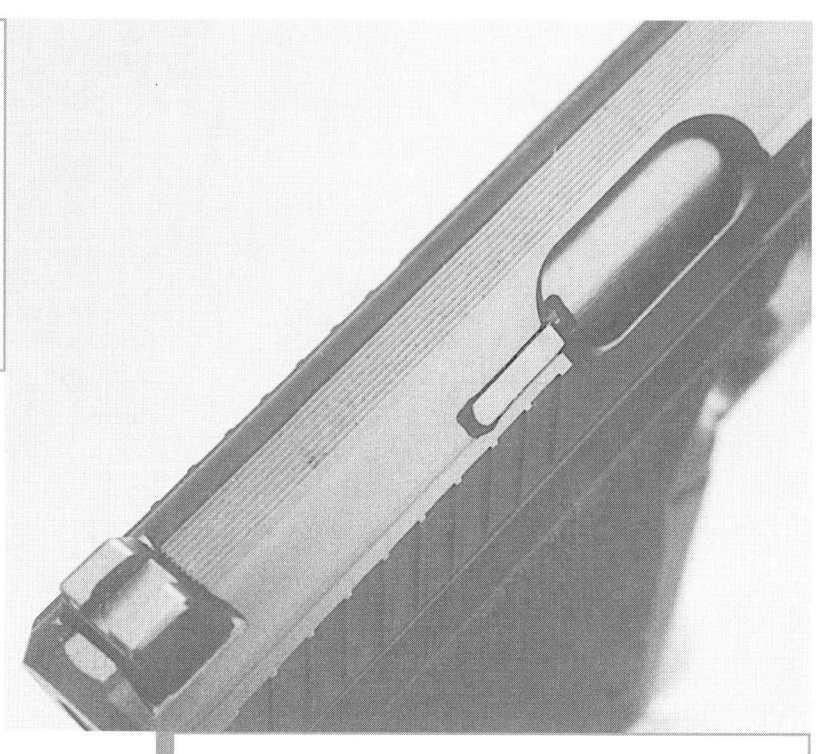

Below. Once an adult shooter places three fingers on the P7's squeeze-cocking lever, its 15 pounds of pressure are easily manageable. Note the cocked-striker indicator protruding from the rear of the slide in this view.

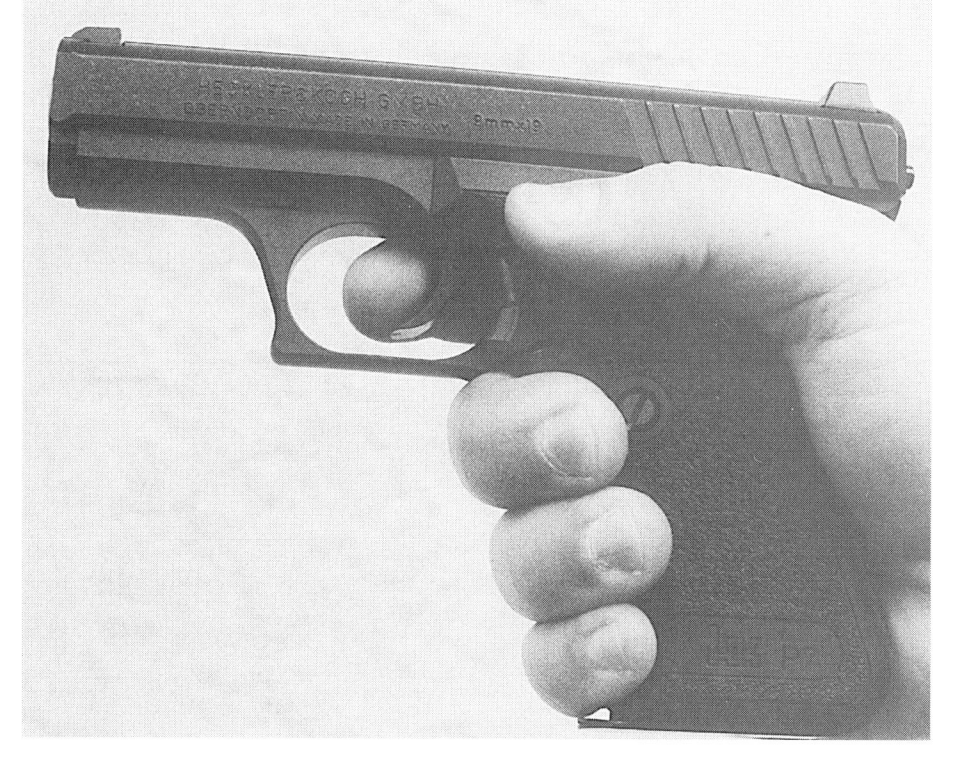

The VP70 allowed this in a fashion rarely equaled since. These sights were not set up for precise target shooting, but rather for a fast sight picture in the rough and tumble of combat at close quarters, where a fast-shooting pistol containing lots of ammunition could make all the difference.

The bane of most machine pistols is poor accuracy, mostly because these weapons climb uncontrollably after the second or third shot of fully-automatic fire, thereby wasting the gun's rapid-fire capability.

Chapter One

AT LEFT — The USP40 is also available in a compact model (photo courtesy of Heckler & Koch)

BELOW — Completing the USP's cartridge options, Heckler & Koch introduced in 1995 the USP in a .45 ACP variant (designated USP45). The stainless steel slide (shown) is optional (photo courtesy of Heckler & Koch).

AT RIGHT: The Mark 23 combines USP technology with some high-performance features demanded by the government (photo courtesy of Heckler & Koch).

BELOW: H&K introduced the USP model chambered for the 9mm Parabellum cartridge in 1993, naming it the USP9 (photo courtesy of Heckler & Koch).

Chapter One 23

After removing the magazine (a) and unloading the firing chamber of the P7 by drawing the slide fully to the rear (b), firing pin (c) can be removed.

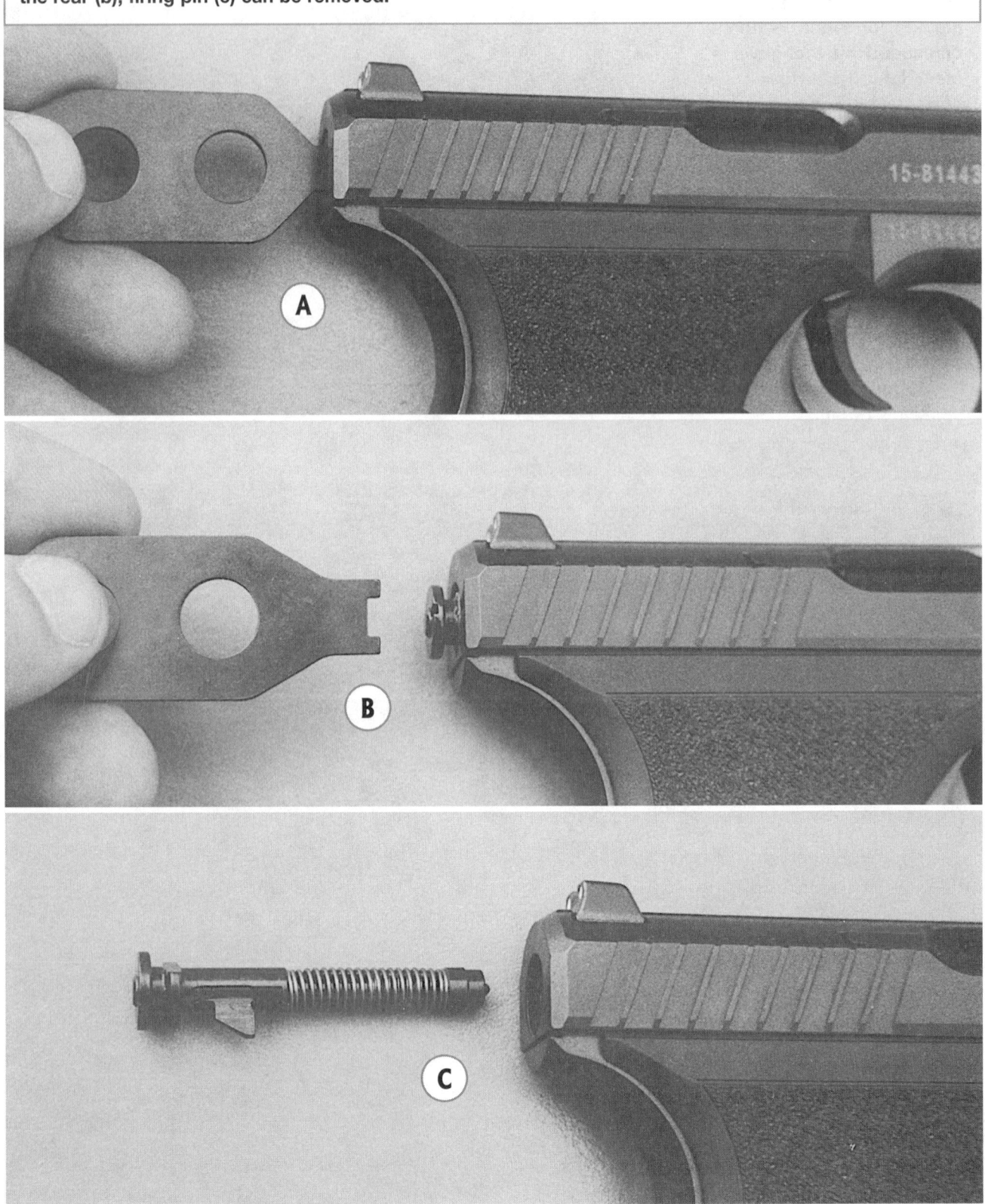

To prevent this wild spraying of ammunition, the Heckler & Koch engineers developed an ingenious rate-reducing mechanism. Located in the stock, the VP70's selective-fire mechanism (when set on "3") produced a three-shot burst for each pull on the trigger at a cyclic rate of 2200 rounds per minute. As a result, the entire burst would hit on or near the target, because there wasn't enough time between shots for the muzzle to climb significantly. In addition, the burst mode would not fire unless the shoulder stock was fitted. Without the stock, the pistol functioned like any other semiautomatic pistol; i.e., limited to one shot for each pull of the trigger. For even greater accuracy, shooters could select single-shot (i.e., semiautomatic fire) capability by implementing "1" on the selector switch.

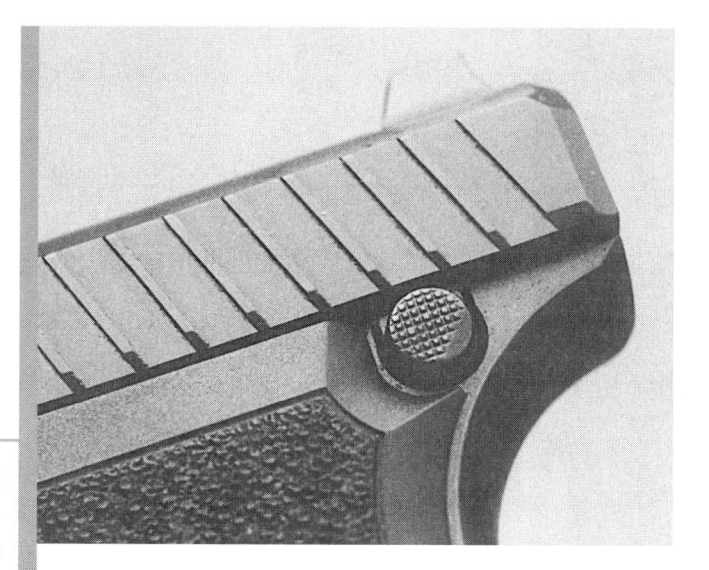

The original disassembly button on the P7, located high on the frame just below the slide, was checkered as shown. Heckler & Koch reintroduced this style with the P7PSP, replacing the circular style of the P7M8 and P7M13 series.

Because of the VP70's size and weight, no locking device was included in its breech mechanism. The inertia of the massive slide, plus the forward thrust of the recoil spring, held the breech closed at the moment of firing. This simple "blowback" system was usually reserved for handguns chambered in much smaller cartridges than the high-pressure 9mm Parabellum. Heckler & Koch also deepened the rifling grooves, allowing some of the propellant gases to blow past the bullet on their way out of the muzzle. A slight drop-off in muzzle velocity—typically around 100 feet per second—could in theory prevent some types of hollow-point ammunition from expanding as desired. Nevertheless, this modified rifling system achieved its goal: making a 9mm Parabellum blowback pistol that worked. Whether a shooter selects fully-

The P7's field-stripped components include (top to bottom) the slide, recoil spring, frame (barrel stays attached), and magazine.

Chapter One   25

burst mode is excellent at ranges within 50 feet or so. In single-shot mode, accuracy is acceptable on man-sized targets out to 50 yards or so, although the stiff double-action-only trigger inhibited accuracy beyond that distance. Up close, however, where a pistol is meant to be used, the VP70 excelled at placing fast, accurate shots on demand. In my experience, automatic pistols with double-action-only trigger mechanisms are as accurate as any competing handgun type out to 25 feet (the distance at which most handgun combat takes place).

The P7M8 differs from the original P7 with an insulation block added around the forward top portion of the triggerguard, shielding the hand from the gas mechanism, which can become extremely hot during extended strings of rapid fire.

automatic or semi-automatic mode, the gun is a pleasure to shoot. It's worth noting as well that Heckler & Koch built this pistol for military service. In most instances, international treaties, such as The Hague Convention (ratified in 1908), prevented military forces from using hollowpoint bullets.

In a bid to interest civilian shooting enthusiasts in its design, Heckler & Koch introduced a commercial variant in 1979 known as the VP70Z (Z="Zivil," or "Civil"), at which time Heckler & Koch renamed the original selective-fire variant the VP70M (M="Military"). The VP70Z, without its shoulder-stock attachment, was limited to only one shot per trigger pull. H&K displayed a sensitivity to liability concerns by adding a crossbolt-type manual safety button to the pistol's lower triggerguard area (it was also offered as an optional feature on the military VP70/VP70M).

The VP70 series—particularly the original selective-fire VP70—offered a number of advantages over conventional handgun design, including increased firepower. Accuracy with the three-shot

Despite its large magazine capacity, the VP70's all-plastic grip ensures a compact unit that's easy to handle. It's rugged as well. The engineers at Heckler & Koch built in a 30,000-round service life for this weapon, despite a more extensive use of plastic than in any previous firearm, while also firing the high-pressure 9mm Parabellum cartridge. Moreover, the VP70 is easy to maintain and service. To disassemble it, the magazine is removed using the bottom magazine release. Next, the slide is drawn back all the way in order to unload the firing chamber. The striker assembly, located at the rear of the slide, is removed, using a cartridge rim or screwdriver blade to turn the striker assembly counterclockwise. The takedown yoke, located in the triggerguard, is then

Heckler & Koch

pulled straight down and the slide pulled to the rear, up and forward over the recoil spring. The barrel remains on the frame and should not be removed.

In 1978, as part of a long series of service trials designed to select 9mm Parabellum handguns for the armed forces, the U.S. Air Force conducted tests

At Right. Whereas the original P7 had a checkered disassembly button latch, the P7M8 and P7M13 had a series of concentric circles etched on it, as shown.

of the VP70. The results were disastrous. The accuracy tests, conducted from both offhand shooting and a clamped machine rest, were failures along with the harsh environment and endurance trials. The last-named was particularly embarrassing. Of 771 rounds fired, 127 failed to load, producing a "mean rounds between system failure" (MRBS) rat-

The P7M8, unlike the original P7, had a lanyard loop (shown) where the original PSP/P7's magazine release was located.

ing of only five rounds. The VP70, like most European handguns chambered for the 9mm Parabellum cartridge, relies on ammunition loaded close to the upper end of the scale. The U.S.-made ammunition supplied for the tests wasn't "hot" enough to operate the VP70 properly. The Spanish Star Model 28 suffered a similarly dismal showing in this test for exactly the same reason.

The VP70's disadvantages in these tests included a bulky slide and a trigger system that was not understood nor appreciated at the time. As a submachine gun design, its stock wobbled slightly when in use, while offer-

Chapter One 27

The P7K3 offers a choice of two popular small centerfire chamberings: .32 ACP and .380 ACP .22 Long Rifle rimfire (photo courtesy of Heckler & Koch).

ing no real size advantage (with the stock fitted) over small submachine guns like the Micro-Uzi, or even Heckler & Koch's own MP5K. In any case, the gun was considered too eccentric for the time period in which it appeared. Had the VP70 come along ten years later, the world might have been ready for it. Indeed, most of its salient design features (except the burst-fire system) that made it an oddity when Heckler & Koch first produced it have since become commonly preferred assets in an automatic pistol.

In retrospect, the VP70's chief shortcoming was Heckler & Koch's attempt to create a highly specialized design for which there could be only a tiny, select market. In 1986, following limited sales to military and police forces, primarily in Africa, the Middle East and Asia, the company discontinued all VP70 production.

SPECIFICATIONS: VP70

Overall Length: 204mm/8.0 (w/o stock)

Barrel Length: 116mm/4.6

Weight: 820g/28 (empty, w/o shoulder stock)

Caliber/Capacity: 9mm/18 rounds

P7 Series

Heckler & Koch's reasoning for its creation of the original PSP was directly traceable to the tragic deaths of Israeli athletes following a terrorist attack at the 1972 Olympics held in Munich, which represented a once-in-a-lifetime opportunity to sell the West German police a new service pistol. A West German police commission given the task of investigating the tragedy laid the fault on West Germany's police for their lackadaisical training, mediocre equipment, and a casual mindset unsuited to the anti-terrorist struggle engulfing Europe. The commission recommended that sweeping changes be made in West German police methods, training and equipment. In 1972, the standard West German police handgun was a .32 ACP caliber automatic pistol, much like the Walther PP. The commission recommended instead that a more powerful 9mm Parabellum handgun be adopted.

The West German government promulgated stringent requirements for this new police handgun. It must first pass a stringent endurance/reliability test of 5,000 rounds with no more than one

H&K's prototype 13-shot P7A13 competed in M9 tests to select a new service pistol for the U.S. armed forces (photo courtesy of Heckler & Koch).

malfunction per thousand rounds. Loaded, it must be safe from accidental discharge, yet be instantly prepared to fire without having to release a manual safety. Size and weight requirements were set low, allowing the same gun to be used as a holstered weapon for open carry by uniformed officers or concealed by undercover officers. Magazine capacity was set initially at six rounds, but later raised to eight. In 1975, requirements were further defined: Maximum length: 7 inches. Maximum width: 1.9 inches. Maximum height: 5.1 inches. Maximum weight (fully loaded): 35 ounces. The endurance test was raised to 10,000 rounds, with no more than one malfunction per thousand rounds. Any pistol adopted would also have to pass a rapid-fire course of 500 rounds in 50 minutes, plus testing for accuracy and reliability in hostile environments.

By 1979, following four rounds of grueling tests, three pistols had been declared acceptable for West German police service: Walther's P5, SIG's P225 (officially designated P6) and H&K's PSP

> **Heckler & Koch developed its 13-shot P7A13 into the P7M13, combining P7 operating features with a high-capacity, 13-round magazine. (photo courtesy of Heckler & Koch).**

(officially designated P6). A fourth entrant, Mauser's HsP, was declared unsatisfactory and was withdrawn. In addition, three Walther entrants—the P1, P38K and PP Super—proved unable to meet the increasingly stringent requirements.

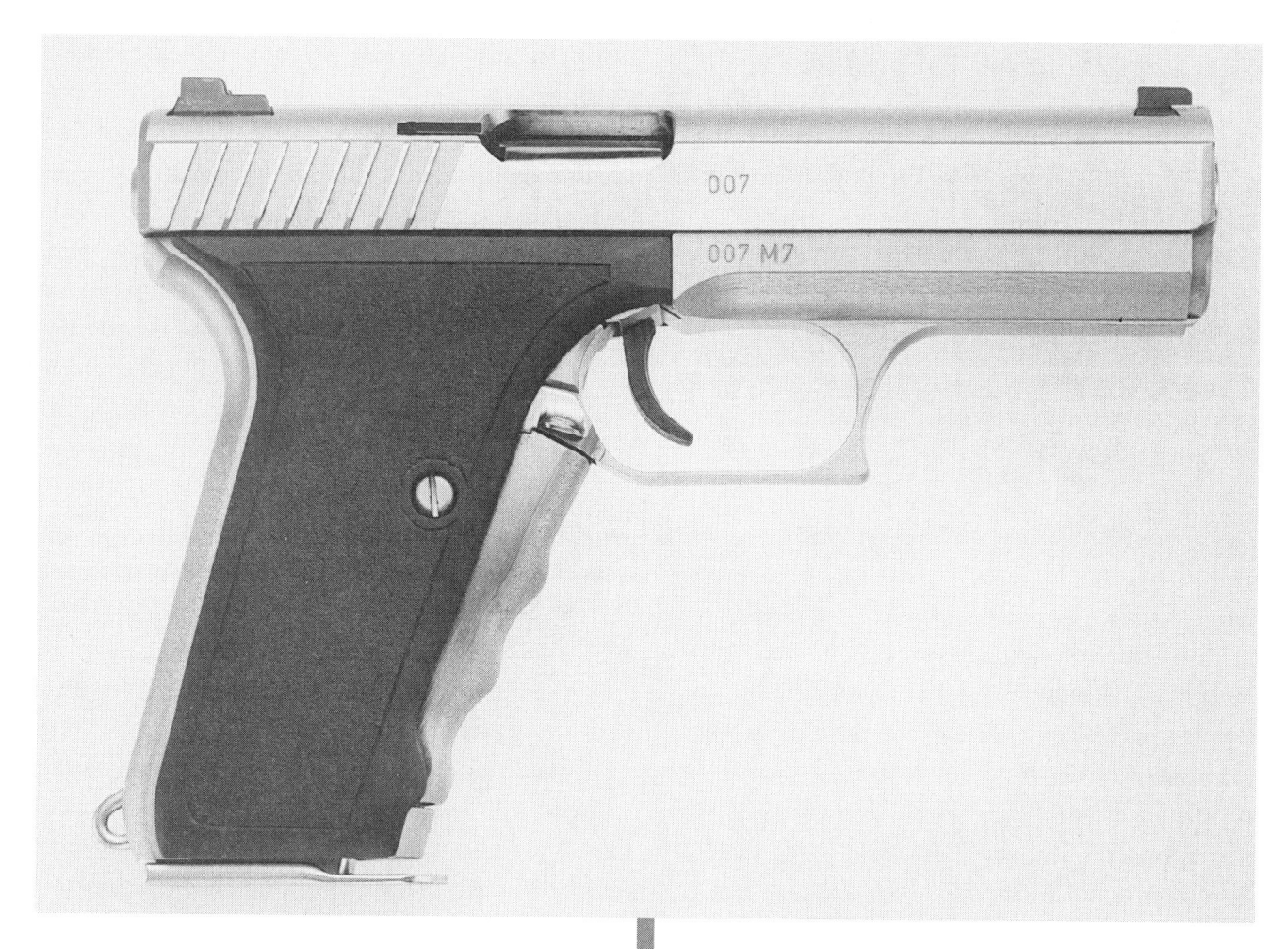

The official designation for the pistol Heckler & Koch created in accordance with West German police requirements was PSP ("Police Self-loading Pistol"). The PSP (**photos p. 8, 9, 24**) featured an interesting method for retarding the rearward travel of its slide. A gas cylinder located beneath the barrel contained a piston rod and a return spring, the former being attached to the inside of the slide. A hole in the gas cylinder allows burning propellant (powder) gases from the barrel to enter the cylinder. Immediately upon firing, some of these gases escape from a gas port in the barrel and pass into the gas cylinder below. These gases force the piston rod to travel forward, which in turn holds the slide all the way forward, shutting it tight until the gas pressure falls. Then, as the bullet leaves the barrel, a rush of propellant gas ensues. Once the gas pressure is depleted, the slide is free to move back, ejecting the spent cartridge case as it travels back as far as possible. A recoil spring forces the slide forward again, and on its way back into battery it strips the top cartridge off the magazine.

> **The P7M7 represented an attempt by Heckler & Koch to apply P7 technology to the popular .45 ACP cartridge. The pistol, having proved expensive and too complex, was abandoned after production of only a few prototypes, one of which was given the evocative serial number "007" (photo courtesy of Heckler & Koch).**

Heckler & Koch did not invent this basic principle of using gas to retard the slide operation firing chamber to ease extraction of fired cartridge casings.

PSP controls include a squeeze-cocker mechanism that combines quick reaction with safe operation whenever the gun is not held in a shooting grip. This squeeze-cocking mechanism, which takes up the entire forward gripstrap below the triggerguard, must be held in fully in order to fire the pistol. The squeeze-cocking lever, which is essentially a grip safety, requires about 15 pounds of pressure to close. But once in, it can be held shut with only a pound of force. Once the

until chamber pressures reached a safe level. A German rifle, the *Volksgewehr VG1-5*, which was built in small numbers late in World War II, pioneered this concept; also, two automatic pistols—an experimental Swiss model of the late 1940s and the Austrian Steyr Model GB—used variations of the same principle. But the P7 (**photo p. 15, 19, 21, 25**) was by far the most successful of these weapons and the only one still in production.

Despite its styling, the Vektor pistol is a P7 under the skin.

The P7 legacy continued in South Africa, where at least two 9mm pistols, the Heritage Stealth and the Vektor (shown), copied Heckler & Koch's gas-delayed breech.

shooter relaxes his grip on the cocking lever, the firing pin automatically returns to its rest position and the gun cannot fire, even when the trigger is pulled or the pistol is dropped. The amount of pressure required to close the cocking lever also contributes a valuable safety factor. For example, a small child cannot exert

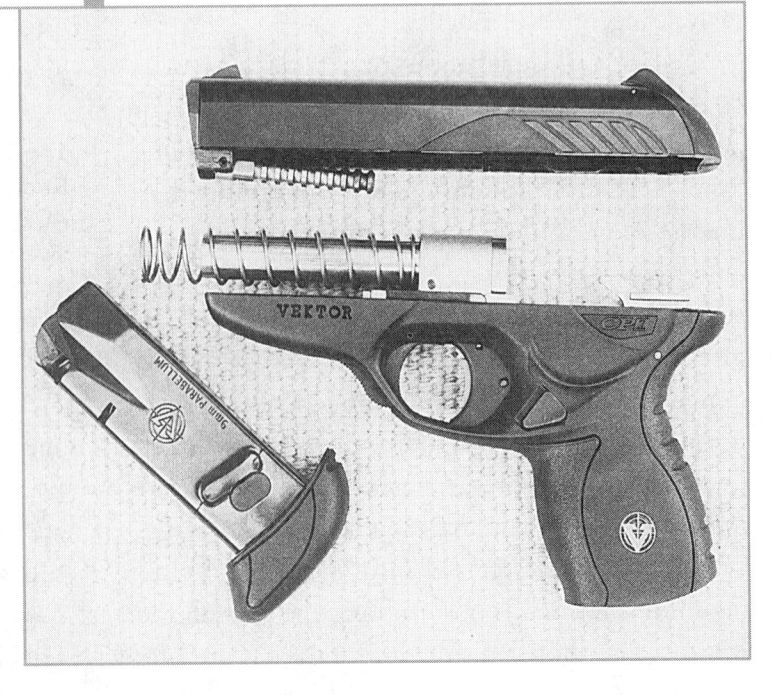

The beauty of this gas-delayed mechanism is that it regulates itself; i.e., using ammunition of greater power generates more gas, causing the slide to stay shut the extra bit longer needed to control the increased power. To avoid the possibility of losing bullet speed, hence reducing stopping power, the P7 pistols use a variation of the polygonal rifling found in the P9. Compared to standard rifling, with its distinctive grooves and lands, polygonal rifling reduces friction between the bullet and the rifling. Thus, muzzle velocities remain close to those generated by other 9mm service pistols, even those with barrels an inch longer. As with the G3 rifles, the P7 uses a fluted

The Mark 23 has been in U.S. armed forces service since 1996 and has performed admirably (photo courtesy of Heckler & Koch).

enough force on the lever to arm the pistol. Once the slide is pulled back after emptying the magazine, a fresh magazine can be inserted and the slide closed by pushing the squeeze-cocking lever all the way in. Should there be a jam, H&K includes a manually operated slide stop on the left side of the P7's frame, just behind the trigger. Once the slide has been pulled all the way to the rear, this slide stop can lock the slide open and enable the shooter to clear the jam.

With the squeeze-cocker held in, the striker protrudes about a quarter-inch from the rear of the slide, indicating a readiness to fire. The striker establishes this readiness position and, when released, returns into the slide with an audible click. In some circumstances, this clicking sound could conceivably give one's position away. The only way to avoid this would be to retract the slide slightly while operating the squeeze-cocking lever, then easing it forward gently.

The PSP's sights are the three-dot variety now so popular in police/military and self-defense circles. These consist of two white dots on the rear sight between which the shooter aligns the single white dot on the front sight. Illuminated radioactive dots of greenish tritium have also been sold commercially since 1993. Ironically, though, these night sights have been standard on Wet German guns since the P7's first appearance in 1978. While these greatly aid in aligning the sights under low light conditions, they also show up to the rear. Should an adversary sneak in behind you, these night sights might well make you vulnerable.

Heckler & Koch improved the handling characteristics of the P7 by lightly sandblasting and stippling the front of the squeeze-cocking lever and the rear gripstrap. This enables the shooter to get a firm purchase

The Mark 23 comes in a military-style carrying case with a pocket for the owner's name tag.

on the gun under most circumstance. In the same vein, the sides of the grip pieces are more heavily roughened.

After Heckler & Koch released the PSP in early 1978, the West German states of Baden-Württemberg, Bayern (Bavaria), Lower Saxony and Niedersachsen all adopted it as the P7, as did *Grenzschützgruppe 9* (GSG-9), the elite West German police anti-terrorist special unit. Heckler & Koch received an even greater accolade in 1980 when the West German *Bundeswehr* adopted the P7

AT RIGHT

Threading the muzzle of the commercial Mark 23's barrel allows a suppressor to be added, but the federal government strictly regulates such devices. This capability may be a selling point for some police special units, however.

BELOW

The USP-series guns contain a rail on the frame's bottom forward portion which allows the shooter to fit an auxilliary aiming device to the gun.

Chapter One 35

The SP89, which resembled the MP5K submachine gun, could fire only a single shot for each pull on the trigger (photo courtesy of Heckler & Koch).

as its next service pistol to replace the glamorous P1 (formerly P38) which had been Germany's premier service pistol since 1940.

In its original form, and as the P7 German service pistol, the newly-released PSP uses a variation of the heel-mounted magazine made famous in generations of great European handguns, chief among them the Beretta Model 1934 and Walther P38. Unlike these older guns, however, the magazine release on the PSP pushes forward, not to the rear, when releasing the magazine. Heckler & Koch spent the first three years of its P7 production run filling West German official orders, with exportation beginning in early 1981. Then, in 1986, the company replaced the original PSP/P7 with the P7M8, which differed from the PSP in several respects. One was its use of an ambidextrous magazine release mounted on the sides of the frame (near the top of the cocking lever) rather than on its heel. The P7M8 also carries a heat shield in the upper front portion of the triggerguard. Tests had revealed that the original P7 heated up in this area and could, under certain situations, become too hot to hold. Some shooters objected to the new magazine release, claiming it widened the pistol grip and greatly increased the likelihood of accidentally releasing the magazine. Thanks to the continuing popularity of the PSP/P7 in its original configuration, Heckler & Koch reintroduced it, first in a limited production run of about 150 pistols in 1990, and then restoring it to full production in 1999.

Because the PSP/P7 and P7M8 (with an 8-shot magazine) lacked the high capacity magazine feature considered *de rigeur* in American police and military circles, Heckler & Koch introduced in 1984 its modified P7M13. As the name indicates, the company took the P7M8's basic slide and barrel design while enlarging the grip frame to accommodate a 13-shot magazine, stacking the extra five rounds in a wider double column. Regrettably, thanks to the widened grip, this pistol sacrificed much of the eight-shot model's desirable handling characteristics.

Upon discontinuing the small caliber HK4 pistol, Heckler & Koch adapted a P7 variant to replace it in 1987 as the P7K3 **(photos p. 16, 28)**. The model designation tells the story: the P7K3, having been modified from the P7 design, fires either 9mm Browning Short (.380) caliber or 7.65mm Browning (.32 ACP) or .22 Long Rifle calibers. While the P7K3 retains the basic shape and squeeze-cocking mechanism of the standard full-powered P7s, it fires less powerful rounds and therefore lacks the gas-delay system used by the other models, reverting instead to a simpler straight blowback mechanism. As a training weapon, the P7K3 holds considerable promise. But while it is superbly accurate, its high price gave many would-be buyers considerable pause, finally forcing Heckler & Koch to discontinue the model in 1994.

Following its introduction in 1990, when U.S. police were switching to the .40 S&W cartridge in droves, H&K decided to chamber a P7 variant in the powerful new handgun round so as to maintain its competitive edge. The result was the Model P7M10, which appeared in 1991. Built on the P7M13 frame, the P7M10 fired the larger .40 S&W cartridges, leading to a loss of three rounds in magazine capacity. While its accuracy was excellent—something that cannot be said about all .40 S&W handguns—the P7M10's high price and poor handling hampered its acceptance with U.S. police, considered the best market for a handgun in .40 S&W caliber. Consequently, sales were slow, which forced Heckler & Koch to halt P7M10 production in 1994.

The SP89 (top), though manageable as a handgun, dwarfed the P7M8, which was made specifically for compactness. This is an early-style SP89 with a vertical forward handgrip later disallowed by BATF.

Chapter One 37

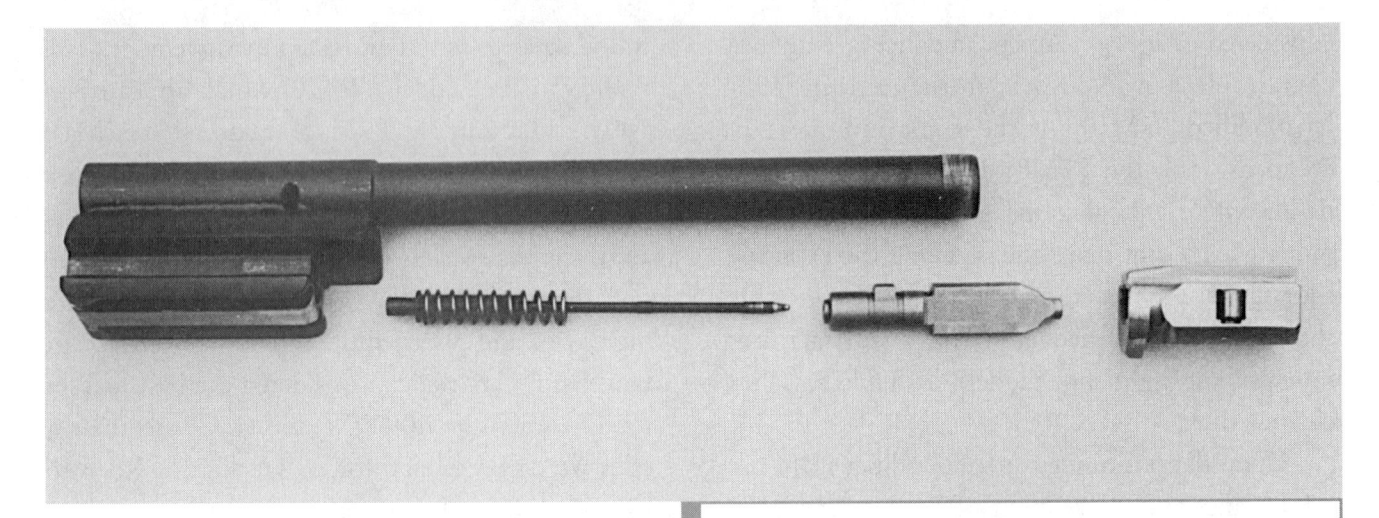

The SP89 used a G3-style roller-locking bolt system for enhanced accuracy and reliability.

The company also tried out a .45 ACP caliber P7 variant, called alternately the P7M7 (reflecting reduced magazine capacity) or the P7M45. This interesting technical exercise, developed in 1987, utilized a cylinder filled with oil rather than the original gas-delay system. This new system worked but was complex and expensive to manufacture. Having predicted low acceptance of such a radical design in the all-important U.S. market, Heckler & Koch accordingly gave up the idea of series manufacture after building only a few prototypes. The company's most recent iteration of the long-lived P7 series is, remarkably, a reversion to the original PSP concept. The so-called "P7PSP," introduced in 1999, is simply a P7M8 without the heat shield underneath the gas system (as introduced in the later series P7s), redesigned to take the original eight-shot magazine and bottom magazine release.

Heckler & Koch briefly offered a deluxe target version of the SP89 equipped with adjustable target grip and "claw" type scope mount (photo courtesy of Heckler & Koch).

Although the P7 series has not been a bestseller by any means, the PSP and P7M8 versions remain in production and have attained modest use outside of Germany. Several police departments in the U.S. have adopted P7 variants. Use

38   Heckler & Koch

Even in its standard form, the SP89 produces excellent accuracy.

of the P7 abroad includes the Greek armed forces. The P7M13 sought acceptance with the U.S. Armed Forces during the XM9 pistol trial of 1984, but the Army then rejected it. The full story follows.

Analysis

Like all Heckler & Koch products, the P7 series is well-made, reliable and highly accurate. In my experience, the only pistols that exceed the P7 in accuracy are the even more expensive SIG P210 series—but not by much. Some of the later Walther P88/P99 designs compete with the P7, whose efficient fixed-barrel design doubtless contributes to the pistol's stellar accuracy. The gas-retarded operation allows the gun to perform reliably with a wide variety of ammunition loaded to various power levels. The eight-shot 9mm variants in particular are quite thin and handy, offering low recoil due to a low bore axis. Still, they're relatively heavy all-steel pistols. I consider the PSP quite desirable as a service pistol, with the P7M8 close behind.

Regrettably, the P7-series pistols also possess some inherent weaknesses. To begin, they are unusual in shape, causing some shooters to find them awkward. This can create problems in terms of holsters and concealed carry. Those who wish to carry a P7 concealed should talk to Mitchell Rosen (Mitch Rosen Extraordinary Gunleather). A top-

Chapter One 39

The USP40, introduced in 1993, was the first of a new series and became H&K's most successful pistol line in the U.S. to date. (photo courtesy of Heckler & Koch).

notch holster craftsman, he has considerable experience outfitting shooters with excellent leather holsters for this unusual gun.

The P7 handles differently from any other automatic pistol. As soon as you grip a loaded P7 firmly—which you'll do instinctively once danger is perceived—this pistol is ready to fire with a remarkably light pull on the trigger. As a result, the P7's arming system demands even more than the usual vigilance required when handling any firearm. The P7's high cost is another disadvantage. Firearms built by Heckler & Koch have never been cheap. The P7 is a classic case in point. For less than half of what a P7 costs, you can buy an excellent service handgun from CZ, Ruger or Taurus. Finally, because of the P7's unusual characteristics and high price, it will remain a rare and special handgun—at least in the United States. Let it be said, however, that many shooters who have worked with these pistols long enough to be proficient in their use do like them and find them excellent companions in time of need.

SPECIFICATIONS: P7 SERIES

PSP/P7	P7M8	P7K3	P7M13
Overall Length (in.)	6.7	6.7	6.3	6.9
Barrel Length (in.)	4.1	4.1	3.8	4.1
Width (in.)	1.14	1.14	1.14	1.3
Height (in.)	5.1	5.1	4.9	5.3
Weight (lbs.)	29.5	29.0	26.5	31
Capacity (rounds)	8	8	8	13/10*

*Note: *Magazine restricted to 10 rounds in sales to private citizens (in USA only).*

US M9 Trials

The story of how the United States military tested the 9mm Parabellum caliber service pistol (designated M9) as a replacement for the M1911A1 involves several Heckler & Koch handguns. By 1977, the U.S. Armed Forces had recognized a definite need to replace its dwindling and aging stock of Model 1911A1 automatic pistols, plus a hodgepodge of .38 Special revolvers. The cartridge choice, 9mm Parabellum, was never in doubt. It had been the standard NATO pistol caliber ever since the alliance began.

Choosing a pistol became one of the first projects of a new organization, the Joint Armed Services Small Arms Program or JSSAP. This group was formed in December 1978, comprising members of all the U.S. service branches, including the Coast Guard. One of JSSAP's first goals was to identify an "off the shelf" handgun for use by all the services as a replacement for existing .45 and .38 caliber service handguns. Whatever the company name, the pistol's official designation was to be "M9." During the testing phase, all candidate pistols submitted for possible adoption under the terms of this project would be designated: "XM9."

The first round of these handgun tests occurred in 1979-1980 at Eglin Air Force Base

The USP40 (bottom) provides stiff competition for the 9mm Parabellum service pistols, such as the Beretta Model 92 (top) in U.S. police work.

Chapter One 41

AT LEFT The USP9 Compact (bottom) is much handier and more concealable than the full-sized USP45 (above), making this a useful combination for on- and off-duty use.

BELOW The right-side view of a Mark 23 indicates the pistol's ambidextrous safety. Ambidextrous operations have been strongly emphasized in all U.S. service pistols since the M9 trials of the early 1980s.

AT RIGHT

The Mark 23 (top) is much larger than the P7 (below), but both share Heckler & Koch's tradition of innovative features combined with first-rate materials and workmanship.

BELOW

The Mark 23, which is available commercially, closely resembles the U.S. military model, including a threaded muzzle for accepting a sound suppressor. Note the decocking lever provided on the upper frame (in front of the manual safety).

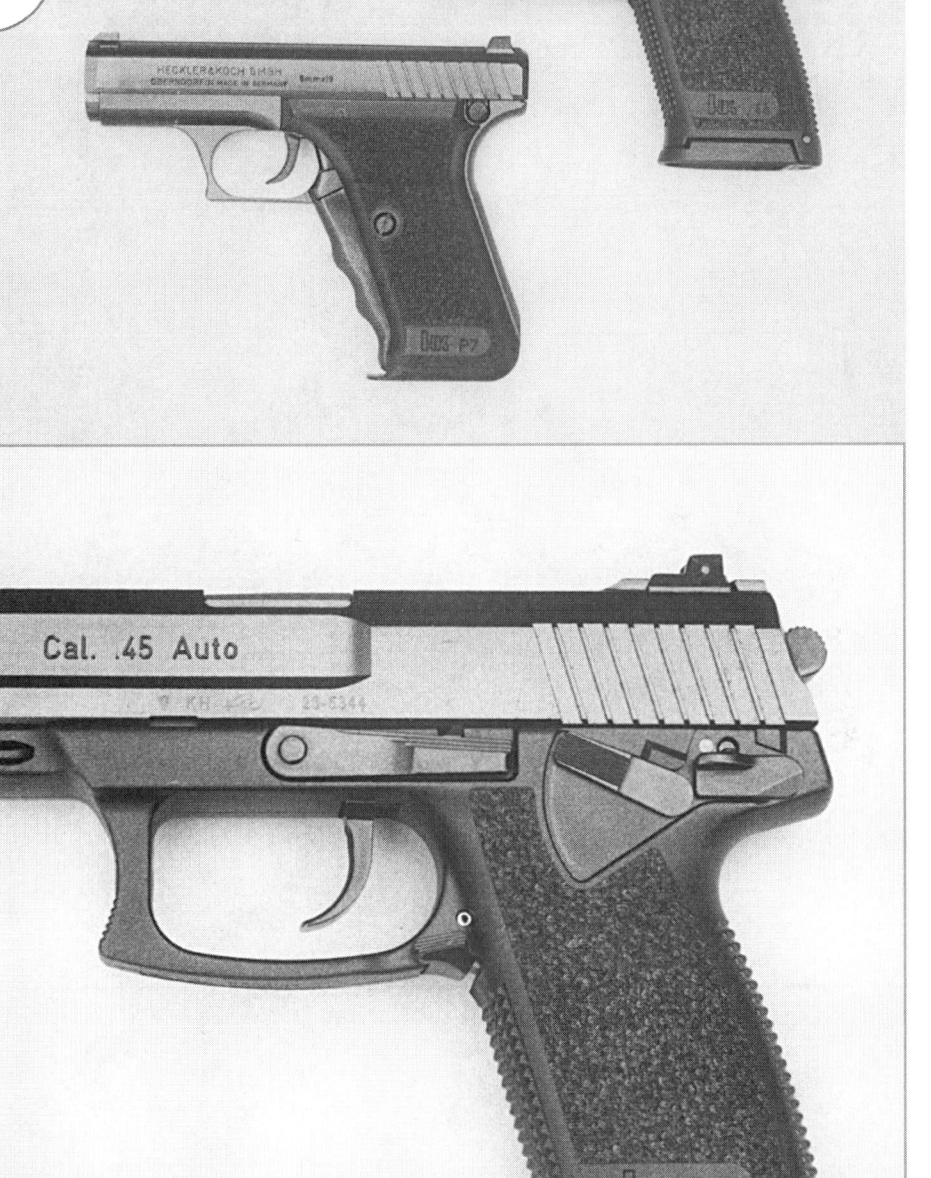

Chapter One 43

The three cartridge options in the USP line are: .45 ACP (bottom), .40 S&W (center) and 9mm Parabellum (top) (photo courtesy of Heckler & Koch).

in northern Florida. Of the nine pistol types tested, two were submitted by Heckler & Koch: the P9S and the VP70. The former carried the smallest magazine of all the pistols tested, while the VP70 boasted the highest capacity magazine. The other guns tested included the Beretta Model 92S-1, the Colt Stainless Steel Pistol (Model SSP), the Fabrique National (FN) High Power, FN Fast Action and FN double-action (FN DA) models, the Star Model 28 and the Smith & Wesson Model 459A.

A whole series of tests arranged by the Air Force included accuracy, environmental testing, and an endurance trail in which Mean Rounds Between Stoppages (MRBS) was tallied. Heckler & Koch's P9S easily won the accuracy phase of the testing but fell into disfavor when its operating controls failed to adapt themselves to left-handed use (an official requirement). Also, its magazine capacity (nine rounds) was one short of the desired (later required) capacity. The VP70, with its then unusual trigger mechanism, allowed only double action firing and failed the hand-held accuracy portion of the tests. As for the endurance tests, the four P9S specimens fired a total of 18,697 rounds with 360 stoppages, producing an MRBS number of 52 (18,697/360). The VP70 performed far worse, firing a mere 771 rounds with 137 stoppages for an MRBS of only 5. In fairness to the VP70, the ammunition used for these tests was extremely suspect. None of it approached the "hot" power ratings of the European 9mm ammunition for which Heckler & Koch—and indeed all European manufacturers—had designed their guns. Star's Model 28, ordinarily a strong, reliable handgun with an excellent service record, also stumbled over the low-powered cartridges, recording the same dismal MRBS number as the VP70. Beretta's Model 92S-1 performed the best overall, but it failed to pass every test and therefore was not accepted for service. While Heckler & Koch's two handguns did not perform as well as hoped, neither had any other pistol clearly outdistanced the others by the end of the first round of XM9 testing in 1980. And so the potentially lucrative, enormously prestigious U.S. M9 service pistol contract remained up for grabs. Heckler & Koch remained in the running and planned to try again.

On May 22, 1981, the U.S. government announced a second round of XM9 testing, soliciting 30 pistols of each type to be tested, starting at the end of September 1981. All pistols were tentatively designated "Pistols, 9mm, XM9" and had to meet the following specifications: **Maximum loaded weight:** 2.77 pounds. **Maximum Overall Length:** 8.7 inches. **Barrel Length:** 4 inches. Each candidate must also contain ambidextrous safety

Eventually Heckler & Koch sought outside help with a suppressor for the Mark 23, choosing a design developed by Knight's Armament Company (photo courtesy of Heckler & Koch).

and magazine controls; and each magazine must hold at least 10 rounds and must fall freely from the frame when released.

By this point, Heckler & Koch had withdrawn its P9S and VP70 from JSSAP testing. The former's low magazine capacity and the VP70's dismal showing in the earlier testing were the cause. Instead, Heckler & Koch chose as its standard-bearer the

Chapter One 45

newly developed P7M13. In this round of testing run by the U.S. Army, the P7M13 passed the energy tests (mud, dust, firing pin, etc.) but failed the saltwater corrosion resistance and reliability tests with an MRBS of 169. The U.S. Department of Defense terminated this second round of XM9 pistol testing in February 1982, including a terse announcement that all handguns submitted had failed to meet the requirements.

The third XM9 pistol trial began in 1984. Once again Heckler & Koch sent its P7M13 with 30 test samples (submitted at the manufacturer's expense), but again the pistol came up short. The U.S. Army did not even allow H&K to bid, failing the pistol in the saltwater corrosion phase of the adverse conditions testing. Over a 10-day period following their immersion in saltwater, the two P7M13s tested in this phase of the XM9 trials experienced 55 malfunctions out of 390 rounds fired, with 36 malfunctions occurring in the last five days of the test. In contrast, the two Model 1911A1 pistols used as controls in the saltwater testing scored 99 percent for reliability, with only two malfunctions out of 210 rounds. Because passing the saltwater test with a better reliability rating than the control M1911A1s was mandatory, the U.S. Army eliminated the Heckler & Koch P7M13 from further consideration.

The Big SP89

This large pistol was created simply by converting Heckler & Koch's remarkable Model MP5K submachine gun (see Chapter 4) to a semiautomatic-only mode. Following its introduction in 1989, the SP89 **(photos p. 37-9, 61)** fell afoul of restrictive government regulation through no fault of its own. Like the G3 rifle, the SP89 had a roller-locked breech. Its operating controls were placed much like the G3/HK91's, with the trigger mechanism limited to semiautomatic fire. The safety catch

A disassembled Mark 23 reveals a strong resemblance to the company's USP series, though many of its specific details differ.

utilized a two-position switch, "up" being safe and "down" allowing a single shot for each pull on the trigger. Similar to the selective-fire MP5K on which Heckler & Koch based its design, the SP89 used either 15 or 30-round magazines. H&K installed HK91's pushbutton magazine release on the right side of the frame rather than using the G3's ambidextrous lever-type release. The SP89's sights and cocking handle were set up exactly like the G3's. A claw mount for installing a telescopic sight also fit on this pistol. In tests conducted by the author, the SP89 featured excellent accuracy and total reliability using a variety of ammunition.

The Mark 23 mounts an accessory module located beneath the suppressor, adding to the pistol's versatility (photo courtesy of Heckler & Koch).

Early SP89s included the same vertical forward handgrip featured on the MP5K, but the U.S. Bureau of Alcohol, Tobacco and Firearms (BATF) decided this was illegal—apparently because it made the pistol look too much like a submachine gun—and pressured H&K into dropping the handgrip. All SP89s retained a slight bulge below the muzzle designed to keep the shooter's fingers of the support hand from straying dangerously in front of the muzzle.

Because of the SP89's large size and relatively high cost, commercial sales were limited. But politics hastened the pistol's demise still more. In 1993, certain guns were officially designated "assault pistols" and further importation was barred, marking the end of the SP89.

The USP Series

By 1990 the P9 and P7 series pistols had established Heckler & Koch's reputation as an excellent handgun manufacturer. Its guns, however, had not experienced great commercial success in the U.S. The reason for disappointing U.S. sales was twofold. First, the P9 and P7 were such a departure from

SPECIFICATIONS: SP89

Overall Length: 12.8

Barrel Length: 4.5

Width: 2.4

Height: 7.9

Weight: 70 (unloaded)

Magazine Capacity: 15 or 30 rounds

Chapter One 47

the norm in terms of their handling, appearance and operating features that many American shooters were put off. Second, the guns were too costly to earn widespread approval by American shooters. Accordingly, H&K created an entirely new pistol series, one that addressed these concerns and hopefully would create a new generation of American shooters. The project was named "USP" (Universal Self-loading Pistol) **(photos p. 16, 22, 23, 35, 40, 42, 44, 55, 57, 59, 60, 70)**.

Featured was a traditional Browning-style short-recoil locking system. H&K also

The USP9 Compact (top) is only slightly larger than SIG's Model P239 (bottom), another popular concealed-carry pistol.

developed a polymer frame to lower the cost and reduce weight. In these respects, H&K was following the lead of Glock, whose Model 17 9mm Parabellum pistol was then well on its way to establishing a dominant market share both in the U.S. and abroad. To avoid battering the frame and lowering recoil, Heckler & Koch developed a unique buffer system involving a heavy spring unit located behind the traditional recoil spring. H&K subsequently received a U.S. patent for this innovative feature.

The first two USP variants—a 9mm pistol called the USP9 and a .40 S&W model of similar size called the USP40—appeared in 1993. From the start, the USP was designed for the .40 S&W caliber, making this model one of the strongest .40 S&W caliber handguns on the market. A .45 ACP caliber service model, the USP45, **(photo p. 58)** appeared in 1995. This is slightly larger and heavier than the 9mm and .40 caliber variants by virtue of the larger cartridge it fires.

Later, Heckler & Koch, recognizing that a slightly smaller version of the USP would have more appeal in the marketplace, created the USP Compact, now available in 9mm, .40 S&W and .45 ACP caliber. The USP quickly established itself as an unusually accurate pistol. H&K then took further advantage of this pistol's inherent accuracy potential by creating the USP Tactical pistol (1998). It combines some of the Mark 23 features developed for U.S. special forces (see following section) with the basic USP design. Those features inspired by the Mark 23 for use on the USP Tactical model include a threaded barrel muzzle, an O-ring (partway down the barrel), and a carrying case with plenty of space for accessories.

The Tactical model features an adjustable rear high-profile sight, an adjustable match trigger, and a magazine with a prominent fourth-finger rest on the bottom. The manual safety lever, operable from the left side only (for right-handed shooters) pushes up to safe, down one notch to fire, then down a second notch for decocking the hammer. Other features, such as a polymer frame with integral rails for mounting accessories and a dual-spring buffer/recoil-reduction system, are common among all pistols in the USP series.

Heckler & Koch also offers the USP Tactical with a 10-shot magazine. Its market is either the private citizen (witness the 10-shot magazine) or some police forces who like the Mark 23 except for its price. In 2001, list price was $999 compared to the Mark 23's retail price of $2,169.

Building on the USP Tactical, H&K introduced in early 1999 the USP Expert and USP Match variants. The former is similar to the Tactical model but with a longer slide, while the USP Match has the same features with an added barrel weight.

One of the most interesting design features used in the USP series is a modular fire-control mechanism. Heckler & Koch offers ten different variants that will appeal to any shooter's taste. The USP can be tailored to any type of single or double action mode. Buyers may select between a traditional manual safety or a decocking lever, and they may have a manual safety/decocker placed on either or both sides of the frame. The table below summarizes these and other permutations:

The magazine release for the USP appears on either side of the triggerguard, making it fully ambidextrous. A slight swell in the bottom edge of the triggerguard—before it abuts the frame—helps shield the magazine release from operating inadvertently. Too many police officers, soldiers and private citizens have accidentally dropped a perfectly good (loaded) magazine under the stress of a life-threatening situation. With the USP, Heckler & Koch has created a truly remarkable series of pistols. In a very short time span, these pistols have developed a strong following among police and private citizens. At this writing more than 200 law enforcement agencies in 37 states issue USP pistols.

Compared to previous Heckler & Koch offerings, the guns in the USP series are much more affordable. This factor alone contributes greatly to the appeal of these guns. H&K did not achieve this cost reduction, however, by lowering the high standards of quality for which the company is rightly renowned. The USP handguns are accurate, extremely reliable and durable. In the company's

USP FIRE MODES

	DA	SA	DAO	Left-side Control	Right-side Control	Manual Safety	Decocking Lever	No Decock
Variant 1	•	•		•		•	•	
Variant 2	•	•			•	•	•	
Variant 3	•	•		•			•	
Variant 4	•	•			•		•	
Variant 5			•	•		•		•
Variant 6			•		•	•		•
Variant 7			•		•			
Variant 8								
Variant 9	•	•		•		•		•
Variant 10	•	•			•	•		•

own pre-production evaluation phase, one test gun fired over 10,000 rounds of .40 S&W ammunition without a single malfunction. In addition, several passed 20,000-round endurance shoots in company testing with no problems. In 1998, the U.S. Drug Enforcement Agency (DEA) subjected seven sample .40 S&W caliber USP 40 Compact models to a testing regimen that included abuse testing, accuracy testing and endurance testing. The results can only be described as incredible. In the endurance testing phase of the DEA's grueling evaluation process, for example, three USP pistols fired a combined total of 30,750 rounds, with a mean failure occurring only once every 10,250 rounds. Accuracy testing also went extremely well, with an average group size of 2.42 inches for 25-yard targets

The author found the Mark 23's roughly stippled grip ideal for operation with wet hands.

Below. The Mark 23's oddly-shaped triggerguard suits it well to operation with heavy clothing.

fired from a rest. Faced with results like these, the DEA signed a contract on November 19, 1998 for up to 10,000 USPs, including the USP40 Compact in both double action only and double/single action. All DEA guns have tritium night sights and 12-round magazines, with six magazines provided for each pistol **(photo p. 19)**.

In the USP, Heckler & Koch has created a pistol line admirably suited to the intense demands of North American police and private citizens. Not only is it a tremendous success, both mechanically and commercially, but it has proven so successful that

The hole in front of the Mark 23 trigger guard adds versatility to the gun, allowing the use of other aiming devices.

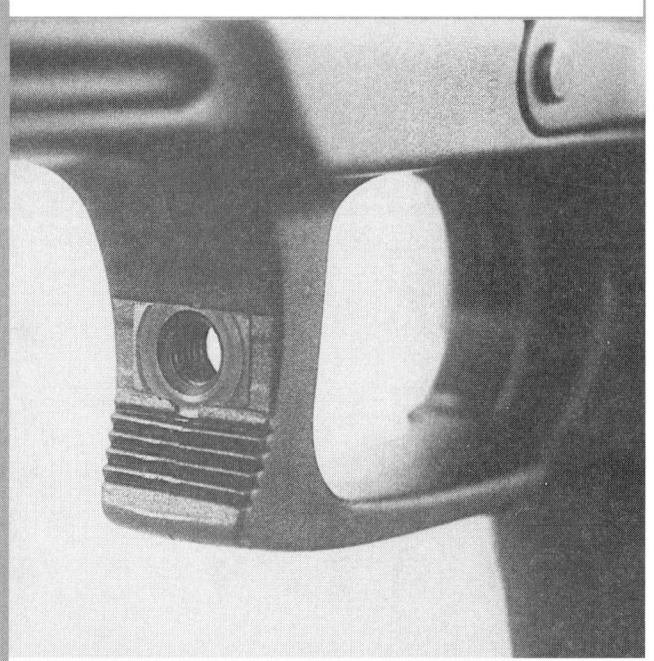

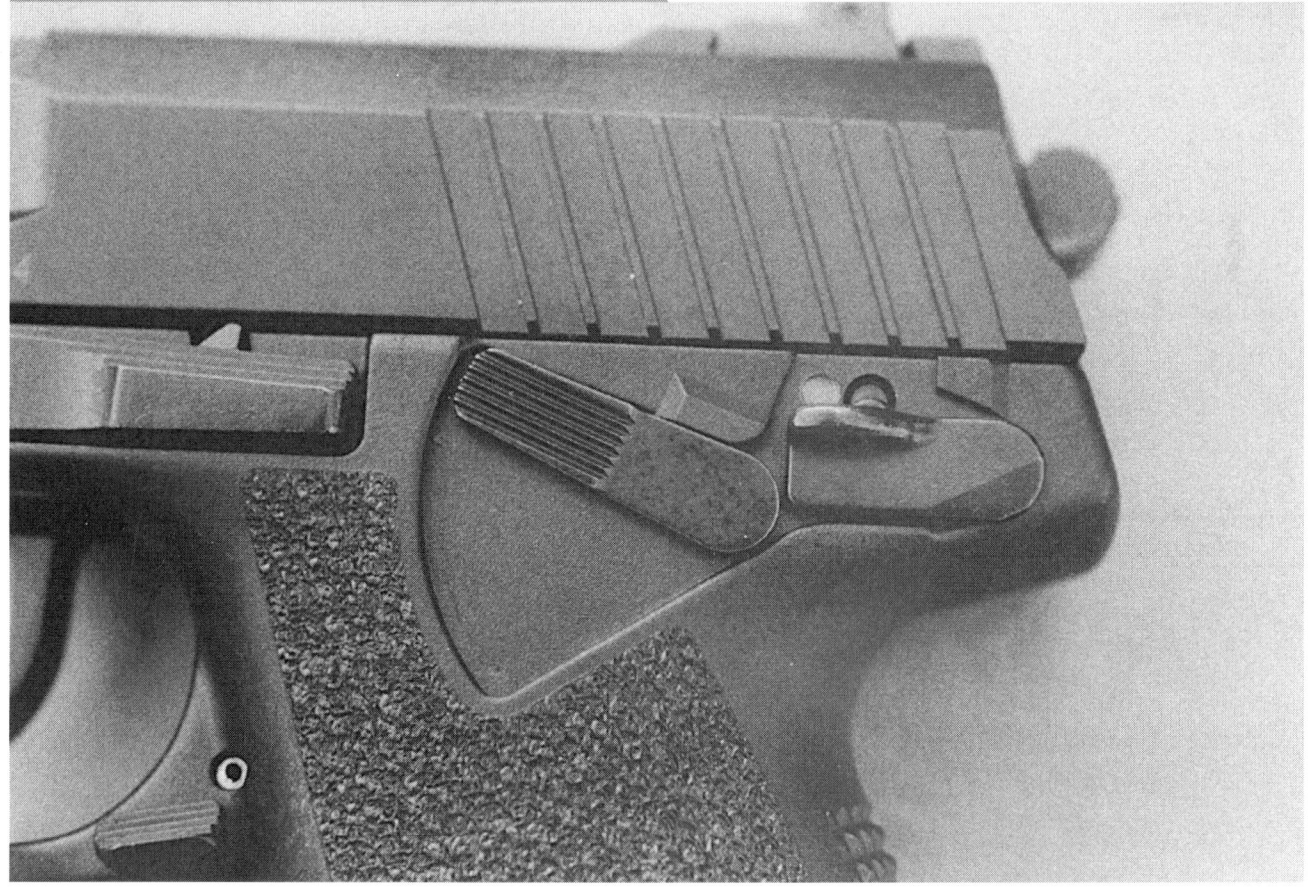

After loading the firing chamber, a right-handed shooter may elect to lower the cocked hammer of a Mark 23 with the decocking lever; or the shooter may want to keep the hammer cocked and apply the manual safety (located behind the decocking lever).

For right-handed shooters the left-sided manual safety lever on the Mark 23 is sized adequately for rapid operation.

The author found the Mark 23's decocking lever a little too low in profile to apply consistently, it would prove even more difficult to lower the hammer with it when wearing gloves.

the company was able to use much of the technology it developed for this series when it created the Mark 23 pistol for the U.S. special forces (see below).

USSOCOM/MARK 23

After the U.S. armed forces had adopted the Beretta Models 92F and SIG P228 (as the M9 and M11 pistols, respectively), many military personnel continued to express a strong preference for a .45 caliber handgun. Among these military agencies was the elite Special Operations Command, also known by its initials as USSOCOM. Unlike other armed forces agencies, which view the pistol in primarily a defensive role, USSOCOM sought an

AT RIGHT The Mark 23 includes twin dots on the rear sight and a single dot on the front sight to assist in aiming.

BELOW The Mark 23 can be carried cocked and locked for a quick single-action first shot, a feature not available with the military's M9 and M11 9mm service pistols but specifically called for in the Mark 23.

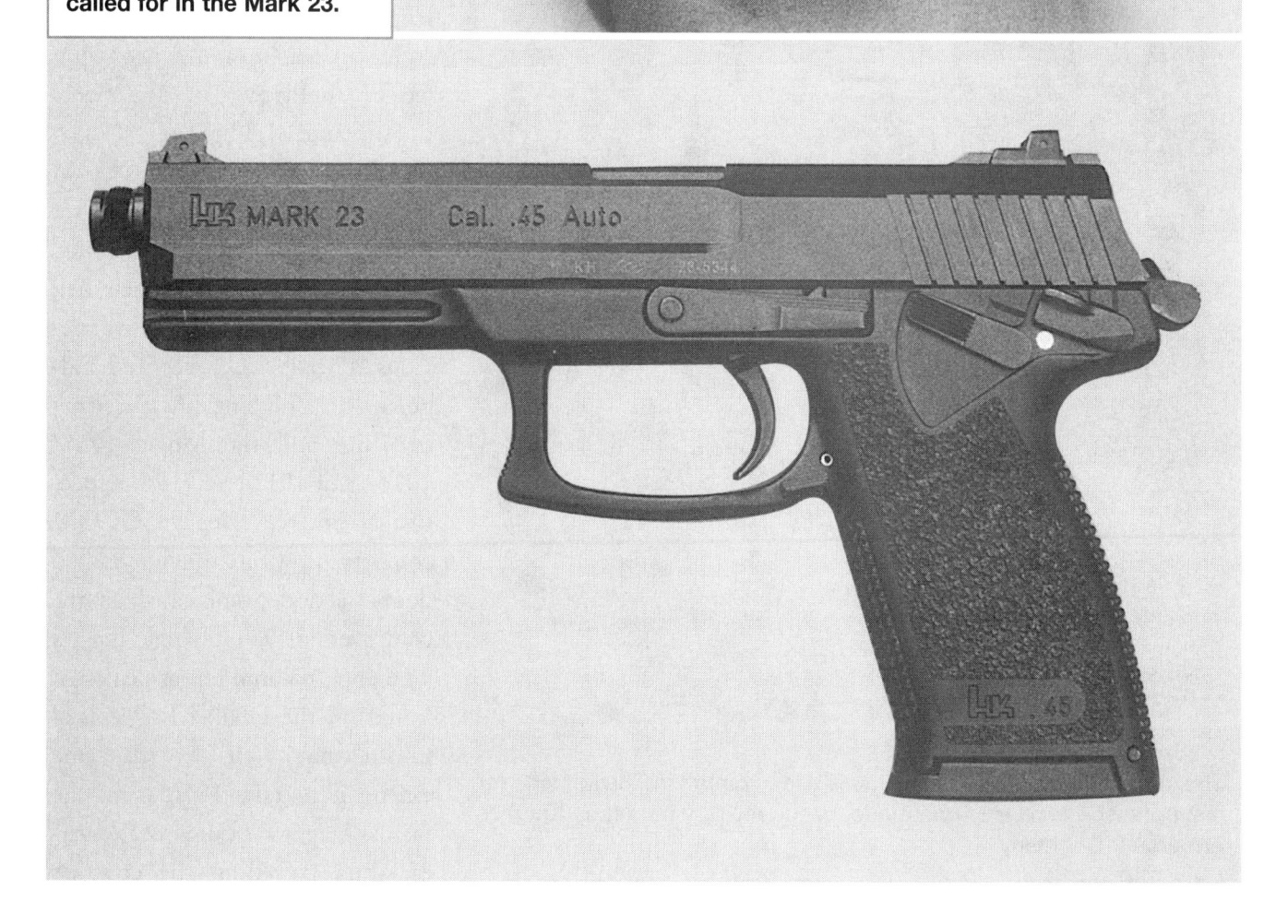

Chapter One 53

The Mark 23's carrying case includes a long pouch on the left side for a suppressor, similar to one made for the military model by Knight's Armament Company.

automatic pistol as a dedicated offensive weapon. Hence the request for a return to the heavier .45 ACP round, the 9mm Parabellum being deemed inadequate for the kind of offensive handgun USSOCOM envisioned. Other USSOCOM requirements included ambidextrous operation, modern safety features, an ability to mount a silencer (sound suppressor), and various alternate aiming devices. A return to the Model 1911A1/ Government Mo-del pistol was obviously not feasible. Moreover, maximum allowable sizes were set at 9.84 inches in length x 1.4 inches in width x 5.9 inches in height, and a maximum weight (unloaded) of 46 ounces (2.86 pounds/1.3 kg).

These and other USSOCOM requirements were formally set forth in an 85-page proposal dated February 1990. Colt, which had manufactured three of the five previous .45 caliber U.S. service handguns—the Colt Single Action Army of 1873 and the Model 1911/ 1911A1 of 1911 and 1926, respectively—entered the USSOCOM competition with a much modified double action pistol based on the controversial Double Eagle design. The single column magazine design found on the Double Eagle pistol meant that with the magazine extended to take 10 rounds, the pistol's height measured 6.25 inches, thus exceeding the contract specifications. Nevertheless, Colt received a $1.4 million developmental contract for this weapon in September of 1991. As a result of its competition with Colt, Heckler & Koch created its own version of the USSOCOM pistol, basing it largely on the evolving technology the company was developing for its USP. Thus did Heckler & Koch receive its own $1.4 million contract a week after Colt received theirs.

H&K submitted its SOCOM pistol prototypes first, sending the required 30 sample pistols to the U.S.

Above. The USP45 in this right-side view displays its one-sided manual safety, but ambidextrous manual safety levers are also available.

Below. Despite its considerable size, the Mark 23 handles well. Note the extended triggerguard, a useful feature for shooter's encumbered with heavy gloves for winter weather or chemical/biological warfare.

Chapter One 55

Navy Surface Warfare Center in Crane, Indiana, on August 30, 1992. Colt submitted its 30 sample pistols two months later.

The durability requirements set forth by the U.S. armed forces were daunting indeed. These included 30,000-round endurance shoots, plus mud and saltwater corrosion tests far in advance of what even the XM9 and XM11 pistols had been required to endure. Under tests run by the U.S. Army, the all-steel Colt pistol fell short. By contrast, H&K's experimental USSOCOM model, while its suppressor design proved deficient, showed enough promise for

The author found the right-side safety lever of the Mark 23 undersized for rapid operation, particularly when raising the lever to its safe setting.

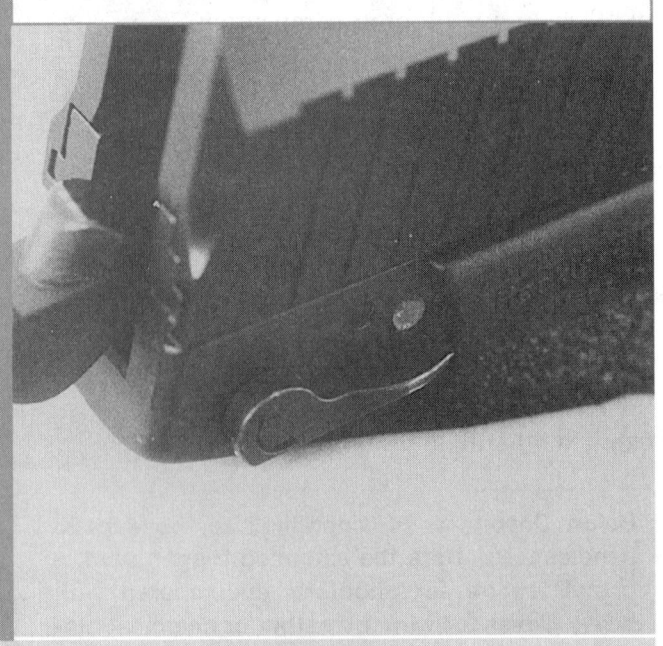

The USP45 (top) followed the lead of the Glock 17 (bottom) by using a polymer frame for enhanced corrosion resistance, recoil control, weight reduction and cost containment. Actually, H&K's VP70 appeared with a polymer frame more than a decade earlier than the "trend-setting" Glock.

the government to pursue it further. Knight's Armament Company (Vero Beach, Florida), an expert in suppressor technology, entered the project to develop a more efficient suppressor that would meet government requirements. Heckler & Koch's failed suppressor had a rectangular profile, while Knight's featured the classic rounded "muzzle can" appearance now common among firearm silencers. Colt's failed prototype and Heckler & Koch's pistol design both employed variations of the Browning short-recoil pistol mechanism with a tilting barrel, proving that the Browning system could be adapted to a suppressed pistol.

The magazine release on the Mark 23 appears on either side of the triggerguard. To release the magazine, simply press down on the release.

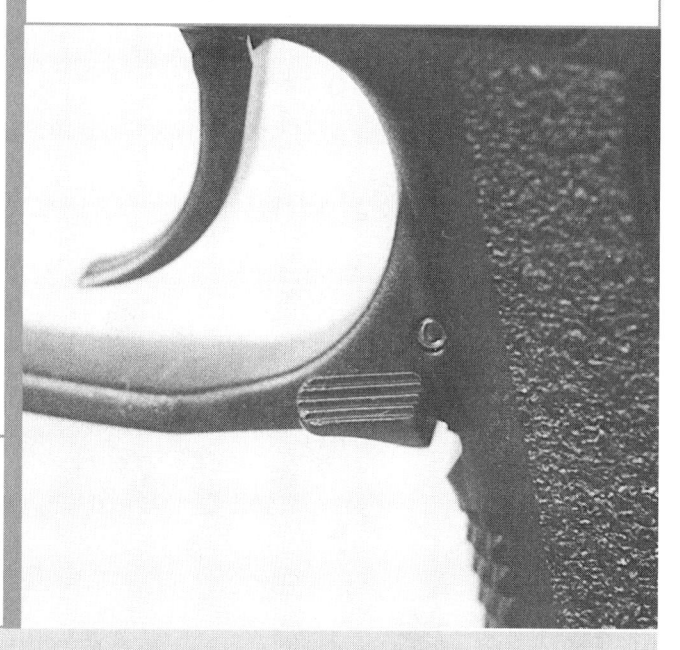

The USP9 Compact combines the excellent mechanical features of the full-sized USP with a sleek and compact size which makes it a versatile and surprisingly concealable gun.

Satisfied with the results, the U.S. Navy Surface Warfare Center, on behalf of the U.S. Special Operations Command, awarded Heckler & Koch on June 29, 1995 a production contract worth $4.5 million in exchange for 1,950 Mark 23 Mod 0 pistols and 10,140 matching magazines. Deliveries began on May 1, 1996, with more to come, setting a total contract price of $12 million. Units under USSOCOM direction include the Special Operations Wing of the U.S. Air Force, the U.S. Army's Rangers, Special Forces and Special Operation Aviation, and the U.S. Navy SEALS, any one of which might use the Mark 23 Mod 0 pistol in the future.

To meet civilian demand for its pistol, Heckler & Koch introduced the Mark 23 in 1996 (**photos p. 17, 23, 33-5, 42-43, 45-7, 50, 51**). Virtually identical to the SOCOM pistol, it includes threads on the muzzle end of the barrel for mounting a silencer (a strictly regulated item not supplied with the package). Its design features include a lightweight polymer frame which, despite the gun's imposing size, weighs only 11 ounces. Heckler & Koch had pioneered this frame design in its USP series. The frame has been reinforced with steel rails, however, and is immensely strong. Adding to its durability is a patented buffer system, representing still another example of what H&K learned while developing the USP. This two-spring captive system reduces recoil at the rear of the frame.

The lower part of the front frame features a slot for easy attachment of lights or laser sights. Likewise, a hole has been drilled and tapped into the triggerguard. The USSOCOM's military version uses a Laser Aiming Module, or LAM, developed specifically for this pistol by Insight Technologies. The LAM incorporates both a laser aiming point and an infrared flashlight which can illuminate an area using night-vision goggles. A "white light" unit can also be fitted to the LAM. Civilian shooters may opt for H&K's Universal Tactical Light (UTL). To ensure a secure hold on the pistol, the front and rear gripstraps have been deeply checkered and heavily stippled on the sides.

Despite its size, the Mark 23 includes operating features designed to make the pistol reasonably

The well-made USP45 is pleasingly accurate.

58   Heckler & Koch

The USP40 is an accurate .40 caliber service pistol. Many handguns chambered for this cartridge deliver only lackluster accuracy.

ergonomic. The trigger mechanism, for example, is smooth and responsive in both single action and double action firing modes. The trigger is wide and deeply grooved, reflecting current practice. There's also plenty of space in the triggerguard for a gloved trigger finger. The sights also reflect modern trends by employing a three-dot aiming system, in which a white dot on the front sight is aligned between two white dots on the rear sight for aiming.

Because of Heckler & Koch's extensive experience with different operating modes gleaned from its development of the USP series, the safety system adopted by the Mark 23 is remarkably versatile. It includes a safety catch, which is am-bidextrous, and a de-cocking lever on the left side of the frame. Thus, after being loaded, the pistol can be carried "cocked and locked," or the shooter may elect to lower the hammer (using the decocking lever) and rely upon a double action first shot. When applied, the safety catch does not lock the slide. The shooter may now load or unload the gun while leaving the safety mechanism on to deactivate the firing system. This ability to load and unload without having to disable its safety mechanism removes a major complaint against the Model 1911 series. Unlike some modern double action pistols, the Mark 23 safety can be set on the safe setting when the hammer is cocked (there is no half-cock setting). Unfortunately, in common with ambidextrous safety mechanisms, the lever on the left side of the Mark 23 frame (for right-handed shooters) is slightly larger than the right-side lever. This makes it difficult for left-handed shooters

Chapter One 59

—for whose convenience an ambidextrous safety was fitted in the first place—to reapply the safety lever. Although it pushes down easily enough with the thumb of either hand, it is difficult to move upward, especially using the left thumb. Applying the safety deactivates the decocking lever altogether. To use the decocking lever to lower the hammer, therefore, the manual safety must first be moved down to its "fire" setting.

The decocking lever on the Mark 23 is also mounted low to the frame, making it seem difficult to operate with a gloved hand. However, the machined striations on the outer portion of the lever ensure a firm purchase, even with gloves on. The slide stop is also mounted quite low. While its operation by right-handed shooters is not a problem, left-handers need to draw the slide back a little further before releasing it when overriding the slide stop. Given the pistol's imposing size, one wonders why the controls are set so low. Did Heckler & Koch seek the pistol's sleek profile with too much zeal?

The magazine release on the Mark 23 is located on both sides of the triggerguard and pushes down to release the magazine. In keeping with preferred practice in the U.S., depressing the magazine release ejects the magazine smartly out of the pistol. While Heckler & Koch supplies 12-round Mark 23 magazines to the police and military

Like other guns in the USP series, the USP9 Compact delivers good accuracy.

trade, civilian shooters in the U.S. must be content with a 10-round model. Unlike some manufacturers of polymer-frame pistols, the Mark 23 magazines are almost entirely made of steel. Still another example of ambidexterity in the design of this pistol is an attachment point for a lanyard loop located in the bottom rear ("heel") of the frame.

Despite its imposing size, the Mark 23 has a slim, well-shaped grip and handles well, lending that intangible quality known as a "lively feel." The Mark 23 also shoots with accuracy, being highly responsive in both single action and double action modes. Using the patented buffer system created by H&K for the USP, the pistol is a pleasure to shoot even with ammunition loaded to +P levels. Low recoil allows for fast repeat shots. The sights are highly functional and well-regulated. The gun's large size is a drawback, but in creating this weapon Heckler & Koch was responding to official requirements, which the company has met in an exemplary fashion. • **H&K**

> **The standard SP89 used a variant of the G3 rotary rear sight. Note also the ring on the receiver end-cap, intended to attach a carrying sling.**

SPECIFICATIONS: USP SERIES AND MARK 23

	USP 9/40 (45)	USP Compact 9/40 (45)	USSOCOM/Mark 23
Overall Length (in.)	7.64	6.81	9.65
Barrel Length (in.)	4.25	3.58	5.87
Weight (lbs.)	1.66	1.60	2.66
Height (in.)	5.35	5.00	5.90
Caliber/Capacity	15/13	10/10/8	.45 ACP/12/10

Chapter One

The development and sale of the G3 rifle and related long arms rank as technical and business achievements of the highest magnitude. While certainly not a financial success, the G11 remains high among the major advances in firearms technology. Heckler & Koch may yet offer its innovative genius in the field of military rifles.......

Chapter 2

MILITARY RIFLES

PART 1: BACKGROUND

The German armed forces were well aware of the superb performance turned in by the U.S. M1 Garand rifle during World War II. Germany's own lack of a standard semiautomatic rifle hampered them greatly during the war, and their attempts to get the G41, G43 and StG44 into widespread service in mid-war proved a disappointment. Most German soldiers in World War II still carried the obsolescent Mauser Model 98 bolt-action rifle, causing firepower to suffer greatly.

In one of those ironies that help keep life on this earth interesting, the first armament of the *Bundeswehr*, now part of the Federal Republic of Germany following World War II, consisted of used M1 Garand rifles once belonging to the U.S. military. The West German armed forces received a total of 46,750 of these aging rifles. The M1s gave

> The most controversial feature on the M1 was its clip method of loading. The 8-shot clip (far right) offered less ammunition than box magazines becoming fashionable in military rifles after World War II.

Chapter Two 63

good service, but their Mannlicher-inspired clip ammunition feed and difficulty of disassembly prevented them from being more than stopgaps in Germany's armament program. All M1 Garands had been phased out of German service by 1965.

West Germany's next service rifle was the *Gewehr 1*, or G1 (*Gewehr* = "Rifle"), a Belgian-made FAL (*Fusil Automatique Légere*, or Light Automatic Rifle), a Belgian-made FAL variant. Immediately after World War II, Belgium's giant Fabrique Nationale (FN) took a close look at the assault rifle developed by the Germans during the war. The idea of a selective-fire assault weapon capable of firing a reduced-power cartridge held considerable merit, inspiring FN to develop a similar weapon. By 1948, they had created their first FAL prototype. The original FAL fired the same 7.92x33mm cartridge used by the Germans in their early assault rifle. As a result, it

FN's FAL, called G1 by the Germans, was a commercial version limited to semiautomatic fire (shown). Had FN agreed to West Germany's request to purchase a production license, the G1 might have become standard and the G3 might never have been made.

was lighter and handier than contemporary service rifles. It was also far more controllable in fully automatic fire than the selective-fire weapons built around full-sized service cartridges. By 1950, FAL had two pre-production model 7.92x33mm caliber rifles in a full-scale testing and development program. One used a standard layout and the other featured a "bullpup" arrangement, with its receiver and magazine located close to the shooter's shoulder. In an attempt to interest the new NATO alliance in its gun, the company decided in 1951 to rechamber the FAL for the experimental new British .280

64   Heckler & Koch

(7x49mm) round. The larger British round required considerable enlargement of the gun, thereby losing most of the control in fully-automatic fire it had enjoyed while using the intermediate German cartridge with its mild recoil. When, at the insistence of NATO, this promising cartridge was rejected, the American-sponsored 7.61x51mm (.308) was adopted as FN's service cartridge, which was enlarged still further so that the FAL could fire this cartridge. The result was a rifle with a 21-inch barrel (40 inches overall) and weighing 9.1 pounds. Its selective-fire capability was retained but its .308 version proved all but uncontrollable in automatic fire. As a result, many FALs built for the military and issued to dozens of countries around the world had their firing mechanisms mechanically blocked for semiautomatic fire only. And so, in 1953, the FAL entered series production with NATO's standard .308 caliber.

The FAL, being a gas-operated rifle, had the same tipping-bolt system used in the company's earlier SAFN rifle, which was developed prior to World War II and shelved before starting production in 1949. This efficient and reliable mechanism dates back to the Soviet's SVT-38 and SVT-40 "Tokarev" rifles widely issued in World War II. They were also found in several other military rifles, including the Swedish-designed Ljungman (AGB-42 and Egyptian Hakim) and the German Gew. 43. The gas system was located above the barrel in order to lower the rifle's bore axis as much as possible. Doing so reduced muzzle rise upon fire in contrast to the M1 Garand, whose barrel and gas system locations were reversed.

The FAL, with its clever design, is noticeably simpler to take apart for routine maintenance than any existing self-loading rifle—much more so than the M1 Garand. Among other clever touches, the

> After the G1 decision, the West German government bought a small number of Swiss-made StG 57s, which the armed forces tested for possible adoption as the G2. The StG 57/G2 included features the Germans found desirable, including adaptability to the NATO-standard 7.62mm cartridge and a straight-line stock configuration to aid control in fully-automatic fire (photo courtesy of SIG).

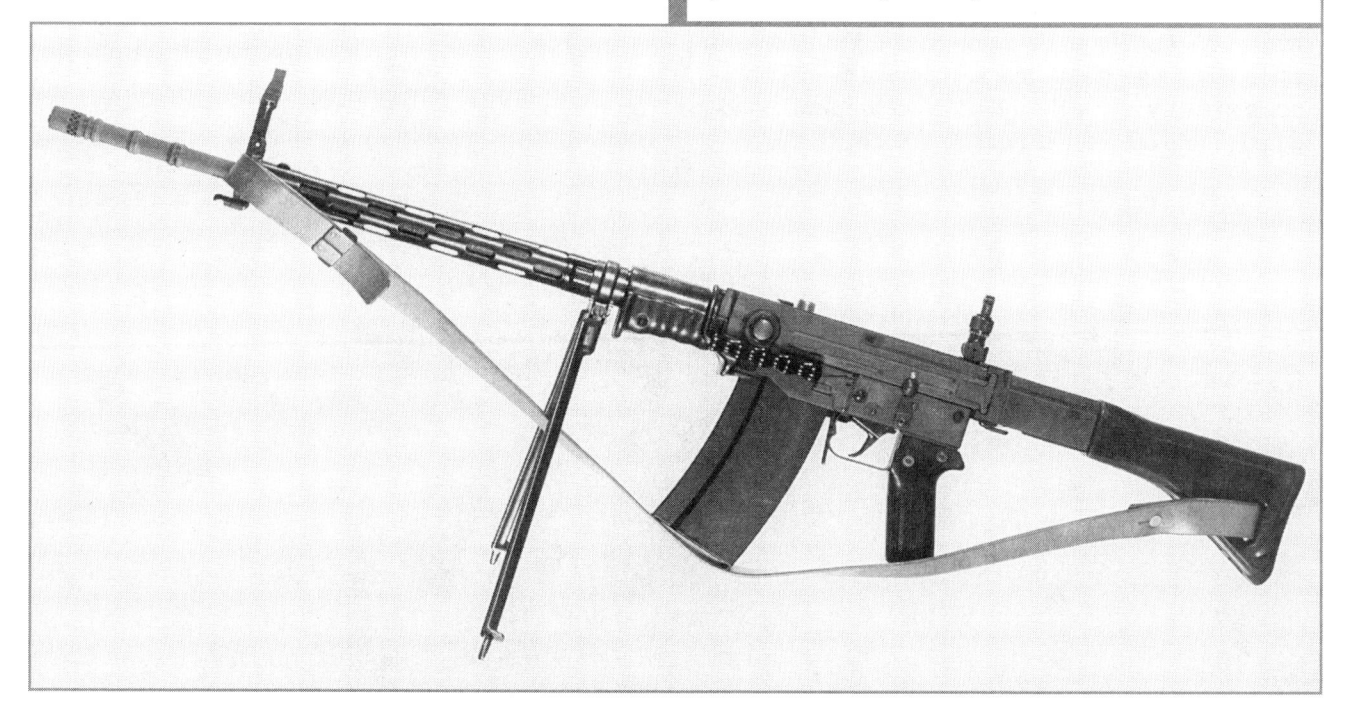

Chapter Two

FAL had a folding carrying handle atop the receiver as an aid in handling. The location of the cocking handle on the left side of the receiver enables shooters to charge the weapon with the left hand, allowing a (right-handed) shooter to keep the dominant hand on the pistol grip. The fire settings on the safety/fire selector, which are placed on the left side of the receiver above the pistol grip, are placed far apart to avoid confusion.

By 1956, the West German government had standardized the rifle type as the "G1" and purchased about 100,000 FAL rifles from Fabrique Nationale. It then sought to buy a production license from FN so it could make its own FALs. While most countries issuing FALs bought them directly from FN, several countries which had standardized the FAL for their armed forces made licensing arrangements with FN to manufacture the rifle locally. Thereafter, FAL licensees included Canada (1956), Britain (1958), Austria (1958), Australia (1959), India (1963), South Africa (1963), Brazil (1964) and Argentina. When FN management learned that the Germans wanted to produce the FAL domestically, it was reluctant to grant a manufacturing license. Having seen Belgium invaded twice by the Germans within living memory, and with the FN plant occupied by the Nazis both times, FN's managers had no intention of facilitating the rearmament of a former enemy. Whereupon the West German government decided its armed forces needed a new standard service rifle, despite the FAL/G1 having been in service for less than five years.

The Germans were not totally satisfied with the FAL anyway. The difficulty of reaching and changing its safety/fire-selector mechanism was one major objection. They also were aware that because of the FAL's gas operation, short-barreled versions would be limited to something the size of the FAL-Para with its 17-inch barrel. Anything shorter would compromise the rifle's reliability. The FAL was also expensive to manufacture, many of its parts requiring precise machining. In any event, the G3 addressed these concerns while managing to keep most of the FAL's strong points.

By the 1960s, the Germans had begun phasing the G1s out of service even as the G3, which was manufactured locally by Heckler & Koch, came on

The original G3 featured a wooden buttstock, round handguard and L-shaped rear sight that allowed only two distance settings. The fixed-stock G3A3, as issued since 1986, has a plastic stock, improved pistol grip, 4-position rotary rear sight and widened "tropical" handguard (photo courtesy of Heckler & Koch).

line in sufficient quantities to justify the switch. The West German government later sent its surplus FAL (G1) rifles to Burma and Turkey, both of whom later switched to the Heckler & Koch G3 service rifle.

> Most G3s do not feature an ambidextrous manual safety/fire selector, though their markings are repeated on the right side. Heckler & Koch has made an ambidextrous safety/selector unit that appears frequently on the company's submachine guns (photo courtesy of Heckler & Koch).

PART II: THE H&K 7.62mm (.308) G3 SERIES

The G3's **(photo p. 99)** ancestry dates back to 1945, when Mauser-Werke supplied Nazi Germany's armed forces with 30 examples of an improved assault rifle prototype, called the StGW45. While this weapon never went beyond the experimental stage, some of those involved in its design moved to Spain to work for the *Centro de Estudios Técnicos de Materiales Especiales* (CETME) in Madrid. While Heckler & Koch was being created in Germany's western portion, several ex-Mauser technicians also moved to Spain in pursuit of further development of the new rifle under CETME's auspices.

By 1952, a firing prototype was ready. Inspired by the World War II German Sturmgewehr StG44, this experimental CETME rifle fired a special round—in this instance, a 7.9x40mm cartridge—shortened from the standard 7.92x57mm Mauser cartridge. Unlike full-sized rifle rounds, this cartridge offered good control in fully-automatic fire while still offering reasonable levels of long-range power and accuracy.

By 1954, CETME was ready to put its design on the world market, turning to Heckler & Koch for technical help. By the following year, CETME was forced to accept the inevitable conclusion: nobody would buy a gun chambered for a proprietary cartridge, no matter how efficient. And so the rifle was redesigned to take the larger 7.62x51mm (.308 caliber) NATO standard cartridge. To do this, the rifle had to be enlarged, just as FN had done with the FAL two years earlier. This larger CETME rifle then competed against the FAL as a candidate for West German service the following year, only to lose to the FAL.

The CETME later became a Spanish service rifle in several versions. The *Modelo B* (also called *Modelo 58*) was approved for service in 1958, the improved and strengthened *Modelo C* in 1965, and the shorter and lighter 5.56mm (.223 caliber)

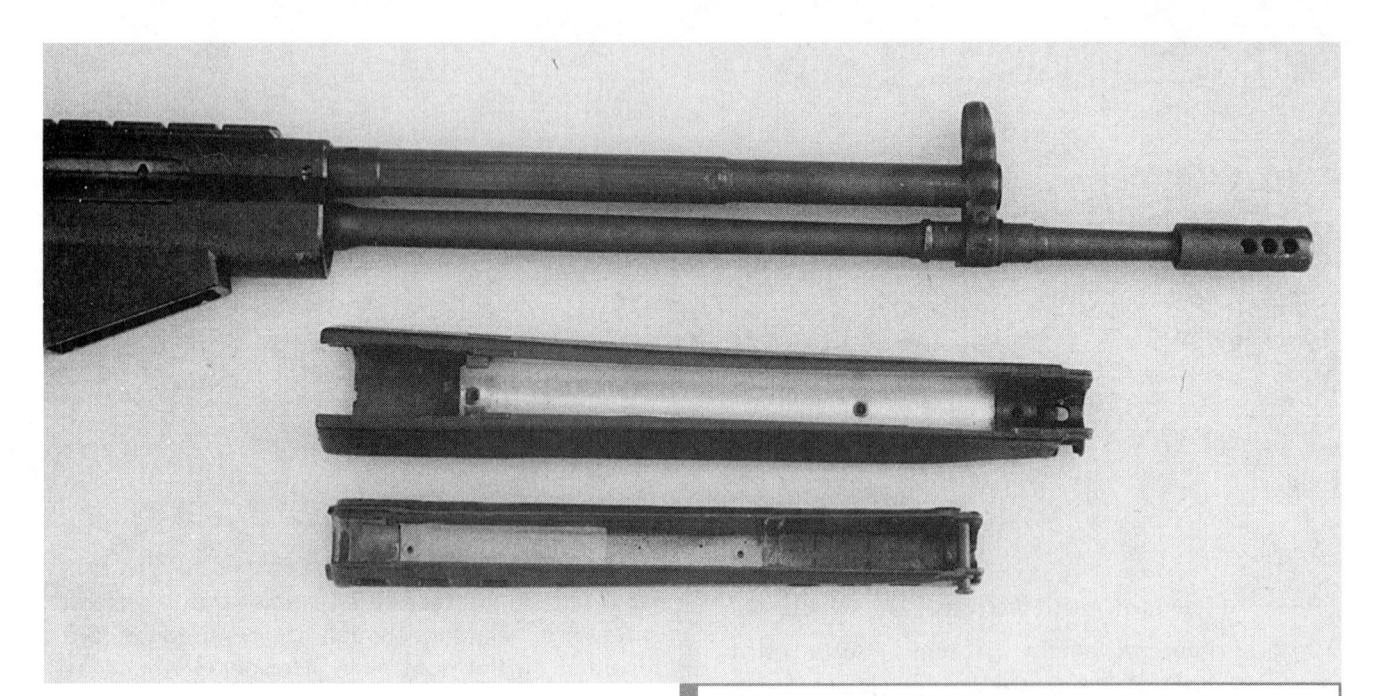

Modelo L in 1984. An even shorter version, for use as armament for armored personnel carriers shooting through special firing ports, appeared in 1982 as the *Modelo R*.

Among the countries who purchased CETME rifles for issue to their armed forces were Chad, Congolese Republic, Djibouti, Dominican Republic, Equatorial Guinea, Guatemala and Mauritania

A major advantage of the broad tropical handguard (shown immediately below the rifle) is a metal heat deflector, which helps prevent barrel heat from injuring the shooter's hand. The older, smaller circular handguard (bottom) lacks this feature.

(all *Modelo B/58* or *Modelo C*) and *Malawi (Modelo L)*. Denmark, Norway, Pakistan, Portugal and Sweden each purchased several hundred to a few thousand CETME rifles for military trials before adopting Heckler & Koch's own G3 rifle in each instance.

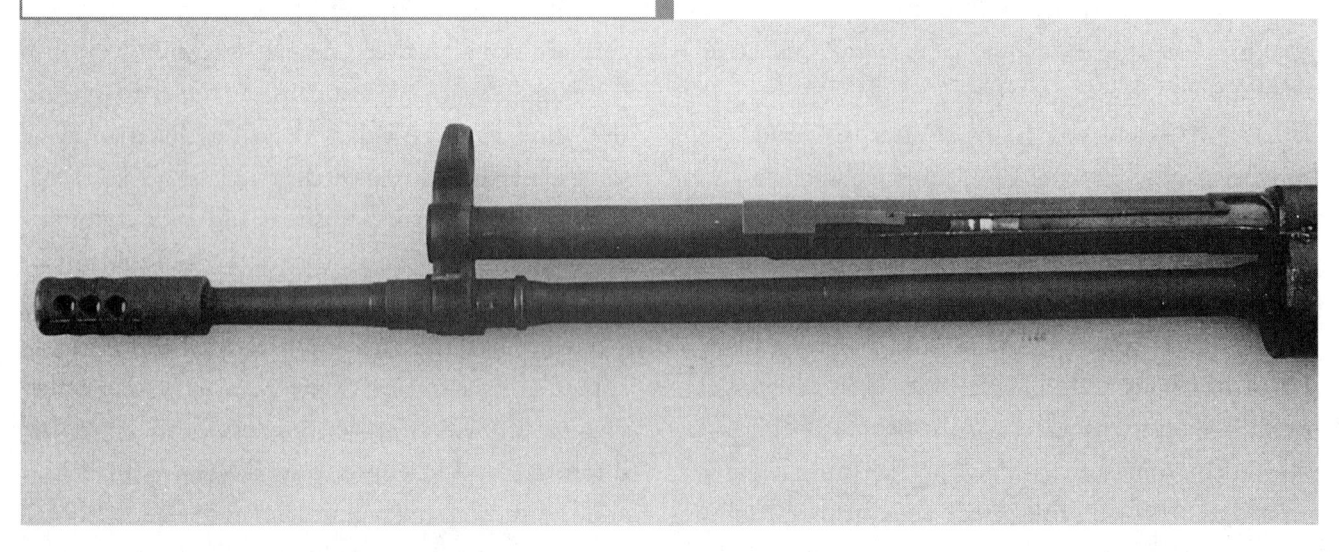

What looks like a gas tube atop the barrel of a G3 actually holds the rifle's cock-ing mechanism and supports the front sight.

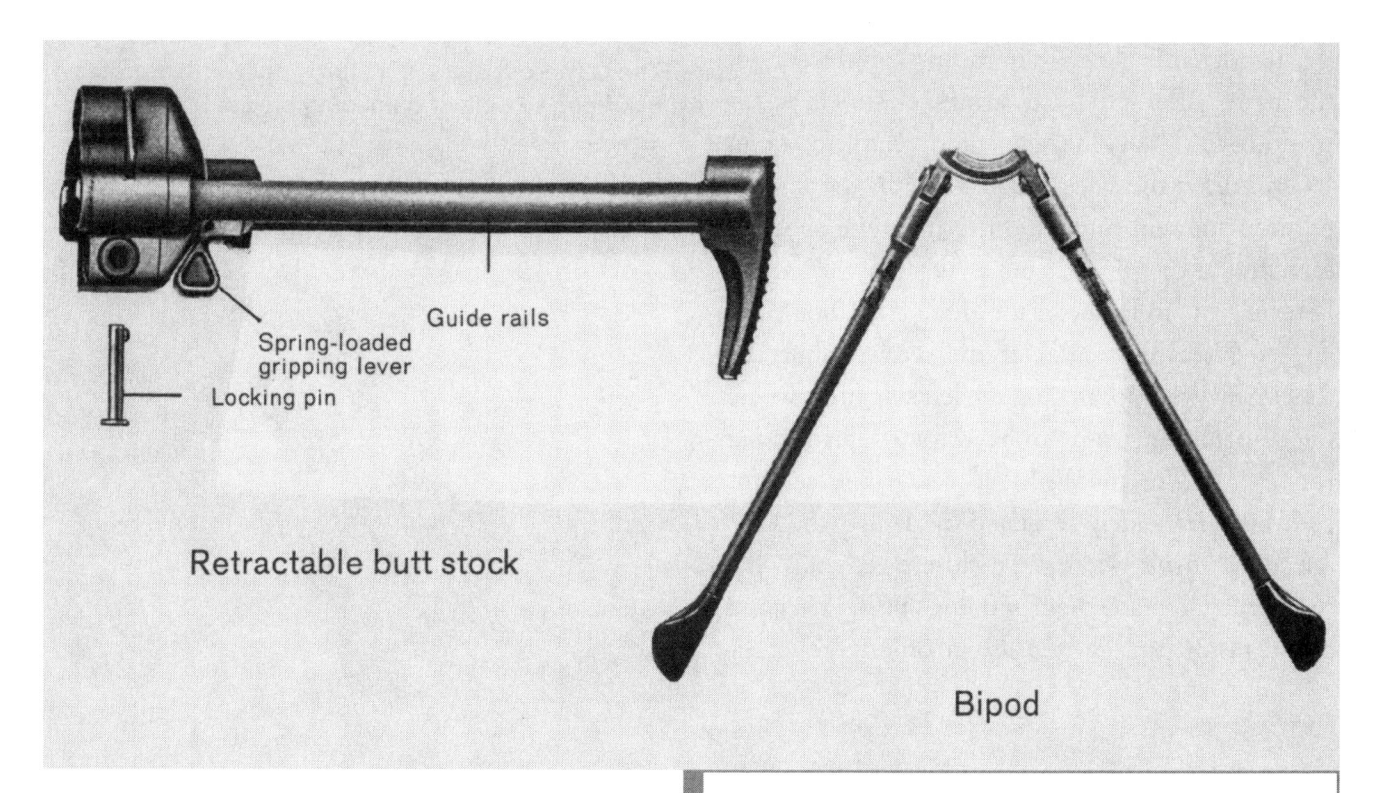

Heckler & Koch's retractable buttstock and folding lightweight bipod have added to the flexibility of the G3 series (photo courtesy of Heckler & Koch).

CETME also offered its basic 7.62mm rifle as a commercial development known as the "CETME Sport." The Mars Equipment Corporation (Chicago, Illinois) imported these rifles into the U.S. during the 1960s. Later on, Heckler & Koch refined the CETME design even further to create the company's legendary G3 battle rifle.

In 1959, West Germany purchased several thousand Modelo B CETME rifles, designating them as G3 (the Swiss StG 57/SIG 510 rifles purchased at the same time had already been given the German designation G2, while the Armalite AR-10 was called G4 by the Germans). Field trials conducted by the *Bundeswehr* confirmed the usefulness and general suitability of the CETME rifle and it was recommended for adoption, albeit with some small changes (see below).

The West German government decided in 1960 to adopt the CETME, slightly modified to suit local requirements, and retain the designation *Gewehr 3* (or G3 for short). Its adoption by the West German armed forces assured its future with an initial order of several hundred thousand. From there, the G3 went on to arm dozens of other countries, being outsold in the noncommunist world only by the FAL. Although Heckler & Koch has not released total G3 production figures for several years, production is said to have reached nearly seven million by 1978.

The G3

During its service in Germany, the original G3 variant had a carrying handle and bipod, both of which folded when not in use. The L-shaped rear sight had two settings which rocked into whatever setting the shooter desired. This sight was replaced in June 1961 with the rotary rear sight now standard on G3-type rifles. The buttstock was wooden, while a slim handguard, rounded in cross-section, was made of sheet metal. Ventilation holes cut in the handguard allowed air to enter and cool off the barrel after extended strings of fire. Selector markings on the G3's trigger group consisted of an "S" (top) for the safe setting, a "1" in the middle position for semiautomatic fire (i.e., one shot for each pull of the trigger), and a "D" or an "F" at the bottom for fully-automatic fire. The markings appeared on both sides of the receiver, but the selector switch appeared on the left side only, where the control came easily to hand for a right-handed shooter. Unlike the FAL, in which the selector controls were widely separated by design, the G3's selector controls were spaced close together, so the shooter could reach them without shifting his hand on the pistol grip. The G3 also incorporated a cock-

The G3's front sight is a sturdy post with a protective hood to deflect damaging blows.

The USP45, in a left-side view, shows the pistol's clean lines.

ing lever located on the rifle's left side, alongside the barrel. This allowed shooters to cock their rifles while maintaining their dominant right hand in the firing position. Early G3 production took place in Spain until Heckler & Koch tooled up. Once that happened, production shifted entirely to West Germany, with Heckler & Koch getting the lion's share.

The G3A1

Because of the delay, the G3A1 finally made its appearance in October 1963. Heckler & Koch immediately took pains to perfect its retractable stock. It was worth the effort, though, because the stock served extremely well. In the ensuing years, its

Since the original model was introduced, the G3 has used a four-position rotary rear sight adjustable from 100 to 400 meters.

The West German military's first issue rifle after Worl War Two was the superb M1 Garand, of which 46,750 were supplied to the country from the United States.

Chapter Two 71

The G3A4 and G3KA4 (shown) both use a collapsible tubular metal stock for greater compactness. This rifle's barrel is under 13 inches in length and its stock when retracted as shown is only 28.4 inches long (photo courtesy of Heckler & Koch).

design has been used throughout the company's product line. To deploy the stock, its release, located beneath the receiver cap, is first set into operation. The stock then slides out along tracks on either side of the receiver. With the stock retracted, the rifle is only 31½ inches long, making it far more compact than the standard rifle with fixed stock. This stock-retracting mechanism, by the way, adds weight to the entire mechanism when compared to the standard rifle (unloaded weight of the G3A1 rose to 10.23 pounds). The G3A1 has been extremely popular with the German police and armed forces.

The G3A2

When the G3A2 first appeared in June 1962, it featured a free-floated barrel designed to improve accuracy. Many other guns in the past shared this feature as they were returned to various *Bundeswehr* armories or to Heckler & Koch for periodic rebuilds in accordance with West Germany military mandates. Such older rifles, having been converted to G3A2 standard, are marked "FS" on their magazine housings.

The G3A3

The G3A3, which was approved in December 1964, replaced the original wooden stock with a sturdy plastic one. Its handguard was also changed to a plastic type, initially with a rounded cross-section. Later on, the triangular-shaped "tropical" handguard was introduced, at first on H&K's .223-caliber rifles. Both the G3A3 and G3A4 (below) incorporated in their designs a strengthened front sight and an improved flash suppressor/muzzle brake. The latter made use of NATO-standard 22mm rifle grenades. Many older G3-type rifles sent back for rebuilding were retrofitted with the new plastic stock/handguard furniture.

The G3A4

The G3A4, appearing at the same time as the G3A3, carried all the G3A3 improvements, but featured the retractable stock developed for the G3A1.

72 Heckler & Koch

The G3A4 has since become one of Heckler & Koch's most popular variants, both in its original German form and in foreign copies.

The G3K

One of the FAL's shortcomings is its gas operation, which precludes shortening the barrel much beyond 17 inches. Reducing it any further decreases combustion of the powder charge, causing failure to develop adequate pressure. As a result, the gas system lacks the proper amount of propellant gas needed to cycle the action. The same problem surfaced in the mid-1960s with the U.S. M16 rifle, which was also gas-operated. The 10-inch barrel of Colt's SM177E "Commando" looked sharp but functioned poorly because consumption of the propellant charge in such a short space proved inadequate to operate a gas-operated loading system reliably. The M16-type M4 Carbine currently in use by U.S. Special Forces has since switched to a 14-inch barrel, representing as such the shortest barrel length known to function with reliability.

Fortunately, the G3 suffers no such barrel-length limitations. Its roller-locked design does not rely directly on gas pressure in order to operate its reloading mechanism. Thus, barrel length is of no consequence—at least not where the rifle's self-loading function is concerned. The only real concerns that arise with the short barrel length in a G3-type rifle are its cartridge power, accuracy and the shooter's health and safety.

As a result, Heckler & Koch developed the short-barreled G3K (*K=Kurz* or "Short"), whose abbreviated 12.9-inch barrel barely extends beyond the handguard. This rifle usually appears with a retractable stock (as pioneered in the G3A4), but a standard fixed stock may also be used. With its A4-type retractable stock fully closed, the G3K is only 28.4 inches long. Muzzle flash and blast are, as a result, increased over those of a standard rifle with a longer barrel. But the improved portability and concealability of this weapon often outweighs ballistic considerations, particularly when used at distances of 100 yards or less.

> **Unlike most modern military self-loading rifles, the G3's roller-locking mechanism does not depend upon gas pressure to operate, so the short-barreled G3K functions as reliably as the standard G3. The collapsible stock is shown extended for accurate long-range shooting (photo courtesy of Heckler & Koch).**

Important Changes Emerge

With the simultaneous adoption of the G3A3 and G3A4, Heckler & Koch and West Germany's armed forces remained satisfied with the basic design for some time. Then, beginning in 1974, the company made a series of changes, starting with the pistol grip and selector lever. In addition, a modified and enlarged handguard with a triangular cross-section replaced the rounded handguard. Sometimes called the tropical handguard, this new design first appeared in the HK33 series **(see below and photo, p. 78)** and eventually became standard on all Heckler & Koch military rifles (its machine guns have, however, kept the rounded handguard).

Further changes occurred in 1986. On standard German military models made prior to that year, the selector switch went all the way up to safe (marked S for *Sicher*, meaning "safe"), down to an intermediate position (marked E for *Einzelfeuer*, meaning "single shots") for semiautomatic fire (i.e., one shot for every pull of the trigger), and all the way down to a setting marked D (for *Daueurfeuer*, meaning "automatic fire") for fully-automatic fire. Rifles shipped abroad had the exact same settings, except that a letter "F" replaced the "D" for fully-automatic. Heckler & Koch called this trigger group the SEF group. Originally, this group appeared as a separate piece of wood (early G3s) or plastic attached to the steel frame of the pistol-grip assembly. The triggerguard was a separate piece of steel bent to shape and welded to the lower receiver. The safety/fire-selector control appeared only on the left side of the pistol grip. The settings were repeated on the right side but there was no control on that side for shooters who adopted a left-handed hold. The two-position, semiautomatic-only trigger group released for commercial sale as the HK91 repeated this early trigger group design.

Since 1986, German-made G3s and their look-alikes have used a single plastic molding that unifies

> **In an effort to extract even greater accuracy from the G3 design, Heckler & Koch created the G3SG1 in 1973 with set trigger for an improved trigger pull, provision for a stabilizing bipod, a cheekpiece on the buttstock and a "claw" mount for a telescopic sight. (photo courtesy of Heckler & Koch).**

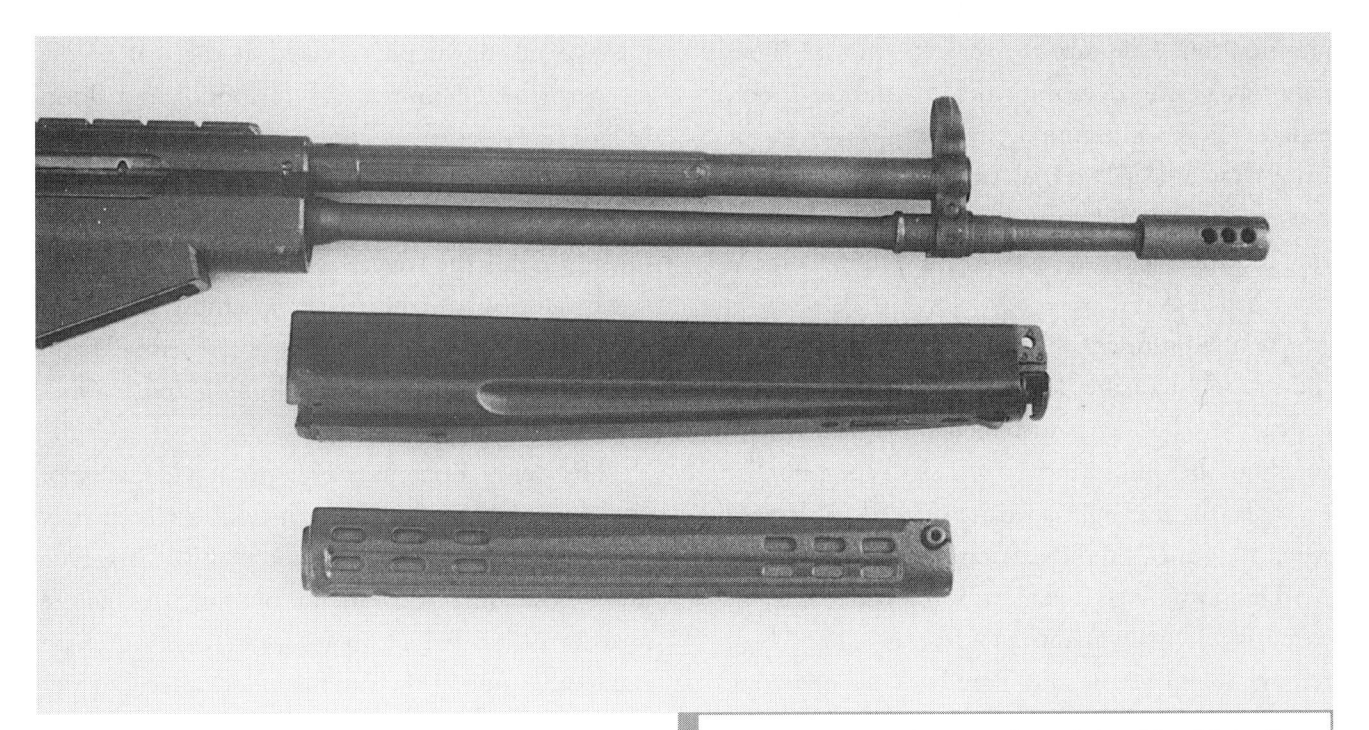

Heckler & Koch has marketed the G3 with both a narrow handguard (bottom) and a broader "tropical" handguard (center). Grooves in the side of the latter are for optional bipod legs to fold up close to the rifle when not in use.

grip, triggerguard and lower receiver. Controls are almost always ambidextrous. Markings at present consist of the following: a white bullet marked with an X to denote the safe setting; a single red bullet for the semiautomatic option; a row of three red bullets for the three-shot burst option; and a row of seven red bullets for fully-automatic use. For recently manufactured guns made for commercial sale on the open market—and thus limited to semiautomatic fire (one shot for each pull on the trigger)—two settings are available: "S" for safe and "F" for semiautomatic only fire.

G3 Operation

Operating procedures for the G3 deserve close attention, because they serve as the prototype for the entire Heckler & Koch rifle and submachine gun series. To load the weapon, the rifle is held by the pistol grip using the right hand. The operating handle is simultaneously drawn back with the left hand until the operating handle can be inserted all the way back into its retaining notch. While still holding the pistol grip, the front of a loaded magazine is inserted in the magazine well, meanwhile rocking the rear portion of the magazine until the magazine release clicks, announcing that the magazine has been seated successfully. Next, the operating handle is pulled down and moved forward under spring pressure, thus loading the first round. It's important not to hold the operating handle or attempt to "ease" it forward. Since the full force of the spring is required, it will not be hurt by "slamming" forward. Check the manual safety and, if not already set for the desired level of fire, adjust the selector accordingly; i.e., "1" or "E" for single shots, or "20" or "F" for fully-automatic fire. This gun does not include a hold-open feature on the bolt once the last round has been fired. The traditional method is to load the last few rounds (generally three) as tracer ammunition, so once the tracers appear the shooter will know he's almost out of ammunition. Contrary to what the movies show, counting rounds does not work. Should the shooter lack tracer ammunition, or fails to notice it, the firing pin may fall on an empty firing chamber, causing the shooting to stop. The procedure for getting the gun back into operation is then the same as described above.

Sight adjustment is simple. One simply rotates the rear sight to the desired range settings, which appear in 100-meter increments marked with a small number just below the rear sight aperture. For example, the rear sight aperture marked "3" is used when shooting 300 meters from the target.

Disassembling (field stripping) the G3 for cleaning and maintenance proceeds as follows: first, remove the magazine and draw back the operating handle all the way to the rear, making sure the firing chamber is unloaded. Let the operating handle run forward again, leaving the hammer cocked. Do not dry-fire the rifle. The hammer should remain cocked during disassembly. Next, remove the two takedown pins located at the rear of the receiver (the 5.56mm (.223 HK33/93 and 9mm MP5/HK94 series use only a single pin in this location). Set these pins aside in a safe place. With the pins removed, pull the stock sharply to the rear. Once it clears the trigger assembly, that will hinge downward. When the trigger assembly has fallen open, reach up and remove the bolt assembly from the rear end of the receiver. Cleaning and maintenance may now proceed.

Heckler & Koch has developed a wide range of accessories for the G3. These include a winter trigger, scope mounts, a bayonet and many others. Due to the close similarity of the various long arms in the Heckler & Koch line, many accessories are interchangeable among the various models (see Chapter 6 for further details).

Distribution of The G3

In addition to Germany, G3 rifles are (or have been) military/police issue in the following countries: Bahrain, Bangladesh, Bolivia, Brunei, Burma, Burundi, Canada, Chad, Colombia, Cyprus, Denmark, Djibouti, Dominican Republic, El Salvador, Ethiopia, Gabon, Ghana, Great Britain (SAS),

The introduction of the ArmaLite/Colt CAR-15 and its military acceptance as the M16 caused worldwide interest in creating 5.56mm/.223 caliber rifles to compete with the popular "black rifle."

Greece, Guyana, Haiti, Indonesia, Iran, Ivory Coast, Jordan, Kenya, Lebanon, Libya, Malawi, Malaysia, Mauritania, Mexico, Morocco, Ni-ger, Nigeria, Norway, Pakistan, Paraguay, Peru, Philippines, Por-tugal, Saudi Arabia, Somalia, South Africa, Sudan, Sweden, Tanzania, Togo, Turkey, Uganda, United Arab Emirates, United States (primarily for Special Forces use by Navy SEALS and Army Rangers), Zaire, Zambia and Zimbabwe.

At least ten countries have arranged licensed production of the G3 (see chapter 7). While sales of the G3 have inevitably slowed down with the deluge of handier, more compact .223 caliber/56mm military assault rifles now available, these H&K guns remain reliable and sturdy. Many will doubtless stay in service for decades to come.

> The 5.56mm HK33A2 is the company's standard fixed-stock variant. The improved broad "tropical" forend/handguard first introduced with this model later became standard with the larger 7.62mm/.308 caliber G3 (photo courtesy of Heckler & Koch).

company's first sniper rifle on the G3 platform—the G3 Zf (Zf.=*Zielfernrohr*, meaning "telescopic sight")—appeared in 1964. These specially selected rifles, whose test-firing results at the factory proved them to be unusually accurate, were then mated to an optical sight. Since the stamped sheet steel used in the G3's receiver did not lend itself to drilling and tapping holes for an optical scope mount, Heckler & Koch developed a special "claw" mount, so that an optical scope could be attached to any of H&K's G3-type rifles.

PART III: 7.62mm (.308) SNIPER RIFLES

The G3 Zf

The G3's exemplary accuracy, even in its standard models, encouraged Heckler & Koch to challenge the commonly held supposition that only bolt action rifles provide top-notch accuracy. The

The G3 SG/1

In 1973, H&K added a special trigger mechanism to this selection process. It included a set trigger, allowing a much lighter trigger pull, and led to the G3 SG1 (SG= *Scharfschützengewehr*, meaning "sharpshooting rifle"). Most G3 SG1 variants were equipped with a bipod and a cheekpiece on the left side of the buttstock for easier sighting with the

Chapter Two 77

Safe	Single fire	Burst
Safe	Single fire	Burst

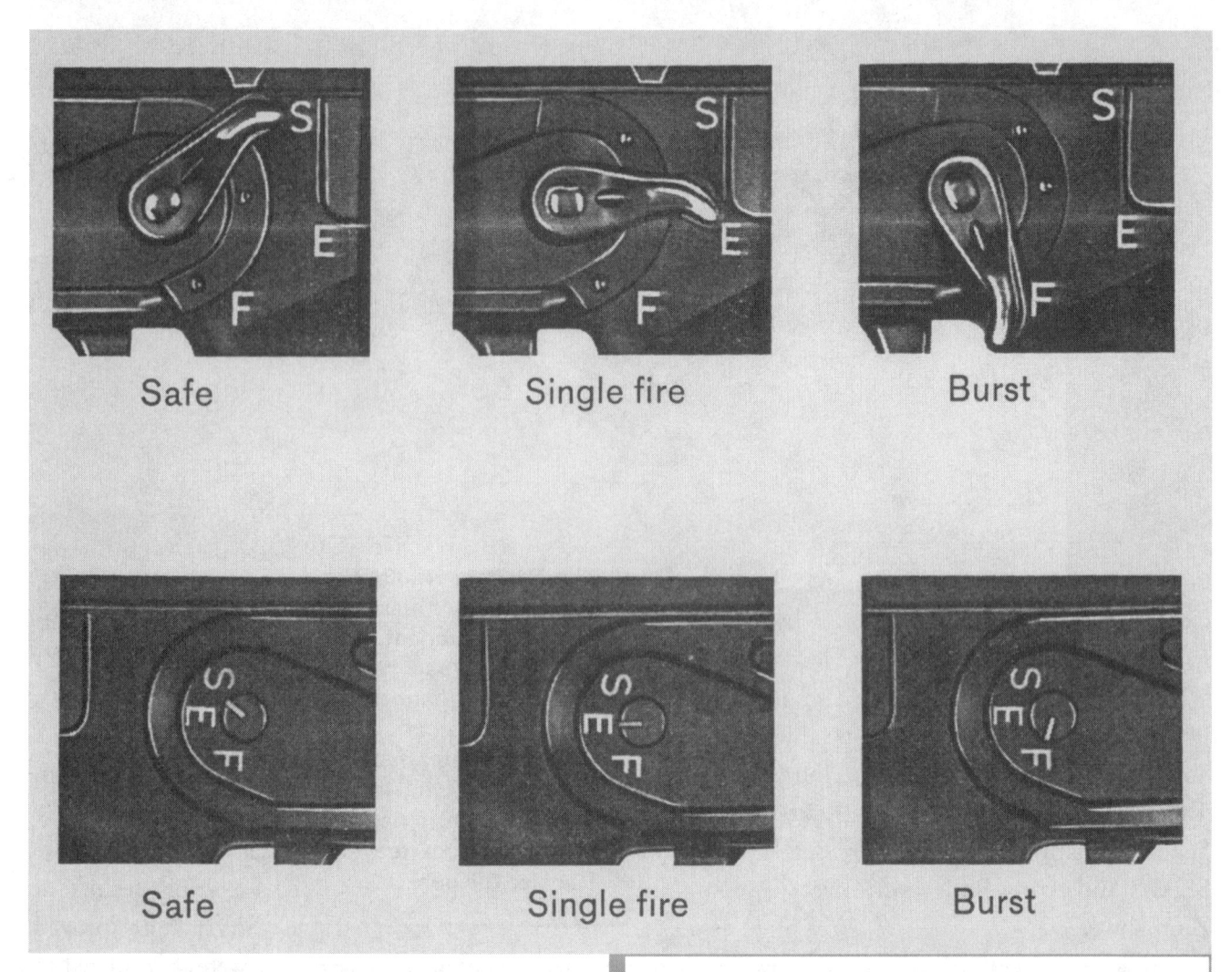

> The early G3's fire selectors were marked with an S for "safe," an E for semiautomatic fire and an F for fully-automatic fire (photo courtesy of Heckler & Koch).

standard 1.5-6 power adjustable scope. In addition to Germany, several countries, including Italy, Malaysia and the United States, sill issue the G3 SG1 to a limited number of military and police forces.

The PSG-1

While the G3 Zf and G# SG1 rifles improved on the already impressive accuracy, Heckler & Koch still had not succeeded in creating a rifle that could shoot with the best bolt action models. Accordingly, the company began a no-holds-barred competition to create the ultimate semiautomatic sniper rifle. This effort led to still another variation, the PSG-1 (PSG= *Präzisions Schützen Gewehr*, meaning "Sniper Rifle"). It made its debut **(photo p. 100)** in 1985 after a five-year developmental period. This rifle still employs the G3's basic roller-locked mechanism, but it also adds a fully adjustable stock and pistol grip, plus a heavier, longer barrel and fixed 6-power telescopic sight. Even more important was H&K's decision to address the G3's greatest shortcoming as a serious sniping rifle by creating a much more responsive trigger mechanism. Unlike the standard military G3, however, the PSG-1 has no provision for fully-automatic fire. Since few snipers have ever had a serious need for fully-automatic fire

78 Heckler & Koch

in the performance of their duties, this seems a small price to pay, particularly when a responsive trigger pull is a must on a sniping rifle.

Total weight of the PSG-1 rises to an impressive (and unwieldy) 17.9 pounds, nearly double that of the standard G3. Not surprisingly, H&K offers with each rifle a special tripod mount for use by, among others, police counter-snipers who stand long watches in stakeout or hostage situations. In addition to its marvelous accuracy, the PSG-1 is also fabulously expensive, limiting its use to the wealthiest governments.

The MSG 3

Despite the PSG-1's high efficiency, its cost made it less successful than H&K had anticipated and forced the company to continue its search for less costly alternatives. First among these was the MSG 3. This consisted of carefully tuned G3 actions combined with a less elaborate stock than that issued with the PSG-1, even though it remained adjustable for comb and length of pull, a sturdy (but non-adjustable) bipod and fixed sights, including a drum rear sight similar to those found on the H&K machine gun designs derived from the G3 (see Chapter 5). The MSG 3 appeared in 1987 and was used by the German police, who were impressed by the PSG-1 but appalled by its high cost.

The MSG 90

A year after introducing the MSG 3, H&K announced the slightly more elaborate MSG 90, which split the difference between the MSG 3 and the PSG-1. The MSG 90 adds to the MSG 3 an adjustable bipod and, like the PSG-1, eliminates fixed sights altogether in favor of NATO's standard scope mount. The MSG 90 trigger features an adjustable shoe fitted to reduce overtravel. All H&K sniper rifles use NATO's standard 7.62x51mm (.308) round, thereby assuring a place in the inventories of various NATO countries and other Western-aligned nations.

Part IV: Heckler & Koch's 5.56mm (.223) Rifles

In addition to its sniper rifles, Heckler & Koch has downsized the basic G3 to fire the newer 5.56x45mm (.223 caliber) round. This ammo was first used in combat by the U.S. in its M16 rifles in Vietnam and later, in the 1980s, standardized in modified form by NATO as the SS109. Even though the West German armed forces had made a decision in the late 1960s to skip the 5.56/.223 round altogether, Heckler & Koch developed a series of G3-type rifles modified to fire the 5.56mm cartridge as a private venture. The company reasoned that, once it changed calibers (from the 7.62mm/.308 to the 5.56/.223, its many customers around the world might opt for the tried and proven G3 operating system. H&K's assumption proved at least partially correct. The resultant HK33 family, while not sold in enormous quantities like the G3, has certainly had its share of success.

The HK33

The first of H&K's 5.56mm rifles based on the G3 mechanism was the HK33 **(photo p. 77)**, which the company introduced officially in 1965. The first major sale took place in 1968, when Brazil bought several thousand for its air force, even though it was also building FAL variants in both standard and shortened forms.

In its mechanical operation and features, the HK33 owes a great deal to the G3; in fact, they look a lot alike. The dimensions have been reduced proportionally, however, to reflect the smaller size and lower power level of the .223 caliber cartridge.

This reduction in cartridge size allows H&K to fit a 25-round magazine to the 5.56mm rifle, as opposed to the G3's bulkier 7.62mm magazine, which holds only 20 rounds. The HK33 and its descendants also weigh appreciably less than the G3—a definite selling point in the rugged tropical terrain in which many of these rifles are carried and used.

Given the similarity between the two types, the HK33 series can use most of the accessories developed for the G3 line. Thanks to a kind of reverse borrowing, the improved and widened "tropical" style handguard, which Heckler & Koch pioneered on the HK33 series, later became standard on the G3 series as well.

Although the HK33 has not achieved anywhere near the popularity of the ubiquitous G3, its rifles are well distributed. The main areas of interest in the HK33 are the Americas, Africa and Southeast Asia, though other continents are also represented. In addition to Brazil, both Chile and El Salvador issue the weapon. Moreover, various 5.56mm/.223 caliber HK33-type rifles, including the semiautomatic-only HK93, have gained a following among police forces in the U.S. In Southeast Asia, Malaysia and Thailand also issue the HK33 to elements of their armed forces. The European countries include Ireland, the Netherlands, Portugal, Spain and Switzerland. In Africa and the Middle East, HK33 purchasers have included Ghana, Lebanon, Senegal and Tanzania. By the way, not all HK33s were made in Heckler & Koch's home factory in Germany. The story of license-built Heckler & Koch firearms merits a whole chapter to itself (see Chapter 7).

The new HK33A2 that was first placed into series production had a fixed stock, a 15.4-inch (390mm) barrel (36.2 inches overall), and a total weight (unloaded) of 7.95 pounds. Handy as this rifle was, Heckler & Koch made it even easier to carry by applying the same collapsible-stock technology used in some G3 variants. Though mechanically identical to its predecessor, the HK33A2, the A3's stock, when completely retracted, reduced overall length to only 29.15 inches. This reduction in size made the HK33A3 ideal for paratroopers and other airborne personnel, along with drivers and other vehicle operators, artillerymen, officers and the like.

The HK33K

As convenient as the HK33A3 proved to be, Heckler & Koch decided an even shorter version would appeal to various police and military forces in need of firepower at the HK33 level in a small-sized package. Noting that the HK33's self-loading system did not depend directly on gas pressure, the barrel, as a result, could be shortened at will. Accordingly, Heckler & Koch created the HK33KA1 (k=*Kurz* meaning "short"). Barrel length on this HK33Ka1 version is only 12.7 inches, with a total length (including a retractable stock fully extended) of only 34.06 inches. With the collapsible stock fully retracted, the overall length is 26.75 inches.

The U.S. Navy's elite SEAL teams took to the HK33KA1 in modest numbers. Considering its compact size, the rifle delivered good power and excellent reliability. Compared to the .223 caliber HK53 (see Chapter 4), the KA1 rifle offers slightly more barrel length, plus improved accuracy and terminal ballistics, while retaining extremely compact dimensions and easy handling. The HK33KA1 was used extensively by the SEAL teams in the mid-1980s, before Colt's M4 .223 caliber carbine version of the M16A2 became available.

The HK33E Series

The improved HK33E line appeared in 1983. Two years later, Heckler & Koch added an improved fire-selector system, which is not only ambidextrous—its controls appear on both sides of the receiver—but adds a fourth position. In addition to the safe, single-shot and fully-automatic settings, it now provides the three-round burst. The rate of fire on full-auto (750 rpm) remains the same as the original HK33A2's, but unloaded weight has risen slightly, from 8.05 to 8.4 pounds.

To improve sales potential in a variety of markets, Heckler & Koch created several minor variants of the HK33E. The HK33ECA2, for example, featured a forest green finish instead of the usual black. Its purpose was partly to endow the rifle with superior camouflage potential. Another was to reduce the rifle's absorption of heat. The buttstock was fixed, not retractable. The HK33ECA3 was also painted forest green, but it retained the popular collapsible buttstock. Still another variant, the HK33KC, had both a shortened barrel (K) and a retractable buttstock. The HK33ESA2 featured a fixed buttstock along with a two-tone desert sand camouflage finish. Much of Asia, the Americas and northern Africa have desert regions, so it seemed a logical step for Heckler & Koch to create a rifle painted to match. The HK33ESA3 kept the desert camouflage pattern but substituted a collapsible buttstock for the fixed unit. And finally, the HK33KS was painted in the same desert-camouflage scheme but came equipped with shortened barrel and retractable buttstock.

G3 magazines made by Heckler & Koch include a manufacturing date (month and year) stamped near the bottom. Magazines may be steel (shown), aluminum or plastic.

HK33 Sniping Variants

As with the G3 in .308 caliber, Heckler & Koch also created sniping versions of its .223 caliber (5.56mm) HK33. First among these was the HK33 Zf, which was the same as the fixed-stock HK33A2 but with a telescopic sight and scope mount. No trigger work, nor any other work usually associated with converting a military-issue weapon into a sniping rifle, was undertaken. Nevertheless, for this relatively minor addition, the cost of the rifle was so high that the HK33 Zf enjoyed little success. Anyone not wanting the enhanced accuracy potential of an optically-sighted rifle could easily accomplish an equivalent conversion at relatively modest cost.

Heckler & Koch created a more elaborate sniping conversion in the early 1980s, called the HK33 SG1 ("SG"= *Scharfschüt-zengewehr*, or "Sharp-shooter's Rifle"). Compared to the standard HK33E, this model featured a slightly longer and improved stock with an adjustable cheekpiece. The barrel was heavier, causing the rifle to weigh nearly a pound more than a standard HK33. Heckler & Koch added a set trigger to compensate for the long, heavy trigger pull for which H&K's military rifles are notorious. A claw mount and a 4-power (4x) telescopic sight completed the package. Interestingly, the HK33 SG1 retained the original trigger group on the HK33A2, including selective-fire capability—an odd feature on a rifle designed for precision sniping. At least two countries, the Netherlands and Switzerland, issued these rifles, but there are probably others.

The HK41

In 1977, the North Atlantic Treaty Organization (NATO), which at the time included West Germany, the U.S. and 12 other members, launched a series of trials to determine a new standard cartridge to replace the then standard 7.62mm/.308. The U.S. Army's decision in 1969 to re-equip its

> The HK33K, with its shortened barrel, was the compact version of the HK33 series. The "claw" mount allowed a telescopic sight to be mounted atop the receiver (the sheet metal receiver cover was not suited to the drilling and tapping process). Heckler & Koch offered this model as the HK33 Zf (photo courtesy of Heckler & Koch).

82 Heckler & Koch

Cartridge — Bolt head — Locking piece — Firing pin

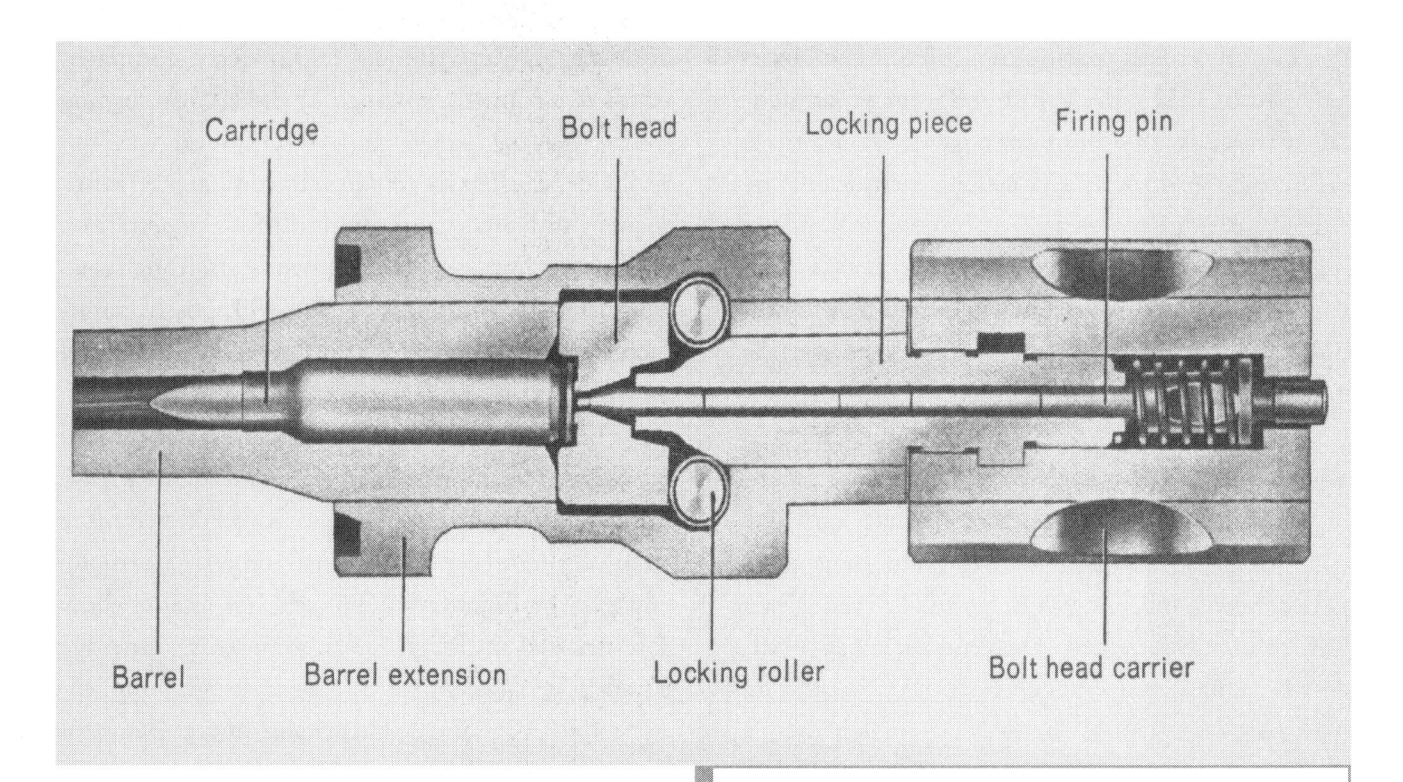

Barrel — Barrel extension — Locking roller — Bolt head carrier

soldiers stationed in Europe with the M16A1 (5.56mm/.223 caliber) as a replacement for the M14 (7.62mm) helped bring about a crisis in NATO. The other NATO member countries liked the improved controllability of the .223 round in fully-automatic fire, nor did they dispute the fine record of this little cartridge following ten years of use by the U.S. in Southeast Asia. However, they did not want to give up the superior range and penetration of the .308 round. They also wanted assurances that a test program would be set up in a manner that would eliminate the national bias which had allowed the United States to force the 7.62mm round upon the other, weaker NATO member nations back in 1951.

As a result, the NATO Small Arms Test Control Commission set up to test cartridges and weapons submitted by various member countries in an impartial and manageable way. Accordingly, the NATO Army Armaments Group sent member nations a list of desired characteristics that included the following: reliability, maintainability, suitability to tactical mission, hit probability and probability

> The G3 and most other Heckler & Koch self-loading rifles use a roller-locked mechanism first developed in Nazi Germany near the end of World War II and subsequently refined in Spain and West Germany. In this system the recoiling cartridge base acts to force the locking rollers outward against the receiver walls. This ensures the breech will remain closed until the bullet has left the barrel and chamber pressures have dropped to a safe level.

of incapacitation. NATO also expressed a desire for an integrated weapons system consisting of an individual weapon or rifle, a light support weapon (automatic rifle or light machine gun) and a medium support weapon or medium machine gun. Getting the 15 member nations—most of whom had significant capability for manufacturing weapons of their own—to agree to this much in principle was a major accomplishment. It didn't come easily; indeed, a NATO commission had been formed to oversee these standardization talks.

As matters evolved, five distinct types of cartridges were submitted for NATO testing in 1977:

the 4.7mm caseless ammunition (fired in the Heckler & Koch G11); the British 4.85mm experimental cartridge (with 49mm cartridge case); and three separate 5.56x45mm/.223 caliber cartridges. The British cartridge represented a conversion from the U.S. .223 round, for which rifles like the M16A1 could be adapted quite easily. It fired a 48-grain bullet, which was seven grains lighter than the 55-grain bullet most commonly used with the .223.

Of the 5.56mm/.223 caliber rounds entered as candidates, one was the U.S. M193 that served in Vietnam, one was a U.S. candidate cartridge (the XM777) modified for improved long-range performance, and one was Belgium's SS109, which was eventually adopted. France, which had withdrawn from NATO in 1966, joined the testing with its own weapon, the FAMAS, which fired a steel-cased variant of the proven U.S. M193 (.223 caliber) cartridge.

These five cartridges appeared with six different weapons submitted as candidates and two light support weapons. A third light support weapon—the West German MG3E—fired the NATO-standard 7.62x51mm/.308 cartridge. As things turned out, while the NATO test panel liked the light weight and small size of the 5.56mm and even ended up recommending one for the alliance, the panel could not agree on a standard weapon among all those submitted. The test panel left each member nation to choose its own weapons, declaring that those submitted for evaluation varied too widely in maturity of design for a small testing commission like theirs to make an informed choice for the entire alliance.

Of great importance to the Heckler & Koch story was NATO's decision on October 28, 1980, to standardize its SS109 version of the 5.56mmx45mm/.223 caliber cartridge. This round, developed by Belgium's Fabrique Nationale (FN), demonstrated superior terminal ballistics—especially at ranges between 500 and 800 meters—compared to the two rounds developed by the U.S. According to the NATO panel, the M193 round was too unstable, causing it to wound combatants inhumanely and producing inferior armor penetration. The U.S.-sponsored XM777, while affording superior armor penetration to the M193, posed manufacturing difficulties caused by its reliance on a steel penetrator core.

The West Germans were not altogether pleased with the test commission's report, arguing in a 1980 publication that their 4.7mm cartridge offered more than enough power against targets normally engaged by infantry. Moreover, no matter how sophisticated in design, no 5.56mm/.223 cartridge could hope to compete in a machine-gun application with the much larger and more powerful 7.62x51mm/.308 caliber SS77 cartridge as originally standardized by NATO. The Germans also pointed out the enormous cost of converting from 7.62mm to 5.56mm, a project that could not be justified in light of the meager results it might achieve. This document, released with West Germany's approval, argued further that the best ammunition/weapons mix in the foreseeable future would consist of 4.7mm individual weapons and 7.62mm support weapons. Since the Bundeswehr had plenty of 7.62mm G3s on hand, it would carry on until the late 1980s, at which time the G11 could replace them.

Shortly after releasing this document, West Germany reversed itself and withdrew its funding for the G11 project, adopting instead a 5.56mm /.223 caliber weapon for the Bundeswehr. Heckler & Koch, while continuing development of the G11 on its own, obliged by creating one of the best assault rifles built to date: the HK41. This rifle is far more than a revamped HK33, though the family resemblance is obvious. With nearly two decades of experience in building HK33 variants, Heckler &

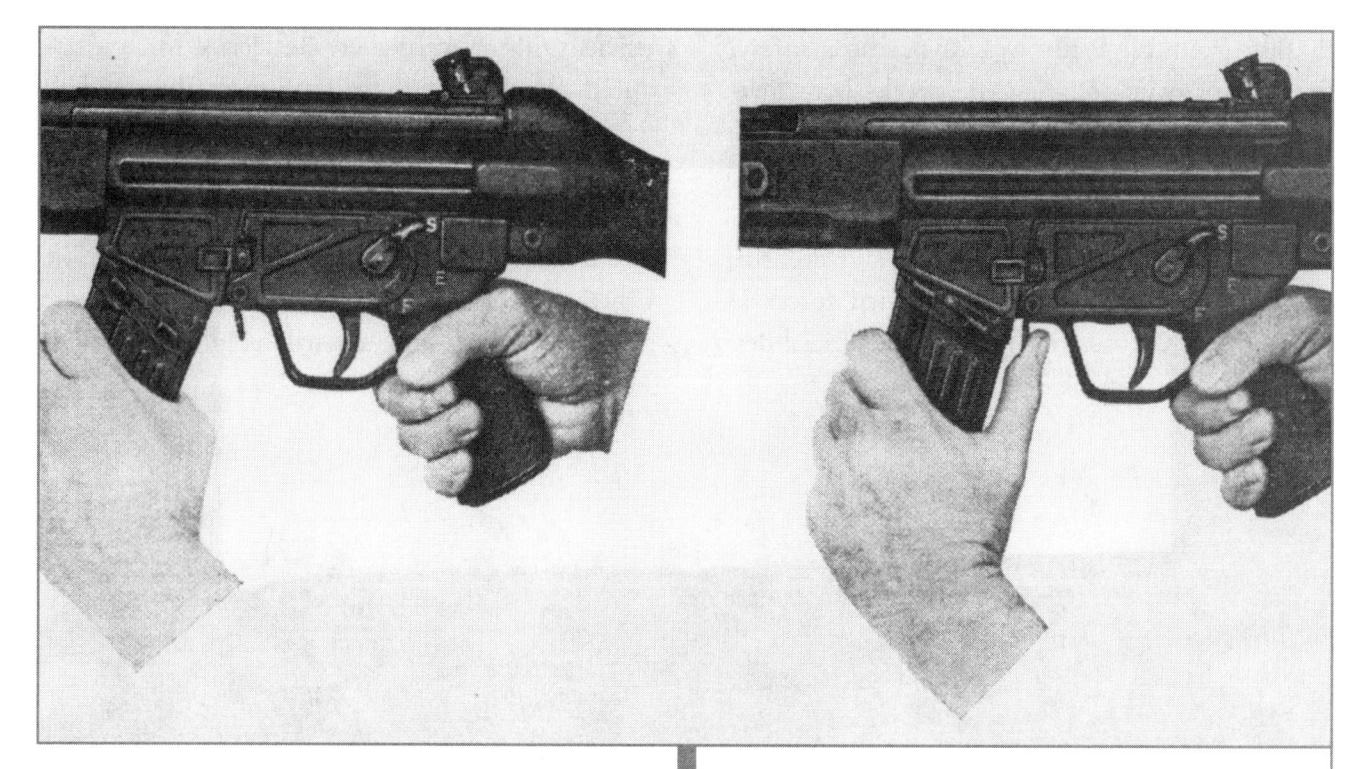

The military-issue G3 has an ambidextrous flipper-type magazine release. It was replaced in the commercial HK91 variant with a one-sided magazine release button (photo courtesy of Heckler & Koch).

Koch had plenty of ideas about how to improve the rifle. The changes and improvements added to the HK41 included a mechanical hold-open device on the bolt, which was activated once the last shot left the firing chamber. The absence of this hold-open device had been a perpetual source of complaint for all previous G3-type rifles. With its new HK41, Heckler & Koch had eliminated still another complaint directed at earlier rifles based on the G3; i.e., the difficulty of cocking them for the first shot. To do so, the shooter had to overcome the considerable mechanical inertia of the bolt-locking rollers in pulling back the operating handle. Simply by enlarging the HK 41's operating handle, cocking the rifle was made noticeably easier without sacrificing the functionally desirable G3 mechanism. A bolt-closing device, a forward bolt assist and a hinged ejection-port cover, all inspired by the U.S. M16A1, appeared on the HK41. Moreover, its magazine well was designed to be compatible with the M16 magazine. Heckler & Koch also added NATO-standard scope mounts and tritium inserts on the iron sights, providing the HK41 with improved night-fighting capability. A folding carrying handle, inspired by one found on the FAL, was hinged to the right side of the rifle. And, to use the SS109 variant of the 5.56mm/.223 cartridge more efficiently, Heckler & Koch gave the new rifle a heavier, longer barrel (17.7 inches) with a faster twist of rifling (one turn in seven inches) as compared to the HK33's 15.35-inch barrel and a rifling twist of one turn in 12 inches.

All changes made to the basic HK33 in creating the HK41 did not come without cost. Compared to the HK33 series, its weight rose slightly (9.04 pounds unloaded) and became noticeably more expensive to produce. Basic disassembly procedures remained the same as for the popular G3. The HK41 was built sturdily, with a minimum service life of

20,000 rounds. With a four-position safety/fire selector switch offering safe, single-shot, three-round burst and full-auto settings, the HK41's cyclic rate of fire in fully-automatic mode rose to 900 rounds per minutes.

Upon its introduction in 1981 and eventual adoption by the West German armed forces in 1983, the HK41 was finally given the official designation *Gewehr 41*, or G41. Now considered Germany's new standard rifle, it was about to replace the G3, which was slated for gradual withdrawal for rebuilding purposes, a process that took place about once every five years.

At first, the G41's term of front-line service with West Germany's armed forces seemed limited to only five or six years at most. The *Bundeswehr* really wanted the much more advanced G11, assuming Heckler & Koch could perfect it. However, with plans to introduce the new rifle shelved in 1990 (see below), the G41 and the later G36 (see below) will undoubtedly remain Germany's standard military rifles for some years to come.

Considering the inherent problems of the 5.56mm/.223 caliber cartridge, the G41 is an efficient rifle. Nevertheless, Heckler & Koch introduced several variants to supplement the standard fixed-stock G41A2, thereby making the rifle even more suitable for a variety of missions. Thus did a retractable-stock version—the G41A3—go into service along with the fixed-stock variant. The G41K added a shortened barrel (14.9 inches) to the retractable-stock variant, making a total length (with the stock fully extended) of 36.65 inches, reduced to 30.1 inches when the buttstock was retracted all the way to the receiver end plate.

When the G41 TGS appeared in 1985, a 40mm grenade launcher—the HK79—was added to the underside of the barrel. To aim the grenade launcher, early G41 TGS variants included a ladder-style sight on top of the receiver in front of the front sight, while later TGS variants placed a more compact, rounded grenade launcher sight on the right side of the forearm (see also Chapter 6).

> The HK33K was offered with a collapsible stock as the HK33KA1. With its 12.7-inch barrel and its collapsible stock retracted, this model measures less than 27 inches long (photo courtesy of Heckler & Koch).

86 Heckler & Koch

In 1986, Heckler & Koch introduced important changes to the G41's pistol grip, trigger group and fire-selector assembly. Instead of a plastic grip screwed to a steel support frame, the entire assembly was now made from molded plastic. The shape of the pistol grip was improved and given a more ambidextrous character, with the safety/fire-selector switch repeated on the right side, enabling left-handers to operate it. Simple bullet symbols, understandable to shooters of any language, replaced the previous letters and numbers used on the selector to indicate firing modes.

Still another G41 variant—the G41 INKAS—appeared in 1987. This variant has an active infrared laser projector located in the cocking handle tube for use with special night-vision goggles. The system appeared at the same time in a modified G3 7.62mm rifle (see also Chapter 6).

In addition to West Germany, Great Britain's elite Special Air Services (SAS) antiterrorism team has used G41s to a limited extent. The Italian armed forces, also involved in the NATO alliance, had a close look at the G41, albeit in slightly modified form. The G41's sponsor in the Italian service trials of 1985 was the famous Italian shotgun manufacturer, Luigi Franchi SpA, Heckler & Koch's business partner at the time. One stipulation of the ensuing competition was that the winning entrant, if selected for the Italian armed forces service, must be built in Italy. Had Heckler & Koch's G41 won, however, Franchi would have made the rifles locally. Among the changes made by Franchi to the basic G41 were a fixed, M16-style carrying handle with the rear sight placed on top and the front sight elevated to match. The handguard was rounded, with ten ribs molded into it. The shape of the fixed buttstock was also changed and the rifle acquired a slightly more substantial bipod than that usually fitted to the German-issued rifle. Although the modified G41 put in a good performance, the Italians decided to do with a wholly local design, namely Beretta's Model AR70/90 (see Chapter 8 for additional H&K/Franchi connections with the manufacture and merchandizing of shotguns).

For sniping purposes, Heckler & Koch created a G41 Zf variant by taking a rifle that had performed well in H&K's thorough test-firing procedure prior to leaving the factory. In this case the rifle was given a 4-power telescopic sight. While the 5.56mm/.,223 caliber cartridge has never had a sterling reputation for accuracy, the NATO-standard SS109 round now in use has improved its long-range performance somewhat. With the G41 Zf rifle fired with compatible ammunition, good accuracy results are attainable to 300 or 400 meters. Nevertheless, the 5.56mm will never be a match for the 7.62x 51mm/ .308, despite the many efforts expended in making the new NATO cartridge perform as well as the old one did.

One might have expected the HK41/G41 to replace the HK33 series altogether, but this did not happen. Even though the HK33K short-barreled variants went out of production in favor of the G41K, the HK33E remained in production, in part because Heckler & Koch can sell it for considerably less than the G41.

The GR3

Heckler & Koch began development of the *Gewehr R3* (GR3) series around 1985 as a modification of the HK33/41 line intended mainly for export. Following the example of the popular 5.56mm AUG rifle produced by Austria's Steyr GmbH, the H&K GR3 rifle featured a fully adjustable 1.5-power telescopic sight permanently attached to the receiver. Experience with the Steyr AUG revealed that this sight, with its highly visible aiming reticle, offers an aiming advantage over the standard iron sight, while keeping the magnification low enough to allow a shouter to keep both eyes open.

The GR3CA2 variant first appeared in 1988 as the standard model. It had a forest-green finish with fixed buttstock, a barrel measuring 15.35 inches (36.2 inches overall), weighing 8.65 pounds (unloaded) and firing from a 20-, 30- or 40-round magazine. Heckler & Koch then added in quick succession a number of variant models, starting with the GR3SA2 (the same gun as the GR3CA2, except it was finished in a two-tone desert camouflage. Then came the GR3CA3, also forest green in color but with a collapsible stock. A GR3SA3 variant also made use of a collapsible stock but was especially finished for desert operations. Finally, Heckler & Koch introduced two short-barreled "K" GR3 variants with collapsible stocks: the green GR3KC and the desert-camouflaged GR3KS.

Part V: The 7.62x39mm Family

The HK32 made its debut around 1965. Similar to the 5.56mm HK33, it was made instead to fire the 7.62x39mm M1943 Soviet intermediate rifle cartridge. Clearly, Heckler & Koch hoped to compete with weapons like the Czech vz 58 and the SKS, AK-47 and AKM models designed by the Soviets. Standard Heckler & Koch terminology applies, beginning with the HK32A2, the basic model with fixed buttstock. The HK32A3 has a retractable buttstock, exactly the same one used on the G3, HK33 and G41 families.

Heckler & Koch also created an HK22A1 machine-gun version. Belt-fed, and with a higher rate of fire (800 rounds per minute vs 750 rounds per minute for the standard barrel and 700 rounds per minute for the short-barreled variants), this rifle offered formidable competition to the obsolescent RPD light machine gun designed by the Soviets. As with Heckler & Koch's other belt-fed machine guns, this one had a drum-type rear sight offering 11 adjustments compared to the four-position rotary rear sight found on most G3-series rifles.

Finally, Heckler & Koch devised the HK12 light machine gun (or automatic rifle, depending on one's terminology). Box-fed from a 40-round magazine, this model also accepted the standard 30-round magazines issued with the A2, A3 and K-series rifles. This would have been an interesting answer to the Soviets' RPK. Heckler & Koch's weapon supplied a quick-change barrel with its HK12, a feature that would have allowed a far higher degree of sustained fire than the RPK could muster, limited as it was by a fixed barrel. Based on the HK21 machine gun family, the HK22 and HK12 used the same bipod, which is much more rugged than the standard H&K bipod offered as an optional feature. The HK12 employed a four-position, rifle-style rotary rear sight rather than the HK11's bulkier but more precise drum rear sight.

Regrettably for Heckler & Koch, no one who might have had an interest in a weapon in this caliber was willing to compete against the well-entrenched Communist designs made to fire the 7.62x39mm cartridge. As a result, Heckler & Koch sold only a few of these guns and stopped making them altogether around 1982.

An Analysis

The G3, along with other related rifles made by Heckler & Koch, is nearly unique among modern military self-loading rifle makers in not using a gas system for the purpose of operating its action. Instead, a pair of rollers located in a removable breechblock unit at the rear of the receiver holds the mechanism shut for that brief period of maximum chamber pressure upon firing. Within milliseconds, residual chamber pressure exerts force through the spent cartridge casing, which in turn pushes the bolt back to finish the extraction. It then ejects the empty cartridge, strips a fresh cartridge from the magazine, and loads it into the firing chamber for another shot.

Primary extraction is always the chief weakness of the delayed-blowback system. To make it work, the designers must find a way to loosen the fired cartridge casing in the firing chamber before starting the vigorous full ejection stroke. In the past, designers would wax the cartridge casings. They even included oil pumps on automatic rifles or machine guns in an effort to gain a more gentle primary extraction. Obviously, such measures added to the complexity of manufacture, but the need remains. The G3 and related guns would have pulled empty cartridge casings out of the firing chamber with excessive force had not CETME, in concert with Heckler & Koch, fluted the chamber. This enabled the propellant gases to force the brass cartridge casings away from the firing chamber walls, thus easing the cartridge out more gently and avoiding extraction difficulties. The fluted chamber gives cartridge brass fired from the G3 a unique etched appearance. The

This official U.S. Navy photograph shows members of a SEAL team carrying (front) an M16A2 with M203 grenade launcher. The U.S. Navy SEALs have used G3 and HK33-type rifles on many occasions, one appearing in the far right in this photo.

Chapter Two 89

A soldier demonstrates Heckler & Koch's promising but ill-fated G11, which saw only limited military issue in West German service. The cost of rebuilding East Germany's shattered infrastructure caused the government to cancel the G11 project (photo courtesy of Heckler & Koch).

ejection which follows is extremely vigorous, with empty brass sometimes flying 20 feet or more to the right side and slightly forward of the shooter.

Aside from the unusual feature of fluting the firing chamber to allow a gentler primary extraction, the G3 shows some affinities in handling to the FAL, including its pistol grip and left-sided operating handle. The latter allows right-handed shooters to maintain their hold on the pistol grip while loading. The G3's operating controls are straightforward and easy to master. The fire selector is located on the left side of the receiver, just above the pistol grip and accessible to the shooter's left thumb. Rifles intended for commercial sale (and thus limited to semiautomatic fire) have an "S" at the top for safe and an "F" at the bottom for fire setting.

Almost all G3-type rifles now use the rotary rear sight, one of the rifle's most distinctive features. It consists of four settings: an open notch for ranges up to 100 meters (109.36 yards), and peep (aperture) sights that steadily decrease in size for distances of 200, 300 and 400 meters.

Like the FAL, the G3 is easy to disassemble for cleaning and maintenance, a feature that endears this rifle to its many users. The easier a weapon is to maintain, after all, the more likely it is to get the care and attention it deserves. Moreover, the lack of a separate gas system simplifies maintenance beyond what shooters have come to expect in today's military rifles. Both the AK-47 and FAL rifles have separate gas systems requiring special attention after firing beyond the cleaning of the firing chamber and barrel bore.

As we have learned to expect from German rifle makers, the G3 design displays mostly positive, well-engineered traits despite a few problem areas. The rotating rear sight, for example, can be difficult to adjust without a special tool provided by Heckler & Koch for this purpose. While it can be locked open manually for disassembly and for unloading, the bolt on G3-type rifles does not automatically remain open upon firing the last shot. Few other highly regarded rifles share this undesirable characteristic. Many, including the M14 and the FAL, do include a bolt hold-open on the last shot. In any event, this complaint ranks high among the most forceful negatives one can cite regarding the G3's design features.

The bolt is more difficult to move manually by means of the cocking handle than on some competing designs, though in the writer's experience the force required to move it is really not excessive, and the charging handle does tend to loosen up with continued use. Construction of the G3s also lacks aesthetic appeal, both for its blocky shape and for the visible welding and stamping marks on the metal. Despite these criticisms, the rifle has more than proven its durability and ruggedness under every conceivable condition of arduous military service. It is, however, fairly heavy and, according to some, poorly balanced with a recoil impulse that's heavier than normal in .308 caliber. None of these problems presents any serious difficulties for strong young military personnel; but the G3 definitely lacks appeal for less well-endowed individuals compared to smaller, handier rifles such as the M16.

A more cogent complaint expressed by some shooters concerns the humpbacked shape of the G3's stock made necessary by the high receiver, which can cause the stock to strike a shooter's face upon recoil. This can occur both with the military G3 and the sporterized versions (both fixed- and collapsible-stocked versions). While not painful in semiautomatic fire, the possibility of striking one's face against the receiver can be annoying and disconcerting to a serious degree in automatic fire, when recoil forces are necessarily much greater.

The G3's most serious shortcoming, however, concerns *ammunition feed*. This rifle, unlike the M14 and some FALs, cannot be loaded from the top of the open action by means of stripper clips with an empty or partially loaded magazine in place. Once the supply of pre-loaded magazines runs out, ammunition resupply becomes a problem. The standard 20-shot magazine on the G3 is also quite bulky, extending as it does downward about four inches from the underside of the rifle. This protrusion tends to catch in gear, clothing and even vegetation encountered along the route of march. It also interferes with shooters who adopt a prone firing position for protection. In fairness to Heckler & Koch, this problem of ammunition feed, and the rifle configuration that stems from it, effects virtually every modern military rifle design. The problems are real, nevertheless, and military shooters must work around them somehow.

Despite these problem areas, the G3 remains an excellent high-powered battle rifle which continues to serve widely in military and police forces throughout the world, including extensive use by U.S. Navy SEAL teams. As for accuracy, reliability and ease of maintenance, the G3 rifle equals or surpasses its main competition, including the FAL and M14, in every respect.

PART VI: BEYOND THE G3 FAMILY: AN INTERMEDIATE STEP

Heckler & Koch developed its Model 36 in the period 1967 to 1968 as part of a joint venture with CETME. The goal was to combine a new lightweight cartridge (the 4.56x36mm) with the G3-style roller-locked bolt mechanism. The proprietary cartridge developed a muzzle velocity of 2,560 feet per second. An asymmetrical bullet core made of tungsten encouraged tumbling once the bullet hit its target, ensuring increased soft-tissue destruction and compensating, in part, for the bullet's small diameter and light weight.

The rifle that evolved was fed from a 30-round box magazine and weighed much less (6.33 pounds unloaded) than the HK33. Total length was 35 inches with a 14.95-inch barrel. A fixed carrying handle was fitted above the receiver.

Because of its small, lightweight bullet, the cyclic rate of fire for the HK36 rose to 1100 rounds per minute, considerably more than that of any previous Heckler & Koch automatic weapon. Despite this, the weapon's controllability in fully-automatic fire was significantly better than with the 5.56mm/.223 HK33 series. The HK36 is also significant for having been the first Heckler & Koch selective-fire weapon to offer a two-shot burst setting on its fire selector. This feature was later included on the company's submachine guns and has become very popular with combat personnel.

By 1975, Heckler & Koch was making encouraging progress with its even more advanced G11 design (see below). With NATO's rifle and ammunition trials just a year away, the company decided to concentrate its efforts on getting the G11 ready for that milestone. As a result, Heckler & Koch terminated the HK36 project. Despite its eight-year span, Heckler & Koch and CETME made only a handful of experimental rifles for this interesting and unusual project.

New Technologies: Caseless Ammunition and the G11

While its use so far has been limited to German special forces, the process by which Heckler & Koch developed the 4.73x33mm *Gewehr 11* (**photo p. 90**) and its unique caseless ammunition may yet exert a strong influence on future arms development. The G11 project began in 1969 with a West German armed forces requirement: a greatly improved hit probability in automatic fire compared to existing weapons. Firing the relatively large and powerful 7.62 NATO round, the G3 was quite accurate in its single-shot mode but a dismal performer when firing fully-automatic. This poor showing was not unique to the G3. Indeed, all existing rifles of average weight and selective-fire experienced the same difficulty with this cartridge. The simple fact was, the 7.652x51mm NATO-standard round was too powerful for hand-held automatic weapons of conventional rifle weight and design. The U.S. military tried solving the problem of inaccurate automatic rifle fire by introducing the smaller and less powerful 5.56/.223 cartridge (replacing the 7.62mm), but the *Bundeswehr's* specifications were even more challenging. Ever the innovators, Heckler & Koch decided on a radically new design to outpace 5.56mm technology altogether in what has to be considered a quantum leap forward in terms of improved performance.

This ambitious and daunting task occupied Heckler & Koch for almost 20 years. The company chose four of its most talented engineers—Tilo Möller, Günter Kästner, Dieter Ketterer and Ernst Wössner—and tasked them with the development of a new rifle for the *Bundeswehr*, one that would far outperform all previous attempts at building a superior assault rifle. Möller's design team strove to create a rifle that would enhance hit probabilities, be light enough to allow a soldier to carry enough ammunition, and be sturdy despite its light weight.

Early in the process, the design team settled on an altogether new type of ammunition as the key to

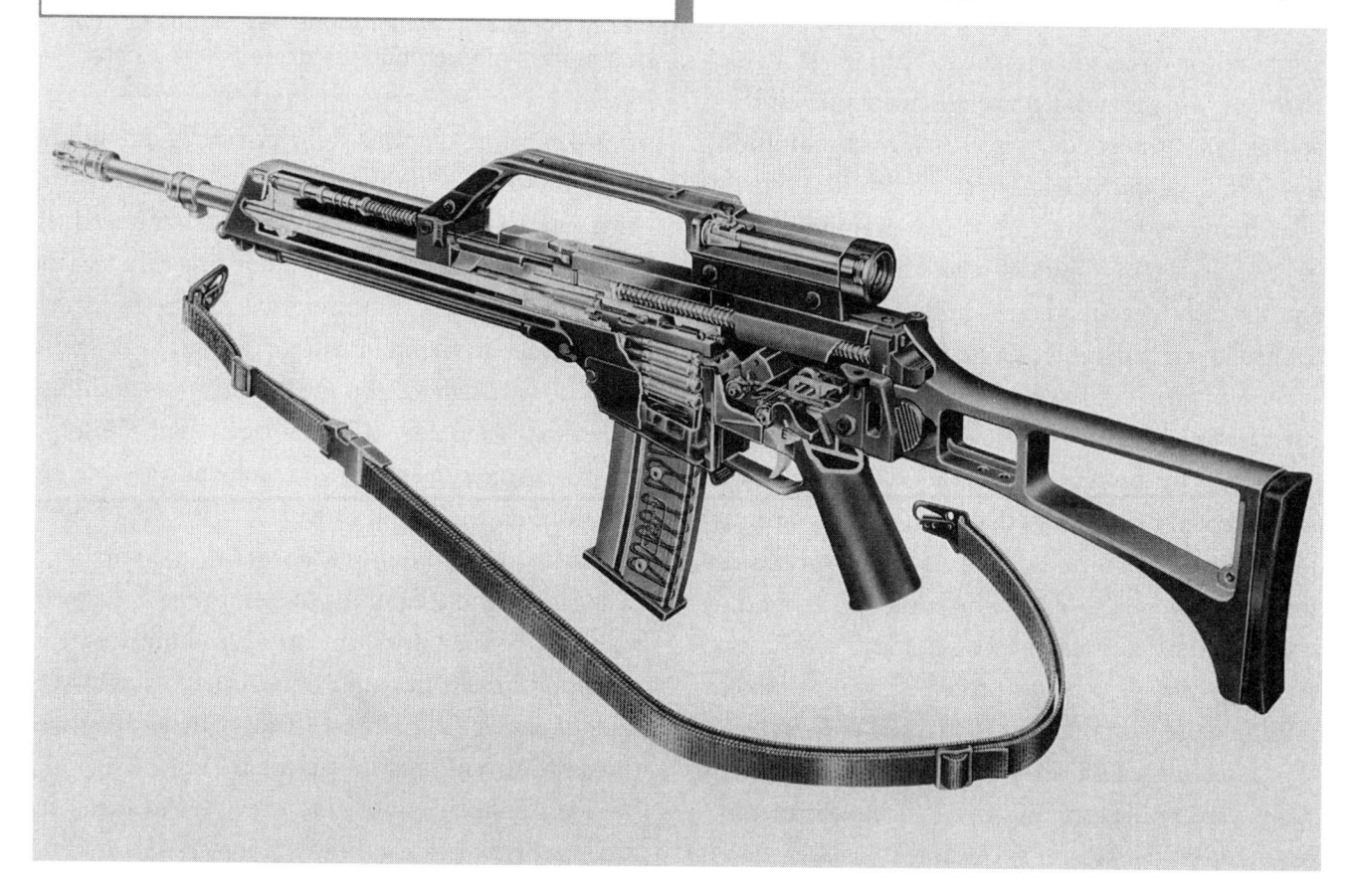

A cutaway view of Heckler & Koch's new G36 displays the rifle's Stoner-type rotating bolt, a departure from usual Heckler & Koch practice. Note also the ambidextrous cocking handle located atop the receiver, ready to be turned to either side (photo courtesy of Heckler & Koch).

Chapter Two 93

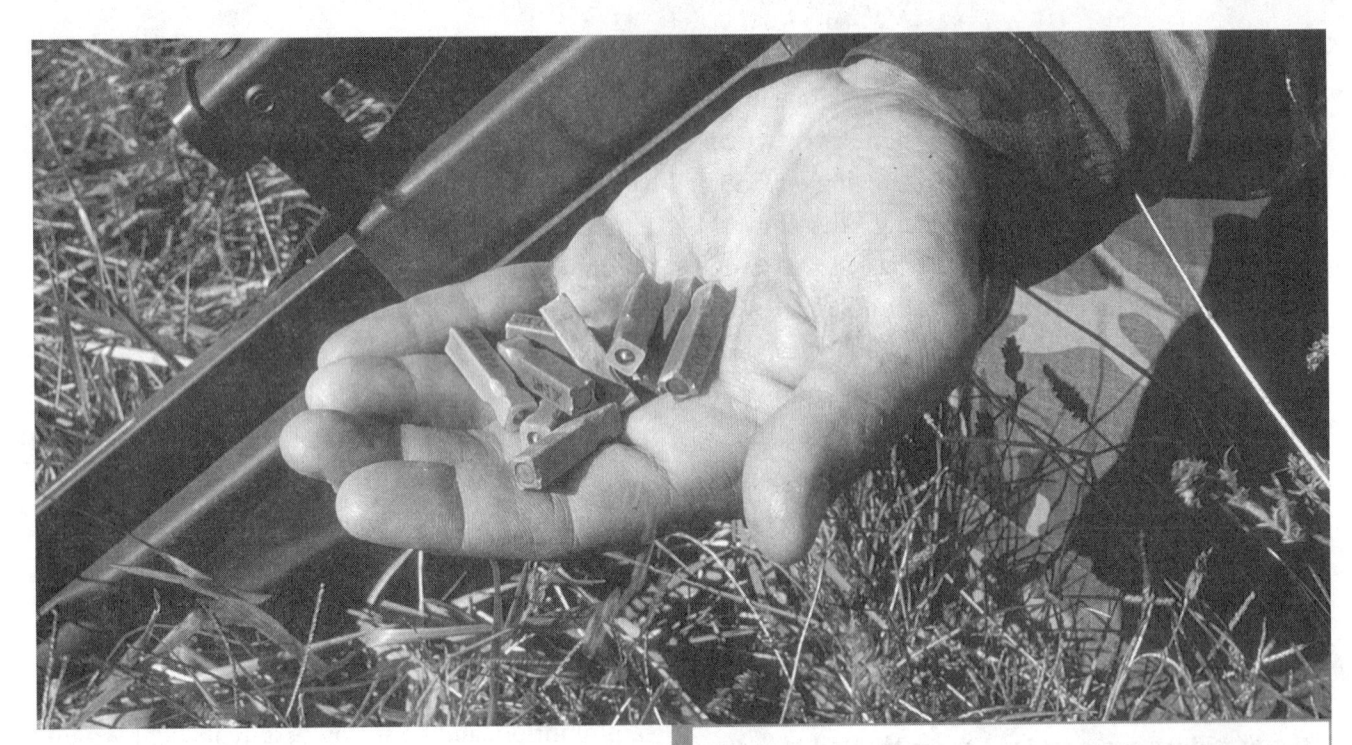

The G11's caseless ammunition, developed in cooperation with Dynamit Nobel, was a major technical triumph which nevertheless fell short due to political considerations beyond the company's control (photo courtesy of Heckler & Koch).

the improved performance sought by the *Bundeswehr*. They decided that ammunition which totally consumed itself in the act of firing (i.e., caseless ammunition) was vital to their creation of a rifle that met first-shot accuracy requirements. Their reasoning was threefold: first, caseless ammunition would reduce the weight of each individual round, allowing a soldier to carry more ammunition. Second, this ammunition would be significantly shorter than the standard round and would have a metallic cartridge case located behind the bullet. A shorter cartridge would provide a more compact breech mechanism that cycled faster between shots. Finally, by eliminating the entire extraction and ejection cycle, a rifle that fired caseless ammunition would eliminate a significant source of unreliability in an automatic weapon. It would also produce a weapon whose mechanism was enclosed and thus better protected against water, mud or sand.

Caseless ammunition, however, presented significant problems of its own. Reliable obturation, or sealing of the breech, which metal (usually brass) cartridge casings automatically ensure by expanding under the heat of firing, simply doesn't take place with caseless ammunition. It has to be arranged. If obturation of the breech does not occur, hot gases from the powder combustion will escape from the mechanism at the moment of firing, a situation fraught with danger for the shooter. In addition, cook-offs, or spontaneous combustion of the powder charge, become an even bigger problem with caseless ammunition fired in automatic weapons than with standard ammunition made with metal cartridge casings. The propellant in a caseless round is exposed to direct contact with the firing chamber, which is already heated from previous firings. Finally, the odds of damage to caseless cartridges are greater than those of conventional ammunition.

Despite the new ground they had to break in order to perfect an assault rifle firing caseless ammunition, Heckler & Koch decided the advantages of such a radical new design far outweighed the difficulties that must be overcome. To assist the team in developing the ammunition, Heckler & Koch enlisted the aid of one of Europe's leading ammunition manufacturers, Dynamit Nobel. Together, the two companies created one of the most interesting cartridges ever developed in the history of small arms: the 4.7x21mm O.H. (O.H. = *Ohne Hulse*, "Without Case" or "Caseless"). The propellant and booster charges, equivalent to the powder and primer of a conventional cartridge, are formed by pressure and then covered with a sealant before the bullet is inserted. The entire length of the molded propellant block at first was 20.9mm, hence the "21" in the cartridge's original designation. More recently, it's become known as the 4.73x33mm, while in the U.S., as part of the Advanced Combat Rifle (ACR) testing in the late 1980s, it was called the "4.92x34mm."

The 4.7mm bullet itself is 23mm (almost an inch in length) and weighs 52.5 grains. It contains a lead core surrounded by a steel jacket and covered in gilding metal. Ammunition types include ball, tracer, plastic bullets for training and blanks. While one might think this bullet too small for military efficiency, West German military theory centers on "the infantryman's half-kilometer" (500 meters, or 547 yards) as being the area within which standard infantry rifles must assert their presence on the battlefield with confidence. Heckler & Koch has demonstrated that the G11 and its 4.7mm cartridge can put a hole in a West German military helmet at a distance of 600 meters (656 yards). Accuracy out to 300 meters is fully competitive with the best 5.56mm/.223 caliber ammunition. The rapid muzzle velocity (3,050 feet per second or 930 meters per second) undoubtedly contributes to the round's excellent accuracy.

The mechanism, which H&K developed while ammunition testing was still underway, has a metal breech (firing chamber) that rotates as each round is fed into it from above (the cartridges are stored in the magazine with their bullets pointing straight down). As soon as the round enters the firing chamber, it rotates 90 degrees to align with the barrel. Once the cartridge is fired the barrel recoils, rotating the breech/firing chamber so it can receive the next round.

In the 1977 testing procedure with NATO, the ammunition, which was based on a nitrocellulose compound, cooked off at about 178 degrees centigrade (352 degrees Fahrenheit). The firing chamber of the early G11 prototypes reached this temperature after only seven or eight rounds of fully-automatic fire, causing frequent premature discharges. This disappointing performance caused the West German government to drop its financial support. Fortunately, Heckler & Koch continued the project on its own.

Throughout the late 1970s, H&K refined the design of the G11, improving and simplifying the mechanism of the rifle. The company developed methods for transferring heat away from the firing chamber more efficiently than in the fifth-generation prototypes found wanting by NATO. While Heckler & Koch's design was evolving, Dynamit Nobel developed a new propellant, called HTIP (for "High Temperature Ignition Propellant"), which raised the cook-off threshold at least 100 degrees centigrade (212 degrees Fahrenheit) compared to the original nitrocellulose compound. With the G11's 10th prototype finally completed in the late 1970s, its design changes and improved ammunition mastered earlier problems to such an extent that the West German government resumed financial support of the whole project. The *Bundeswehr's* large-scale purchase of 5.56mm/.223 G41 rifles also helped Heckler & Koch's financial situation, which in turn allowed the company to invest more capital into the enormously expensive G11 project.

In October 1981, Heckler & Koch displayed its 13th-generation G11 prototype to the American Defense Preparedness Association's Second International Small Arms Symposium, at which time Dieter Rall test-fired the weapon for an appreciative ADPA audience. As its development continued in the early 1980s, Heckler & Koch managed to reduce the G11's weight from 13.15 pounds to 9.41 pounds. This was later trimmed to 8.18 pounds in 1989, achieved in part by substituting a composite polymer outer casing for the sheet-steel type used in earlier versions. An advertisement placed by H&K in the later 1980s claimed that with the same total weight of 16 pounds (7.35 kilograms), a soldier could carry either a 7.62mm G3 with 80 cartridges, a 5.56mm M16A2 with 210 cartridges, or a G11 with 500 cartridges.

In early 1988, Heckler & Koch resubmitted the G11 for military testing by the West German *Bundeswehr*. In the course of testing, 50 prototypes were used to fire close to 200,000 rounds. The tests so impressed the participants that the West German armed forces were urged to adopt the G11. A second test series confirmed that decision, with a spare magazine holder added. Although the revolutionary G11 had failed to appeal to any of its NATO allies, West Germany decided to proceed on its own, shouldering the enormous cost of implementing a switch to this totally new weapons system.

The West German military had great plans for the G11. The idea was to issue the rifle to the entire West German armed forces over a period of several years, beginning in 1989. Unfortunately, worldwide political events intervened. With the fall of the East German Communist regime in 1989, reunification of the two Germanys, divided since the end of World War II, became a reality. The East German economy, having been ravaged by decades of Communist mismanagement, required major transfusions of West German money. As a result, rearmament plans for the G11 were shelved after only a few special forces units had received the radical new weapon. Now, with no chance of recouping its enormous development

H&K's standard G36 rifle features a folding stock. Note also the dual-function sighting equipment and ambidextrous S-E-F fire-control group. The magazine release facilitates ambidextrous operation (photo courtesy of Heckler & Koch).

costs, the company was sold in 1991 to Britain's Royal Ordnance plc.

A final chapter in the G11 story concerns U.S. armed forces testing of a slightly modified G11 as a prototype Advanced Combat Rifle, or ACR, with tests beginning in the late 1980s. The goal was to create a rifle militarily at least twice as effective militarily as the existing state-of-the-art M16A2 5.56mm/.223 caliber rifle. Other candidates included Colt's ACR, another from AAI Corporation, and a fourth from Steyr GmbH of Austria. Each entrant tried a different approach to the improvement of lethality and hit probability. For example, the Steyr and AAI rifles fired flechette ammunition instead of bullets. The experimental Colt rifle, on the other hand, fired duplex ammunition, which broke into two projectiles, one landing at point of aim and one close by. The Heckler & Koch entry was, without doubt, the most mature design from an engineering point of view. Even though the candidate rifles all performed well, the U.S. Army decided to stay with the existing technology, because none of the prototype ACRs demonstrated the desired increase of 100 percent in combat capability over the existing M16A2 rifle.

Operating procedures of the G11 include some odd characteristics along with some familiar ones. With the magazine release located beneath the front end of the carrying handle and sight, the magazine slides in to load and out to unload (from the front). Further, the location of the safety and fire selector above the pistol grip is quite similar to the G3's and was probably done that way purposely (the original plan for this rifle was, after all, to serve as a replacement for the G3). With this system, the safe settings are as follows: rotate the selector switch forward (counterclockwise) one notch to "1" for single shots, the next notch (marked "3") allows an extremely rapid (2000 rounds per minute) 3-shot burst for each pull of the trigger; and finally, rotating the selector switch fully forward (to "45" or "50", depending on the version), allows fully-automatic firing at a cyclic rate of 600 rounds per minute. Magazine capacity is 50 rounds.

The G11's long tubular optical sight, which doubles as a carrying handle, offers no magnification. Heckler & Koch made it a 1-power scope so that infantrymen could keep both eyes open while firing their rifles. This was a desirable asset in military situations where a soldier's field of view must remain as wide as possible to protect against approaching threats. While the scope possesses no magnification potential, it does include an illuminated reticle for improved target acquisition.

People who have fired the G11 invariably agree that it is both pleasant to handle and easy to fire. Testers rate its accuracy and engineering as excellent. The rifle's center of gravity, which is located behind the pistol grip, enhances balance. It's a pity, actually, that Heckler & Koch didn't sell more G11s. It could be argued that this revolutionary and advanced rifle was one of the last casualties of the Cold War.

Evolution, Not Revolution: The G36

During the 1990s, Heckler & Koch revived its Model 36 **(photo p. 93)** designation for a new rifle, the G36. Firing the NATO-standard 5.56mm (.223 caliber) cartridge, this rifle was developed after the German army had requested an affordable lightweight rifle utilizing well-established construction features that made it adaptable to a 9mm Parabellum, 5.56mm/.223 and 7.62mm/.308 weapons family encompassing related designs for sub-machine guns, rifles and general purpose machine guns.

In a departure from previous practice by Heckler & Koch, the G3-style roller-locked bolt was supplanted by a rotating bolt and short stroke piston mechanism. Inspired by the Armalite AR-18 rifle (designed by Eugene Stoner after he created his legendary AR-15/M16), the G36 refines the design still further. Its bolt, bolt carrier and gas system, however, still strongly resemble those found in the AR-18. Except for a few steel parts—the barrel, bolt and carrier, receiver rails, springs and assorted small parts—the G36 relies on polymer construction for corrosion resistance and weight reduction. When fully forward, the bolt carrier doubles as an ejection port cover, thus eliminating the spring-loaded ejection port cover that proved troublesome in Stoner's designs.

In light of its strong military role, Heckler & Koch decided to optimize the rifle's performance with NATO-standard SS109 ammunition by giving the barrel rifling a twist rate of 1-in-7 inches. As a result, older ammunition designed for a faster twist rate may not produce acceptable accuracy with this rifle. In a departure from common practice, Heckler & Koch decided not to develop the G36 magazine around that of the M16, which is arguably the world standard in .223 caliber rifles. Instead, the company developed a 30-round translucent magazine unique to this weapon. It includes attachment points on the external part of the magazine, enabling magazines to be clipped together, side by side, to speed up reloading. Heckler & Koch borrowed this feature from SIG, who developed the system for use in its Model 550 rifle (adopted in 1984 as Switzerland's Stgw 90 military rifle).

In keeping with current military thinking, the German army specified good ergonomics and ambidextrous operation. The manual safety/fire selector appears on both sides of the receiver. The magazine release—a flipper located between the triggerguard and magazine well—serves equally well for right-handed and left-handed shooters, as does a bolt release located in front of the triggerguard. The tip of the cocking handle, located atop the receiver, can be raised or turned right or left according to each shooter's preference. Attached directly to the bolt carrier, it can be used as an aid in loading reluctant cartridges into the firing chamber or to minimize noise when loading (a separate component is necessary in the M16). The cocking handle on the G36 is strong enough so that a shooter may step on it hard should a cartridge case get stuck in the firing chamber. In yet another departure from earlier Heckler & Koch service rifles, the G36 boasts a stock that folds to the right, next to the receiver, once the shooter has pressed a release button on the left side.

G36 variants—all of which fire the 5.56mm /.223 cartridge—include the G36 rifle, a G36K short-barreled carbine, and an MG36 machine gun. Heckler & Koch also offers export versions of the three variants with "E" suffixes. These differ from the standard versions only in their sighting arrangements and selector options on the trigger group. The G36 issued by the Germans has a 1.5-power optical sight and a red dot sight using ambient light, thereby eliminating batteries. A Hensoldt night sight, which can also be attached for night operations, uses "starlight" technology to greatly amplify ambient light. An ambidextrous "S-E-F" trigger group is fitted for safe, semiautomatic and fully-automatic modes of fire. The export version has an optical sight, eliminates the red-dot sight and adds iron sights, a blade-type front sight and a notch rear sight, both located in a detachable carrying handle that fits on top of the receiver. Several trigger groups are available with varying combinations of single-shot, two-round burst, and fully automatic fire modes. A police model limited to semiautomatic fire is under development, and the SL8-1 sporting rifle (see Chapter 3) uses much of the G36 technology.

German reunification proved enormously costly. The G36, which was designed with low cost in mind, appeared at the right time and therefore prospered

The G3 magazine is of Portuguese manufacture. Like Heckler & Koch, the Portuguese licensee also marks the month and year. The 1005-series number is the G3's NATO Identification code.

where the G11 failed. The G36 has been issued to Germany's armed forces personnel and advertised for military and police use through Heckler & Koch's worldwide sale network. Reasonably priced for this type of weapon, the G36 series offers excellent controllability in fully-automatic fire. Its modular construction allows easy maintenance and an adaptability to different configurations.

A Look Toward The Future: The SABR

Although the G11 project fell disappointingly short, Heckler & Koch has not remained silent in the field of military small arms. The company joined a development team sponsored by Alliant Techsystems (Hopkins, MN) to aid in the development of the U.S. Army's next battle rifle. Once called the Objective Individual Combat Weapon (OICW), it has since been renamed the Selectable Assault Battle Rifle, or SABR. Alliant's winning design—selected in April 1998—combines an upper gun firing 20mm projectiles with a 5.56mm selective fire assault rifle. The SABR's 20mm portion delivers programmable "smart" projectiles that make allowances for high-explosive airbursts, delayed action fusing and other non-traditional ways of inflicting maximum casualties and damage on the enemy.

Heckler &Koch's task is to develop the shooting components of this weapon, while Dynamit Nobel has been assigned to perfect the ammunition. This is the same team that developed the G11, and the two companies are build-

> **The PSG-1 and MSG 90 represented Heckler & Koch's attempts to bring additional profits from the G3's inherent accuracy potential by modifying the basic platform for improved performance (photo courtesy of Heckler & Koch).**

Special Application Products

Critical tactical situations call for specialized products designed to meet unique demands. Heckler & Koch has developed an extensive line of special purpose products that include precision marksman rifles, light and general purpose machine guns, grenade launchers, and signalling devices. All have been operationally tested and combat-proven.

ing on the experience of that project, along with H&K's creation of the promising but now defunct Close Assault Weapon (CAW), a kind of super shotgun of the early 1980s (see Chapter 8). The SABR's 20mm rifle is recoil-operated and has a titanium barrel for weight reduction. It fires semiautomatic only, while the 5.56mm carbine is capable of selective fire. The same trigger housing fires either the 20mm or 5.56mm weapon as the shooter elects. Rotating the bolt body adapts the weapon for use by either left-handed or right-handed shooters, a necessity because the SABR uses a bullpup configuration with its ambidextrous cocking handle. Weight reduction, which had been a major concern, has been altogether successful. In its current configuration the SABR weighs only 14 pounds unloaded. The Contraves Brashear Company (Pittsburgh, PA) manufactures the "smart" technology employed in the SABR's fire control system. Located in a module atop the 20mm gun, it calls for four fusing modes for the 20mm gun and several imaging and aiming modes to assist the gunner in selecting and engaging a target. The plan, as currently set forth, calls for an initial purchase and issue of 40,000 weapons beginning in 2007. Each SABR is scheduled to cost $10,000, with each round of 20mm ammunition currently priced at $25.

Military Rifles: Conclusion

The Bible tells us that those who live by the sword will die by the sword, a saying that has been all too true for Heckler & Koch. The G3 rifle provided a foundation for success that was nothing short of fabulous. Then the company bankrupted itself trying to bring the G11 project to fruition in the face of tremendous financial pressures involved in reunifying East and West Germany. Sold first to Britain's Royal Ordnance plc and then to British Aerospace, the company has been rebuilding ever since. It seems unlikely that Heckler & Koch, or indeed any single armaments company, can ever achieve the worldwide success experienced by H&K with the G3. There exist too many gun manufacturers in the market today for any one company to gain the market share enjoyed in the past by such giants as Colt, FN, Mauser and Heckler & Koch. Nevertheless, development and sale of the G3 rifle and related long arms ranks as a technical and business achievement of the highest magnitude. While certainly not a financial success, the G11 ranks high among the major advances in firearms technology. With a new lease on life provided by the U.S.-sponsored SABR project, Heckler & Koch may yet offer its innovative genius to the field of military rifles. • **H&K**

SPECIFICATIONS: HECKLER & KOCH MILITARY RIFLES

	G3	G41	G11
Overall Length (in.)	40.2	39.25	29.5
Barrel Length (in.)	17.7	17.7	21.2
Years Produced	1959-	1983-	1989-1990
Weight (lbs.)	9.9	9.0	8.2
Caliber/Capacity	7.62mm/20	5.5mm/30	4.7x33mm/50

The HK91 and the SR9 series were powerful, accurate and efficient rifles, but German-made guns of the 1970s and 1980s were always extremely expensive in the U.S., owing to the strength of the West German Deutschmark against the U.S. dollar. The heavy expense no doublt limited the rifle's distribution even more than the U.S. Government's intervention.......

Chapter 3

THE SPORTING RIFLE STORY

PART I: COMMERCIAL G3 VARIANTS

Noting the great worldwide interest in its G3-type military rifles, Heckler & Koch capitalized on that interest by developing sporting variants of the basic G3 design. The company also created and marketed several sporting guns apart from the G3.

Prior to the creation of Heckler & Koch, Inc., Golden State Arms (formerly located in Pasadena, California) imported a fixed-stock variant of the Heckler & Koch Model G3A2. In order to import and sell this rifle to civilians, the parent company

> **The HK91 A-2 was a semiautomatic-only variant of the standard fixed-stock G3 service rifle imported into the United States for sale to private citizens and police forces between 1975 and 1989.**

Chapter Three 103

The Model 911 appeared in 1990 as a transitional model between the HK91 and the SR9 (photo courtesy of Heckler & Koch).

had to alter the receiver, limiting it to semiautomatic fire only. The receiver could not be altered for fully-automatic fire. The receiver could not be altered for fully-automatic fire, either, nor could fully-automatic components be fitted to convert it. The U.S. Bureau of Alcohol, Tobacco and Firearms (BATF) mandated these changes before approving the importation of the semiautomatic-only version of the rifle. Golden State Arms designated the new Heckler & Koch rifle as Model 41 and imported it from 1968 to 1970.

Beginning in 1971, S.A.C.O., formerly located in Virginia, imported a similar version of the 5.56mm/.223 caliber HK33 rifle (its receiver similarly altered for use with semiautomatic fire only. Picking up where Golden State had left off, S.A.C.O. named its semiautomatic G3 variation the Model 41, corresponding to the HK91 subsequently handled by Heckler & Koch, Inc. (see below). The Model 43 was S.A.C.O.'s designation for the semi-automatic-only HK33 variant. Importation by S.A.C.O. began in 1971 and ended in 1974, after which Heckler & Koch created its own import firm, Heckler & Koch, Inc., to handle future North American sales. Model 41 and 43 rifles marked "S.A.C.O." are today quite rare.

The HK91/SR9 Series

To create a "civilian-legal" HK91 from the selective-fire G3, Heckler & Koch engineers eliminated the G3's fully-automatic capability by redesigning the HK91's trigger housing, subtly altering its dimensions to prevent anyone from substituting a G3-style trigger housing. Despite the change to the fire-control system, the HK91 still resembled almost exactly the military-issue G3. The only sure way to tell them apart was to look at their safety/fire selectors and magazine releases. The HK91's manual safety switch contained only two settings—one for safe and one for fire—the only mode of fire available being one shot for each pull of the trigger. For the HK91, the company substituted a pushbutton magazine release (located on the receiver's right side) for the G3's flipper-type magazine release. The original military G3-style magazine release is the preferred type because of its overall operation and ambidextrous setup.

Heckler & Koch made the HK91 in two versions. The Model 91 A-2 featured the standard black cycolac plastic stock (fixed), while the 91 A-3 utilized the collapsible stock popular with the West German military. The A-3 variant was always more expensive, and even today it commands a premium among collectors. A .22LR conversion kit was also offered for either variant, and Heckler & Koch, Inc. also offered a "package" with a scope mount and telescopic sight added.

Importation of the HK91 lasted until 1989, when it fell afoul of the U.S. Government, which claimed that the rifle's military-style stock (with separate pistol grip), plus its high-capacity magazine, flash suppressor and bayonet attachment made it a

The SR9 was built from 1990 to 1994. The 5-round magazine shown was standard, though the earlier 20-round units standard in the HK91 series would also work. The barrel lacks a flash suppressor but partly makes up for it by being two inches longer (photo courtesy of Heckler & Koch).

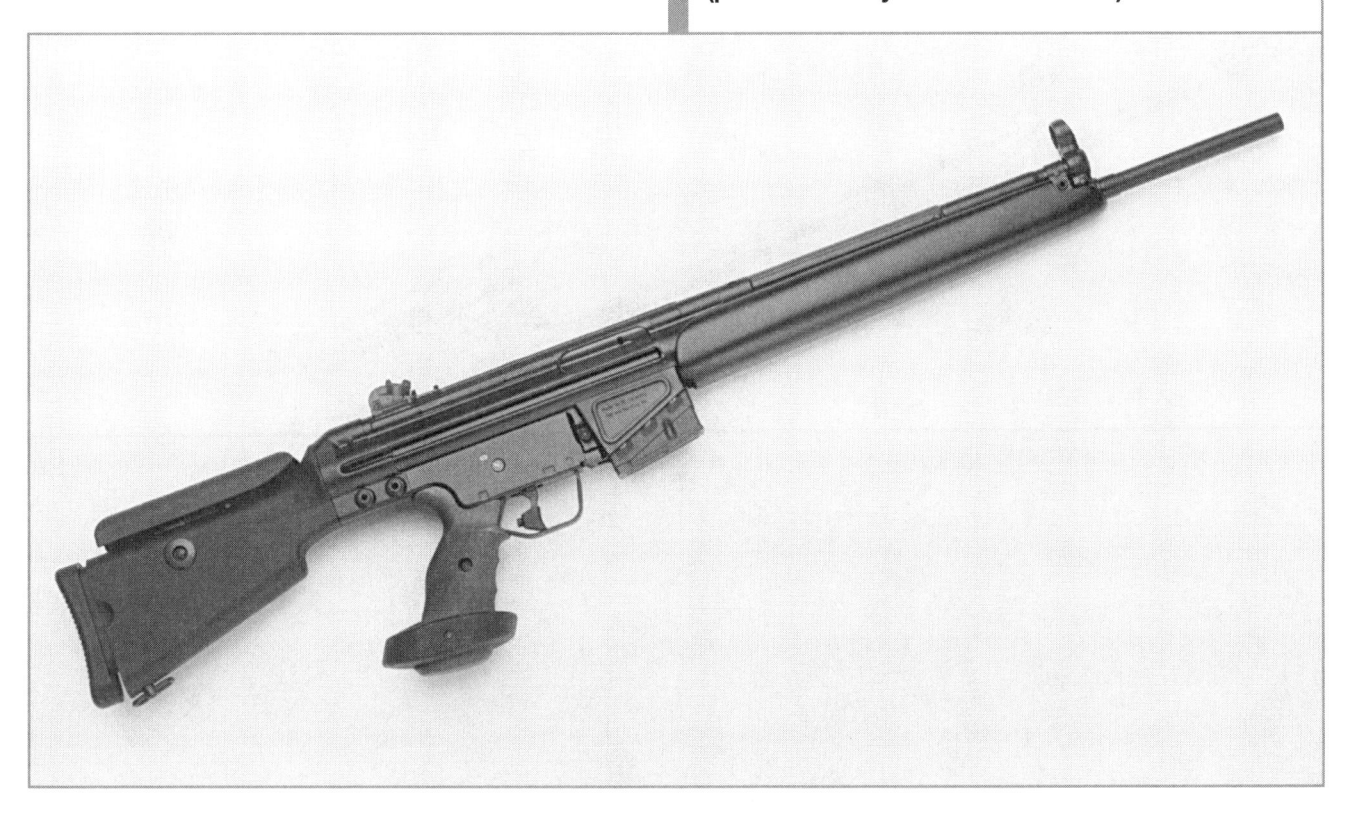

Below. HK93 A-2 was a fixed-stock variant of the HK33 limited to semiautomatic fire. With a telescopic sight (attached by H&K's "claw" mount), this rifle can shoot accurately to 300 yards.

Above. The SR9(T) added a PSG-1 trigger group and adjustable MSG-90 buttstock to the basic SR9 design (photo courtesy of Heckler & Koch).

The full-house SR9(TC), which was introduced in 1993, added the PSG-1's fully-adjustable buttstock to the SR9(T). Importation stopped later that year, making this variation quite rare, collectible and desirable (photo courtesy of Heckler & Koch).

"paramilitary rifle" unsuitable for sporting purposes." At the time, Heckler & Koch, Inc. had nearly 1,000 HK91 rifles on hand which the company could not sell because of their "military configuration."

Accordingly, the company modified these components to create the stopgap Model 911. The chief difference between it and the HK91 was the former's black thumbhole stock made of fiberglass reinforced with Kevlar. Heckler & Koch, Inc. also replaced the HK91-style flash suppressor with a plain cylindrical barrel shroud held in place by a set screw. The Model 911 came with a standard 5-round magazine (as introduced on the PSG-1 rifle four years earlier), though the earlier 20-round units also worked. Heckler & Koch converted fewer than 1,000 HK91s before replacing the 911 in 1990 with the more refined SR9. The Model 911's relative scarcity may in the future transform this rifle into an interesting collector's item.

The SR9 was a more refined, sporterized version of the HK91. It had a Kevlar-reinforced fiberglass, thumbhole-type stock with a built-in recoil buffer system. The transitional Model 911, however, used the standard HK91 buffer. The SR9's thumbhole, sporter-style stock and handguard sometimes wore a wood-colored look, but it also came with a black thumbhole stock and handguard.

When Heckler & Koch eliminated the flash suppressor and bayonet lug from the SR9, it was forced to add two inches to the barrel to make up the difference. This elongated barrel, combined with the improved recoil buffer system built into the stock, made the SR9 more pleasant to shoot than the typical G3. The company was quick to make this point in its advertising, which claimed the SR9 had more comfortable recoil characteristics than any other self-loading .308 caliber rifle.

The SR9 came standard with a five-round magazine, though the earlier 20-round HK91/G3-type magazines also fit and functioned. In 1992, the improved SR9(T) appeared, adding to the basic rifle's design a trigger group similar to that of H&K's super-accurate PSG-1 rifle. The buffer system built into the MSG-90's stock was designed to keep the PSG-1's excellent recoil control while at the same time saving weight. These elements combined with the longer barrel made the SR9(T) a smooth-shooting .308 caliber rifle while adding $430 to its cost.

In 1993, Heckler & Koch, Inc. introduced the SR9(TC), a "target competition" model with a fully adjustable buttstock. This added another $147 to the package, making a total suggested retail price in 1993 of $1,946. This proved another short-lived variation, for in that same year Heckler & Koch, Inc. halted its importation of all SR9-type rifles.

The HK91 and the SR9 series were powerful, accurate and efficient rifles, but German-made guns of the 1970s and 1980s were always extremely expensive

Heckler & Koch offered an HK93 variant with collapsible stock as the HK93 A-3. Such rifles enjoy wide use with several police forces in the US and abroad (photo courtesy of Heckler & Koch).

The 9mm Parabellum HK94 is shown with its short (8.85-inch) barrel, suppressor and forward handgrip. It's limited to police forces or civilians who are legally licensed to purchase Class III firearms.

in the U.S., owing to the strength of the West German Deutschmark against the U.S. dollar. The heavy expense no doubt limited the rifle's distribution even more than the U.S. Government's intervention.

Ironically, Heckler & Koch's PSG-1—the company's costly top-of-the-line sniping/competition rifle—remained on the market the longest of any of its products in the commercial sporting line. Introduced in 1985, the rifle's no-holds-barred design features raised the list price to $5,388. By 1993, the cost to consumers was $8,859; and only three years later the $10,000 barrier was broken, soaring to $10,811 a few years later. While these tremendously expensive guns are marvelous to shoot, their weight (almost 18 pounds) and five-figure price tag have greatly limited sales. More PSG-1 rifles found in the United States were bought by police departments with drug-related seizures of the assets generated rather than by private owners.

The HK93 (**photo p. 108**), another adaptation of a military design—in this case the HK33 5.56mm (.223)

Chapter Three **109**

caliber rifle—featured a new receiver limiting the rifle to semiautomatic fire. Otherwise, aside from being slightly smaller, it corresponded in every way to the HK91 conversion from the G3. In addition to the standard finish, Heckler & Koch offered this model in "desert camo" and "NATO black" finishes, commanding a premium from co-lectors worldwide. As with the Model 91, H&K offered its Model 93 in another variant—the collapsible-stock A-3. The Model 93 enjoyed some sales from police departments in the U.S., and Heckler & Koch, Inc.'s Military and Law Enforcement Division has offered selective-fire HK33s in several different variations to this country's police departments, which can buy them without restriction. The semiautomatic-only HK93, however, appealed to some departments that simply wanted a well-made modern rifle without the "machine gun" image attached to the selective-fire HK33s. After 1989, Heckler & Koch never developed a sporterized variant and, as a result, it is only rarely encountered in the United States today.

The HK94

The HK94, a 9mm Parabellum derivative of the MP5 submachine gun, is still another military knock-off limited to semiautomatic fire. It can appear in standard length (8.85-inch) or extended length (16.54-inch) barrels, the latter meant to solve legal obstacles concerning the minimum rifle barrel lengths allowed for civilian ownership in the U.S. Police forces in

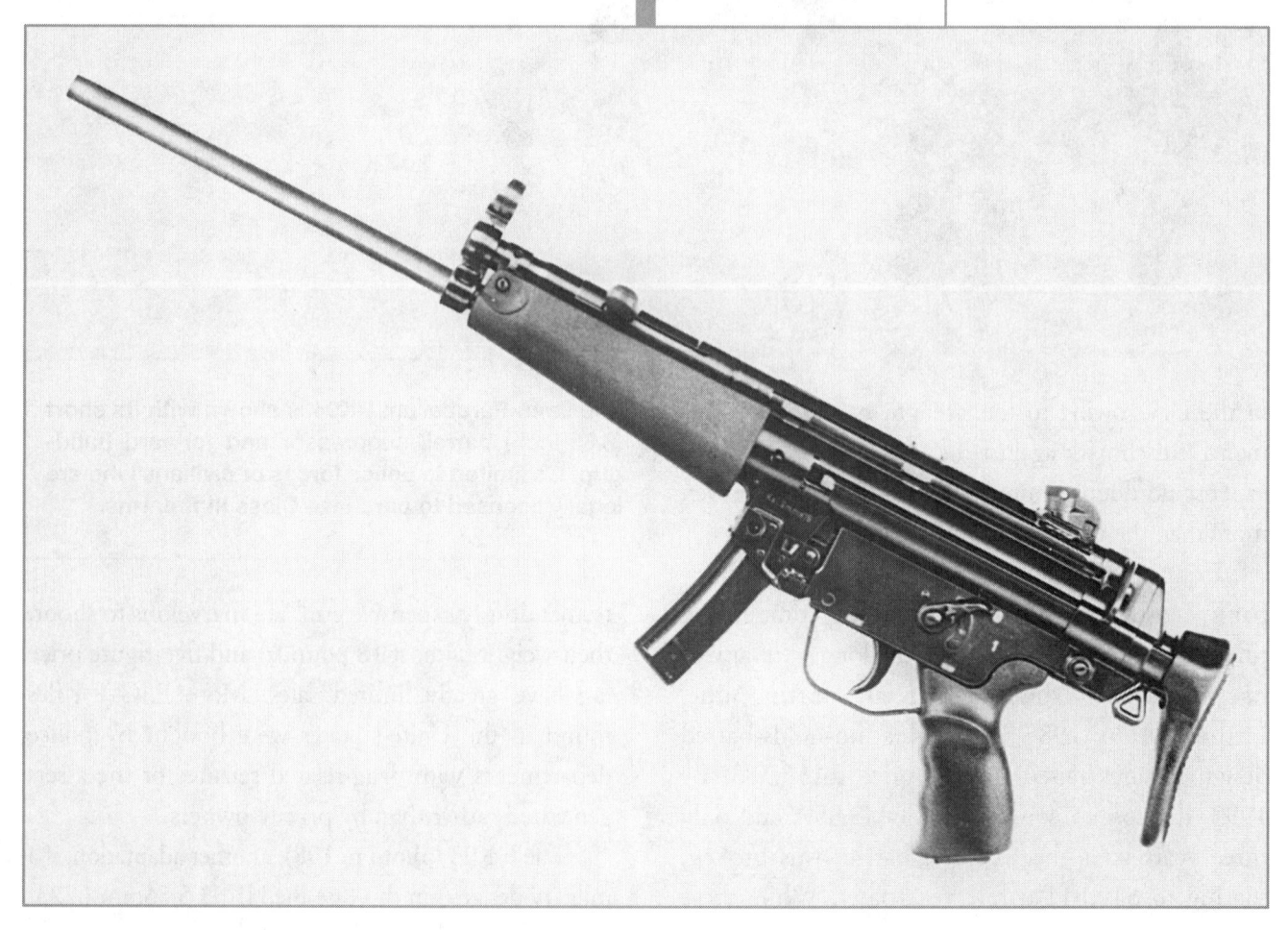

The HK94 A-3 rifle features a barrel measuring 16.54 inches (photo courtesy of Heckler & Koch).

The 5.56mm/.223 caliber SL-6 was a sporterized version of the basic Heckler & Koch roller-locked design. Its G3 parentage is revealed in the rifle's sighting system and receiver configuration. Magazine capacity was two rounds (shown), but a 10-round magazine was also available.

The SL-7 resembled the SL-6 but was scaled up to fire the larger, more powerful 7.62x51mm/.308 caliber NATO round. Note the repositioning of the cocking handle on the right side of the receiver and the rotary safety on the left side. Magazine capacity was ten rounds (photo courtesy of Heckler & Koch).

Chapter Three

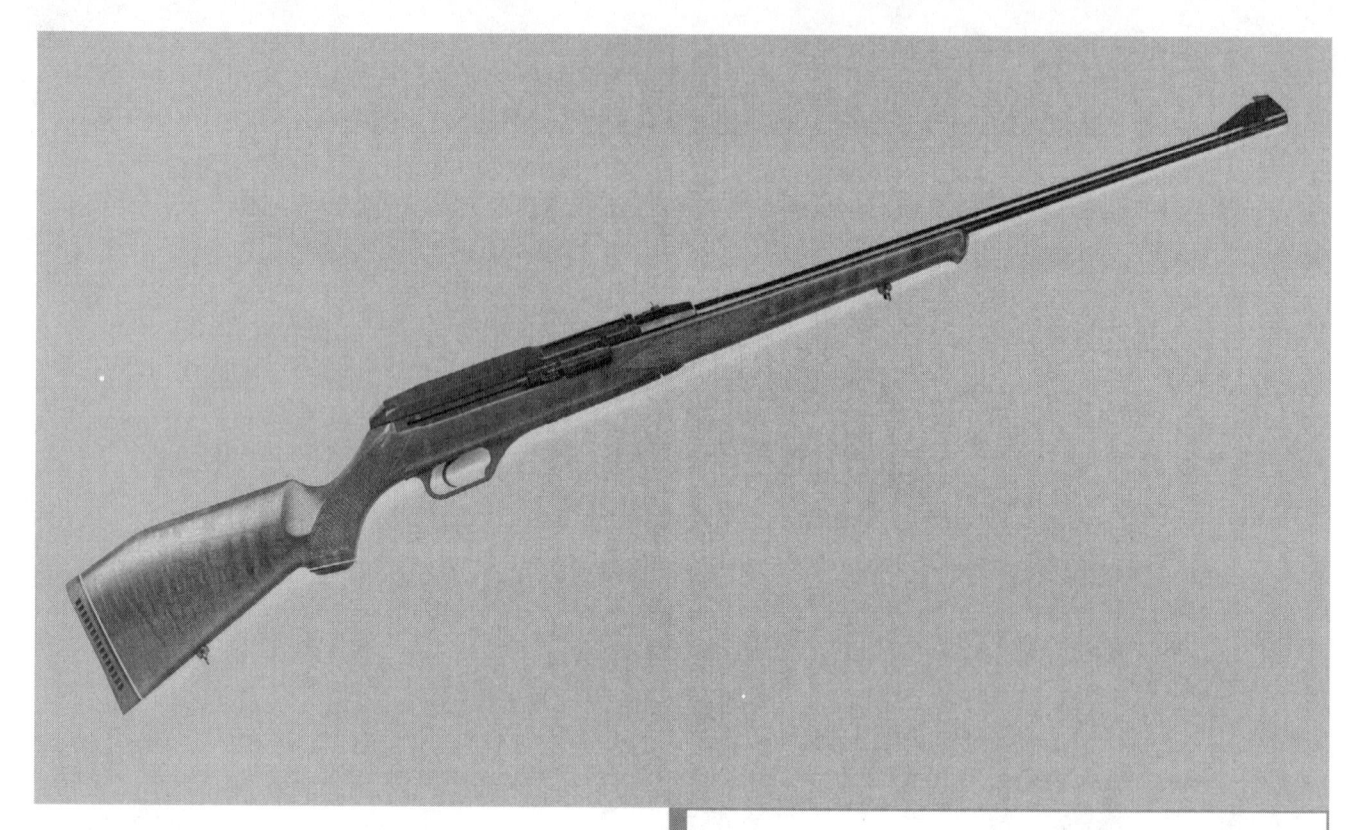

The HK 770 first appeared in 1978 as a more refined SL-7. Note the more elegant stock (photo courtesy of Heckler & Koch).

the U.S. may, of course, use the standard barrel without restriction. Heckler & Koch has actively marketed both selective-fire MP5 variants and semiautomatic-only HK94 carbines to police forces in this country.

The semiautomatic-only HK94 variant of the MP5 submachine gun has proven popular worldwide. Shorter and handier than a rifle, with less danger of bullet overpenetration in the event of a miss (or even in the event of a hit), the 9mm Parabellum caliber HK94 is much easier to shoot effectively than a pistol chambered for the same cartridge. Many governments have discovered the secret that semiautomatic fire is more accurate on average than automatic fire and is still quite fast. Some people translate firepower as a gun that makes a lot of noise, but I agree with the definition offered by Melvin Johnson, a Marine Corps officer turned firearms designer: "Firepower is bullets hitting people." By that definition, the HK94, though limited to one shot for each pull of the trigger, is capable of firepower equal to or greater than that of the fully-automatic MP5.

Heckler & Koch, Inc. offered the HK94 in three configurations: fixed-stock (A-2), sliding collapsible stock (A-3), and scoped "package." There was also a Model 94 SG1, which attempted to create a 9mm target rifle of sorts out of the HK94. Announced in 1986, this package offered as well a bipod made of aluminum and a six-power Leupold target scope. The apparent goal of this target rifle was as a weapon for police use in hostage situations requiring pinpoint accuracy to avoid loss of innocent life. In this context, the 9mm Parabellum makes some sense, but only within 50 yards or so. A strange little gun, the Model 94 SG1 failed to produce the kind of accuracy the company had hoped for. Consequently, sales were soft and Heckler & Koch, Inc. had to quit importing it after only one year.

The SL-6

The 5.56mm (.223 caliber) SL-6, which first appeared in 1975, used the HK33 mechanism in a commercial-style stock, leaving the last few inches of the barrel exposed up to the muzzle. The stock featured a hog's-back comb to facilitate scope mounting, but H&K also retained its traditional rotary rear sight. The front sight, a hooded post, lay on the barrel at the muzzle. The company changed the cocking handle's location from the left side, as in its military rifles, to the right side, where it was more often encountered. The company did, however, retain the folding feature of the cocking handle, again demonstrating the gun's military ancestry. The manual safety became a rotary-style unit located on the left side of the stock, just above the triggerguard.

The SL-6 had a detachable box magazine, but unlike the HK33's 20-, 30- or even 40-shot box found on the Hk33, the SL-6's magazine held either two rounds (the legal limit in West Germany) or ten. The 10-round magazines were intended for use with a large order (25,000 rifles) from the police of Colombia, but the order never came to fruition. Because the Colombian order failed to materialize, Heckler & Koch stopped production by 1986 after building about 15,000 of these rifles.

The SL-7

When Heckler & Koch introduced the SL-6, it decided on a slightly enlarged version, one made to fire the 7.62mm (.308) round. What resulted was the SL-7, which shared all the SL-6's mechanical features and appurtenances; indeed, the two rifles are all but identical except for their size and markings. The SL-7 proved no more successful commercially than the SL-6, and both designs died out quickly.

PART II: THE MODEL 770 SERIES

The HK 770

The HK 770 made its first appearance in 1978 as a more refined, civilianized SL-7, eliminating the G3-style rotary rear sight altogether in favor of a folding leaf rear sight and blade front sight (but without the SL-7's prominent G3-inspired protective hood. The rear sight on the Model 770 was placed forward of the receiver and folded down to facilitate scope mounting (Heckler & Koch also offered an optional scope-mounting bracket). This rifle was available in the predictable .308 caliber (7.62mm). To make things interesting though, it was advertised in several other calibers as well. These included the .243, 6.5mm and 7mm, all of which are exceedingly rare, at least in the United States.

Unlike the G3, which employed a stamped steel receiver, Heckler & Koch chose for its HK770 an investment cast receiver unit instead, polished to a high blued luster. This shiny, slab-sided receiver, along with its top quality hardwood stock and precision cut checkering—sometimes highly embellished and decorated at great expense—combined to give the rifle a more refined look as "sporting purposes" than any of the company's previous rifle offerings for civilian use. Magazine capacity choices included two rounds (again as mandated by the West German government), three rounds (the one seen most), and ten rounds.

Meteoric price increases halted further importation of the Model 770 in 1986, although some remained on hand until 1988. From 1978 to 1986, the suggested retail price doubled, from $394 to $797, curtailing sales. In truth, this was never a particularly good rifle. Though accurate enough from the bench—indeed, some are sensationally accurate when propped in a rest—many shooters found its

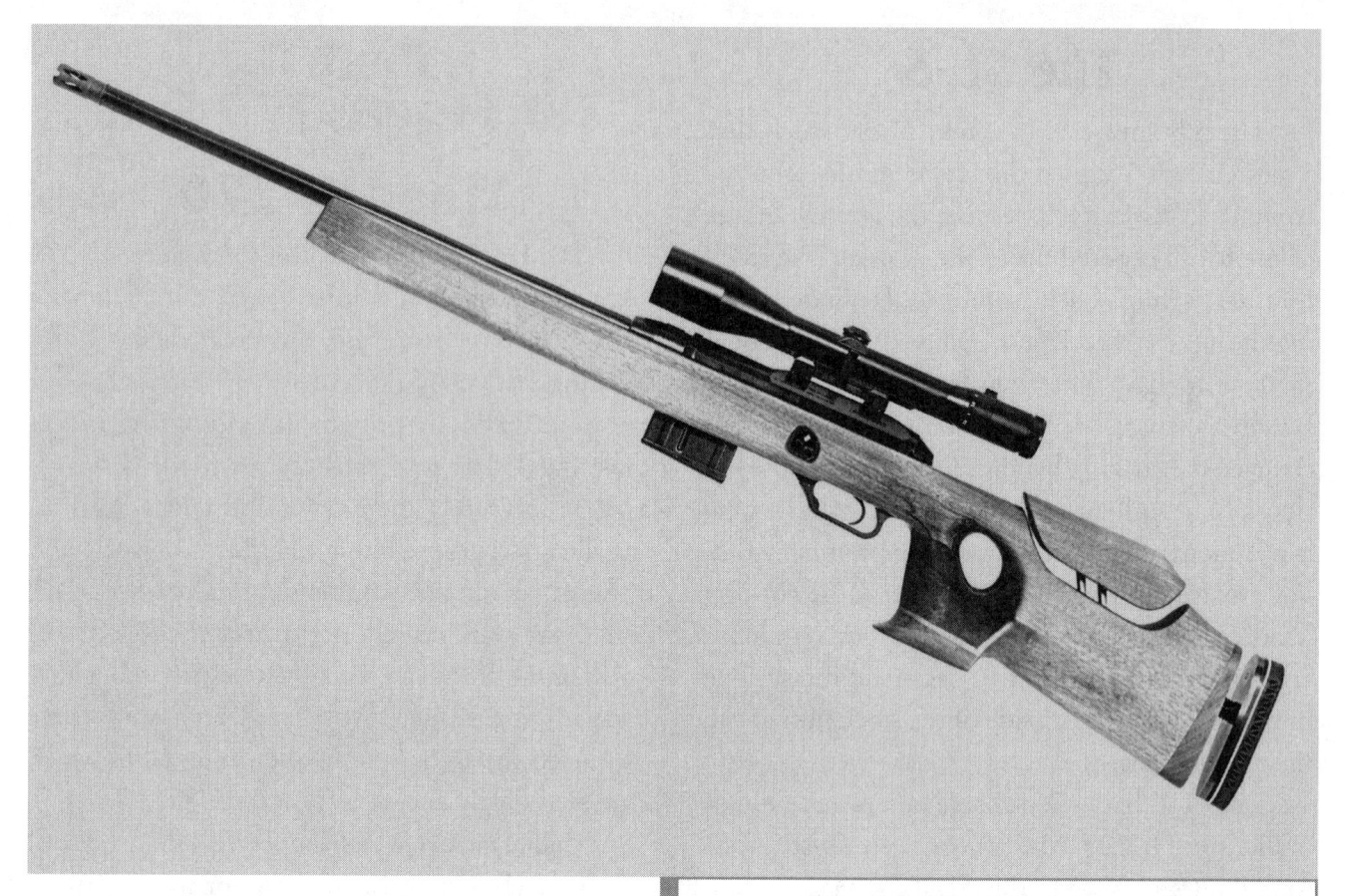

Mechanically and externally, the HK 630 was identical to the Model 770, firing smaller cartridges such as the .223. The example shown featured an adjustable target-style stock (photo courtesy of Heckler & Koch).

stock too long and too poorly balanced overall for accurate or comfortable offhand shooting. Rapid repeat shots, a "must" for a semiautomatic sporting rifle, proved a difficult challenge with the HK770.

The HK 630

When Heckler & Koch introduced the HK770, it also brought out the slightly smaller Model 630. Mechanically identical to the 770 and sharing the same appearance, this rifle fired smaller-caliber cartridges, including the .22 Hornet, .221, .222 and .223 (5.56mm). Again, only the .223 variation has appeared in any numbers in the U.S. For a time, however, the .222 Remington variant enjoyed some popularity in France.

Heckler & Koch had no more success with the Model 630 than the Model 770, despite its being some three inches shorter, half a pound lighter and firing a softer-recoiling cartridge. Certainly, this combination would make for a more pleasant shooting experience than the larger Model 770. In 1987, Heckler & Koch, Inc. was still advertising Model 630s from stock on hand, but they are long gone by now and only rarely encountered at gun shows and in private collections.

The HK 270

The HK 270, which appeared in 1978, outwardly resembled the Model 770-series guns but in a small caliber format firing the .22 Long Rifle cartridge. Because of the comparatively low-powered rimfire cartridge for which it was chambered, the HK 270 used a simple blowback mechanism.

No roller-locking system was needed to retard the bolt's rearward movement. Magazines came in two-shot (for West German sales), five-shot and 20-shot sizes. Despite the high-polish finish on the blued metal parts, the stock typically has a plain finish, probably because most people who buy a .22LR rifle aren't looking for something too fancy.

Without a locking system in this model, Heckler & Koch was able to produce the HK 270 with less expense than its other rifles cost. Due to the currency exchange rates between the German Mark and U.S. dollar, however, the Model 270 remained expensive for its type. At its discontinuance in 1985, the suggested retail price was $200.

> **The HK 940 was Heckler & Koch's "big gun," made to fire larger cartridges like the .30-06. Despite its excellent workmanship, it was clumsy and not well balanced (photo courtesy of Heckler & Koch).**

The HK 300

Another sporting rifle following the outward appearance of the HK 770 was the Model 300. Externally and mechanically, this blowback model closely resembled the .22LR Model 270 enlarged to handle the .22 Winchester Magnum Rimfire (.22 WMR) cartridge. The .22 Magnum, as it's often called, has, since its introduction in 1959, become popular for the varmint shooters. As such it represents a significant step up from the .22 Long Rifle in terminal power and ballistic trajectory.

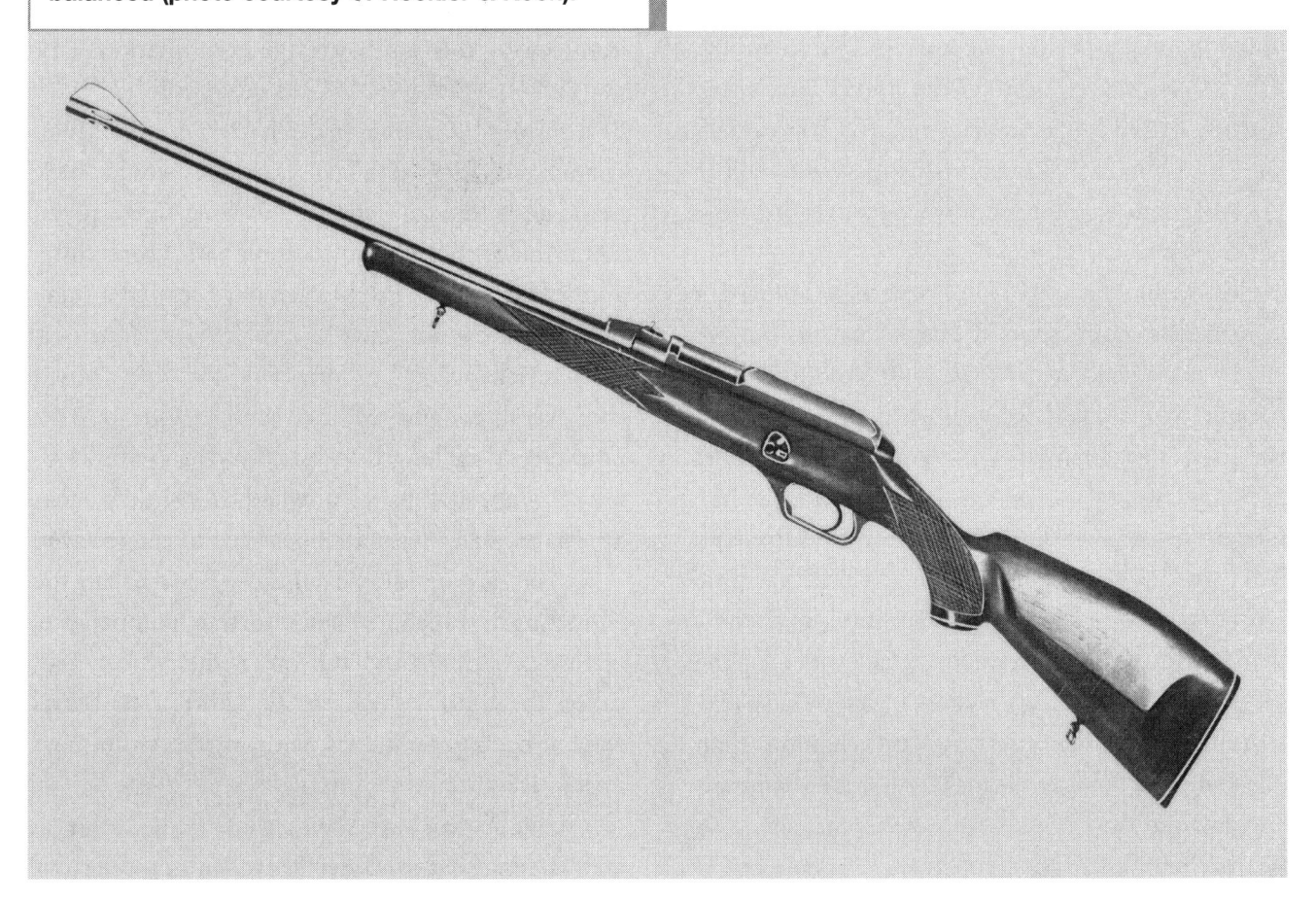

For this model, Heckler & Koch chose a stock design of higher quality than the smaller Model 270's. The Model 300 stock included cut checkering on the pistol grip and forearm and a cheekpiece on the left side for those who wanted to scope the rifle. While H&K offered good adjustable iron sights on its Model 300, apparently the company assumed most shooters would mount a scope on this rifle, so they frequently advertised it with scope mounts. The Model 300 offered both a factory scope mount and an A.R.M.S. scope mount package option, the latter including a Leupold variable-power 3-9x telescopic sight.

The HK 940 Series

Once the various guns of Model 770 type showed signs of success, Heckler & Koch followed up with the Model 940 series, which looked virtually identical to the Model 770 but fired the .30-06 caliber instead. Like its twin, the HK 940 came with good integral sights and an optional scope-mounting system.

The .30-06 cartridge has a 63mm cartridge case, as opposed to the 51mm case employed by the .308; otherwise, the two are remarkably similar, the .30-06 being one of the .308's ancestors. Because of the longer cartridge case (12mm translates into almost half an inch), the .30-06 caliber HK940 required a longer, heavier receiver than the Model 770.

Knowing that the .30-06 cartridge enjoyed a tremendous popularity in the U.S., Heckler & Koch chambered the Model 940 accordingly. It became the standard service cartridge in 1906 and was used in such famous U.S. weapons as the Model 1903 Springfield, the Model 1917 Enfield, the M1 Garand, the Model 1918 Browning Automatic Rifle, and the various M1917 and M1919 machine guns designed by Browning. In addition, U.S. commercial rifle designers have long made rifles for the .30-06 cartridge, in part because of its military reputation but also because it has proven more than adequate for killing virtually all game animals encountered on the American continent. The .30-06 also enjoyed a good following overseas, but it remains in the eyes of many an "American" cartridge. Because the longer receiver made it possible to chamber the Model 940 in a whole class of "long action" cartridges unavailable in the Model 770 series, Heckler & Koch also decided to make a bid for stronger international sales. It did so by chambering the series in a few popular European sporting cartridges in the .30-06 size and performance class, specifically the 7x64mm and the 9.3x62mm.

Oddly enough, Heckler & Koch did not attempt to manufacture or market the Model 940 in .270 Winchester caliber. Introduced in 1925, it consisted of a .30-06 cartridge case necked down to accept a small-diameter bullet. The increase in velocity gained over the .30-06 bullet made the .270 Winchester an excellent long-range cartridge against medium-sized game. The Model 940's G3-style roller-locked mechanism and crisp, single-stage trigger could have brought out the inherent accuracy of this gun/cartridge combination. The conversion would have been accomplished with ease simply by changing the barrel. A Model 940 chambered for the .270 cartridge would have made an interesting choice as a long-range precision rifle for sports shooters looking for something a little different. It might even have created a small but loyal niche for itself.

The change to a "long-action caliber" raised the overall weight of the Model 940 to 8.62 pounds and its length to 47.25 inches (with 21.6-inch barrel), making an unwieldy, top-heavy package, particularly with a scope fitted to the receiver. Since the rifle handled even more poorly than the Model 770, H&K, in an effort to compensate, introduced a car-bine version of the Model 940, called the 940K (*K=Kurz*, or "short"). Its barrel was cut back to 16 inches, with corresponding savings in weight and length.

While it may have been an interesting technical exercise, none of the Model 940 variants proved commercially successful. As with the other Heckler & Koch sporting rifles, the exchange rates of the early- to mid-1980s caused an unavoidably steep price increase. The guns had never been a bargain, and competition from other good manufacturers was strong. Hence, these rifles did not remain on the market long enough to build a following. Despite considerable advertising in the mid-to-late 1980s, Heckler & Koch, Inc. was never able to find a market for the Model 940. The Model 940K is a particularly rare entity, with only two of these rifles finding their way into the United States, both in 1984.

The S*A*T*S*

One item Heckler & Koch has not offered to date is a "bullpup" rifle. A bullpup rifle has a short buttplate attached to the rear end of the breech which, when placed against one's shoulder, eliminates the commonly used buttstock assembly—and, in the process, reduces overall length by almost a foot. The trigger assembly migrates well forward, ahead of the magazine, thus enabling shooters to reach it easier. Indeed, most conversions of rifles to a handier carbine length involve lopping several inches off the barrel. Heckler & Koch has used that approach to create models like the G3K and HK53 from the basic G3. The problem with this barrel-shortening approach is that a radically shortened barrel leads to inferior shooting characteristics. This is especially true in high-powered rifle cartridges, where loss in velocity and increased muzzle flash and recoil are the result. The bullpup configuration, on the other hand, doesn't require the barrel to be shortened at all. And yet, by adopting the changes outlined above, one has already achieved a length reduction of a foot or more.

Though by no means commonplace, bullpup rifles are not particularly rare, either. One of FN's

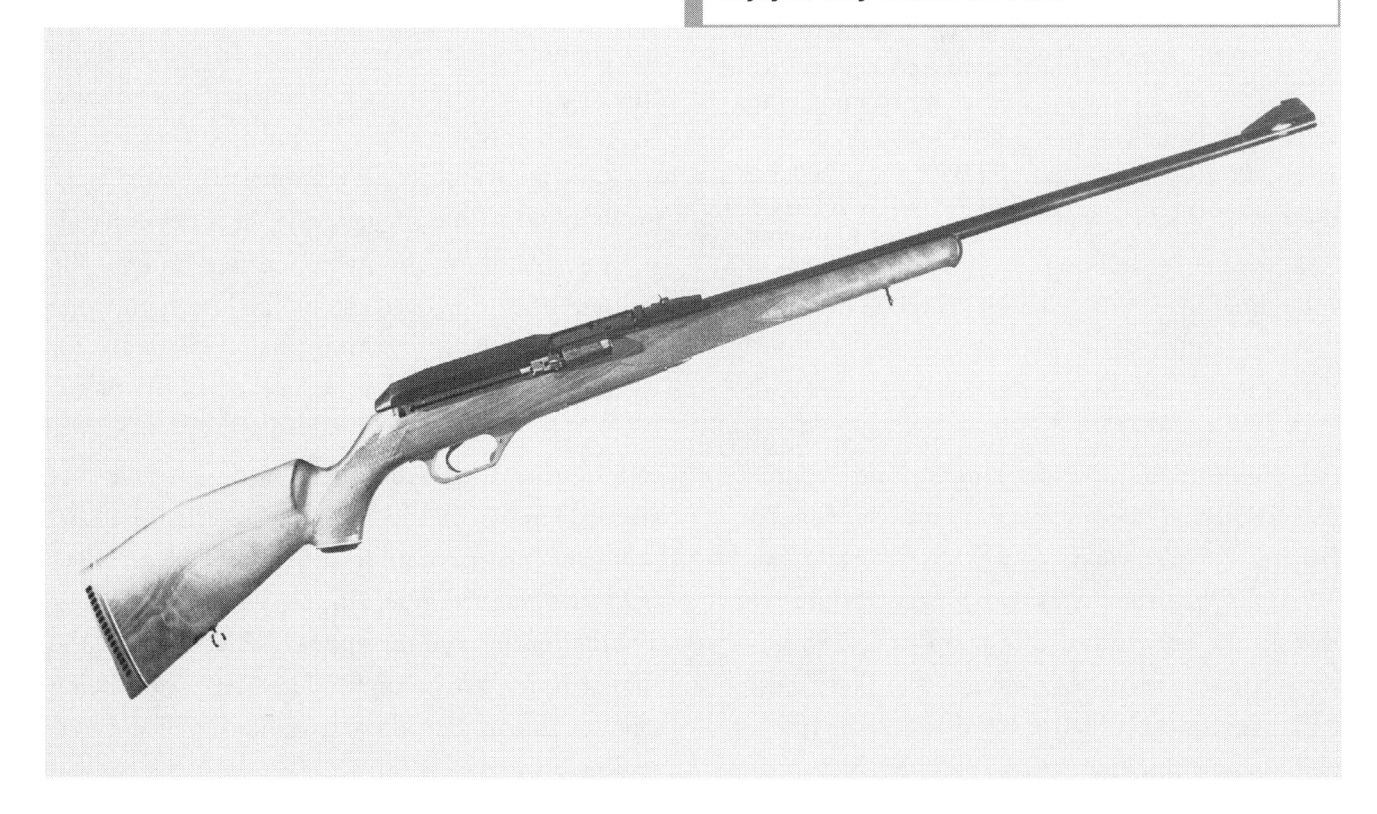

> **The HK940 was the last Heckler & Koch commercial rifle descended directly from the G3. While an interesting technical exercise, the Model 940 enjoyed only limited success.**

> **Heckler & Koch's latest semiautomatic rifle for the sporting and police markets is the .223 caliber SL-8. The example shown contains standard iron sights. Note the transparent magazine sides, an excellent feature not often seen in firearms. Magazine capacity is 10 rounds.**

first prototypes of the FAL, dating from the late 1940s, featured a bullpup configuration. In the mid-1980s, the Chinese and Finns, working separately, made successful adaptations of the AK-47/AKM assault rifle design to bullpup configuration. Official interest never materialized, however, and both projects soon lapsed. In 1977, the Austrians introduced the excellent Steyr AUG .223 caliber military rifle, which has since become the world's most successful bullpup rifle design to date, including sales to Austria, Australia, Ecuador, Ireland, New Zealand, Omani, Saudi Arabia and Tunisia. Once the AUG had broken the ice, the British also introduced a bullpup—the L85A1—which now serves as their service rifle. The French, too, have since 1980 marketed a service rifle of bullpup configuration, called the FAMAS.

As we've seen, the rationale behind the bullpup design is a radical shortening of overall length while retaining most of the original barrel length, thereby enhancing concealability and handiness while maintaining good firing qualities. In fact, bullpup rifle designs do involve a few inherent compromises. One involves the trigger linkage, which is by necessity longer and more complex than usual, generally resulting in a trigger pull that is not especially amenable to improvement and fine-tuning. The bullpup rifle, moreover, can be fired from only one side of the body, which means the ejection port for spent cartridge casings must lie close to the shooter's head. With the French-made FAMAS, the shooter can reverse the direction of cartridge-case ejection to accommodate left- or right-handed shooters; but accomplishing this switch involves field-stripping the rifle. An alternative when using a bullpup rifle from the opposite side is to hold the rifle at nearly arm's length. That may avoid being struck by spent cartridges, true, but it will also lead to poor accuracy.

Several American companies have adapted the bullpup configurations of other companies, one being Tomark Industries, which once offered a conversion of the HK91/G3, called the S*A*T*S*. In redesigning this rifle, the G3's barrel length remained the same, but with an overall length reduction of about eight inches. The magazine doubled as a pistol grip for the shooting hand. This S*A*T*S* conversion enjoyed some notoriety from the late 1970s to the early 1980s. Its use of the magazine as a handgrip left something to be desired, mostly because the .308 caliber, 20-shot magazine was quite bulky. Moreover, the S*A*T*S* conversion placed the rear sight too close to the shooter's face and eyes, presenting the likelihood of injury caused by recoil.

This SL-8 features a 3-power telescopic sight and an electronic red-dot sight. It also sports a slim forearm with integral bipod developed for the company's G36 military rifle (photo courtesy of Heckler & Koch).

PART III: MORE COMMERCIAL DESIGNS

The BASR

In 1986, Heckler & Koch briefly marketed its only bolt-action rifle, the BASR. As so often happens in the firearms business, the company started out with ambitious plans for this model. H&K intended to offer a wide choice of cartridge chambering options, including .22 Long Rifle, .22-250, 6mm PPC, .308, .30-06 and .300 Winchester Magnum. A Kevlar stock and stainless-steel barrel ensured good weather resistance. Regrettably, the BASR never really came to fruition. The original plan was for Heckler & Koch, Inc. to offer this advanced rifle design through its extensive dealer network as a special-order item at a suggested retail price of $2,199. However, the U.S. manufacturer and Heckler & Koch could not come to agreement on pricing and marketing procedures. As a result, fewer than 135 complete BASR rifles were made, with Heckler & Koch receiving none of them. The BASR is now a collector's item only, with a mint-conditioned specimen bringing well over $5,000.

F.W. Heym GmbH

In 1865, German gunsmith Friedrich Wilhelm Heym began operations in the eastern German industrial city of Suhl. The company he created—F.W. Heym GmbH—became world famous as a manufacturer of high-quality sporting long guns. The company achieved particular fame in 1891 when it introduced the first drilling: a three-barreled hammerless rifle/shotgun combination.

Following a year's absence after World War I ended, production of Heym sporting guns continued almost without interruption until the conclusion of World War II. With the Soviets having occupied Suhl, the Heym firm was relocated to West Germany, reestablishing itself first in the Bavarian (south German) town of Münnerstadt (1945-1996) and, since 1996, to Gleichamberg in eastern Germany.

From 1989 to 1993, Heckler & Koch, Inc. imported Heym rifles into the U.S. Drillings and other custom rifles were available through Heckler & Koch, Inc. until 1993, but the mainstay of the line was the bolt-action SR 20 series. Introduced in 1975, this series ultimately included the following models: SR 20G, N, L, M, Classic, Alpine, Trophy, Classic Sportsman and Classic Safari. Common features of the SR 20 series included twin opposed locking lugs near the head of the bolt, and a sliding three-position manual safety located on the tang. Rifles of the SR 20 type appeared in a wide variety of cartridge chamberings, including .243 Winchester, .270 Winchester, 6.6x55mm Mauser, 7x57 Mauser, .308, .30-06, 7x64mm, 8x57JS, 7mm Remington Magnum, .300 Winchester Magnum, .338 Winchester Magnum and .375 Holland & Holland.

The Heym Express bolt action rifle, which appeared in 1989, shared a general similarity to the Heym Classic Safari model. However, the Mauser-style three-position manual safety on the Express (located at the rear end of the bolt shroud) was reinstated. Due to the powerful cartridges it fired, Heym also reinstated Mauser's Model 98-type third (safety) lug located on the bottom rear portion of the bolt, adding a measure of protection against bolt failure should the front two locking lugs ever break. Cartridges chambered in the Heym Express included the following: .300 Weatherby Magnum, .338 Lapua Magnum, .375 H&H Magnum, .378 Weatherby Magnum, .404 Jeffery, .416 Rigby, .425 Express, .450 Ackley, .458 Winchester Magnum, .460 Weatherby Magnum, .500 A-Square and .600 Nitro Express.

The Heym rifles were well-made but costly. In 1993, the year Heckler & Koch, Inc. dropped the line, the SR 20s ranged in price from $2,285 for a Classic Sportsman in standard calibers to $2,725 for a Classic Safari model (rifles adapted for left-hand operation added $450 to the total price). The Express models were even costlier, starting at $6,245 ($575 more for a left-handed model) and peaking at $10,900 for the .600 Nitro Express version. By contrast, a Remington Model 700 could be bought in 1993 for as little as $519 in standard calibers and $1,264 for the costliest Safari Model in most of the heavy calibers offered by Heym.

The SL8-1

Heckler & Koch announced its latest commercial rifle venture, the SL8-1 (**photos p. 118, 119**), in late 1999. It marked a return to the commercial market by Heckler & Koch after a long absence. In some ways, the SL8-1 is a typical 1990s high-tech rifle. Eschewing the roller-locked breech expected in a Heckler & Koch rifle, the SL8-1 has the same gas-operated rotating bolt one might see on any number of similar .223-caliber assault rifles and sporters worldwide. The SL8-1 also boasted extensive polymer construction, a thumbhole stock, an ambidextrous manual safety, and an extensive choice of sighting systems (including red-dot, scopes or iron sights).

The SL8-1 also featured a variety of unusual characteristics guaranteed to set it apart. Its magazine's clear plastic sides allowed the shooter to check his ammunition supply at a glance. The forearm was easily removed by driving out one pin and replacing it with other forearm configurations, including one with an integral bipod developed originally for the G36. The rifle also had an adjus-table/removable cheekpiece on the stock, an excellent feature in any rifle with a telescopic sight.

The operating controls on the SL8-1 are well laid out. The ambidextrous manual safety/fire selector is accessible below the shooting hand, whether the shooter is right- or left-handed. The selector pushes down and forward to fire—the best movement for rapid response. The buttstock can be extended up to two inches in length by pulling the buttplate out and adding (or removing) spacers.

The SL8-1 remains scarce in America, despite its wide acceptance in Europe. Heckler & Koch has high hopes for this rifle, both in the civil market and for police/paramilitary service. Its sturdy construction, wide variety of optional aiming devices and good ergonomics all indicate future success. At its introduction, the SL8-1's suggested retail price ($1,600) made it competitive with Colt's Match Target HBAR, H&K's chief competition in the U.S.

In Conclusion:

While not a household name among sport shooters, the Heckler & Koch sporting rifle line has been quite extensive and endowed with a rich history. The company has also demonstrated considerable technical innovation in pursuing this line. For shooters who desire a powerful, accurate and reliable rifle for hunting, there's enough variation in the Heckler & Koch sporting rifle line to engage the interests of even the most ambitious firearms collectors. • **H&K**

SPECIFICATIONS: SELECTED H&K SPORTING RIFLES

	Overall length (in.)	Barrel (in.)	Weight (lbs.)	Caliber	Magazine Capacity
HK91	40.38	17.7	9.7	.308	20 rounds
SR9	42.5	19.7	10.9	.308	5 rounds
HK93	37.0	16.14	7.94	.223	25 rounds
HK94	34.6	16.54	6.43	9mm	15 or 30 rounds
SL-6	39.95	17.7	7.7	.223	4 rounds
SL-7	39.7	17.7	8.4	.308	3 rounds
770	44.5	19.7	8.1	.308	3 rounds
630	42.1	17.7	7.1	.223	4 rounds
300	39.4	19.7	5.7	.22 WMR	5 rounds
940	47.25	21.6	8.6	.30-06	3 rounds
SL8-1	38.58	20.8	8.6	.223	10 rounds

While the Germans had led the way with military deployment of submachine guns in both World Wars, they limited their use of such weapons afterwards, becoming instead converts to the assault-rifle concept. In those carefree days before the 1972 Munich Olympic debacle, the West German police also made relatively little use of submachine guns, contenting themselves with......

Chapter 4

Submachine Guns

While Germany led the way in submachine gun design during the early days, their development lay dormant for a few decades following World War II. The combatant nations had churned out so many submachine guns during the war that the international arms markets were awash in them. This period largely coincided with Germany's inability to develop and produce new firearms because of restrictions enforced by the victorious Allies. But as West Germany began to rearm during the mid-1950s and beyond, the natural inventiveness of German designers in this field reasserted itself.

Although Heckler & Koch was not the first West Germany company to build submachine guns after World War II, the company's submachine guns have become some of the most durable weapons ever created in this category of firearms.

Initial postwar issue of submachine guns to the West German armed forces included the DUX Model 53, which was basically a wartime Finnish redesign of the Soviet Model PPS43 7.62mm Sudayev gun altered to fire the more

The MP5A2 is the basic fixed-stock derivative of Heckler & Koch's chief submachine gun design (photo courtesy of Heckler & Koch).

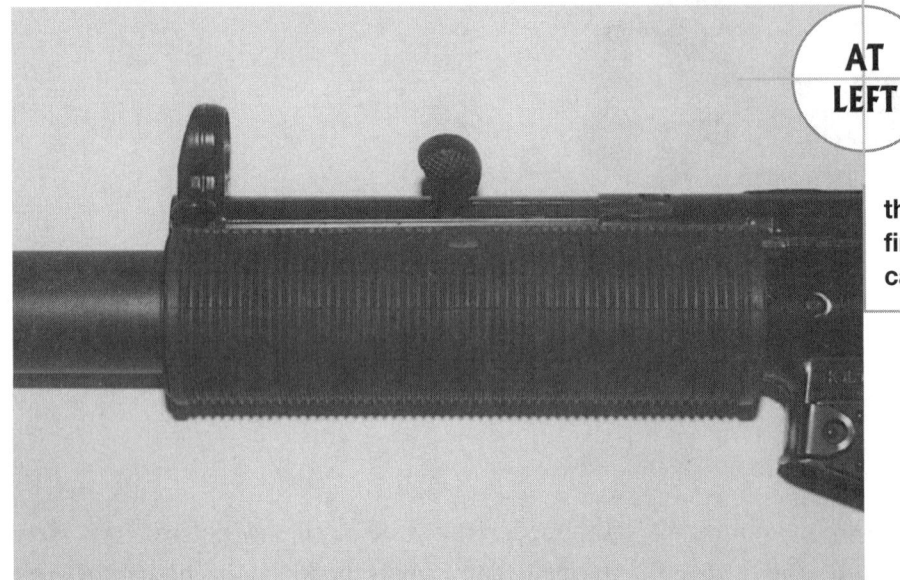

AT LEFT — The MP5SD's barrel shroud and integral silencer do an extremely effective job muffling the sound of the cartridges being fired, though they do add significantly to the weapon's bulk.

BELOW — Heckler's & Koch's advertising for the MP5/10 stresses its acceptance by the FBI, who adopted the 10mm Auto cartridge after a disastrous shootout in Miami in 1986 in which FBI agents armed with .38 Special +P revolvers and 9mm Parabellum automatic pistols sufered grievous losses in a battle with two murderous bank robbers (photo courtesy of Heckler & Koch).

AT RIGHT

A front view of the MP5SD shows that its barrel is much shorter and smaller than the hefty shroud which surrounds it.

BELOW

A typical firing stance for the MP5K places both hands on the weapon for optimum recoil control, eyes on the target and firing in short bursts to control muzzle rise, conserve ammunition and determine effect on the target. However, if necessary the weapon is small enough to carry and shoot one-handed like a pistol.

Chapter Four 125

widespread 9mm Parabellum cartridge. The DUX design migrated to Spain, where about a thousand of these guns were made for the West German border police. Walther then stepped forward with the MPL and MPK, two related designs differing only in barrel length. These useful and reliable weapons drew heavily on stamped-steel construction techniques first developed late in World War II and perfected later by Heckler & Koch, among others. From 1963 until Walther stopped their manufacture in 1987, the MPL/MPK series saw limited service with the West German military and police (whose special units were active at the hostage crisis during the 1972 Olympic Games held in Munich).

Meanwhile, an Israeli designer, Uziel Gal, had created the Uzi submachine gun. The Israeli armed forces made extensive use of this versatile weapon from the start, and the West German armed forces were quick to adopt it as well after the Allies allowed German rearmament in the mid-1950s. The rapidity with which the Allies adopted this design gave credence to the suggestion that doing so was a way of apologizing to Israel for the horrible treatment Nazi Germany had meted out to the Jews during World War II. West Germany bought Uzi submachine guns from both Israel and Belgium's Fabrique Nationale (FN), once that company began manufacturing the gun in the early 1960s. FN dropped the Uzi in 1985 in order to manufacture the Italian-designed Beretta Model PM-12S instead. The West Germans chose not to adopt this design, though one wartime Beretta design—the Model 38/42—had seen limited service in West Germany as the MP1 during the early postwar period.

The MP5A3 has a collapsible stock for greater compactness, but it is otherwise identical to the A2 variant. The weapon shown features a white-light attachment popular with police forces who use the MP5 as an "entry gun" (photo courtesy of Heckler & Koch).

While the Germans had led the way with military deployment of submachine guns in both World Wars, they limited their use of such weapons afterwards, becoming instead converts to the assault-rifle concept. In those carefree days before the 1972 Munich Olympic debacle, the West German police also made relatively little use of submachine guns, contenting themselves with small numbers of Walther MPLs and MPKs. That all changed after 1972, with Heckler & Koch positioning itself to capitalize on this new interest among the German police forces in submachine guns.

The MP5

Heckler & Koch's first foray into the field of submachine guns—the MP5 **(photo p. 124)**—proved extremely significant. The company built the first prototype in July of 1964 (hence the original company name, "Project 64"). Basing much of the submachine gun on H&K's phenomenally successful G3 greatly speeded up its development. A second prototype, finished in November of 1964, served as a pre-production model.

The MP5 was introduced in 1965 and remains in production to this day. West Germany's military issue of the MP5 has been limited, though, because its armed forces now make only modest use of submachine guns, whereupon West Germany's police quickly took to the design. In Europe, submachine guns have been viewed traditionally as the "politically and socially correct" long arm of law-enforcement personnel, whereas the shotgun has been considered rather barbaric. Credit for the gun's current designation belongs to West Germany's *Bundesgrenschütz* (Border Police), whose original model designation of "HK54" has been supplanted, even in the company's own literature, by the MP5 (an abbreviation of *Machinen Pistole*, or Machine Pistol). This term had been used since the creation of the first such weapon in 1918; that is, one may regard a submachine gun as a miniature machine gun that fires pistol ammunition. Originally, Heckler & Koch wanted the MP5 to fire the 9mm Parabellum pistol cartridge exclusively, since that is the all-time favorite submachine gun round in Germany and, indeed, throughout most of the world.

The MP5 differs from virtually all other submachine gun designs by eschewing a simple blowback mechanism for the roller-locked breech system used in the P9, the G3 and various machine gun designs. The West German government acknowledges these similarities by placing the

> **The MP5/10, introduced in 1991, is an MP5 chambered for the 10mm Auto cartridge. Note the straight magazine, which has been standard with this variant from the beginning. Since 1977, though, all Heckler & Koch's MP5s chambered for the 9mm Parabellum cartridge have used a curved magazine (photo courtesy of Heckler & Koch).**

Chapter Four **127**

Heckler & Koch offers the MP5/10 in an A3 collapsible-stock version. The twin-magazine clamp is an option also available for H&K 7.62mm and 5.56mm rifles and 9mm submachine guns (the transparent magazine is currently limited to the 10mm MP5/10 series) (photo courtesy of Heckler & Koch).

7.62mm G3 and the 9mm MP5 in what it calls the "Group 1" category of Heckler & Koch weapons. The MP5's sights, operating controls, locking mechanism, furniture and other structural and operational characteristics are essentially identical to those of the G3. While this similarity may detract slightly from the MP5's function, compared to that of a submachine built to fill a specialized role, the similarities work to the advantage of soldiers who train with weapons having a common operating system, not to mention production efficiencies, availability of spare parts and the like. By using the basic G3 operating mechanism, the MP5 becomes noticeably more accurate than the typical submachine gun, which generally relies on a shorter barrel and a blowback bolt mechanism. That may be fine for spraying bullets at a big target up close, but not when more precise shot placement is required.

The original MP5 issued to the West German police had a fixed stock, but Heckler & Koch soon added a collapsible-stock version, called the MP5A1. After other refinements, including adoption of the G3-style rotary rear sight, were made, the MP5A2 (with fixed stock) and the MP5A3 (with collapsible stock) were added.

Regrettably, the MP5's advanced construction makes it more expensive than the simpler blowback mechanisms used by H&K's competitors. For that reason, ironically, a few competitors managed to survive. This competition included the French-built MAT-49 and the British Sterling, both of

The MP5/40, introduced in 1993, is the .40 S&W caliber equivalent of the MP5 series. Note the straight magazine inherited from the MP5/10 (photo courtesy of Heckler & Koch).

which have since gone out of production, as well as the numerous used submachine guns available on the world arms market, such as the MP-38 and 40, the British Sten, the U.S. Thompson and M3, and the Soviet PPSh-41. Not only has the MP5 outlasted all of these well-known firearms, but it has gone on to outpace even the Uzi and the Beretta PM-12 series in overall sales, not to mention the number of military forces and police agencies that issue it.

As a result of this phenomenal success, the MP5 today represents the world standard in submachine guns. In addition to its native Germany, the following countries are known to use MP5s for official issue to military and/or police forces: Bahrain, Belgium, Brazil, Canada, Chile, Denmark, El Salvador, France, Ghana, Great Britain, Greece, Honduras, Hong Kong, Iceland, Iran, Italy, Japan, Kenya, Kuwait, Luxembourg, Mexico, Mor-occo, the Netherlands, New Zealand, Niger, Nigeria, Norway, Pakistan, Qatar, Saudi Arabia, Singapore, Spain, Sri Lanka, Sudan, Switzerland, Thailand, Turkey, United States, Uruguay, Venezuela, Yugoslavia, Zaïre and Zambia. Of special interest is the fact that Brazil and Italy, both of whom produce variants of the highly-regarded, Beretta-designed PM-12, and Britain, whose Sterling submachine gun remained in production until 1988, also use the MP5. Why? Because all three countries issue MP5s to elite police units where first-rate accuracy is a necessity. The MP5 is unmatched among sub-machine guns for precise bullet placement, whereas other submachine guns are known as "bullet hoses," spraying the target area and endangering innocent civilians.

The MP5 and related submachine guns carry either 15-shot or 30-shot magazines, the 15-rounders generally considered best for improved handling and ease of carry, while the 30-rounders are kept as spares. When using an MP5, it's smart to keep a number of

Heckler & Koch's MP5SD features an integral silencer, adding bulk to the front portion. In some special operations, this gun's quiet operation is much appreciated (photo courtesy of Heckler & Koch).

At Right. The MP5SD is available in both fixed-stock and collapsible-stock configurations. The collapsible-stock SD3 (left) uses the curved pistol grip, while the fixed-stock SD5 (right) utilizes the straight post-1986 style of pistol grip.

spare magazines (loaded) on hand, because these guns gobble up ammunition at a cyclic rate of 800 round per minute. Until 1988, both 15- and 30-round magazines were straight, but since then Heckler & Koch has converted to a slightly curved profile on the 9mm Parabellum MP5 magazines in order to reduce the overall height slightly. All MP5s made to fire the .40 S&W and 10mm automatic cartridges use a straight magazine.

Below. The H&K trigger group (introduced in 1986) combines the trigger group and lower receiver in a single molding. The company also introduced that year its well-known red and white bullet symbols on the safety/fire selector.

Chapter Four 131

Despite its success with the MP5, Heckler & Koch has not rested on its laurels and continues to develop the basic design even as it makes plans for an eventual replacement. The company has also developed a number of specialized MP5 variants to suit roles a submachine gun might be tasked with, as covered below.

The MP5 SF

Realizing that some official customers, notably European police agencies, preferred using their MP5s in semiautomatic fire only, Heckler & Koch offered this model in an SF (for "single fire") model, beginning in 1989. Similar to the commercial HK94, but available only in the short (8.85-inch) barrel configuration, this weapon shared most of the parts in common with the MP5's standard selective-fire model. The only difference lay in the removal of parts that allowed more than one shot for each pull on the trigger. As a result, the MP5 SF accepted virtually all of the accessories developed by Heckler & Koch during the many years of MP5 production.

The MP5/10 and MP5/40

In 1991, spurred on by developments in the United States, Heckler & Koch added a 10mm automatic caliber variant to its MP5 line **(photo p. 124)**, called the MP5/10. American shooters have never been thrilled with the 9mm Parabellum round as a pistol or submachine gun cartridge, despite its near-universal acceptance elsewhere. In the late 1980s, Heckler & Koch, noting the interest among U.S. shooters in the powerful new 10mm auto cartridge, decided to develop an MP5 variant that could take this round. The FBI's adoption of the 10mm cartridge followed a near-disastrous shootout with 9mm pistols in Miami in April of

When disassembled the MP5SD clearly indicates its debt to Heckler & Koch's G3 design. Except for the sound suppressor, all of its major operating components are virtually identical, except for size, whether as a rifle or a submachine gun (photo courtesy of Heckler & Koch).

An MP5KA4 of recent manufacture displays the modern trigger group and G3-style front and rear sights (photo courtesy of Heckler & Koch).

1986, giving Heckler & Koch even more reason to develop the MP5/10.

The variant, following the basic design of the 9mm MP5 inside and out, shares the same dimensions. In developing the MP5/10, though, Heckler & Koch made several small but interesting changes that would suit the weapon to U.S. needs and desires. Its 9mm magazine, while retaining the straight profile of the pre-1977 MP5, is made of smoked plastic through which shooters can more easily determine the state of their ammunition supply. The weapon also has a hold-open latch for the bolt, located just above the fire-selector switch. It's modeled after a unit used with great success in the M16/AR-15, eliminating a major objection raised for decades by critics of the G3 rifle line. Another interesting feature (first introduced in 1993) was an optional 2-shot burst selector on the fire-control unit, replacing its three-shot counterpart more commonly found on the four-position fire-control group. In theory, any MP5 submachine gun variant can be ordered from Heckler & Koch with this two-shot selector rather than the three-shot (both selectors are ambidextrous). The barrel of the MP5/10 comes threaded for a sound suppressor, offered by Heckler & Koch as an option to qualified buyers.

The MP5/40, introduced in 1993, is the same weapon as the MP5/10, only made to fire the .40 S&W caliber cartridge. Another of those automatic pistol cartridges with greater power than the 9mm

Chapter Four 133

Parabellum, the .40 S&W cartridge became tremendously popular among U.S. police circles within five years following its 1990 release. Consequently, it makes sense for Heckler & Koch to build a submachine gun for the round in the hope that U.S. police forces who have chosen the .40 for their duty pistols will purchase submachine guns so chambered as well.

The ultra-compact MP5K can be carried in a "Special Case," as shown (photo courtesy of Heckler & Koch).

The MP5 SD

Introduced in 1971, the MP5SD (SD is an abbreviation for *Schalldämpfer*, or "silencer") is Heckler & Koch's silenced MP5 variant **(photos p. 124, 125)**. After shortening the normal MP5 barrel from 8.85 to 5.75 inches (146mm), Heckler & Koch drills 30 holes into the barrel and surrounds it with a two-chamber sound suppressor assembly. Hot supersonic gases flow from the barrel holes at the moment of firing and vent into the first chamber immediately

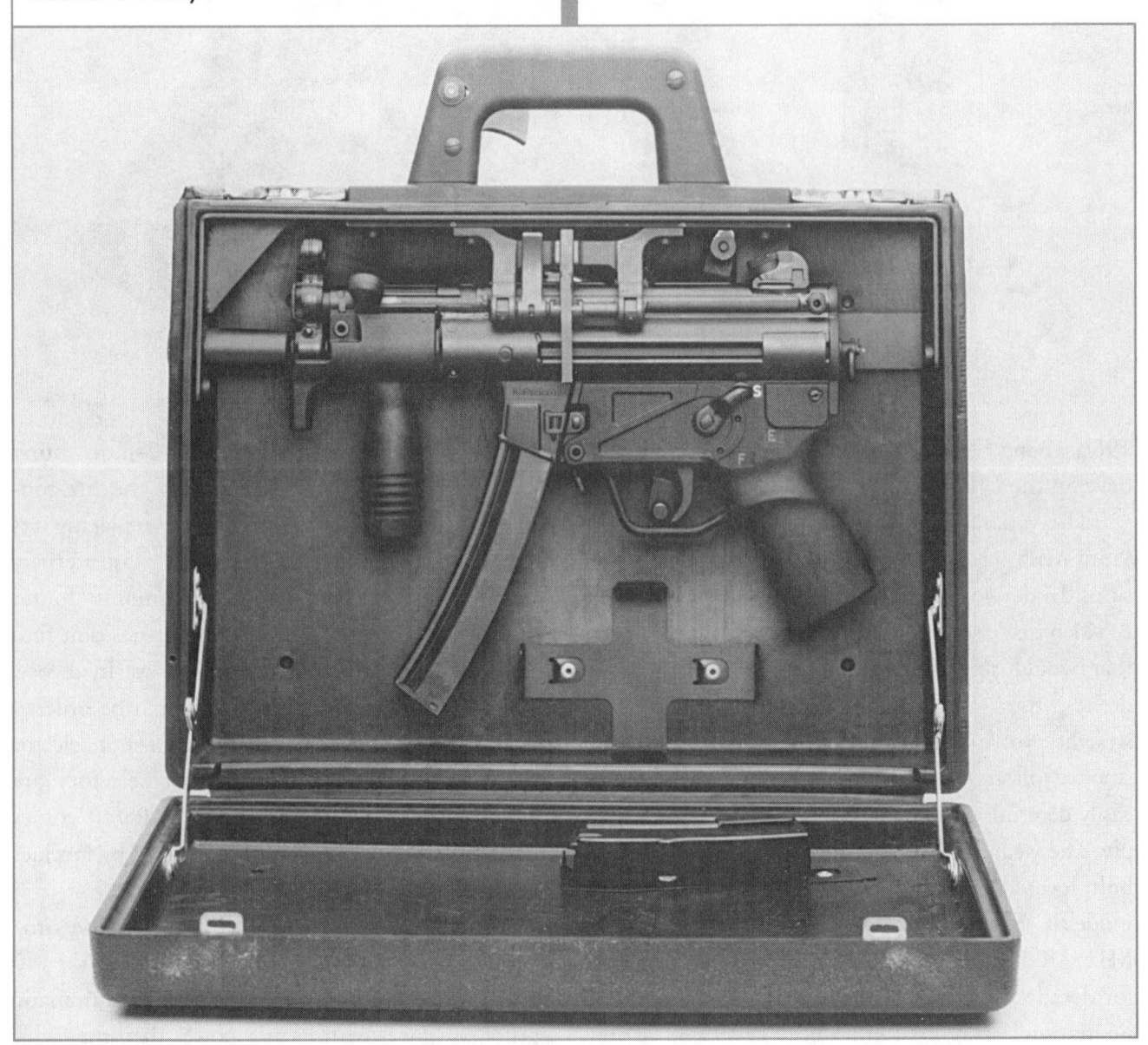

The MP5KA1 eliminates the bulky rifle-style sights of the standard MP5K in favor of two tiny nubs on the receiver top (above the trigger housing). By smoothing the profile, Heckler & Koch created an MP5K variant that is especially useful for shooting from the company's "Special Case" and "Special Bag." In such scenarios, the shooter is unlikely to use sights anyway.

surrounding the barrel. As the gases begin to slow down and cool, they work their way into the second, outer chamber. There they continue to cool and slow down until, having been reduced to subsonic speeds, they vent out the muzzle. Heckler & Koch engineered the MP4SD's suppressor mechanism so that the cyclic rate would remain the same as that of the standard MP5. This decision makes sense in terms of training and in its simplified transition from the MP5 to the MP5SD. Actually, I believe 800 rounds per minute is too fast a cyclic rate to begin with (see below).

The sound suppressor feature does work, but there's still plenty of noise from the bolt clacking back and forth. In terms of handling, the MP5SD is more awkward than the standard MP5 because of the bulky silencer assembly. By comparison with a standard 9mm MP5, the SD's accuracy is unimpaired. The Parabellum bullet's reduction to subsonic velocity does, however, reduce its stopping power to something on the order of a .380 ACP. Moreover, the MP4SD requires careful attention in one's selection of ammunition. Ammunition loaded with a powder charge that's too feeble will not provide the weapon with enough energy to cycle the mechanism, causing feed stoppages to occur.

Chapter Four 135

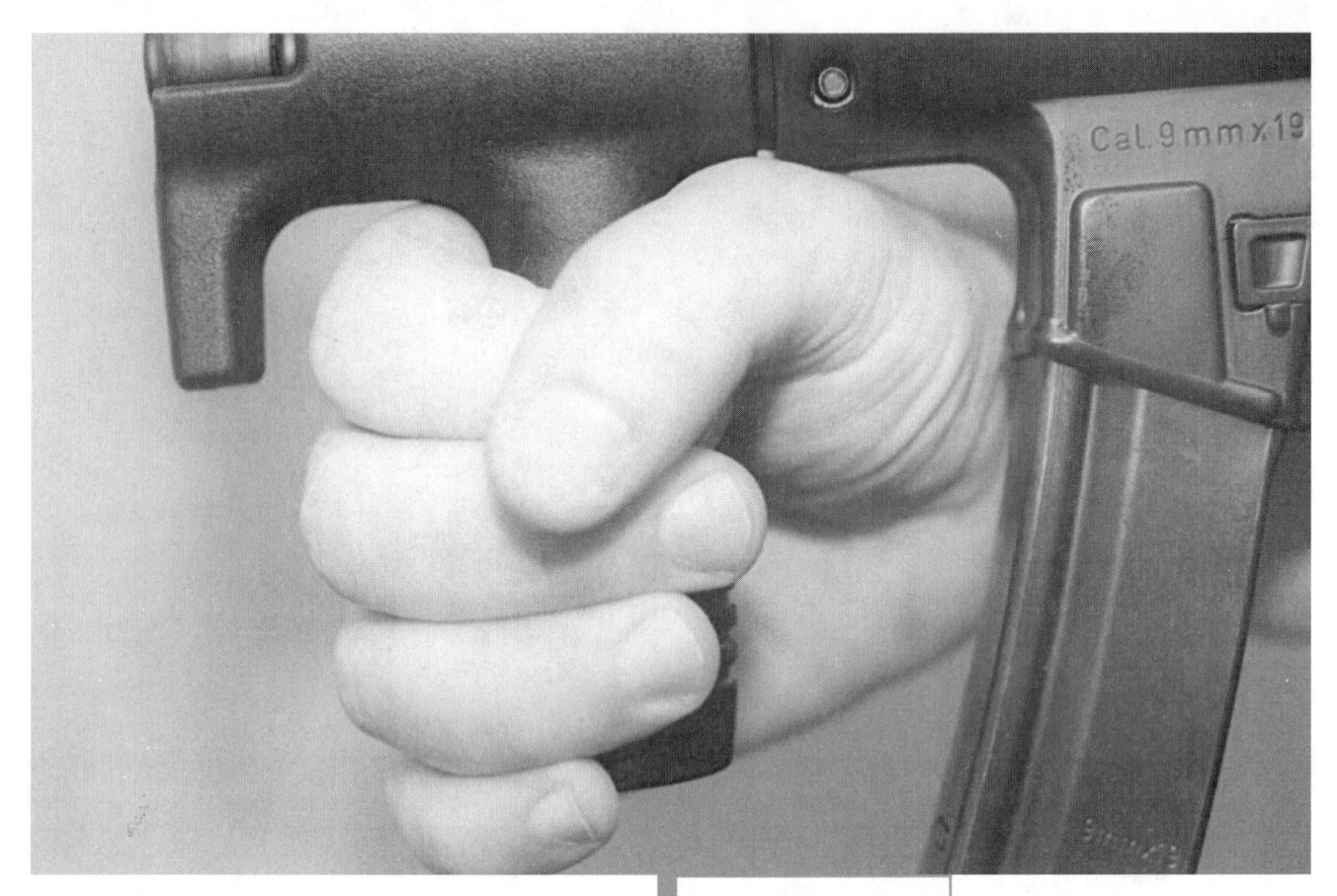

The MP5K's vertical handgrip and the projection shown beneath the muzzle help prevent the shooter's support hand from straying in front of the muzzle on this rifle's short barrel.

Heckler & Koch has actually made half a dozen MP5SD variants to provide the widest variety of possible uses, as follows: The **SD1** is a compact model with no buttstock and the standard three-position manual safety/fire selector (safe, semiautomatic and fully-automatic fire settings). The **SD2**: Fixed plastic buttstock and three-position fire selector. **SD3**: A collapsible buttstock and three-position fire selector. **SD4**: No buttstock and a more recent four-position fire selector with safe, semiautomatic, three-shot burst and fully-automatic settings. **SD5**: A fixed plastic buttstock and four-position fire selector. **SD6**: A collapsible buttstock and four-position fire-selector.

Though not quite as widespread as the parent MP5 design, the MP5SD has become quite popular in the past three decades. Countries that have issued the MP5SD include Brazil, France, Germany, Great Britain, Honduras, Italy, Kuwait, the Netherlands, Saudi Arabia, Singapore, the United States, Uruguay and Venezuela. Most go to elite counter terrorist or military special forces. In France, for example, the elite *Groupement d'Intervention de la Gendarmerie Nationale* (or GIGN) uses them regularly, helping to make it one of the world's most respected counter terrorist units. The same applies to Germany, where the government issues MP5SDs to the elite *Grenschutz-gruppe-9* (GSG-9) antiterrorist unit. In Great Britain, the Special Air Services (SAS) use these weapons. In Italy, when accuracy and silent operation are essential to a successful mission, it's the *Nucleo Operativo Centrale di Sicurezza* (NOCS) which favors the MP5SD over its own home-grown

Beretta PM-12S. In the United States, the Navy SEALS and a few elite police SWAT teams use the MP5SD. It would appear that—in many countries at least—silence is golden.

The MP5K

Heckler & Koch's smallest submachine gun to date is the MP5K (*K=Kurz*, or "short") **(photo p. 125)**. In 1976, after shrinking the basic MP5 design to the size of a large pistol, work began in earnest. After two years of hard developmental work, Heckler & Koch introduced the new variation in 1978; since then, it has become a classic submachine gun design. While its mechanism is basically that of the standard MP5, the barrel length has been reduced to slightly over 4.5 inches (overall length is less than 13 inches). A simple end cap on the shortened receiver has a ring for sling attachment, with no buttstock for shooters to place against their shoulder. Although these characteristics suggest that the MP5K is actually a fully-automatic pistol, that's not really the case. Should someone try holding and firing this gun as he would a pistol, he would soon lose control—especially since the smaller mechanism results in a higher rate of fire (900 rounds per minute) than the standard MP5.

This is not an easy weapon to master; indeed, it requires a set of handling techniques unique to the weapon. A small vertical handgrip placed in front of the magazine offers shooters a place for their support hand. Beneath the muzzle is another downward projection, a lip made of plastic whose function is to prevent shooters from accidentally

The MP5K (bottom) is appreciably smaller than the MP40, Germany's seminal submachine-gun design of World War Two.

Chapter Four

raising their fingers into the path of the muzzle with tragic results.

The usual firing technique is to hold the weapon at arm's length, or perhaps hold it against the pressure of a sling. Then point the gun at the target and fire, pressing the trigger rapidly and vigorously, then quickly releasing the trigger without waiting for the sound of the shots to begin. Using this "press-release" method allows shooters to fire short bursts of three to five shots or so. Anything longer wastes ammunition, because the muzzle rises under recoil causing subsequent shots to fly over the top of the target. This "press-release" method may sound easy, but it's actually quite difficult for even an experienced shooter to master. It works exactly the opposite of the "surprise break" one experiences when shooting any gun that fires only one shot for each pull of the trigger. With a fully-automatic weapon, especially one with as fast a rate of fire as the MP5K, waiting until the first shots are heard before releasing the trigger guarantees a long, wildly inaccurate burst of uncontrolled gunfire. Because the MP5K possesses much greater concealment potential than other members of the MP5 family, those who value this asset are generally willing to tolerate the difficulties inherent in handling the weapon.

Because of the shortened receiver, the accessories that relate to altering the buttstock fail to work on the MP5K variant. By virtue of the weapon's comparatively small size, Heckler & Koch developed two unusual concealment accessories for the MP5K. In addition to the hand-held mode of fire, the designers created a "Special Case" and a similar "Special Bag." Their purpose was to conceal the gun in something that didn't look like a weapons container. Shooters may deploy the weapon for one magazine load (from the case or bag) without having to open it and withdraw the gun. The "Special Case" held a remote trigger linkage built into the handle. The shooter had only to squeeze and hold this element to fire. A hole at the edge of the case held the muzzle and directed its fire. To fire an MP5K from the Special Bag, the hooter had only to reach into the bag—which had a hole in one end—and pull the trigger in normal fashion while supporting the bag with the other hand.

The favorite MP5K variant for these "briefcases" was the MP5KA1, which eliminated the standard

The most sophisticated MP5K variant to date is the MP5K-PDW, which adds a Choate folding stock (here shown fully extended) and a sound suppressor to the basic design.

Heckler & Koch originally offered the MP5K-PDW as a survival wea-pon for downed aviators (photo courtesy of Heckler & Koch).

G3 rifle sights used by most MP5 variants in favor of a smooth top. The MP5KA1 can also be adapted for mounting laser sights or a scope. Once Heckler & Koch had developed the improved trigger group (offering the four-position manual safety/fire selector) and offered this option, the nomenclature changed. The MP5KA4 is an MP5K with standard rifle-style sights and a new trigger group, while the MP5KA5 is a sightless MP5KA1 with the new trigger group.

Opinions vary on the three-shot burst feature used in the four-position trigger group currently in favor among Heckler & Koch's military long arms, i.e., rifles, machine guns and submachine guns. Those who dislike the four-position fire selector claim it tries to substitute a mechanical gadget—the three-shot burst setting—for proper training in good technique. Adding more settings to the fire-control mechanism, these critics warn, means more moving parts, hence more potential for those parts to break down—and more confusion in terms of coordinating fire control among the various components. Their points are valid. The problem is, becoming skilled at delivering automatic fire is very difficult until one has expended a great deal more ammunition than most military training budgets allow. All too often, armed forces prefer

Chapter Four 139

The MP5K-PDW, while a versatile weapon, proves bulky as an aviator's personal defense and survival weapon when carried on the leg in a harness, as shown (photo courtesy of Heckler & Koch).

investing in the latest gimmickry instead of providing their people with the proper education on how to use their materials properly. When troops are well-trained, the equipment really doesn't matter so much. But the world's armed forces insist on "keeping up with the Joneses" when it comes to acquiring the latest weaponry. Given that way of thinking, using gadgetry over trigger control appears to be a permanent feature. At least, Heckler & Koch's mechanism doesn't compromise the quality of the trigger pull anything like the dreadful three-shot burst control device found on the U.S. M16A2 rifle.

Because the modest size of the MP5K offers better concealment than other submachine guns, it has found a niche arming numerous groups, including aviators, bodyguards, soldiers and special operations teams around the world. Countries known to issue MP5Ks—almost invariably to special police or elite military units—are Canada, Germany, Great Britain, India, Japan, Jordan, Kuwait, Malta, the Netherlands, Pakistan and Saudi Arabia. The Royal Canadian Mounted Police issue the MP5K to their special operations and antiterrorist units, while in Germany it's a favorite among the GSG-9.

The MP5K-PDW

Upon its appearance in 1992, the MP5K-PDW became Heckler & Koch's successful entry in a competition to create a "Personal Defense Weapon" suitable for downed aviators and those who required portable but potent firepower. The U.S. military first became interested in H&K's submachine guns in 1983, when the U.S. Navy SEALS approached the company to inquire about the possibility of developing a submachine gun for special operations use. The U.S. Marine Corps was also in need of a submachine gun with an improved design for issue to its guards at sensitive installations. And the Coast Guard was looking for a submachine gun for use by its crews while boarding ships suspected of smuggling. The U.S. Navy's Naval Weapons Support Center signed a contract with Heckler & Koch in April of 1983 for an experimental submachine gun (later called the HK54A-1) that embodied certain features. These included an integral silencer, a 50-round drum magazine, and a fire selector allowing single-shot, three-shot and fully-automatic modes. As talks continued between U.S. armed forces and company representatives, it became clear that several existing Heckler & Koch products already offered much of what the Navy and Marine Corps wanted. It made more sense, obviously, to modify an existing design at modest cost than to build an expensive new weapons system from scratch. By 1993, three submachine guns—the MP5, MP5SD and MP5K **(p. 33-4, 136-40)**—all suitably modified with ambidextrous safety/fire selector groups, tritium-illuminated night sights and other slight refinements—entered into service with the U.S. Navy and Marine Corps.

The basic design of this weapon echoed that of the MP5K, to which the H&K engineers added (in addition to the refinements noted above) a "muzzle-can" type of sound suppressor. To accept this innovation, the barrel was lengthened by an inch and threaded. The suppressor, or silencer, featured a stainless steel outer body. The projected service life of the MP5K-PDW's suppressor is an impressive 30,000 rounds, a far cry from those World War II models that required considerable maintenance and, in some cases, total parts replacement after only a few dozen rounds were fired. The suppressor, while slim and lightweight, does not adversely affect the gun's handling; and as a bonus it greatly reduces the weapon's muzzle flash. When employing an automatic weapon at night—especially a short-barreled one like this—a good silencer is essential.

Another interesting refinement for the MP5K-PDW was its folding stock, which was developed for H&K by Choate Machine and Tool Corporation, known for its quality line of synthetic rifle stocks and related shooting accessories. In one type of harness created by this company, the stock deployed itself as the shooter pushed it away from his body. The stock locks open firmly and remains rigid under the relatively gentle 9mm recoil. To fold and unlock the stock, the shooter merely depresses a small button. Adding this folding stock to the PDW model was a brilliant move. It adds nothing to the length of the weapon and very little to its weight or bulk, while at the same time improving the weapon's accuracy and ease of handling.

Heckler & Koch's company literature of that period shows a man dressed in a flight suit drawing a bead with an MP5K-PDW. This heavy weapon is shown being carried in a leg holster with a 15-round magazine in the gun and a four-magazine pouch beneath it, each spare magazine holding 30 rounds. I seriously doubt many flyers would agree to being burdened with that much defensive gear. Aviators already have more than enough equipment to wear and carry around without having to deal with all those extra encumbrances. Something along the lines of a Glock Model 26 compact pistol makes much more sense in this instance; or, if selective-fire capability is an absolute necessity, the slightly larger Glock Model 18 should work. It's difficult to imagine the MP5K-PDW as a serious choice for military personnel whose primary mission is to fly aircraft—unless it's carried in a survival pack and is not actually worn when not in a combat situation. Despite these reservations, the MP5K-PDW fits a number of applications in which a relatively small but highly potent package, blessed with good concealment potential and the ability to take a sound suppressor, might come in handy.

The MP in Action

On October 17, 1977, the British SAS (Special Air Service) and the West German GSG-9 combined forces to attack a group of four terrorists who had hijacked a Lufthansa jet. The terrorists—two men and two women—were playing for high stakes: the release of the infamous Baader-Meinhof gang. The terrorists had displayed their own brutality by killing the Lufthansa pilot after he had flown the plane full of passengers to Mogadishu, the capital of Somali.

With the prospects for some 80 passengers taking a turn for the worse, an elite counter-terrorism task force went into action. Germans and Britishers together entered the plane from both wings, throwing "flash-bang" grenades ahead of them in an attempt to disorient the terrorists. A firefight ensured, in which three terrorists died on the spot and the fourth, a woman, was captured after being shot nine times. The last terrorist to die was the group's leader, who threw two grenades of his own in an attempt to destroy the airplane and kill as many hostages as possible. The reign of terror ended when the terrorist was struck by a burst of 9mm Parabellum bullets from a Heckler & Koch MP5.

Later, in May of 1980, seven terrorists took over the Iranian Embassy in London, taking a number of hostages. After the terrorists had executed one of the prisoners, the SAS was called upon to rescue the remaining hostages. The SAS had recently switched from its previous submachine gun, the American-made Ingram, to the Heckler & Koch MP5, due largely to the good results obtained with that weapon during the hostage rescue two years earlier in Mogadishu. The SAS liked the MP5's excellent accuracy potential in semiautomatic mode, which they felt made it superior to the Ingram. Attacking from two directions at once, SAS troops broke into the embassy and freed it, killing six of the terrorists

To demonstrate how the **MP5K-PDW** (top) is small enough for personal defense, survival and clandestine uses, H&K distributes this publicity photograph comparing the submachine gun to the Beretta Model 92F (U.S. M9) pistol (bottom).

The HK53 (left) is Heckler & Koch's smallest weapon made to fire the 5.56mm/.223 caliber cartridge. Only slightly larger than the MP5 (right), it uses the 5.56mm/.223 rifle cartridge for greater accuracy, range, penetration and stopping power as opposed to the MP5 chambered for the 9mm Parabellum cartridge. Heckler & Koch has also adapted the HK53 as a Firing Port Weapon.

and capturing the seventh, losing only one hostage killed and another wounded.

In 1985, following several terrorist incidents and close calls at London's busy Heathrow Airport, the Heckler & Koch MP5 became the standard weapon of issue to antiterrorist police units. Despite the high profile status and furor that followed, the British police recognized the MP5 as superior to the 9mm automatic pistol, their second choice. Compared to a 9mm pistol, such as Britain's then-standard Browning High Power, the MP5 was inherently easier to shoot accurately, especially in the semiautomatic mode the British police were trained to use most of the time. There were also the MP5's fixed buttstock, its superior stabilizing weight, and its longer sight radius. The MP5 could also be fitted with auxiliary sighting devices to improve the gun's accuracy still more. In dire emergencies, it could even be fired fully automatically.

In the U.S., the MP5 has enjoyed widespread approval for police work. Following the long reign of the Thompson, the Heckler & Koch now became the most popular submachine gun in use for police duty. The MP5SD variant has proven itself highly useful as well among SWAT units for shooting out lights, puncturing car tires and killing watchdogs with minimal noise prior to launching raids on well-fortified houses of wealthy—and frequently well-armed—drug dealers. In 1992, the U.S. Drug En-forcement Agency (DEA) decided to test the MP5 against other designs. The MP5 passed these incredibly grueling examinations, which included saltwater corrosion tests, drop tests, accuracy tests and, finally, endurance tests. In four days of testing, each of four trial MP5s fired 10,000 rounds in 500-round increments. In 40,000 rounds fired, only two malfunctions occurred. Although the DEA selected Colt's 9mm submachine gun instead, theirs was a political decision, not a technical one. Colt's submachine gun was similar in its operational controls and handling to the M16, which was already familiar to many ex-military DEA agents who undoubtedly played a role in the selection process. In Germany, the same selection process favored the MP5 because of its similarity to the G3 and G41. In any event, the MP5 un-questionably demonstrates better operational reliability than Colt's 9mm weapon and most competing weapons. Given its excellent performance, good accuracy potential, ruggedness, reliability and versatility, it comes as no surprise that the MP5 submachine gun has set the standard around the world.

HK53

When it was introduced in 1975, the Heckler & Koch Model 53 "submachine gun" was in reality a radically shortened assault rifle, what with its overall length of only 8.3 inches. The collapsible stock developed for the G3 series realized its ultimate application here, creating a miniaturized assault rifle chambered for the .223 caliber rifle round, and less than 24 inches in length. With its stock extended, the HK53 was only three inches longer than a fixed-stock MP5 (29.7 inches with the stock extended vs 26.8 for the MP5). By chambering the .223/5.56mm rifle cartridge instead of the 9mm Parabellum pistol cartridge, the HK53 represented a significant step up in power, even considering the gun's relatively short barrel. What makes such a short-barreled .223 caliber weapon possible is that the H&K operating system is recoil operated. Barrel length is therefore not a major concern as it would be with the kind of gas-operated design more commonly encountered in military automatic weapons. Making a gas-operated weapon function reliably with such a short barrel would seem next to impossible, but the Heckler & Koch system accomplishes it without any difficulties whatsoever.

Chapter Four

One might assume that muzzle blast and flash from such a short-barreled weapon in .223 caliber would be excessive, but the Heckler & Koch engineers have developed a remarkably efficient four-prong "flash hider" for the HK53. Similar in concept to the type used on early AR-15/M16 rifles, the HK53 flash hider tames muzzle flash quite effectively. Obviously, muzzle velocity, range and accuracy are degraded compared to full-sized rifles using the .223 round. But comparing the HK53 to an M16 or even H&K's own Model 33 or 41 rifle models misses the point. In competition with submachine guns firing pistol calibers, the HK53 surpasses all other models in combat capability, simply because the .223 rifle cartridge possesses far more power than the pistol cartridges used in almost all competing submachine guns.

Much like several other Heckler & Koch long arms, the HK53 appears in both a fixed stock A2 and folding stock A3 variant. Many other countries like the concept of a portable and concealable weapon that fires standard rifle ammunition. Those countries whose military and police forces issue the HK53 include Germany, Great Britain's SAS, and the armies of Ireland, Mexico, Senegal and the United Arab Emirates.

The MICV Firing Port Weapon

Bitter experience in World War II revealed the need for a firing port weapon that would protect the occupants of military fighting vehicles from attack by enemy infantry carrying explosive charges. While conventional handguns and submachine guns were used sparingly during the war to protect armored vehicles, especially tanks, in close-range encounters, such employment was far from ideal. Firing conventional weapons in the enclosed space of a crew's compartment generated clouds of annoying smoke that hampered visibility and even produced poisonous carbon monoxide. With the postwar adoption of the armored personnel carrier and its widespread use by the United States, the Soviet Union and many others, various countries sought a solution to this problem: How can an armored vehicle crew best defend itself? While some of these vehicles had ports or firing slits that enable military passengers to fire their rifles from inside the vehicle, the trend in Western armies has been to create specialized weapons for the firing-port role.

In 1972, the U.S. Army began searching for a Firing Port Weapon (FPW) to be used for the XM723 Mechanized Infantry Combat Vehicle, or MICV. A major requirement was that any system adopted must exhaust all gas residues that resulted from firing to the outside. A high cyclic rate of fire was another requirement. Also, all weapons under consideration must have a barrel sleeve that could fit into a ball-and-socket joint mounted on the side of the MICV.

Heckler & Koch, among others, decided to compete for the U.S. Army's FPW contract. The Army was already in favor of the .223 caliber (5.56x45mm) cartridge over the 9mm Parabellum (the adoption by U.S. armed forces of its first 9mm pistol, the M9 Beretta, still lay 13 years in the future). While Heckler & Koch might have preferred that the U.S. select a variant of its own MP5, its 9mm chambering precluded that choice. Instead, the company chose a prototype (still in the developmental stage) of its HK53 5.56mm submachine gun (see above) as the basis for the extensive conversions required.

Barrel modifications involved removing the front sight and attaching the barrel sleeve, which was needed to lock into the ball and socket joint. A canvas bag was fitted over the ejection port to catch cartridge casings as the operator fired his weapon, thereby keeping cartridge casings from rolling all over the floor of the vehicle. At the rear end of the weapon, a simple end cap replaced the buttstock. The pistol grip was retained, as was the fire control safety/fire selector group.

The most significant design change required by the U.S. Army was for Heckler & Koch to modify its weapon so that it fired from an open bolt. To do this, the bolt had to remain open each time the trigger was released, allowing the barrel to cool down from both the muzzle and breech ends between bursts. The idea behind firing from an open bolt was simple: the faster the barrel cooled down between strings of fire, the less likely a cartridge would ignite spontaneously ("cook off"), a dangerous condition akin to an accidental discharge. The chief disadvantage of open-bolt fire is that it tends to throw off the shooter's aim as the heavy bolt slams forward, shifting the weapon's balance and center of gravity a split second before firing. The Army was willing to overlook the accuracy problem, reasoning that the range of engagements with this type of weapon would be close. Besides, the weapon would be so well-supported in its mount that the instability problem would be reduced.

In the end, the U.S. Army turned down Heckler & Koch's entry in favor of a modified M16A1 variant called the XM231 (now the M231). The company continued to develop the FPW idea, however, in the hope of attracting business from other customers. H&K soon developed its own combination firing port/vision block for installation in armored personnel carriers. In this system, the weapon's integral sights are used to direct fire, much like the Soviet's APC designs. With Colt's M231, the shooter aims indirectly by looking through a periscope (above the firing

The .45 ACP caliber UMP45 is Heckler & Koch's latest foray into submachine gun technology. As shown, it differs significantly from the MP5 series (photo courtesy of Heckler & Koch).

Chapter Four 147

port), directing fire by watching where the tracer rounds impacted.

In addition to the modified HK53, Heckler & Koch demonstrated its firing-port technology with the German MP2 (uzi) and the MP5. It appears unlikely that any submachine guns firing pistol ammunition will see active service, at least not in this role. Rifle cartridges are still much preferred, primarily because of their greater striking power.

The MP5PT Series

When they first appeared, submachine guns were deemed controversial mostly because gangsters adopted them. They remain controversial weapons to this day. Indeed, the submachine gun, despite its solid record in military service and widespread police use, has been challenged by many analysts who question the need for them. These authorities cite the creation of shortened assault rifle-type weapons firing rifle cartridges, arguing that no technical need for this weapon even exists in the 21st century. The best response to this assertion is the fact that, even though they've repeatedly come into and out of favor, designers continue to create new submachine gun designs. The armed forces of the world, which had rejected or ignored the submachine gun for years, appear to be finding uses for them once more. For instance, from the late 1960s to the early 1980s, the United States armed forces virtually ignored the submachine gun. Beyond storing a handful of aging M1 Thompsons aboard ships and equally archaic M3A1 "Grease Guns" aboard tanks, the U.S. military showed no interest in submachine guns whatever. Then the wheels turned, and ever since the mid-1980s our armed forces have kept Heckler & Koch busy with orders for the new guns.

Whatever else one might argue about, all who work with them agree that it takes a lot of work to master these weapons. Learning how to control the trigger to place shots with a modicum of accuracy, rather than spraying bullets everywhere, is an ongoing challenge. The need for training personnel on how to use the submachine gun has prompted Heckler & Koch to create a pair of MP5 training guns. The company announced these in 1989 as the fixed-stock MP5A4PT and the MP5A5PT with a collapsible stock. These training versions of the MP5 look and handle exactly like any other MP5, but they only fire special plastic bullets, designated the 9x19PT, which cannot be interchanged with 9mm Parabellum ammunition. To prevent the gun from chambering live ammunition, the PT-series submachine guns use a special chamber insert held in place by a metal clip. The mechanism is removable for cleaning, but it must then be replaced before the gun will function. Aside from firing inert ammunition, the PT-series submachine guns function much like a "live" MP5, including the four-position selector switch on the trigger group.

Heckler & Koch's intent in creating the PT cartridge and guns to match was to make training as realistic as possible, while at the same time reducing costs and risks to trainees and bystanders. We must recognize, however, that the PT rounds can injure or even kill when handled carelessly. For that reason, trainees who use these guns must exercise extreme caution, especially at close ranges.

The UMP45

Starting in the late 1980s, Heckler & Koch gave serious consideration to replacing the aging MP5 series. Initial design efforts centered around a weapon called the SMGI, followed by a new prototype (called the SMGII). A third potential replacement submachine gun, the MP2000, also went nowhere. The problem was, none of these three candidates offered much, if any, advantage over the thoroughly tested and widely accepted MP5 series. This is not an

A covey of Heckler & Koch submachine guns (from left to right) MP5K; MP5A3; MP5SD3 and MP5SD5.

indictment of Heckler & Koch's diligent design staff; rather, it's recognition of the MP5's technical excellence.

Finally, in 1999, Heckler & Koch was on the verge of a breakthrough with a new submachine gun design, the UMP45. The UMP45 offers at least three important advantages over the MP5: it chambers the .45 ACP cartridge; it uses a lower rate of fire; and it costs less to manufacture. And, because it's chambered in a round the MP5 cannot use, the UMP45 is not so much a competitor with the MP5 as it is a weapon designed to round out Heckler & Koch's already impressive submachine gun line.

The company's decision to chamber the UMP45 for the .45 ACP cartridge makes its marketing plan quite clear: the weapon is meant, first and foremost, to attract potentially lucrative sales in the U.S. military and police market. Despite competition from the 9mm Parabellum, .38 Special and .40 S&W cartridges, the .45 ACP remains an extremely popular handgun cartridge in the U.S., even though the rest of the world has long since switched to the 9mm Parabellum.

The .45 ACP is also an excellent choice for an "SD" (silenced) submachine gun variant. This round is almost always subsonic to begin, and yet it packs as much energy as a 9mm Parabellum simply by virtue of its weight (about twice as much). Compared to a 9mm submachine gun, the .45 caliber sound-suppressed version would be both easier to build in a silenced variant and, once built, more powerful as well.

Since Heckler & Koch already has a successful submachine gun series based on its popular MP5, one wonders why the company has elected to add the UMP45 to its product line. Apparently, Heckler & Koch senses a comeback for the submachine gun, and perhaps rightly so. This decision also demonstrates the company's strong desire to stay ahead in what has become one of its strongest product areas. Historically, the UMP45 represents the first time since the Ingram Model 10 was created in 1970 that a major manufacturer has offered a submachine gun in .45 ACP. In years gone by, several .45 caliber submachine guns have followed the path blazed by the famous Thompson of 1921, including the U.S. M3. During World War II, submachine guns played an important role among the best-equipped armed forces. In the Soviet Union, for example, some divisions carried submachine guns almost exclusively.

However, as the world's armed forces continued to de-emphasize the submachine gun from the 1950s on, and 9mm pistols had replaced the Model 1911 pistol in military service, it seemed the few submachine guns still being produced in 9mm Parabellum caliber would suffice to handle whatever demand there was. With the increasing numbers of women in police service, the semiautomatic carbine and its cousin, the submachine gun, offered improved recoil control compared to the shotgun (the traditional heavy armament among police forces). Submachine guns also offer certain advantages to military forces—at least in limited use scenarios—over shotguns or assault rifles. While the MP5 continues to enjoy success among certain police and military organizations, Heckler & Koch foresees enough interest in a new .45 caliber submachine gun to justify the expense of tooling up for the new model.

Although the UMP45 has the same general appearance and operating controls of the MP5, it also demonstrates considerable updating. For one thing, the UMP45 now features mostly polymer construction, including the receiver, trigger housing unit and even the magazine. Steel is reserved for the bolt, the barrel, the recoil spring and its guide rod, a few pins and other small parts. This extensive use of plastic helps Heckler & Koch to make the UMP45 appreciably lighter than other submachine guns.

Unlike the roller-locked MP5, but similar to classic submachine gun designs, the UMP45 utilizes blowback operation by means of a bolt heavily weighted with a tungsten carbine insert. Manufacturing expenses are thus reduced even further. Thanks to the heavy bolt, the UMP45's rate of fire (less than 600 rounds per minute) is much slower than an MP5's, making the UMP45 easier to control in burst fire despite its use of a heavier cartridge in a lighter gun. A high rate of fire in a hand-held automatic weapon is nothing but a waste of ammunition, not to mention an expensive noisemaker. Keeping the rate of fire low and controllable is the key to getting bullets to their intended targets, which, after all, is the essence of firepower.

A folding, skeletonized plastic stock and front handgrip are a big help in handling the UMP45. Its combination of mostly plastic construction and blowback operation also holds down the cost significantly. At slightly less than a thousand dollars, this weapon becomes affordable for most police departments, in sharp contrast to Heckler & Koch's far more costly roller-locked weapons.

The sights on the UMP45 consist of a front post with protective hood and a two-position, L-type rear sight, similar to that used in the FAL-Para rifle, rather than the famous H&K "diopter" rotary rear sight unit. In addition to its integral sights, the UMP45 includes a rail atop the receiver for easy mounting of optical sights and red dot projectors (such as the Swedish-made Aimpoint system).

The UMP45 represents a major effort by Heckler & Koch to retain its commanding lead in submachine gun sales worldwide, while at the same time updating the state of the art in submachine gun design. With its .45 ACP cartridge, this model seems a natural for the U.S. police market. Its blowback operating system and mostly plastic construction also bring the price down to not much more than what some armsmakers charge for their automatic pistols.

Conclusion

Heckler & Koch has been a leader in submachine gun technology since early in the company's history. But even after creating the MP5, which became one of the most successful submachine gun designs ever made, the company has chosen not to rest on its past accomplishments. H&K's willingness to invest tremendous time and energy in this product makes it likely that the company will continue its role as a world leader in the development, manufacture and sale of submachine guns well into the future. • **H&K**

SPECIFICATIONS: H&K SUBMACHINE GUNS

	Overall Length (in.)	Barrel Length (in.)	Weight (lbs.)	Cyclic Rate (rounds/minute)	Caliber/ Capacity*
MP5	26.8	8.9	5.6	800	9mm/*
MP5SD1	21.7	5.7	6.2	800	9mm/*
MP5K	12.8	4.5	4.4	900	9mm/*
HK53	29.7	8.3	6.0	700	5.6mm/25
UMP45	27.2	7.9	4.6	580	.45ACP/25

*Notes: Heckler & Koch submachine guns chambered for 9mm accept both 15-shot and 30-shot magazines.

With this formidable weapon well in hand, Heckler & Koch seemingly had little reason for inventive activity in the machine gun realm, but such proved not to be the case. Using the basic roller-locking mechanism already developed and perfected in the StG45/CETME/G3 series, the company went on to develop a whole series of heavy automatic rifles and machine guns......

Chapter 5

Farther And Faster: The H&K Machine Gun

Germany's military use of machine guns in the two World Wars was extremely innovative, both from the technological and tactical points of view. World War I had witnessed German troops fighting the French and British to a virtual standstill for three years and bringing the Russians down to defeat and surrender. These victories on the battlefield were due to

> **The HK21A1—the second version of the HK21 series—eliminated the magazine-feed capability of the early HK21, adding a caliber conversion capability from 7.62x51mm NATO to 5.56mm/.223 or Soviet 7.62x39mm. For testing by the U.S. Army, this machine gun (chambered for 5.56mm/.223) was overweight, forcing Heckler & Koch to create a smaller version specifically for the .223 cartridge. This became known as the HK23A1 (photo courtesy of Heckler & Koch).**

> **This variant—the HK21A1—kept the belt feed, but the ammunition belt was placed into a box for convenience when advancing. Most of its components derive from the G3, but the bipod on the HK21A1 is heavier and adjustable for height. The stock includes a projection for the gunner's support hand and the enlarged drum-style rear sight is adjustable to 1200 meters (photo courtesy of Heckler & Koch).**

Germany's skillful use of the Maxim machine gun. Virtually an entire generation of young French men had been wiped out, with German machine guns claiming the most victims.

In World War II, the Germans created the world's first practical general-purpose machine guns, or GPMGs. The first of these, the MG34, was a versatile and efficient weapon, combining rifle-like accuracy with a blistering rate of fire (900 rounds per minute). However, the MG34 was complex and, because of the many parts requiring precision machining, slow and expensive to produce. In response, German engineers developed the even better MG42. This remarkable weapon improved on the MG34 in both rate of fire—which rose to a daunting 1200 rounds per minute—and ease of production. Numerous stamped parts replaced many of the MG34's machined parts, further simplifying its manufacture.

Following World War II, the victorious Allies restrained Germany from arms production for about a decade. Once West Germany received permission from the Allies to renew its armaments industry and re-equip its army units, the German armed forces expressed a strong preference for the remarkable MG42. The result was the MG3, which differed only slightly from the wartime MG42. The two most salient changes made were the substitution of the

7.62x51mm (.308) NATO-standard rifle cartridge for the wartime 7.92x57mm (8mm Mauser), plus a choice of two bolt buffer mechanisms. The lighter one offered a rate of fire of about 1200-1300 rounds per minute (RPM), while the heavier buffer limited the rate of fire to a more sedate 800 rpm. The latter was considered a better choice for infantry fire support, even though it was still fast by American standards, where a cyclic rate of 500-600 rounds was preferred.

> **The HK21E, introduced in 1990, incorporates the post-1986 four-position safety/fire selector: a white bullet for safe, a red bullet for semiautomatic, three red bullets for a three-shot burst, and seven red bullets for fully-automatic rates of fire. The HK21E's barrel (22") is longer than the 17.7" units found on the G3, HK21 and HK21A1. The optional front handgrip (shown) may be placed in any of the cooling slots cut into the barrel jacket to suit each gunner's carrying style and arm length (photo courtesy of Heckler & Koch).**

With this formidable weapon well in hand, Heckler & Koch seemingly had little reason for inventive activity in the machine gun realm, but such proved not to be the case. Using the basic roller-locking mechanism already developed and perfected in the StG45/CETME/G3 series, the company went on to develop a whole series of heavy automatic rifles and machine guns.

Heckler & Koch's first efforts in the machine gun arena centered, not surprisingly, on developing weapons chambered for the NATO-standard 7.62x51mm cartridge. The company's goal was to create a weapon that used as many parts of the popular G3 mechanism as possible, but which improved on that weapon's limited automatic-fire capability. Later on, as the 5.56mm/.223 cartridge became popular, additional machine guns were developed to fire that round as well.

Chapter Five 155

Part 1: The 7.62mm (.308) Guns

The HK21 Series

The first Heckler & Koch machine gun design—and perhaps its most famous—was the HK21. This model, which first appeared in 1961, was a belt-fed modification of the G3 rifle, sharing about half of the G3's parts. Heckler & Koch did make numerous detail changes, however, to make the weapon more suitable for machine gun use. For example, the HK21 had an improved rear sight, consisting of a drum that was adjustable to greater ranges (up to 1200 meters) than the G3's rear sight. This improvement, plus a tripod mount, allowed HK21 gunners to use the weapon for indirect fire techniques largely unavailable to rifles.

The HK21 barrel is also more heavily constructed than the G3's, and it features a quick-detach system, enabling shooters to exchange spare barrels during sustained-fire missions. Most of the right side of the handguard is cut away, exposing that side of the barrel. In addition, a short handle is attached to the barrel for easy removal (it's too hot to handle directly). Given a large supply of ammunition, several spare barrels and a container of water in which to immerse and cool used barrels, an HK21 can go on firing for quite some time. Early H&K21s featured an optional conversion kit for switching from belt to magazine feed, thus enabling the HK21 to accept the same ammunition magazines as the G3 rifle. Heckler & Koch discontinued the magazine adaptor in the next HK21 variant—the HK21A1—though it has since been reinstated on the HK21E (the third and current version).

The HK21 bipod, which is much sturdier than the rather spindly one sometime fitted to the G3, can be moved to different positions on the handguard. The optional tripod, when not deployed, can be folded into a kind of pack frame, permitting gunners to carry the folded tripod and machine gun together as a single portable load. The tripod can be set up in several configurations to allow for various fire missions.

The HK21 buttstock reveals a large projection on the underside where shooters may rest their support hand while keeping the weapon shouldered during long strings of fire. The rounded handguard on the HK21 is larger in diameter than the G3's and includes numerous rectangular ventilation slots cut throughout its length for transferring cool air to hot barrels.

Heckler & Koch quit making the original HK21 around 1990. Meanwhile, H&K has created two HK21 variants, the first (in 1979) following the basic HK21 design as the HK21A1. It featured a hinged feed tray rather than the removable type used on most HK21s. This change eliminated the option of fitting a magazine adaptor to the gun, making it belt-fed only. An early customer for the HK21A1 was Sweden, for whom the HK32A represented that country's first machine gun chambered for the 7.62mm cartridge. The Swedes had earlier used the 6.5mm Mauser cartridge, later re-barreling their machine guns to 7.62mm as needed (see also Chapter 7).

A conversion unit made it possible to switch from the standard 7.62-51mm/.308 NATO-standard cartridge to an 5.56x45mm/.223 or a 7.62x39mm M43 Soviet cartridge simply by disassembling the gun and substituting a barrel, a feed group and a bolt in the desired caliber. Incredibly, no prospective customers at the time seem to have appreciated the tremendous versatility of this system. Even though the U.S. armed forces briefly tested a slightly modified weapon of this type in the mid-1970s, they tested it only in .223 caliber and showed no interest whatever in H&K's ability to interchange calibers.

> In its **HK21E** model, Heckler & Koch reinstated the magazine conversion unit. The choice of ammunition feed adds versatility. Note how the bipod legs fold up against the underside of the barrel when not in use (photo courtesy of Heckler & Koch).

The definitive HK21 variant currently in production is the HK21E (E=Export). Issued mostly with a 22-inch barrel (compared to 17.7 inches for the standard G3 rifle and early HK21s), this version offers added velocity and range. An improved and ambidextrous four-position fire selector (adding the three-shot burst feature) is located on either side of the trigger group. For the HK21E, Heckler & Koch returned to the magazine conversion kit for those who choose to feed the ammunition supply from a G3 rifle magazine instead of a belt. For units on the march, the capability of conversion to box magazine feed makes good sense. Once a unit has reached an area where a permanent stay is called for, shooters can switch back to the belt feed for improved sustained-fire capability. Heckler & Koch has also modified the HK21's feed group to reduce stress on the mechanism and make it more durable, a major complaint directed at earlier variants. In this improved system, the feed advances halfway while the bolt moves rearward, then finishes the motion as the bolt moves forward. The result is a less abrupt reloading cycle. To improve handling while holding the weapon in the "assault" position, the HK21E adds a vertical forward handgrip.

The West German armed forces have made little use of the HK21, though some state police forces have employed variations of its type for certain operations. Heckler & Koch has had

Chapter Five 157

Ready for action, an HK21E reveals on its right side how the barrel jacket is cut away to facilitate rapid barrel changes. It also displays the ambidextrous (post-1986) four-position selector (photo courtesy of Heckler & Koch).

considerable success, however, in selling HK21 variants to foreign countries. These have included Bangladesh, Bolivia, Brunei, Cameroons, Colombia, Greece, Jordan, Kenya, Malaysia, Mexico, Niger, Nigeria, Qatar, Senegal, Sri Lanka, Sweden and Uganda. Most of these countries, being relatively poor, undoubtedly find the versatility of the HK21 a major selling point.

The HK11 Series

While considered a machine gun in H&K's nomenclature, one might better describe the HK11 **(photo p. 166)** as an automatic rifle, similar to the Browning BAR. Heckler & Koch created the HK11 simply by removing the HK21's belt-feed capability altogether. Like the BAR, the HK11 uses a box magazine to stress portability over sustained-fire capability. While the standard 20-round G3 magazines can be used, an extended 30-shot magazine is the usual feed device, with an optional 80-round drum magazine also available.

Heckler & Koch was pleased with the basic concept of the HK11 but saw room for improvement. The company's design staff took the HK11 concept and refined it into the G8, the basic principle being to offer users a highly accurate, multi-purpose weapon suitable for use in the semiautomatic mode as a precision rifle with a four-power telescopic sight (a rotary drum-style rear sight typical of Heckler & Koch machine guns is also fitted).

Compared to the standard G3 military rifle, the G8's barrel is heavier, offering a higher level of accuracy. An adjustable bipod, which is much sturdier than the light (and non-adjustable) unit offered as an option on the G3, helps increase accuracy. When engaged in its automatic rifle or light machine gun role, where firing in bursts is called for, the G8's heavier barrel becomes a useful heat sink. The G8 also incorporates a quick-change barrel mechanism offering convenient exchange of cool barrels for overheated ones. For added versatility, Heckler & Koch includes a three-shot burst selector on the G8's safety/fire-selector mechanism as well as the standard single-shot (semiautomatic) and full-auto switch settings.

Stock furniture indicates intelligent planning as well. The buttstock features an extension for the operator's support hand, a useful feature in preventing the stock from rising off the operator's shoulder. A front handgrip allows operators to handle the weapon with confidence in a full-auto "walking fire" scenario where units are advancing and firing at the same time. These features do not interfere, however, with operating the G8 semiautomatically as a rifle.

The ammunition system reflects various uses for the G8. Standard ammunition feed is the well-proven 20-round box magazine inherited from the G3. But for improved sustained-fire capabilities Heckler & Koch also offers a 50-shot drum magazine, along with a conversion kit that allows belt feed.

Just as the G8 represents an upgraded HK11, so the G8A1 is modified from the HK11E. The major change is the addition of the four-position safety/fire selector trigger group. Normal ammunition feed is the standard 20-round G3 magazine, with an option for the 80-round drum in situations requiring greater firepower. The belt feed is rarely used on this variant, though it can be adapted as requested.

With its unusually versatile design, the G8 has been well received by police and security forces in Europe and especially in its native Germany. The West German *Bundeswehr* have used the G8 and G8A1 weapons both as sniper rifles and as light machine guns, due largely to their exceptional adaptability to different roles, an asset that appeals to the German military mind. Other heavy users of HK11-series automatic rifles/light machine guns have included Bangladesh, Greece, Malaysia, Morocco, Niger, Sri Lanka and Sudan.

Part II: The 5.56mm (.223) Guns

The HK13 Series

As we've seen, Heckler & Koch was one of the first European arms manufacturers to appreciate the potential of the 5.56x45mm (.223 Remington) cartridge (developed in the U.S.). Even though many other companies have since jumped on the bandwagon, machine guns firing the .223 round have remained controversial. Those who have supported the marriage of the .223 cartridge with a light machine gun have approved of its reduced logistical requirements, with one type of ammunition servicing both rifles and machine guns. They also approve of the relatively small, light machine guns made possible by chambering the .223 cartridge. The low recoil of the cartridge also improves accuracy, say its supporters.

However, critics of the .223/machine gun combination cite its reduced lethality compared to .30-caliber weapons, particularly at the extended ranges (500 meters or more) where machine guns have traditionally picked up where rifles left off. Even at closer ranges, the .223 cartridge lacks the penetrative power of the 7.62mm/.308 round, particularly against vehicles and troops under light cover.

Notwithstanding its critics, Heckler & Koch has made several forays into machine gun development in the .223 chambering. The company's first .223 caliber light machine gun, the HK13, appeared in 1972. Featured were a box magazine feed, a 25-round magazine, and much of the internal mechanism identical to that used in the company's HK33 rifle. For more sustained fire, Heckler & Koch added a 40-round magazine for the HK13, though this required a much greater length, causing the weapon to sit higher off the ground and compromising concealment. The barrel of the HK13 is heavier than the rifle's and has a quick-change feature—a welcome improvement over most .223 caliber machine guns, which are merely glorified assault rifles.

The HK13E, which is based on the HK13, appeared in 1978 and offered several improvements, including adaptability to either magazine-fed or belt-fed modes simply by exchanging the bolt and magazine housing. The HK13E also added a three-shot burst selector to the combined safety/fire control switch. Because the 40-round, high-capacity magazine sometimes issued with this model protruded so far below the receiver, Heckler & Koch developed a 100-round drum magazine for the HK13E (it's actually less bulky, though it holds more ammunition). A forward handgrip, which can be positioned as desired in any of the rounded handguard's cooling slots, completed the modifications. Subsequently, Heckler & Koch changed the rate of rifling twist in the HK13E barrel after NATO's switch to the SS109 cartridge was well underway.

Despite many good features, the HK13 series has enjoyed only limited success. The guns have had their greatest use in Southeast Asia.

The HK23 Series

Early in the HK21 production run, as noted above, Heckler & Koch offered buyers the capability of converting a standard 7.62mm/.308 caliber HK21 to 5.56mm/.223 caliber simply by substituting some parts. The result was a larger and heavier gun than was required for the diminutive .223 round. This caused Heckler & Koch to create a .223 caliber light machine gun, which appeared in 1973 as the HK23A1. It can be regarded either as a downsized HK21 made to fire the 5.56mm/.223 caliber cartridge, or as an HK13 modified to include a

Fans of the HK21-series machine guns like to show its high-performance capabilities. Here a shooter demonstrates the HK21A1's light weight and good balance (photo courtesy of Heckler & Koch).

A demonstrator prepares an extremely long ammunition belt to highlight the HK21A1's sustained-fire capabilities. Changing the barrel on an HK21-type machine gun is easier, safer and more convenient than all but the latest U.S. M60 (photo courtesy of Heckler & Koch).

belt-feeding ammunition mechanism, making it a true light machine gun.

Although it proved unsuccessful in two rounds of U.S. SAW testing, Heckler & Koch persevered with the HK23 concept. In 1979, H&K created the improved HK23E, which added a three-shot burst mode on the fire selector. It also added an improved belt-feed mechanism, along with a forward vertical "assault" handgrip (adjustable) and a drum rear sight to improve the weapon's effectiveness at ranges up to 800 meters.

Regrettably, the HK23 series never really caught on. While several countries have followed America's lead in testing the weapon, only the United Arab Emirates have bought enough of them to supply their armed forces. Once factor that helps explain this limited acceptance of the HK23 is its relatively low-powered .223 cartridge. Another factor is that three other well-made .223 caliber light machine guns compete with the HK23E. FN's Minimi (see below) has enjoyed great success, with sales to the United States, Australia, Belgium, Canada and Italy among others. The Ultimax from Chartered Industries of Singapore has attracted considerable interest in an area where Heckler & Koch products have traditionally done well. Finally, the Spanish-made Ameli appeals greatly to customers who favor the operating procedures and layout of the MG42, of which it is a miniaturized version. The Ameli also employs the roller-locked mechanism popularized in the G3; indeed, having been designed by CETME, it is a cousin of the HK23.

The SAW

When in the process of evaluating the U.S. Army's weapons in 1966, the Small Arms Weapons Study (SAWS) program came to an important realization: the relatively new M60 machine gun lacked some of the important attributes of a portable weapon for use by mobile infantry. Specifically, the study pointed to the M60's considerable weight—almost 23 pounds unloaded and rising to some 38 pounds with 200 rounds of NATO-standard 7.62x51 ammunition (a mere 20-second supply in continuous fire).

Our Vietnam experience suggested that the SAWS committee personnel were on the right track in their criticism of the M60. While it proved rugged and reliable enough, this model proved extremely difficult to carry in rough terrain. Keeping the "pig" in ammunition became as difficult as carrying the weapon itself into battle, its ammunition belts being fairly heavy (about 7 pounds per 100 rounds) and awkward to handle. And though the M60 can be carried and fired by one man, it needs a two-man crew to be truly effective in a situation requiring sustained fire. In all, it's too much weapon for an infantry squad to utilize effectively in battle over rough terrain.

That the M60 would ever be carried into battle at the platoon, or even squad level, had not been foreseen by U.S. Army planners. In the late 1950s, great optimism had been expressed in the U.S. over the new T44 (later M14) weapons procurement program. The plan then was to introduce the new M14 as a replacement for the M1 Garand, M2 Carbine and M1 Thompson and M3 submachine guns. The plan also called for a squad-automatic variant of the M14, called the M15, which was similar to the rifle but added a bipod, a heavier barrel and other minor improvements, to replace the BAR as the official squad-automatic weapon. Finally, the planned role for the M60 general-purpose machine gun was to replace the various air-cooled and water-cooled Browning M1917 and 1919 machine guns at the company fire-support level.

These plans went awry when the M15 failed, obviously. The Army unwisely dropped the tried and true BAR anyway, and instead pressed the M60 into the squad-automatic role which the BAR had filled so well for 40 years. A subsequent attempt to revamp the M14 into a suitable squad-automatic (as the M14A1) also failed. So when the Army went to Vietnam, it took heavy, belt-fed M60s into battle at the small-unit level. Difficulties with the M60 were made even more galling when the communists fielded two acceptable squad-automatic weapons: the RPD and the RPK.

The Vietnam experience caused the Army to intensify its search for a suitable squad-automatic weapon. Based on comments from the troops in Vietnam, Army planners issued specifications for a new light machine gun weighing no more than 22 pounds (including 200 rounds of ammunition). While not specifying ammunition type or even a particular caliber, the ammunition was to have an effective range of 800 meters.

The modest maximum weight requirements effectively cancelled out any weapon firing the 7.62x51mm NATO cartridge, once 200 rounds of ammunition were factored in. According to the weight specification, only about seven pounds would remain for the weapon itself. Making a machine gun for the 7.62x51mm round within a seven-pound weight limit was impossible. The only other logical choice, in terms of cartridges still available, was

The HK21's adaptability to telescopic sights and other accessories developed for the company's popular G3 service rifle is a major selling point for this machine gun (photo courtesy of Heckler & Koch).

the 5.56x 45mm (.223) round. Army planners initially rejected this choice as having limited range and insufficient power for the machine gun role; in time, this prejudice against the 5.56/.223 would change.

In July of 1970, the Army moved the whole project into high gear by approving an Advanced Development Objective. At this time, the nomenclature changed: the light machine gun, which was the goal, became the Squad Automatic Weapon, reflecting its mission more precisely.

The U.S. Army devoted a great deal of thought and effort to the SAW. The review of numerous weapons already in production, or which, with some modifications, met the requirement, eventually drew in Heckler & Koch. First, the issue of caliber had to be addressed. The 7.62mm/.308 cartridge could perform satisfactorily, but it weighed too much, while the existing version of the 5.56mm/.223 cartridge—the model M193—met the weight requirements with ease but lacked the desired performance. The Army wanted U.S. M1 helmet penetration at 800 meters with the same ball ammunition to be used in the future SAW. It also required a visible trace, in broad daylight, out to the same distance. Beyond about 500 meters, however, the existing U.S. .223 ammunition could not accomplish either task. Because of problems with the existing 7.62mm and

The HK21A1 (shown) does a remarkable job of pulling the unusually long, heavy ammunition belt into the gun. The HK21E, with its improved two-stage belt feed, performs even better (photo courtesy of Heckler & Koch).

Chapter Five 165

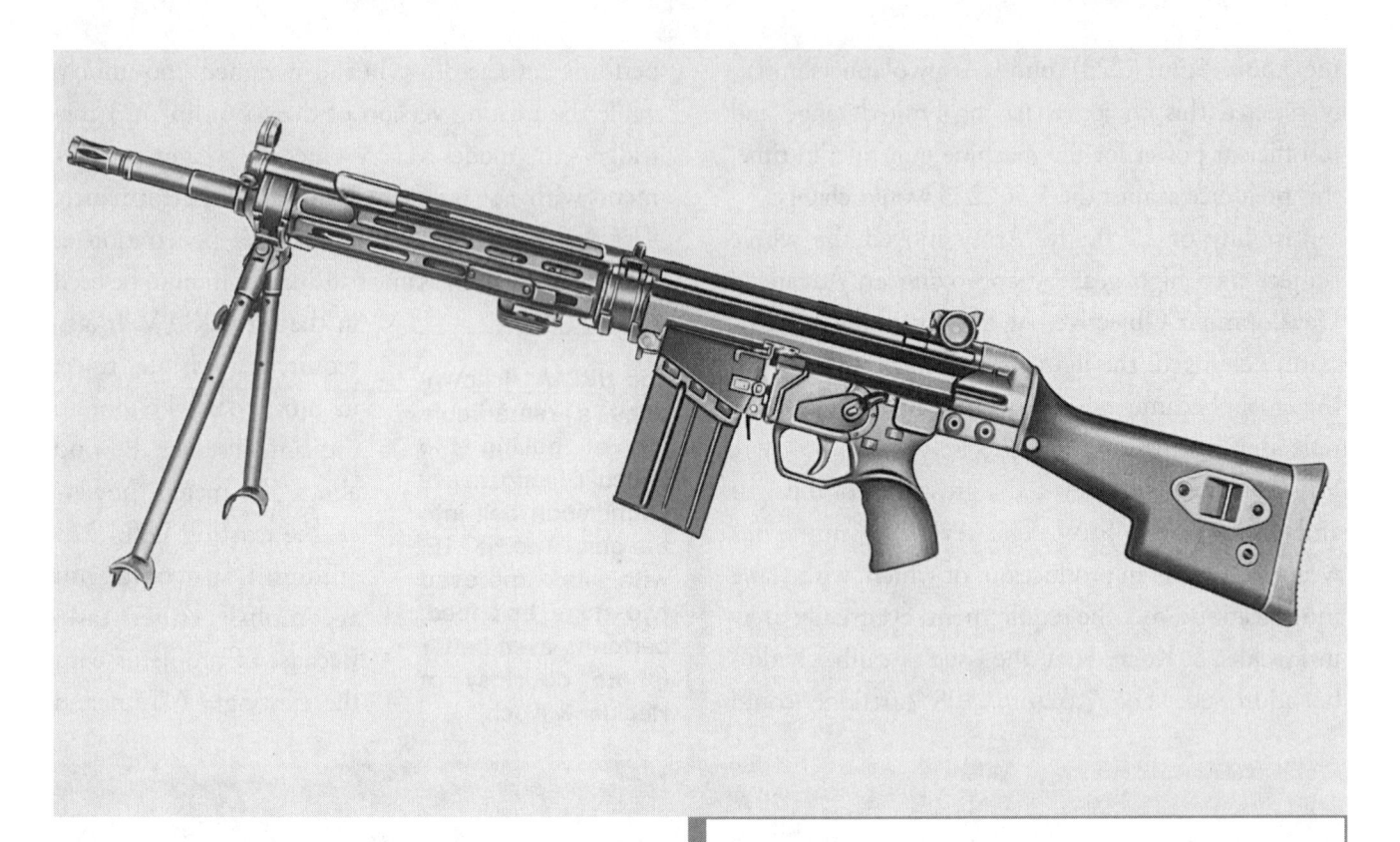

The HK11 (an HK21 modified for magazine feed only) employs a standard 20-round G3 box magazine, an extended capacity 30-shot box magazine (shown) or an 80-round drum magazine. Note that the 17.7" barrel is much heavier and thicker than the G3's barrel, thus serving as a better heat sink during sustained fire. The HK11 formed the basis for the versatile G8 and improved G8A1 (photo courtesy of Heckler & Koch).

5.56mm ammunition, the Army gave serious thought to developing and adopting a compromise cartridge for the SAW. It took the form of a 6.0x45mm cartridge firing a 105-grain bullet at a muzzle velocity of about 2,450 feet per second. This project never went too far, though. Soon the inevitable concerns about ammunition standardization and supply arose, and everyone agreed that adopting a third cartridge would greatly complicate the supply situation in any future war. In February, 1976, the U.S. Army's Training and Doctrine Command, known as TRADOC, recommended on behalf of the infantry that the future SAW use 5.56/.223 ammunition with an improved design to meet the desired performance. TRADOC repeated this recommendation in June of that year. The Department of the Army approved TRADOC's caliber stipulation and made it official in October 1976.

Along with several U.S. firms, plus FN of Belgium (the eventual winner), Heckler & Koch became involved in the U.S. Army's SAW testing early on. The company's HK21A1—an HK21 adapted to fire 5.56/.223 ammunition by substituting .223 barrel, bolt and belt-feed units for the standard 7.62mm units—weighed slightly less than 24.4 pounds with 200 rounds of .223 ammunition, or almost $2\frac{1}{2}$ pounds more than the maximum weight allowed. To meet the weight requirements, Heckler & Koch then created a scaled-down HK21, tailored specifically around the smaller dimensions of the 5.56/.223 caliber cartridge. The resulting machine gun, which Heckler & Koch called the

Features mandated by the Marine Corps on the M1014 include a telescoping stock and a Picatinny-type scope rail on the receiver forward of the rear sight to allow the shooter to attach accessory aiming devices. The M1014's receiver, barrel, pistol grip and magazine design reveal its Benelli ancestry (photo courtesy of Heckler & Koch)

HK23A1, barely came in under the weight limit. With high hopes, the company delivered prototypes to the U.S. Army in late 1973.

The Heckler & Koch HK23A1 prototype now joined other experimental SAW candidates from Maremont Corporation, Ford Aerospace and Communications Corporation, Rodman Laboratory, Colt and FN in a round of testing that concluded in December of 1974. Unfortunately, the testing methodology, like that which led to adoption of the Beretta M9 pistol a decade later (see Chapter 1), was seriously flawed. Experimentation was under way to upgrade the long-range performance (500-800 meters) of the 5.56mm/.223 cartridge with a batch of the newly-developed ammunition. Regrettably, the ammunition itself differed markedly in specifications from the then-standard M193 ball and M196 tracer rounds (for which Heckler & Koch had found a way to work with the HK23A1). For example, the brass used in the cartridge cases was thinner than that found in mil-spec M193 cartridges. When U.S. Army test personnel at Aberdeen Proving Grounds tested the HK23A1 with the new ammunition, results were poor. The HK21A1s in particular suffered numerous stoppages due to swollen cartridge cases and blown primers. Aberdeen personnel placed the blame on the gun's design, while Heckler & Koch understandably blamed the ammunition. H&K personnel were particularly upset that they had not been informed the ammunition was to be used in the HK23A1; also, that no attempt had been made to test their weapon using any other type of 5.56mm/.223 ammunition.

To cloud the situation further, Aberdeen personnel tried to detail-strip the Hk23A1 on their own. Ignoring warnings not to proceed any further, they completely dismantled the gun's trigger mechanism. Then, in the course of botching the reassembly, a meddler at Aberdeen applied excessive force to the hammer catch and release lever. Anxious to cover their own tracks and gloss over the failure to follow correct procedure, personnel there wrote in their report regarding the following incident: "Although this problem is primarily one of personnel error, it is caused by faulty weapon design, which permits this condition to occur."

Heckler & Koch's test representatives, who had spent decades proving the ruggedness of the company's machine guns in grueling test after test, resented the condemnations of the HK23A1. They pointed out that, had the test personnel followed the proper procedures concerning the HK23A1 instead of behaving like amateur gunsmiths, the weapon would have performed satisfactorily. Nevertheless, the damage was done. Aberdeen declared the gun unsafe and flawed in design, and that was the end of the HK23A1 in America's SAW program. At this point, Heckler & Koch discontinued the HK23A1 as a separate design. In 1978, the company made another attempt, converting the HK21A1 to 5.56/.223 for another round of SAW testing, but the U.S. Army chose the FN-designed Minimi instead.

Though it lost the SAW contract, Heckler & Koch did receive some small measure of justification. In April of 1980, the elite Delta Force carried several HK21A1s in its unsuccessful attempt to rescue 52 American hostages held in the Iranian embassy in Tehran. At the time, the U.S. lacked a suitable squad-automatic weapon to provide heavy mobile firepower. Colonel Beckwith, Commander of Delta Force, later complimented the HK21, calling it a "Rolls Royce," and describing the gun as "light, flexible and accurate for the tasks we had to perform." His opinion carries more weight among most experts than that of the testers who damaged a perfectly good gun through disobedience and incompetence, then tried to cover their clumsiness by shifting the blame onto Heckler & Koch.

To reassure potential customers regarding the HK21A1's feed system, a demonstrator (shown) raises the weapon over his head to prove the weapon has plenty of operating power.

A Brief Assortment of Other Machine Gun Models

Heckler & Koch has introduced several other machine guns that, for various reasons, have not enjoyed commercial success. The HK22A1 is a belt-fed machine gun designed to fire the 7.62x39mm Soviet cartridge. It is quite similar in many ways to the HK23E, including the same overall length. Heckler & Koch has also offered a 7.62x39mm magazine-fed automatic rifle—the HK12—that is much like the HK11 or HK13 except for its cartridge chambering. Heckler & Koch has not succeeded in selling these weapons because those countries that might be interested in buying them have traditionally been under Soviet or Communist Chinese domination. Heckler & Koch dropped this caliber line in 1982 because of a general lack of interest.

Another Heckler & Koch development that deserves greater success is the HK23. Based on the HK23E, it features a special "linkless feed box," consisting of a steel box placed in a bracket underneath the left side of the receiver. Loose rounds are placed into the box from which a feeder arm lifts them up and pushes them into the gun's mechanism as it fires. In principle, this loading system resembles that of the Japanese Type 11 machine gun, introduced in 1922 and used throughout the Sino-Japanese wars of the 1930s and in World War II. The box can be replenished before it runs empty or, if the shooter prefers, a 50-round drum, made specifically for this model by Heckler & Koch, can be substituted. The German antiterrorist unit, GSG-9, is the only group known to use this gun. It includes a four-power telescopic sight and bears the official designation G6.

Heckler & Koch was also working on a 4.73mm caseless-ammunition variant of the G11 rifle when German unification caused cancellation of the entire project in 1990. Heckler & Koch's GR6 machine gun retained one part of this design by positioning a G11-type optical sight on top of an HK23E receiver. The G11 sight does not magnify; instead, it is a 1-power scope. It does, however, employ an illuminated reticle and is said to improve instinctive aiming, resembling in that respect the 1.3-power telescope sight used on the Steyr AUG service rifle.

While none of these machine gun designs has achieved much commercial success, they each demonstrate Heckler & Koch's innovative spirit and willingness to experiment with proven design features in the ongoing quest for the "ultimate machine gun."

Bipods and Tripods

Heckler & Koch places a bipod on each HK21- and 23-series machine guns as a standard feature, enabling shooters to get good results out to 500 meters or so. The machine gun bipod is appreciably heavier and sturdier than the lightweight unit offered with the company's rifles. Moreover, these bipods allow shooters to turn the gun 30 degrees either way; they can then fire at targets of opportunity without having to lift the entire gun and shift its position.

Other missions create the need for a tripod. Fire missions requiring a tripod mount include shooting to the limits of 1200-meter sights or even further in plunging or indirect fire. Antiaircraft fire also requires a tripod for best results. Fire missions that involve shooting along a certain compass heading in support of an infantry assault also need tripods to avoid killing one's own troops.

Tripods work best when support crews dig in the legs and weigh them down. Sandbags are ideal. A weighted tripod makes a highly stable mounting for a gun. Stability is especially impor-

AT RIGHT AND BELOW The Heckler & Koch G36K features a shortened barrel but otherwise remains much the same as the standard G36. The transparent magazine sides are an excellent idea, as they allow the shooter a rapid and easy way to ascertain the state of his ammunition supply. See also p. 100, Chapter 2.

Chapter Five 171

tant for the HK21 series models, which are too light for the recoil of the 7.62x51mm/.308 caliber cartridge they fire.

In addition to the bipod and tripod mounts, Heckler & Koch offers a variety of vehicle mountings and other special-purpose mounts. These enable soldiers to fire Heckler & Koch machine guns from jeeps, trucks and armored vehicles, thus adding to the efficiency and versatility of H&K's line of machine guns.

Analysis

The HK21 series has received a great deal of criticism because it doesn't function as well in the general-purpose machine gun role as other designs, such as the MG3, FN MAG, RPK, or even the M60. But comparing the HK21 to one or more of these other guns is rather unfair. After all, Heckler & Koch did not create the HK21 to compete directly with any of these designs. By comparison, the HK21 is quite a bit lighter, approaching an intermediate position between the squad-automatic weapon concept and the general-purpose machine gun. As such, it has the capability of being used as either in a pinch.

One major advantage the HK21 offers over any of the general-purpose machine guns mentioned above is that, unlike any of them, the HK21 is light enough and handy enough to be operated effectively by one man. Despite what the movies sometimes show, the classic GPMGs are really too big and clumsy to be used efficiently in combat by a single operator. Ask anyone who has carried an M60 through Vietnamese terrain what he thinks of that weapon as a "light machine gun" and you'll understand.

A more accurate comparison would be to place the HK21 next to other heavy automatic rifles or light machine guns made from assault rifles. These competing designs would include Belgium's FALO and the American M15/M14 E1. Whatever its faults, the HK21 has put in far more service than either of these guns. Moreover, it is far more controllable in automatic fire while offering belt feed and a rapid barrel change, all useful characteristics shared by neither of the competing models. The HK21 also holds up well against the classic BAR by virtue of its belt feed and quick-change barrel for sustained fire. It's almost as handy, when fitted with a magazine adaptor and front handgrip, as a squad-automatic weapon. Probably the best competitor to the HK21 in the same approximate weight and size class is the legendary Bren gun. While undeniably efficient, accurate and reliable, however, that weapon still lacks belt-feed capability and is significantly more expensive to manufacture.

The Heckler & Koch machine guns, having borrowed heavily from the proven G3 design, naturally share many of its strengths. Changing the barrel of a Heckler & Koch machine gun, being fast and easy to learn, is accomplished in the field with little trouble. Barrel change, by the way, is a critically important aspect of an air-cooled machine gun and remains one of the strongest elements in Heckler & Koch designs.

Good sighting arrangements are another feature of Heckler & Koch machine guns. The rifle-style rotary four-position sight borrowed from the G3 rifle by a few H&K machine gun models is at least adequate, while the 12-position drum-style sight found on most of the company's machine guns is even better—especially at ranges beyond 500 meters. It also makes an excellent iron sight for precise semiautomatic fire. What's more, Heckler & Koch machine guns lend themselves to the mounting of good optical sights. The fact that all H&K machine guns have a semi-automatic mode on their fire selector makes them excellent choices for even high-speed sniping using fast semiautomatic fire. In this role, the HK21 far outclasses the U.S. M60, which lacks a semiautomatic-fire setting altogether and suffers from a heavy trigger pull, making single shots difficult except in the hands of an expert.

Several writers well-informed on gun matters have been highly critical in their articles concerning Heckler & Koch's machine guns, particularly the HK21. Those who cite the fragility of H&K's feed mechanism may have a case, although the improved two-stroke feed mechanism introduced on the latest models should effectively remove that objection. One problem with the feed mechanism that can't be denied, however, is the fact that the belts must be fed from the underside of the receiver, a chore that becomes even more difficult as the weapon heats up. In contrast, most machine guns feature a hinged top cover that's easily opened and loaded simply by laying a belt in position on the exposed feed tray. Unfortunately, the HK21 and related Heckler & Koch machine guns were built originally with a rifle receiver that feeds from underneath; as a result, the more convenient top-feeding mechanism cannot be used. Another potential problem area involves extraction difficulties, always a consideration with roller-locking mechanisms. Again, however, those 12 flutes cut into the firing chambers of Heckler & Koch roller-locked rifles and machine guns have apparently reduced this complaint to a theoretical issue only.

The machine guns made by Heckler & Koch generate a rate of fire about 800 rounds per minute (for the HK21 and 23 series guns) and 700 rounds per minute (for the magazine-fed HK13), which is high considering their relatively light weight. In sustained fire, the guns tend to move around too much, making accurate shooting difficult. In fairness to Heckler & Koch, stability problems related to an overly-high rate of fire have bedeviled German infantry machine guns ever since that country adopted the MG34 prior to World War II. Indeed, European machine gun designs generally develop a somewhat higher rate of fire than do comparable U.S. weapons. The Browning M1917 and M1919 machine guns generate a slower rate of fire (500 rounds per minute), while the M60 produces 550 rounds per minute. All three work much better, both in terms of weapon control and tactically in support of advancing infantry.

In general, it's safe to say that while the Heckler & Koch machine gun line is far from the world's best in terms of ruggedness, it does represent a remarkably diverse collection of versatile, well-made guns. For the many missions in which they may be called upon to perform, Heckler & Koch machine guns, when skillfully employed, can provide the margin between victory and defeat. • **H&K**

SPECIFICATIONS: H&K MACHINE GUNS

	Overall Length (in.)	Barrel Length (in.)	Weight (lbs.)	Caliber/ Capacity	Rate Of Fire
HK11	40.6	17.7	18	7.62/20	800 r.p.m.
GB	40.6	17.7	18	7.62/20, 50, B	800 r.p.m.
HK21	44.9	17.7	20.5	7.62/belt	800 r.p.m.
HK13	40.6	17.7	18	5.56/25	700 r.p.m.
HK23	40.6	17.7	19.2	5.56/belt	800 r.p.m.

Following World War II, the next major breakthrough was the development by the U.S. Army of the M79 grenade launcher in the early 1960s. This weapon, which handled like a break-open shotgun, saw widespread service in Vietnam. Accurate up to 400 yards, the M79 augmented the rifle squad's firepower significantly. It also proved both rugged and reliable......

Chapter 6

A Heckler & Koch Miscellany

Heckler & Koch has not confined its genius solely to such firearms as the P7 service pistol, the G3 service rifle, the MP5 submachine gun, or the HK21 machine gun. The company has also created a host of other devices, including additional weapons systems and useful accessories for existing weapons. All of these devices share one feature common to all Heckler & Koch inventions: great creativity.

Part 1. Flare Projectors

Flares are important in a variety of applications, from calling for rescue to signaling the start of an attack. A good reliable flare projector is a valuable item for a firearms manufacturer to have in its product line, and Heckler & Koch has developed two of the most useful ones. The Emergency Flare Launcher (EFL), for example, fires a 19mm flare to an altitude of 200 feet, its magazine holding up to five spare flares, each measuring 5.75" high, 3.15" wide and 1.45" thick. At only eight ounces

> The EFL is a simple flare launcher with easy-to-follow directions printed on its outer casing. Note the lanyard loop attached to the magazine floorplate and the heel-type magazine release similar to the company's P7 service pistol (photo courtesy of Heckler & Koch).

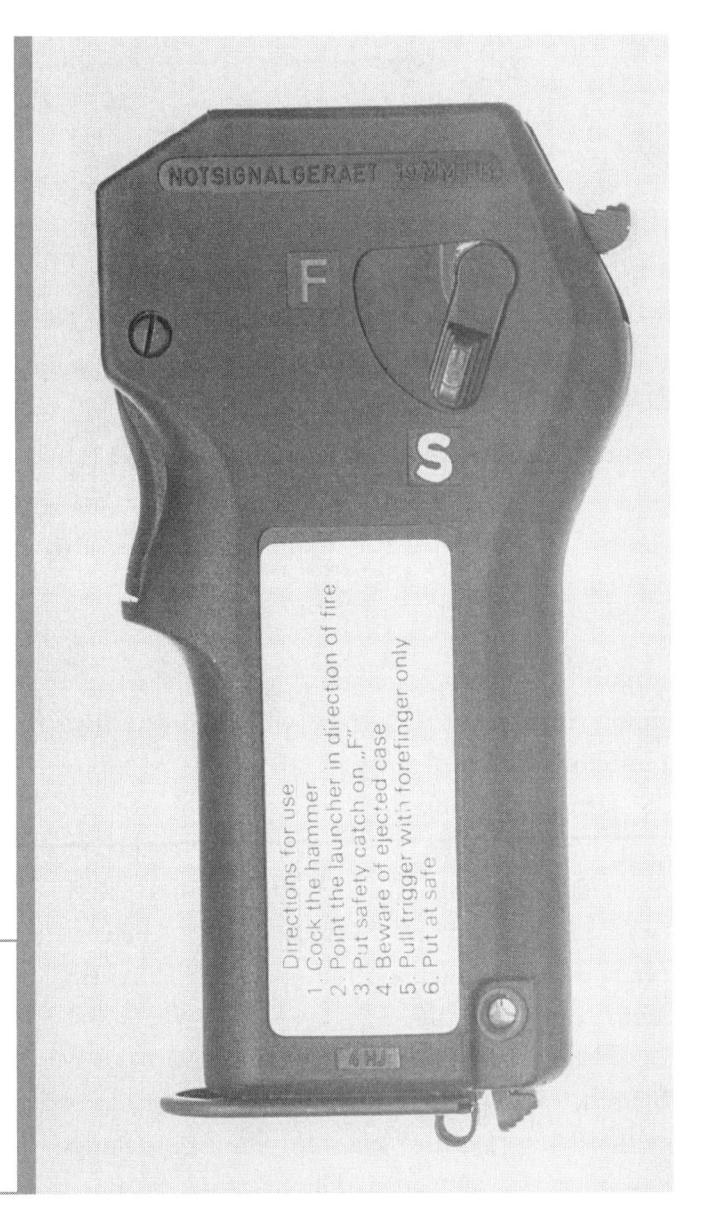

Chapter Six 175

For the Bundeswehr and other German-speaking customers, Heckler & Koch offers the EFL with German instructions. The EFL magazine holds compact 19mm flares (photo courtesy of Heckler & Koch).

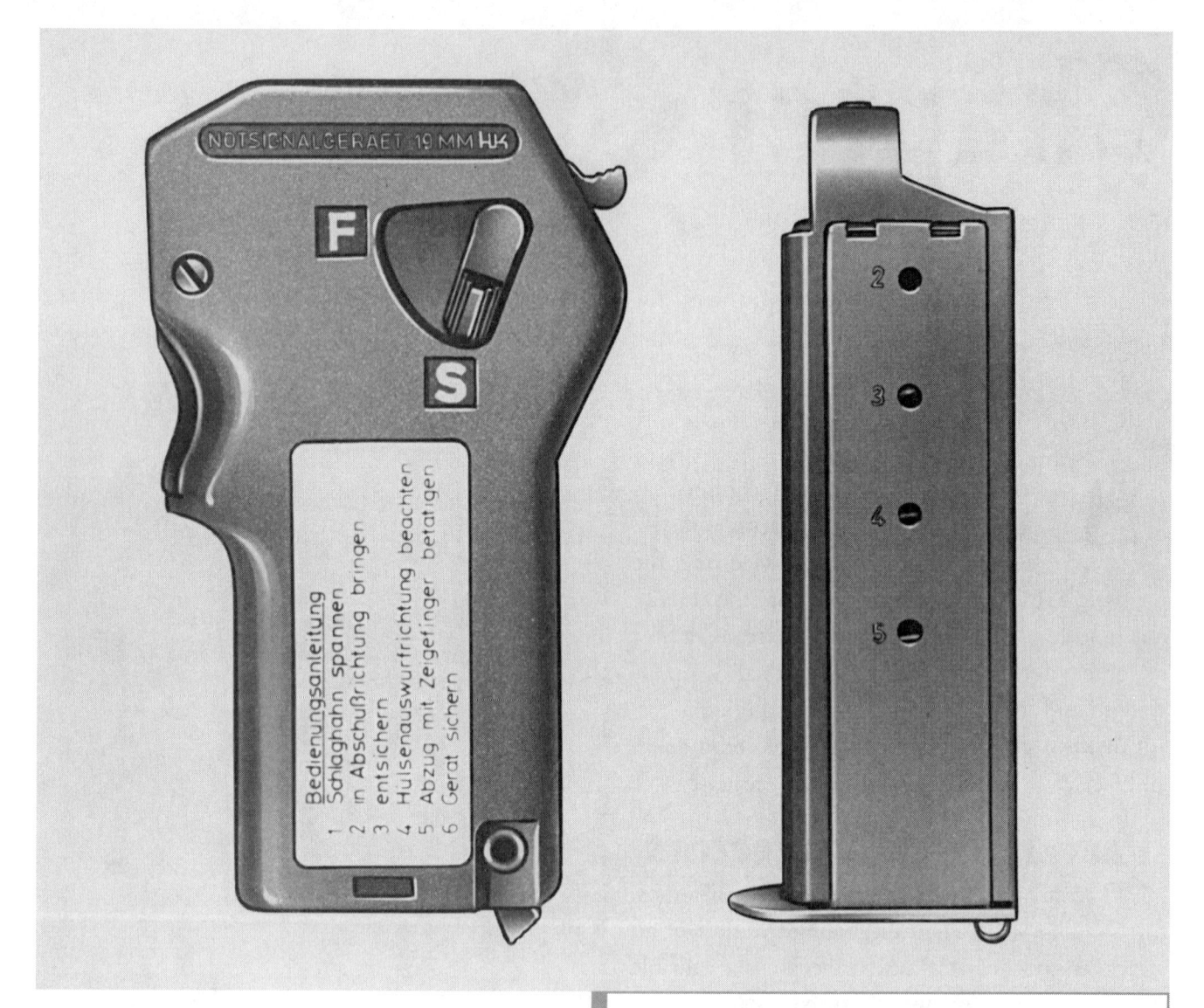

(unloaded), it makes a compact device that's quite simple to operate. It begins with a loaded flare projector, its manual safety placed in the safe (white "S") setting. The operator first cocks the exposed spur hammer, then points the launcher in the intended direction. Finally, the manual safety control is pushed from "S" to the red "F." The trigger is pulled, whereupon the operator returns the safety control to "safe."

The EFL was designed with a number of user-friendly features. Full instructions appear on a label at the flare projector's left side. The EFL handles and operates one-handed. The magazine release—a P38-type, heel-mounted unit—pushes to the rear, releasing the magazine. The EFL's relatively compact dimensions and rectangular shape enable this flare to fit into a cargo pocket.

Heckler & Koch's P2A1 is a more rugged, general purpose flare projector than the Emergency Flare Launcher. It fires larger 26.5mm flares than the EFL (26.5mm has been a standard flare type in

AT RIGHT: The Heckler & Koch multipurpose sling enables this shooter to carry the rifle over his shoulder like an ordinary sling but without the cumbersome extra strap.

BELOW: Heckler & Koch's multipurpose sling allows "assault carry" more easily and conveniently than any competing device.

Chapter Six 177

AT LEFT The Heckler & Koch multipurpose sling, shown from the rear, allows a secure and comfortable "assault carry."

BELOW The multipurpose sling provides fast and easy transition from the "assault carry" mode to a shoulder-typ firing position.

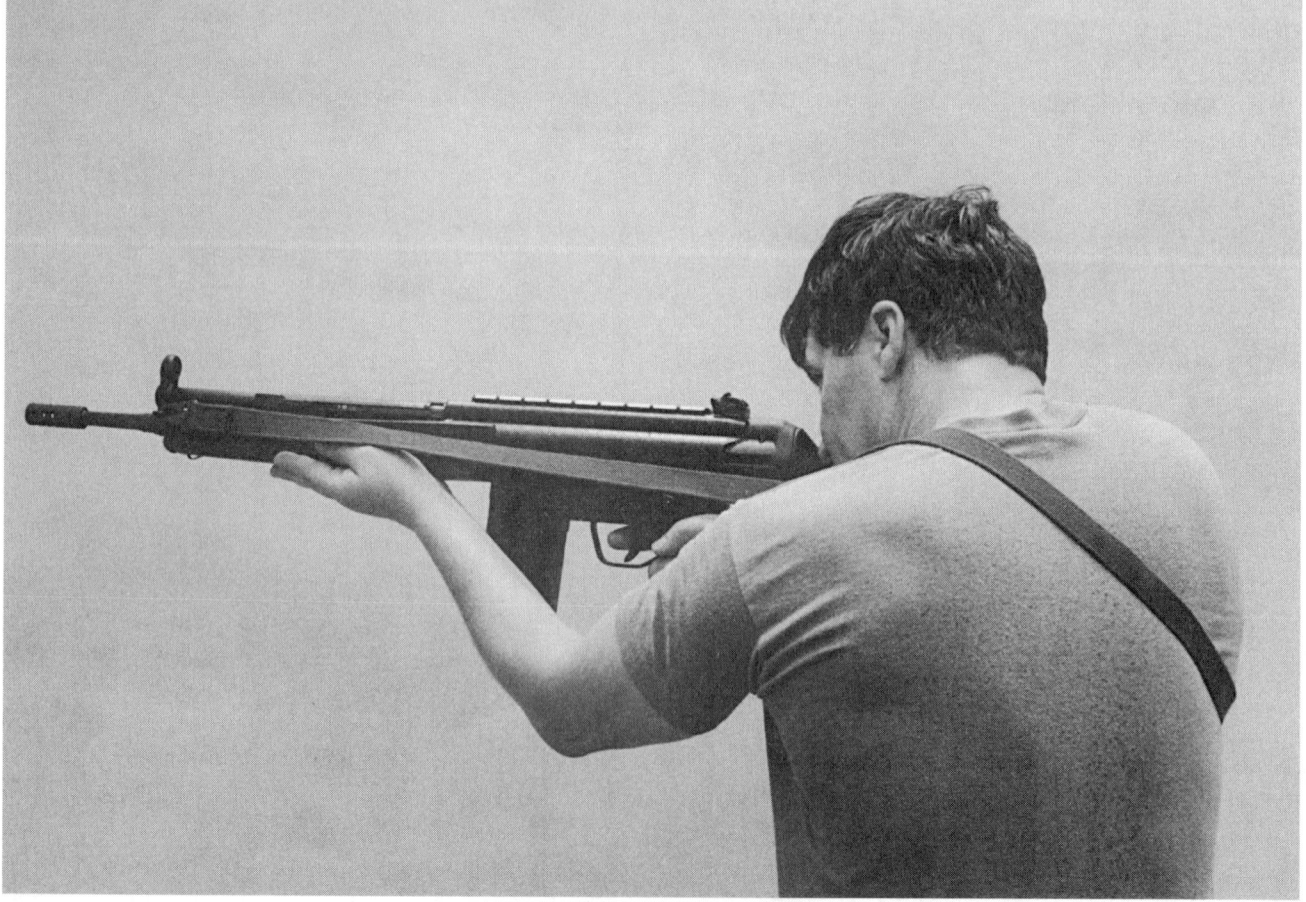

The M79, a dedicated launcher for the 40mm grenade, provided vital firepower to U.S. troops in Vietnam and revolutionized military grenade launching (photo courtesy of Defense Visual Information Center).

Chapter Six 179

Europe since before World War II). Because of its size, the flares from the P2A1 are significantly more efficient signal devices than the pyrotechnics of the 19mm EFL, whose flares are difficult to see in daylight. Flares measuring 26.5mm show up brightly in daylight, while at night the illumination flares available in this chambering can literally turn night into day—for a few seconds, anyway.

Fired from a P2A1, 26.5mm flares reach an altitude of up to 1000 feet and then descend by parachute. Depending on the type of signal used, typical burn time ranges from six to twenty-five seconds. As with the EFL, the P2A1 includes an external hammer (which must be cocked before firing), a manual safety, and two attachment points for a lanyard. The single-shot P1A1 has no magazine; each flare must be loaded individually by opening the breech between launches.

As one might guess, the P2A1 is much larger than the EFL. Shaped roughly like a pistol, it measures 7.9 inches in length with a 6.1-inch barrel. Other specifications include a height of 6.7 inches, a width of 1.5 inches, and a weight of 24 ounces.

REMEMBER AT ALL TIMES: FLARES ARE DANGEROUS IF IMPROPERLY HANDLED. THEY ARE NOT TOYS AND HAVE CAUSED SEVERE BURNS AND EVEN DEATH. BE CAREFUL WHEN HANDLING ANY FLARE PROJECTOR!

This Heckler & Koch police products catalog from the early 1990s shows the Model 69A1 40mm grenade launcher (top right) and the P2A1 flare pistol (bottom left). The long arms are (top to bottom) the HK21E light machine gun, the top-of-the-line PSG1 precision sniping rifle, and the MSG90 precision rifle.

180 Heckler & Koch

Propellant charge

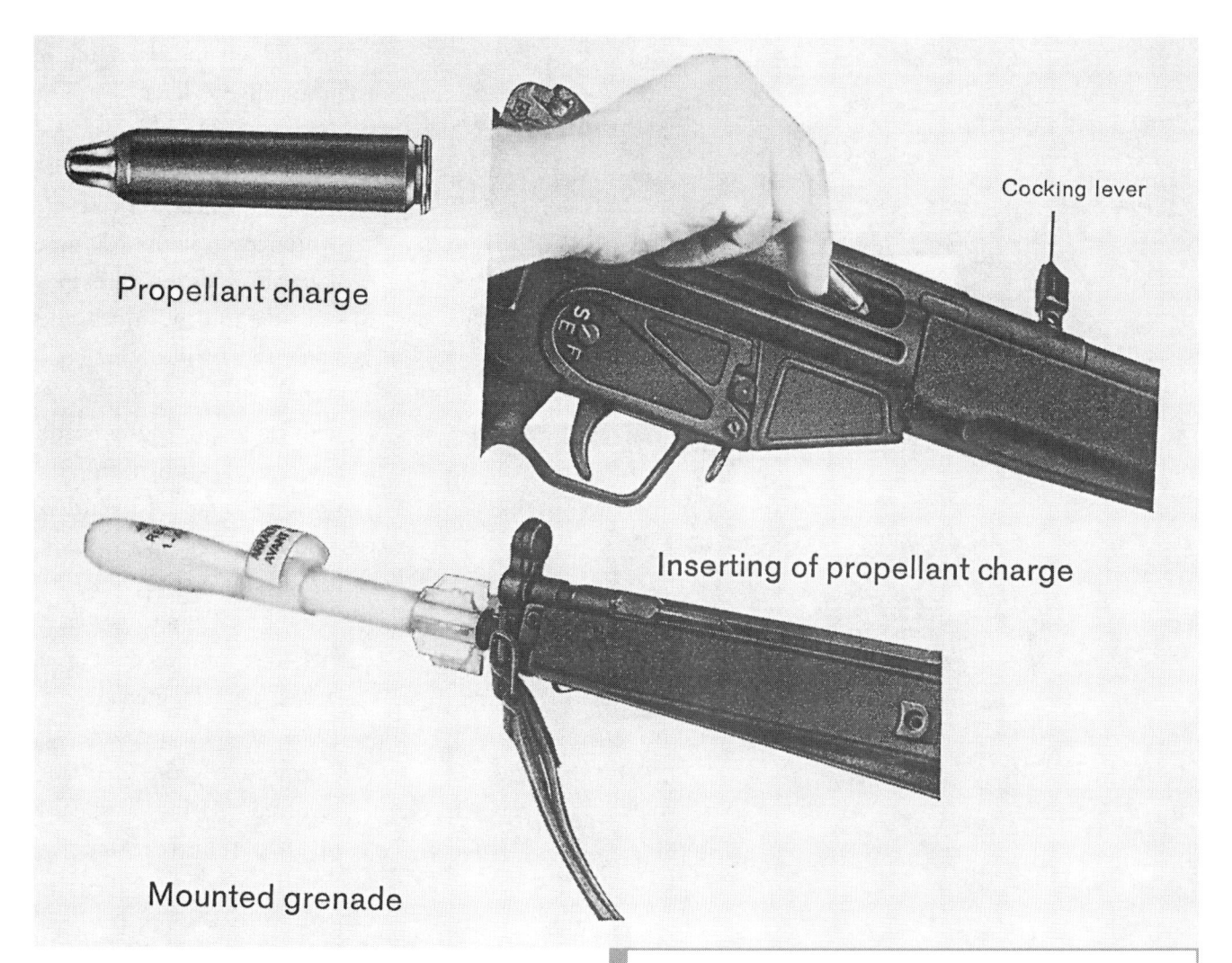

Cocking lever

Inserting of propellant charge

Mounted grenade

The G3 and HK33 are easily modified to fire the popular "Energa" rifle grenade (photo courtesy of Heckler & Koch).

Part II.
Grenade Launchers

Rifle grenades have been an important component of military armament since World War I. Rifle grenadiers in those days were especially important among the French armed forces, who created the remarkably efficient Vivens-Bessières (V-B) grenade launcher for the Model 1886 Lebel rifle. Equally important, the French developed a workable tactical doctrine to go with it. Dating from late 1917, the French infantry employed a method of organization for its infantry units in which a fire team unified one squad around a Chauchat Model 1915 machine rifle, while another squad was built around a V-B rifle grenadier. These small, mobile units made surprisingly effective "machine gun killer teams." The American Expeditionary Force (AEF), which fought in France in 1917-1918, adopted some of these techniques and made use of both the Chauchat machine rifle and the V-B grenade launcher. British, German and Italian rifle grenadiers also served in large numbers throughout World War I.

The rifles developed between the wars continued to feature grenade-launching capabilities. In fact, all World War II combatants used rifle-mounted grenade launchers to some extent. One major prob-

Chapter Six 181

Telescopic sight mount

Telescopic sight

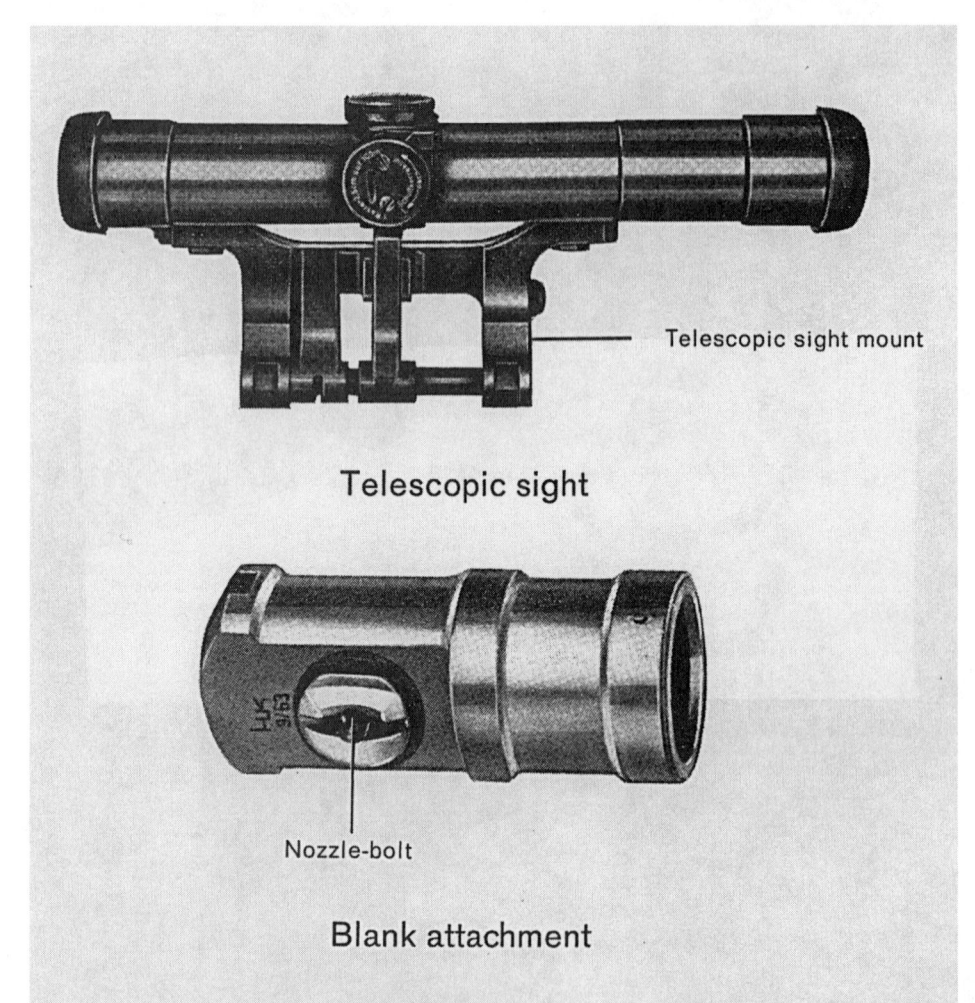

Nozzle-bolt

Blank attachment

nor did anyone else think it up until years later.

During World War II, the Germans developed grenade launchers for use in conjunction with 26.5mm flare pistols fitted with special adaptors in much the same way as rifles were converted to fire grenades. A high-explosive "egg" grenade could be launched from a suitably adapted Walther "Modell Heer" flare pistol, better known as the Wk361. With an adapter in place, this flare pistol could also launch a smoke grenade.

A second adaptation of a flare pistol by the Germans involved placing a special rifled insert into the smooth-

lem for a typical rifle-mounted grenade launcher during that period, such as the U.S M7, concerned the following: a rifle configured to fire rifle grenades could only be used for grenade launching and thus was lost to the rifle squad's firepower. The Carcano Model 28 TS, an Italian rifle introduced in 1928 in small numbers, solved this problem ingeniously by placing a grenade launcher alongside the standard barrel. To fire a rifle grenade, the shooter had only to load a grenade in the launcher's muzzle, transfer the bolt from the rifle breech to the grenade launcher's breech, and fire the grenade. To fire the weapon as a standard rifle, one had only to load the rifle and place its bolt back in the rifle breech, whereupon it could be fired like any other bolt-action rifle. The Italians made only limited use of this innovation,

Heckler & Koch rifles can be adapted to accept a variety of optional sighting devices. The "claw" mount shown with the telescopic sight is effective with the stamped-steel receivers of rifles like the G3 and HK33. The BFA (Blank Firing Attachment) is another popular accessory among military users (photo courtesy of Heckler & Koch).

bore barrel of a Walther 26.5mm flare pistol, narrowing it to 23mm, and then launching a short-range antitank grenade (called the PzWk42LP). The Germans called this conversion the *Sturmpistole*, or "Assault Pistol." By unscrewing and removing the insert, a soldier could instantly return the *Sturmpistole* to its original purpose as a 26.5mm flare pistol. Late in the war, the Germans created a more specialized grenade launcher, called the

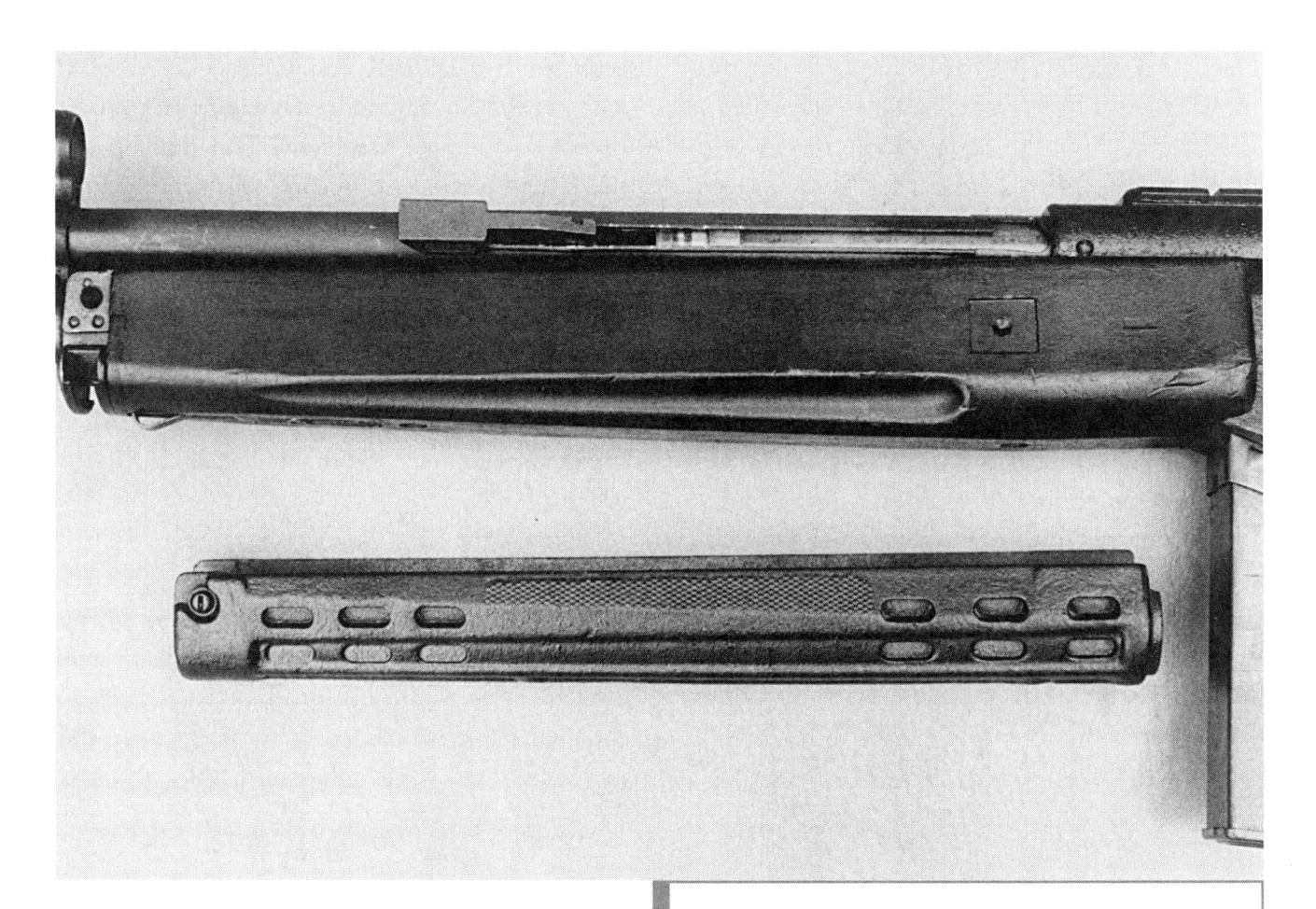

Kampfpistole ("Battle Pistol"). It was fashioned on the same machinery as the flare pistol, but modified to such an extent that it could no longer fire signal flares. To avoid accidents, these *Kampfpistolen* were distinguished from the standard flare pistols (which they outwardly resembled) by a large letter "Z" painted on their receivers. Although the Germans continued to use the standard rifle grenade throughout the war, the various flare-pistol/grenade combinations offered added fire support to the infantryman.

Following World War II, the next major breakthrough was the development by the U.S. Army of the M79 grenade launcher in the early 1960s. This weapon, which handled like a break-open shotgun, saw widespread service in Vietnam. Accurate up to 400 yards, the M79 augmented the rifle squad's firepower significantly. It also proved

> Heckler & Koch G3-type rifles accept either a narrow handguard (shown beneath the rifle), or a broad so-called "tropical" handguard introduced on the HK33 series. Note the indentations for a folding bipod on the tropical handguard installed on a rifle.

both rugged and reliable, which its contemporaries—the early M16A1 rifle and M60 machine gun—most assuredly were not. Several foreign companies, including Heckler & Koch, used the M79 40mm grenade (**photo p. 179**) as the basis for their own grenade-launcher programs.

Another important postwar step forward in rifle grenade development came from the Mecar Company in Belgium. It began in 1965, when Mecar announced its "Universal Bullet Trap," or BTU, with which a rifleman could fire a grenade without having to switch to special ammunition.

One simply attached a BTU to a rifle muzzle, placed a Mecar rifle grenade atop it, then fired a standard military ball rifle bullet into the grenade. As the bullet entered the grenade, its propellant charge was ignited, firing the grenade off the launcher. Previously, rifle grenade launchers had to rely on blanks or special grenade-launching cartridges. Any attempt to use regular bullets, as sometimes happed by accident in the heat of battle, resulted in catastrophic explosions. A device capable of launching a grenade using a regular bullet had long been sought for its simplicity.

Indeed, experimentation along these lines had started as early as World War I. By 1917, the French had developed a prototype rifle grenade launcher activated by standard ammunition. Dissatisfied with its reliability under adverse conditions, however, the French dropped the idea. Mecar thus became the first to perfect a truly safe, reliable bullet-trap system. Since the company had announced its BTU, several other European manufacturers developed their own variations. In some instances, a rifle bullet employed to launch a grenade merely passes through it, allowing the ammo to derive its energy from the powder gases used to fire the bullet. Other systems "trap" the rifle bullet, similar to the Mecar unit.

Even as the M79 was making a name for itself in Vietnam, the U.S. Army was developing its eventual replacement: the M203. The only objection anyone ever raised against the M79 was that it took a rifleman away from his squad, because it was all the grenadier could do to carry the grenade and its ammunition. Given that load, only a Model

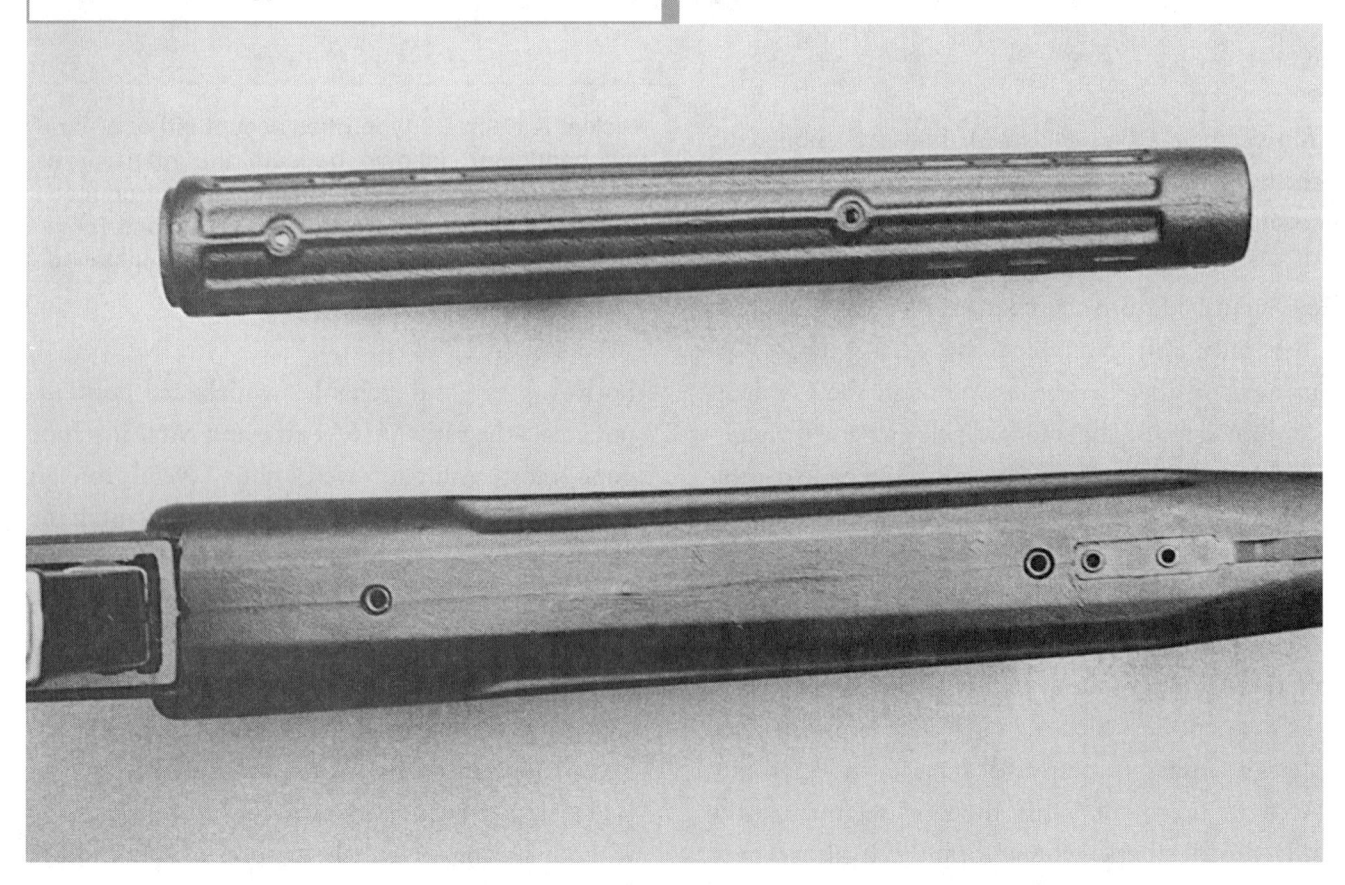

The earlier narrow handguard (shown) works better for small-handed shooters, while the broader tropical handguard allows a superior grip for shooters with large hands.

AT RIGHT — The clip shown connects two magazines for a G3-type rifle as opposed to taping or welding the magazines together (as was often done in the past by soldiers seeking increased firepower).

BELOW — Viewed from the side, the two-magazine clip for a G3-type rifle adds little bulk while offering good protection for the spare magazine.

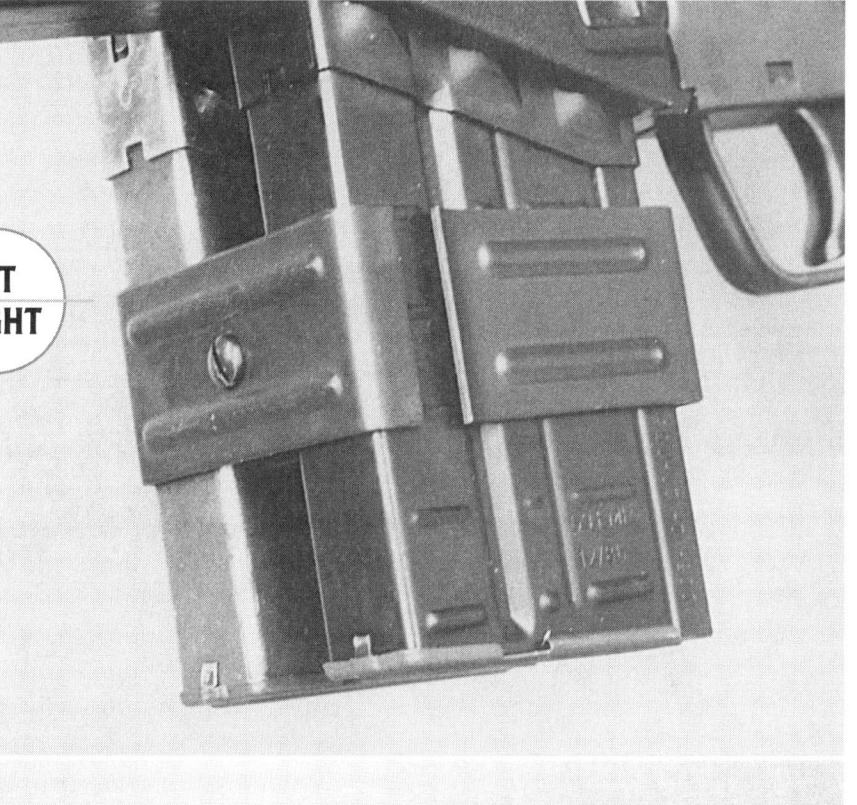

Chapter Six   185

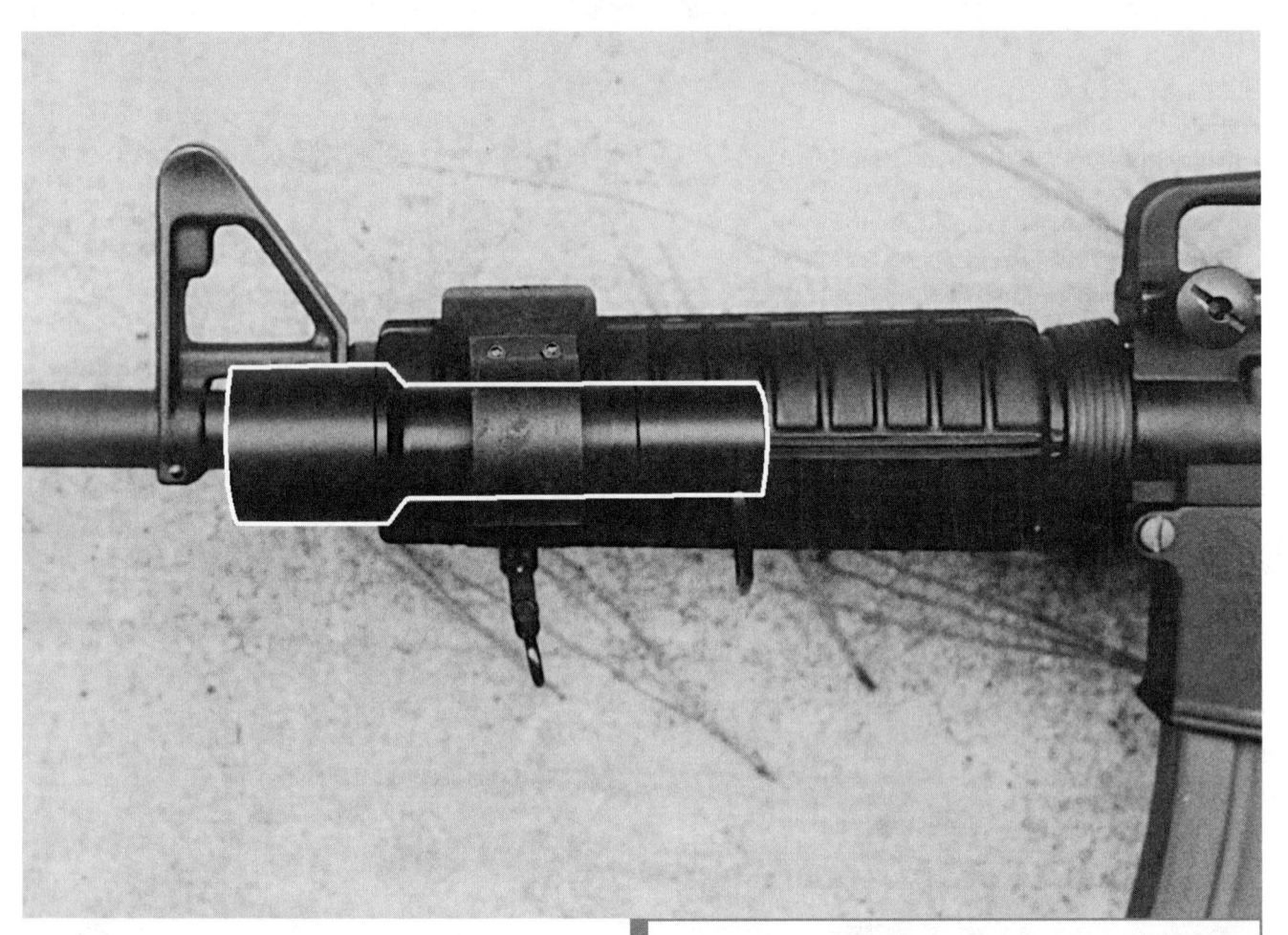

A trend in modern combat rifles is the sighting/target acquisition device, such as a flashlight mounted on the handguard of a Colt CAR-15 for low-light operations.

1911A1 pistol could be carried as a defensive sidearm. The M203's purpose was to combine the M79-type grenade launcher with an M16-type rifle in one unit, allowing the grenadier to double as a rifleman.

The Army formally adopted the M203 in August of 1969. The grenade launcher, which fires the same 40mm grenade used in the M79, attaches beneath the barrel of a modified M16A1 rifle. To make room for the M203, the M16A1 required special rounded low-profile handguards not usable on just any M16A1. Nevertheless, the M16A1/M203 combination, which now allowed one shooter to serve as both rifleman and grenadier, replaced the M79. The M203 has also inspired other countries to adopt it as their own, including a new Heckler & Koch system: the TGS.

Heckler & Koch benefited greatly from all the research that had gone into rifle-launched grenades, combining as they did such striking power, accuracy and ease of use. As a result, it created several innovative grenade launchers of its own. The company has by now developed variations of virtually every grenade-launching system developed since modern grenades first arrived in World War I.

After developing a grenade-launching cup attachment for its 26.5mm P2A1 flare pistol (based on the wartime *Sturmpistole*), Heckler & Koch went on to develop a specialized 40mm grenade launcher, which it placed into production in 1969. Designated the HK69, it fired the standard 40mm grenade—the same used in the U.S. M79 and M203 systems. But unlike the freestanding M79, the HK69 was fitted to a G3, on the left side of the handguard parallel to the muzzle. The HK69 was by no means small, measuring about 14 inches overall and weighing 3½ pounds (unloaded). It was, moreover, a long reach to the trigger; and its position on the rifle meant the shooter had to pull the trigger left-handed, adding to its awkwardness. In addition, being mounted to the side tended to unbalance the rifle. Consequently, interest was limited and sales were small, causing the company to discontinue the unit in the 1970s.

The HK69A1, commonly known in Europe as the GrP (for "Grenade Pistol") is also a launcher for 40mm grenades. Unlike the rifle-mounted HK69, which it strongly resembles, the HK69A1 is a stand-alone unit, with its own stock and firing mechanism. In those respects, it matches the M79 quite closely both in appearance and in conception. Unlike the fixed-stock M79, though, this one features an adjustable, retractable stock and can be fired both from the shoulder or as a pistol. With its stock fully extended, the HK69A1 is 28.9 inches long (18.24 with the stock retracted). Unloaded, it weighs 5.8 pounds.

To operate the HK69A1, simply set the ambidextrous safety lever to "S" for safe and push down the locking latch (located on the left rear of the breech, next to the hammer). The launcher now breaks open like a shotgun, with the barrel tipping down. Next, a 40mm grenade is inserted into the barrel from the rear. The action closes by tipping the barrel back up until the locking catch engages the breech with a clicking sound. The manual safety is them placed into its firing position by pushing it down (from either side) until it points to the red letter "F."

The HK69A1 is capable of impressive accuracy out to a maximum range of 400 meters, but delivering this accuracy takes work. First, the distance to the target must be determined and an appropriate sight selected (the HK69A1 has two of them). The short-range sight, with dual apertures for 50 and 100 meters, is located on the rear end of the barrel. The long range ladder-style sight, which is graduated from 100 to 400 meters in 50-meter increments, lies just ahead of the short range sight. Once the grenade launcher is sighted in, the trigger is pulled and the ordnance is on its way. With practice, the HK69A1 is quite accurate. Many grenadiers learn to drop rounds where they want them instinctively, with minimal use of the sights. Police grenadiers have been noted to place tear gas into the window of criminal hideouts from 200 yards away or more using this system.

Because of its accuracy and the wide variety of ordnance available, Heckler & Koch has enjoyed considerable success with the HK69A1, mostly among police departments, including quite a few in the United States. Though it might appear at first glance to be overly specialized, it's actually quite versatile, thanks to the many different 40mm projectiles the company offers.

Noting the success of the M203 grenade launcher system used in Colt's M16 service rifle, Heckler & Koch went on to develop a similar device, called the HK79, for its own 7.62mm G3 and 5.56mm HK41-type service rifles, calling them the G3-TGS or G41-TGS, depending on the rifle. The TGS (for "Tactical Group System") features a cut-down forearm with a reduced diameter. The HK79 grenade launcher, which weighs about 3.4 pounds unloaded, lies directly below, not off to the side. By releasing a latch on the back end of the grenade launcher, the rear end of the pivoting barrel hinges downward. Once a grenade has been placed in the launcher, the barrel rises until it is held shut by the

Chapter Six **187**

AT LEFT The military-issue G3 includes an adapter on the front of the cocking-handle tube. Its purpose is to accept the mounting hardware at the rear of the bayonet grip. G3s intended for commercial sale use a blank plug on the front of the cocking-handle tube (shown).

BELOW G3-type rifles include a triggerguard for gloved-hand use. For shooters who require heavier gloves or mittens, a detachable winter trigger is available.

AT RIGHT

The oblong hole in the G3-type bayonet's blade combines wih a matching lug on the scabbard to allow the owner to cut through barbed wire. Note also the blade's serrated top edge, adding to its versatility.

BELOW

The combat flashlight, shown mounted on the handguard of a Colt CAR-15, uses a pressure-activated switch turned on and off by the shooter's support hand. H & K rifles can be adapted to accept such devices, inclding the company's own versatile Aiming Point Projector.

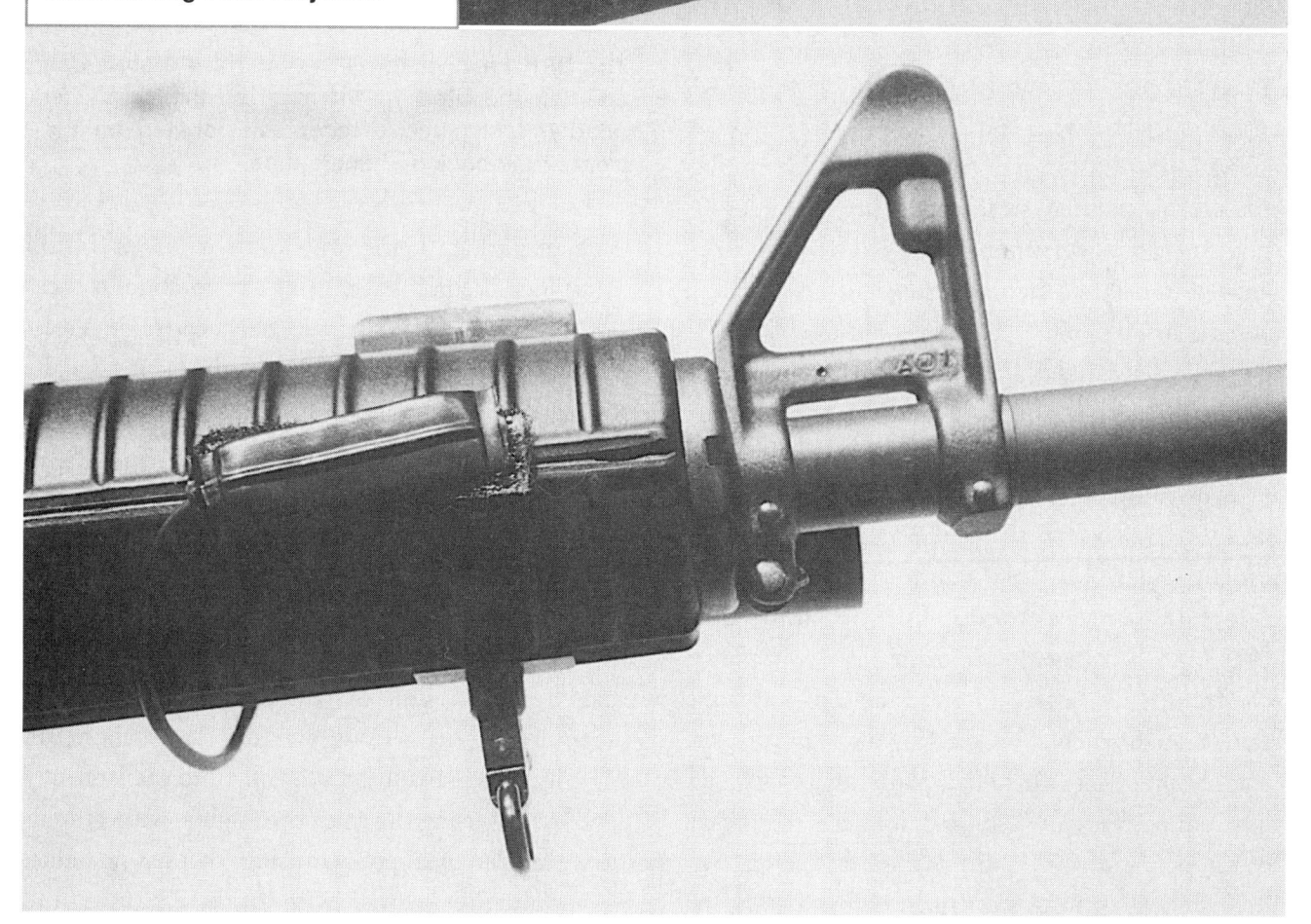

Chapter Six

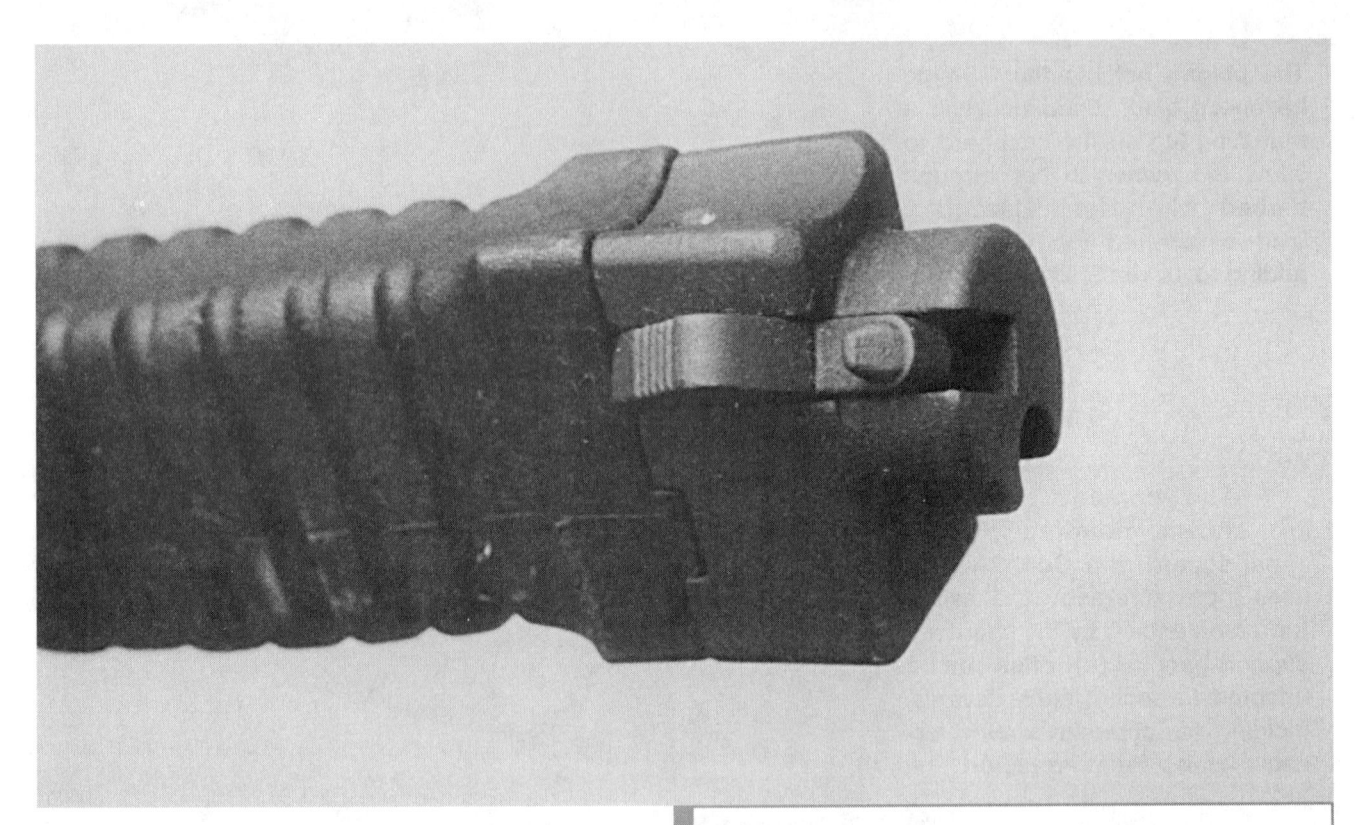

The H&K bayonet for G3-series rifles features an adapter mounted at the rear of the grip. The adapter locks into a receptacle located on the front of the cocking-handle tube.

latch. The grenade launcher's striker, located ahead of the magazine well, is then cocked. The manual safety, a push-button type, moves to the left until a red band is displayed, signaling its "fire" setting. The shooter then sights through the ladder-type sight (located in front of the rifle's rear sight), with range increments noted every 50 meters out to 200. With the range determined, the launcher is fired by pressing the firing control (a rectangular button located halfway down the left side of the grenade launcher).

Still another grenade launcher available for Heckler & Koch rifles is the popular "Energa" system, which has been adapted to several rifles from various manufacturers. Energa consists of a special grenade that fits onto the flash suppressor. The front sight is fitted ahead of the standard front sight, and the grenade is fired by a special propellant, resembling a .308 caliber blank with a crimped nose and no bullet. When fired, it ignites the rocket motor, which then flies to its target. For safety reasons, Energa cartridges do not fit into a standard rifle magazine. Those who carry a G3 or HK33 must lock the bolt back, using the notch for a cocking lever, while inserting an Energa cartridge directly into the rifle chamber. Personally, I consider the Belgian Mecar system, which required no special sights or ammunition, a superior choice, but for some reason the Energa system has become more widely used.

Heckler & Koch also offers a tear gas grenade launcher system of its own design for units (chiefly police SWAT teams) needing to launch such ordnance. H&K's unit has a traditional grenade cup adapter that fits directly over the flash suppressor. The tear gas grenade goes directly into the large cup and is fired using the rifle's own sights, with propulsion supplied by a special cartridge that has no bullet. The launcher works with both 7.62mm and

5.56mm Heckler & Koch rifles with standard flash suppressors.

Still another Heckler & Koch grenade launcher system is made specifically for the MP5 submachine gun. Heckler & Koch makes a flash hider for this gun that is attached to threads cut into the muzzle end of the barrel. Thus it was a simple matter for the company to develop a unit that screws onto the barrel in place of the flash hider.

Part III. Sights

While the integral iron sights fitted to most Heckler & Koch rifles are highly functional and efficient, the company has been at the forefront in the development of high-technology alternative sighting systems. Starting with the G3, telescopic or optical sights have long been a feature on Heckler & Koch rifles. Adapting the G3's stamped sheet-steel receiver to a scope mount, however, was no easy task. The usual method of drilling and tapping threaded holes into the receiver top didn't work, so the company developed a "claw" mount that attaches to the top of the receiver. Heckler & Koch offers two basic types of mounting systems. One fits G3-type rifles and the other fits the G41 German service rifle by means of two blocks mounted on top of the receiver, along with the HK21 and 23 machine guns and related weapons.

One amazing aspect of Heckler & Koch's scope mount design is that it does not "lose its zero" when taken off the rifle and then put back on, as many scope mounts unfortunately do. Even so, it's a good idea to keep a scoped rifle set together as much as possible and not make excessive changes once the combination is set, adjusted and properly zeroed in.

Active infrared scopes work on the principle of illuminating the target area with a burst of infrared energy while at the same time observing the area with a telescopic sight. Such scopes first appeared in World War II, with the Germans and the U.S. developing and fielding them more or less simultaneously in the last year or so of that war. Since we

The Heckler & Koch multipurpose sling, shown mounted on a commercial G3 clone, is one of the most useful devices of its type.

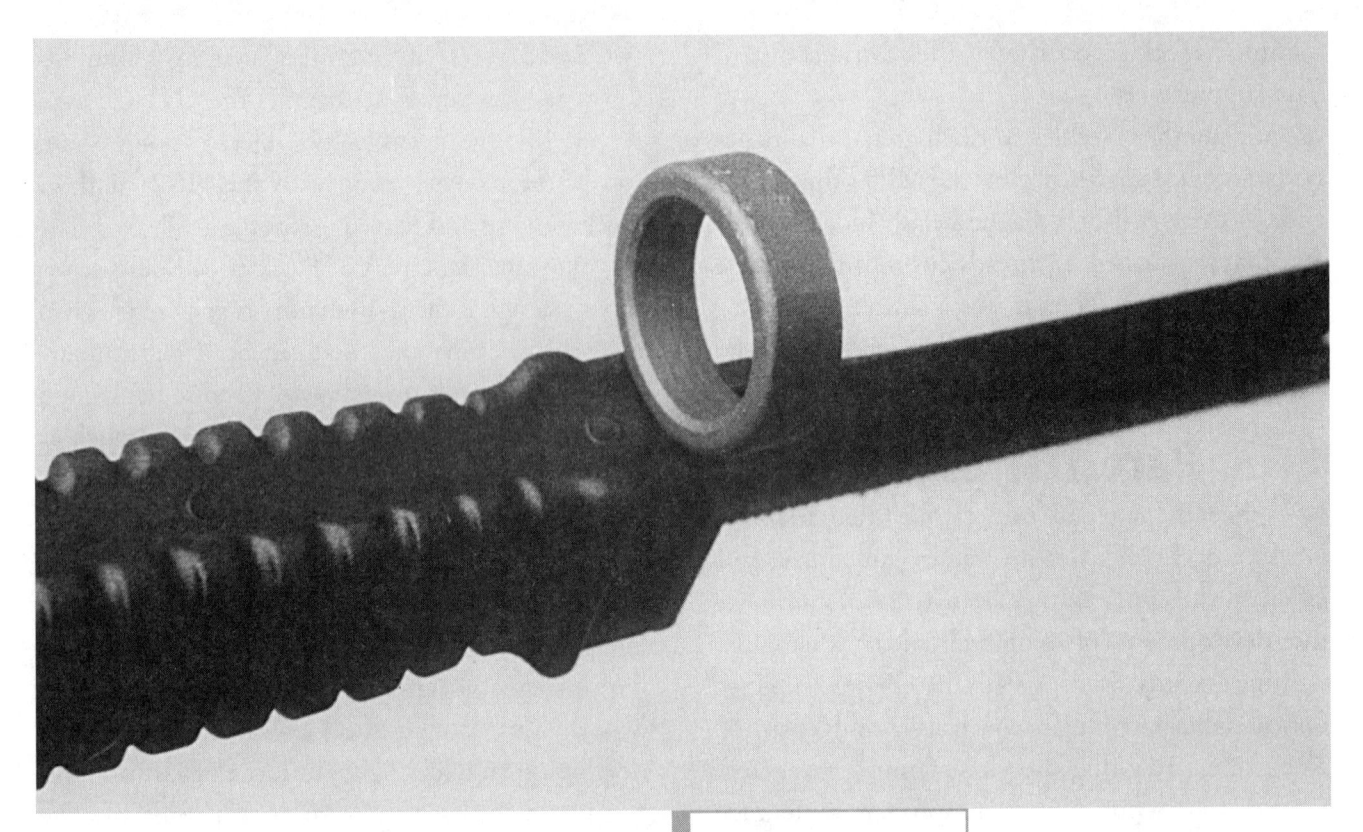

A ring on top of the G3-type bayonet fits over the rifle muzzle.

humans cannot see infrared radiation, it makes a useful system for observing and sighting systems at night against troops who lack the equipment to detect it. This system does have its drawbacks, however. For one thing, it's quite bulky, awkward and heavy. Another problem lies with the passive infrared detecting equipment itself, which is less bulky, undetectable, and available for counteracting the active gear. For example, the Soviet-designed PSO-1 (4-power) telescopic sight fitted to a SVD nipper rifle includes a passive infrared detector in its circuitry. In the event a shooter equipped with one of thee scope/rifle combinations suspects he's been detected by an active infrared system, he need only to select the infrared search mode on his scope, look for red-orange blobs in his scope, and then leave the area or open fire. The PSO-1 is far less bulky than an active infrared system, which calls for an infrared lamp, a scope that can pick up light in that wavelength, and a power supply.

There's also a size and weight penalty associated with active infrared emitters. The World War II German "Vampir" unit had a transmitter (infrared light source) measuring 130mm (5.1 inches) in diameter. The transmitter/ scope combination clamped above the receiver added five pounds to the weight of the rifle and tended to unbalance the gun and make it top-heavy. Worse still, the power pack, which was carried separately, weighed a hefty 30 pounds. Even postwar units, while somewhat lighter, are still bulky and awkward. Nevertheless, they do greatly improve the capability for night-fighting.

Image-intensifying sights work on the principle of amplifying existing ambient light to provide an operator who is suitably equipped with an improved, brightened image resembling daylight. Even a moonless night has enough ambient light to provide useful levels of amplification suitable for detection and aiming. In practice, moonless and overcast nights sometimes won't lend themselves well to this type of night vision, nor would such sights be of any use inside a darkened building, cave, or mine. An important advantage of image-intensifying scopes over the active infrared scopes, however, is the fact that image-intensifying scopes cannot be detected by the enemy.

In the mid-1960s, Heckler & Koch fitted the first generation of the Eltro-Zeiss image-intensifying sight to its G3 rifles and issued them to the GSG-9, which made good use of them despite their added weight and bulk. Second generation image-intensifying sights, such as the "Starlight" scope favored by the U.S. Army, are far less bulky, thanks to improved imaging technology.

The G41 INKAS, introduced in 1987, includes an active infrared laser projector placed in the hollowed-out tube of a cocking handle. The on-off switch for the laser is located in front of the cocking handle. This enables an operator to hold the rifle in an underarm assault position, but not to use the front and rear sights in the usual manner. When employed in conjunction with advanced night-vision goggles (the Phillips Elektro-Spezial BM-8028), this system allows night-fighting effectiveness far in advance of what a shooter may achieve using only the naked eye and tritium-illuminated sights (the usual solution to the problem of accurate shooting in darkness). The INKAS system, with its 48-degree field of view, weighs only 2.24 pounds (1 kilogram), which is not excessive by any means considering the improvement in performance it offers.

> The narrow handguard has no internal heat shield, but the tropical handguard includes this desirable feature in the form of an aluminum reflector that diverts barrel heat away from the shooter's support hand.

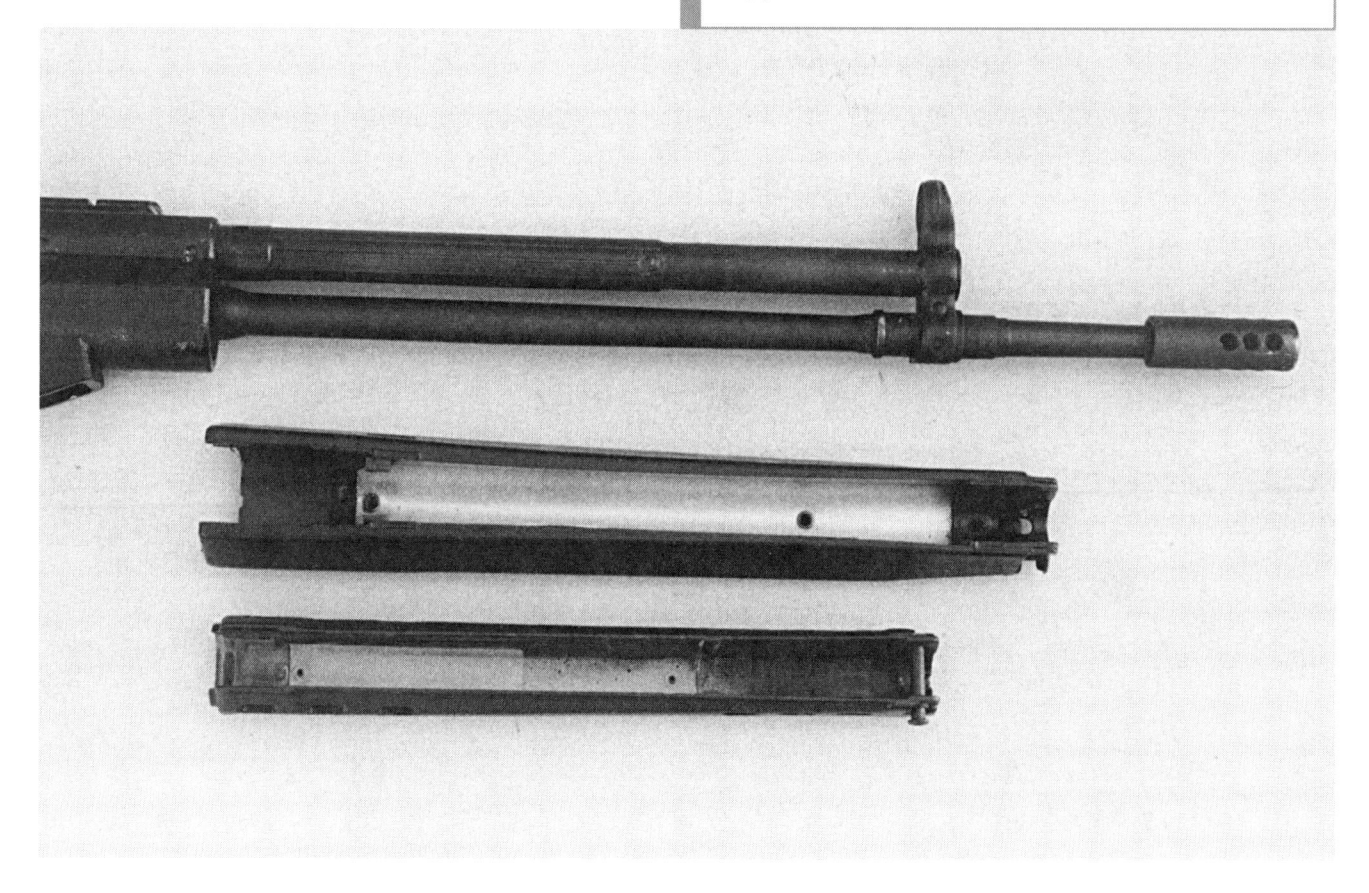

Chapter Six **193**

In addition to the West German armed forces, the West German border police (*Bundesgrenschütz*), carefully selected West German federal police units, and an elite GSG-9 antiterrorist unit use the INKAS system, sometimes on G41s and sometimes on modified G3s. Heckler & Koch offered the G41 INKAS system in both fixed buttstock and retractable buttstock models. A G41K INKAS variant combines the short-barreled, retractable buttstock rifle with the INKAS electro-optical sighting system.

In 1990, Heckler & Koch introduced an "Aiming Point Projector" **(photo p. 186)** which was essentially a large white-light flashlight mounted atop a receiver (using the company's standard claw-type scope mount). This unit illuminates a target and, if necessary, engages it by shooting at the center of the beam. In contrast to more modern laser scopes, which provide aiming points but fail to identify the target, the Aiming Point Projector does both. Unfortunately, it also identifies the shooter as a target for return fire, which explains why it's used so rarely.

Heckler & Koch has also created laser sights for its rifles and some of its pistols. These sights project an intense dot of red light, providing the shooter with an opportunity to aim quickly without having to align the front and rear sights. Laser sights have become especially popular with police forces. An officer can now enter a room and concentrate on possible targets without having to worry about sight alignment. Wherever the dot lands marks the point where the bullet will hit when fired. In some police scenarios, a criminal suspect will give up immediately upon seeing the laser dot. He knows that a rifle or pistol bullet will strike should he continue to resist.

Weighed against these and other advantages of the laser sight are some important shortcomings. In addition to being quite expensive, the laser is prac-

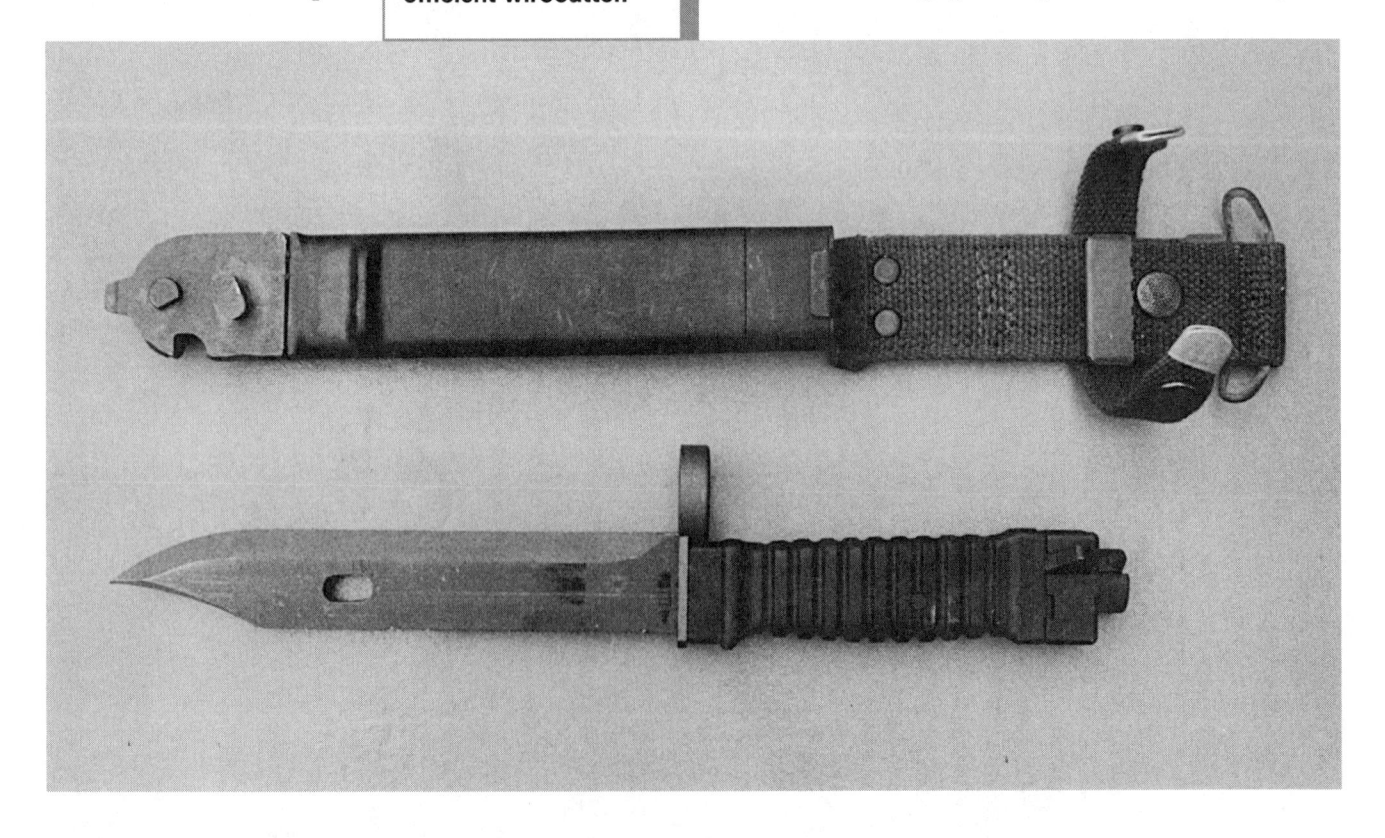

> The G3 bayonet is a useful multipurpose device that, in consort with its scabbard, makes a reasonably efficient wirecutter.

194 Heckler & Koch

tically useless in bright daylight, rain or fog. Furthermore, unlike a flashlight, the laser does nothing to help the shooter identify his target, which means he must first ascertain who or what exactly is under his sights. Also, with several shooters using laser sights simultaneously (which may well happen with a police SWAT team), it's difficult, if not impossible, to know whose sights belong to whom. The laser sight also offers a target for return fire. Finally, a laser sight requires batteries, which must be properly maintained and charged prior to each mission.

For all these disadvantages, laser sights have come a long way. Early units were large, bulky and fragile, while their modern counterparts are surprisingly compact. Heckler & Koch also offers a replacement front sight assembly with a luminous tritium element. It enables a shooter to aim more effectively at night using G3-type rifles and P7, USP and Mark 23-type pistols. As with laser sights, a tritium-illuminated night sight does not illuminate the target, nor does it help shooters identify their targets. Another danger point with luminous sights is that an enemy who manages to maneuver *behind* a shooter who is so equipped can then locate *his* target!

> Since the end of the war in Vietnam, the development of grenade launchers has centered around units attached to the underside of specially-modified rifles. The M203, attached to an M16A1 rifle, went into series production in 1969. This combination has inspired a number of copies, including several from Heckler & Koch (photo courtesy of Defense Visual Information Center).

Chapter Six 195

Part IV: Accessories

Even when it's something as mundane as a rifle sling, Heckler & Koch can create a wonder; specifically, a multipurpose web rifle sling (**photos p. 177, 178**) that allows shooters to carry their rifles either across the chest, on either shoulder, or in the middle of the back. With this in place, the rifle is ready to fire rapidly from the hip or shoulder. Whatever firing position is adopted, the H&K sling will stabilize and keep the rifle close at hand. Heckler & Koch developed this unit originally for the G3, but it works as well with the HK33, G41 and other G3-type rifles. A sling with a traditional leather configuration is also available, though it lacks the versatility of H&K's web sling.

Beginning with the G41, Heckler & Koch began marketing a carrying handle for its rifle line. It now offers a modified carry handle as an add-on feature for all of its service rifles and submachine guns, including the G3/HK91, HK33/93 or MP5/HK94 series. With this accessory, a soldier can carry his rifle like a piece of luggage; witness the world-famous Belgian FN-FAL rifle.

In the past, Heckler 7 Koch has made available two basic handguard types for its military rifles. The first was narrow and had a circular cross section, called the "slimline" handguard. Then, early in the development of the 5.56mm/.223 caliber HK33, Heckler & Koch introduced a broader version. Early HK33s used a slimline handguard, though, which is still available as an option. H&K now offers a choice of

This Heckler & Koch catalog from the early 1990s shows the wide variety of accessories the company offers with its various military and police rifles and submachine guns.

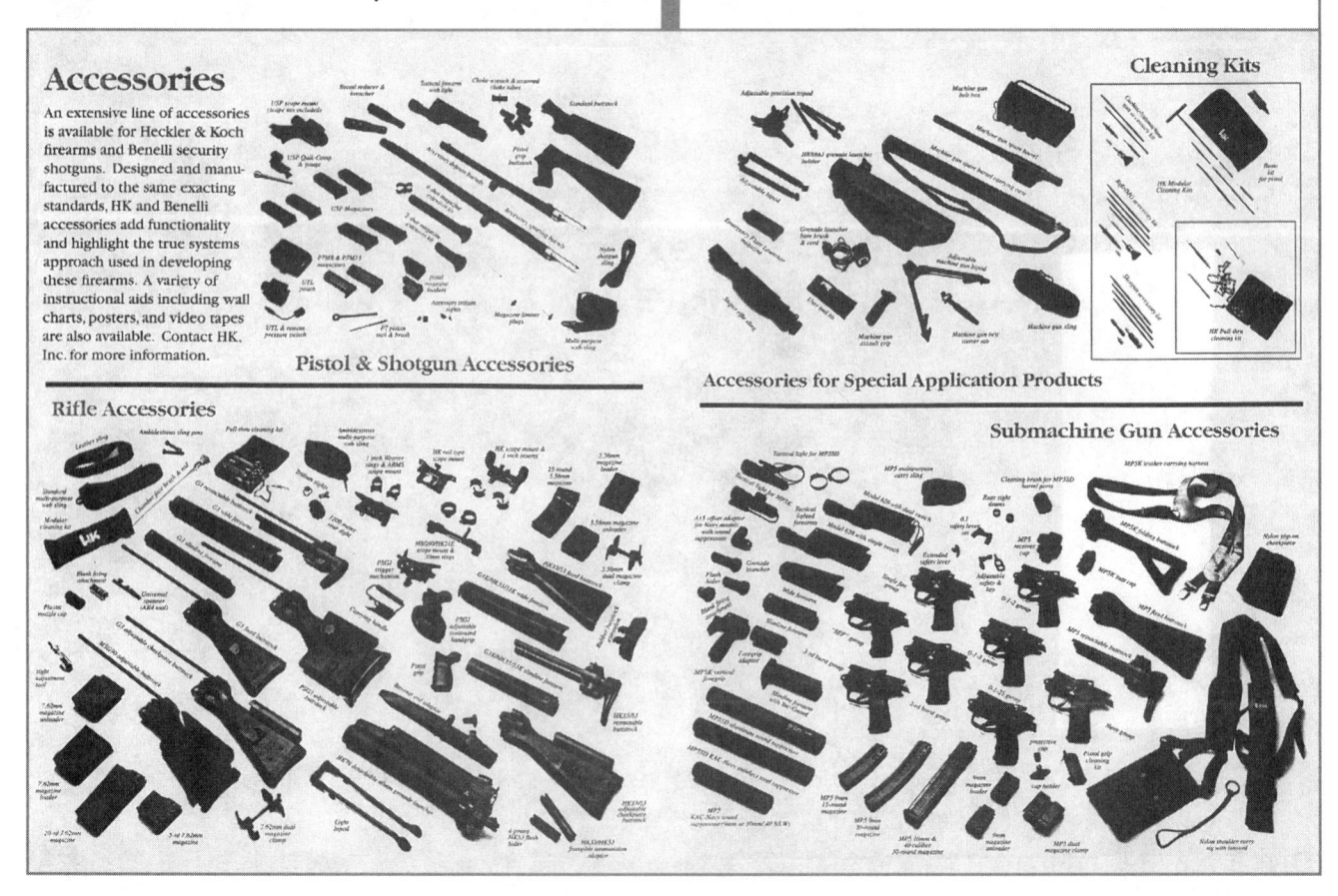

slimline and wide handguards with virtually every long arm derivative of the G3.

While a bayonet is of dubious value in modern military engagements, Heckler & Koch does make one for the G3/HK33 series. It has a special adapter **(photos p. 188, 189, 190)** fitted to the end of the cocking-handle tube. Like many contemporary bayonets, the G3 model features a relatively short 6.9-inch blade, which is actually not a bad combat knife. It also functions as a wire cutter.

Germany is cold for much of the year, so firearms manufacturers there generally manufacture triggerguards large enough to accommodate a gloved trigger finger. Heckler & Koch firearms are no exception to this general rule. In times of extreme cold, however, a glove will not suffice. Instead, the shooter requires mittens, which Heckler & Koch also provides on request for use with a winter trigger assembly, featuring a sheet-steel extension that clips onto the trigger and extends below the triggerguard. The U.S. M1 Garand and M14 rifles use a similar mechanism, as did Germany's Model 98 Mauser bolt action rifle.

Obviously, this setup makes for a potential safety hazard involving the elongated trigger, which can easily catch on brush or some other snag, causing accidental firing. A triggerguard, of course, is supposed to prevent such things from happening, but extending the trigger negates the safety aspect of the triggerguard. Given the potential among military organizations to misplace things when they're most needed, one wonders if such a device would actually be made available to soldiers when they most need them. Perhaps Heckler & Koch will develop a hinged triggerguard, one that a shooter can simply pull down and out of the way when cold weather arrives. Colt did this with its M16A1 rifle.

Another important accessory is a .22 Long Rifle adapter kit made by Heckler & Koch for its G3 (7.62mm/.308) and the HK33 (5.56mm/.223) series. Each of these kits consisted of a barrel insert, a bolt and two spare magazines carried in a hard case. Because of the .22LR's comparatively low recoil, no roller-locking feature is necessary as on high-powered centerfire bolts; instead, it is a simple blowback unit that relies on its own inertia and spring pressure to keep the breech shut until firing chamber pressure has dropped to a safe level. These conversion kits cost several hundred dollars, but they are worth the expense over the long run, what with centerfire rifle ammunition becoming so expensive when shooting several hundred rounds at a stretch.

For military training, Heckler & Koch developed two BFAs (blank firing attachments). One is used with blank ammunition whose cartridge case has no bullet but is instead crimped at the end to emit a bright flash when fired. The other BFA type works with blank cartridges topped with wooden bullets and features a "bullet trap" at the muzzle end to shred the bullets as they pass through, causing them to fall harmlessly to the ground.

Heckler & Koch created a version of the MP5 submachine gun—the MP5SD—with a highly efficient sound suppression system that greatly reduced the noise caused by firing. The company has also developed an add-on silencer of the "muzzle can" type, which clamps over the flash suppressor of a G3-type rifle to provide a useful measure of sound attenuation. While not as quiet and easy to operate as the MP5SD, this unit reduces the noise level of a rifle cartridge by stifling the loud report that ensues upon firing. It also serves an extremely useful tactical purpose by making it more difficult for people who are being fired upon to locate the source of the noise. If greater sound suppression is required, a shooter might also press a .22 Long Rifle adapter kit (see above) into service. The .22LR cartridge lends itself to sound suppression far more readily than do the .223 or .308 caliber cartridges. • **H&K**

On November 17, 1997, all import permits on foreign semiautomatic rifles were rescinded by the government until such time as BATF could determine which of these rifles were in fact "suitable for sporting purposes." Since the changes Springfield had made to the SAR-3 in creating the SAR-8 had already received government approval, the company was naturally upset......

Chapter 7

Worldwide Copying Of Heckler & Koch Designs

Worldwide demand for Heckler & Koch designs, most notably the G3 service rifle, led to the licensed production of H&K designs in a number of foreign countries. Simpler to manufacture than the competing FAL, G3 rifles were built in even more foreign countries under license than the Belgian rifle. Among the foreign licensees were Burma, France, Great Britain,

From 1990 to 1997, Springfield Armory's SAR-8 replaced the SAR-3. Among the differences between it and earlier G3-type rifles was a thumbhole-type sporterized stock and a non-functional muzzle device styled to resemble a flash suppressor.

By G3 standards, the Springfield Armory, Inc. SAR-8 is a pleasure to fire.

Greece, Iran, Norway, Pakistan, Portugal, Sweden and Turkey. Several of these licensees have competed with Heckler & Koch for foreign business, and dozens more have used the G3–and, to a lesser extent, the HK33-for their own armed forces at one time or another. As a result, the practical and efficient G3 mechanism has been, and remains, widely available. Several foreign countries have also undertaken the manufacture of other Heckler & Koch firearms, notably the HK33 service rifle, the MP5 submachine gun and the HK21 machine gun.

Following is a brief history of each major licensee of Heckler & Koch firearms, arranged alphabetically by country.

Burma

The Asian country of Burma (now known as Myanmar) bought its first batch of G3 rifles in 1963. A dozen years later, the country began domestic production, settling on the G3A3, with its fixed plastic buttstock, slightly modified to meet local requirements. A special variant with a heavier barrel and a more substantial bipod came on line in 1980. It was an attempt to provide superior fully-automatic capability, but like most such attempts with the relatively powerful 7.62x51mm cartridge this clone worked better when limited to semiautomatic fire. Nevertheless, the heavier barrel did help to improve accuracy.

AT RIGHT: Springfield's SAR-8 was highly accurate, witness the results of this test at 100 yards.

BELOW: The G-3 Millennium Sporter makes an excellent choice for a police force on a budget.

Chapter Seven 201

Disassembling an SAR-8 rifle reveals the typical G3 mechanism beneath the skin, so to speak.

Burma/Myanmar has since turned to its G3-type rifles often during that country's long civil war with the indigenous Karen tribe. In addition, the lucrative drug trade involving the "Golden Triangle" (including Burma) has increased demand for the G3 among Burmese army and security forces.

Though not originally created for jungle warfare, the G3 has by all accounts served extremely well in Burma and other countries located in extensive tropical rain forest terrain. The G3's ruggedness, reliability and easy fieldstripping for maintenance purposes have all combined to ensure good performance in Burmese service. Its only drawbacks center around its weight and size.

France

The French firm of Manufacture Nationale d'Armes de Saint-Etienne (MAS) began producing G3A3-type rifles under license in the 1960s, mostly by assembling rifles with which to equip the West German police, forbidden by treaty to use German-made weapons. By this technicality—involving the assembly of rifles from German-made parts in a foreign country—West Berlin's native German police force was able to use the same firearms as the rest of the country. The same arrangement had been made for pistols. At first, the West Berlin police carried the .32 caliber HK4 (assembled by MAS) before switching in the late 1960s to the more powerful Walther P38/P1 and, later, the similar Walther P4. The French company Manurhin assembled these Walther-designed pistols from parts supplied by Walther.

After completing its small West German police order, MAS continued to build G3A3s for countries within France's sphere of influence. These countries, who felt that ordering guns directly from Germany would be politically awkward, included Gabon, Ivory Coast, Lebanon, Mauritania, Morocco, Niger, Senegal and Upper Volta. Eventually, MAS' business became quite lucrative, to the point where

The Springfield Armory, Inc. SAR-8 (bottom) joined the Century International Arms L1A1 Sporter (top), thereby making available two of the world's most famous military rifle designs in commercial form.

it added the 5.56mm (.223 caliber) HK33 to its product line. Interestingly, the French armed forces themselves never expressed interest in any of the Heckler & Koch product lines, preferring their native designs. In 1978, MAS and the French government passed over the HK33 for an order of 20,000 guns to equip elements of the French army and the Foreign Legion in favor of SIG's Model 540 (later switching to the French-made FAMAS).

In 1990, financial difficulties brought Heckler & Koch close to bankruptcy. The first to offer the company a way out of its dilemma was GIAT, a giant French arms consortium with extensive foreign holdings, including FN and USRAC, among others. However, Heckler & Koch, with its traditional German outlook, and GIAT, with its French world view, were unable to agree on various matters. These ranged from personnel decisions to pensions to servicing foreign contracts. In any event, negotiations fell through, ending France's involvement in the Heckler & Koch story.

Great Britain

Britain has also produced HK rifles extensively. The Royal Small Arms Factory (RSAF) took up production of the G3 after it had ceased production of the L1A1 (British-licensed FAL) in 1975, before the plant had tooled up for the SA-80 service rifle. The British military concentrated on the fixed-stock G3A3 variant, while also making the collapsible-stock G3A4 on special order. Enfield sold some G3A3s to Kenya, Nigeria, Qatar, Tanzania, Zaïre and Zambia, while G3A4s went to Kenya. The RSAF also built the HK33 and sold some to Ghana, Lebanon and Tanzania.

Unlike France, the British Army showed some interest in the G3 and HK33. The elite SAS, along with some counterterrorist units of the British police, employed the G3 and HK33 along with

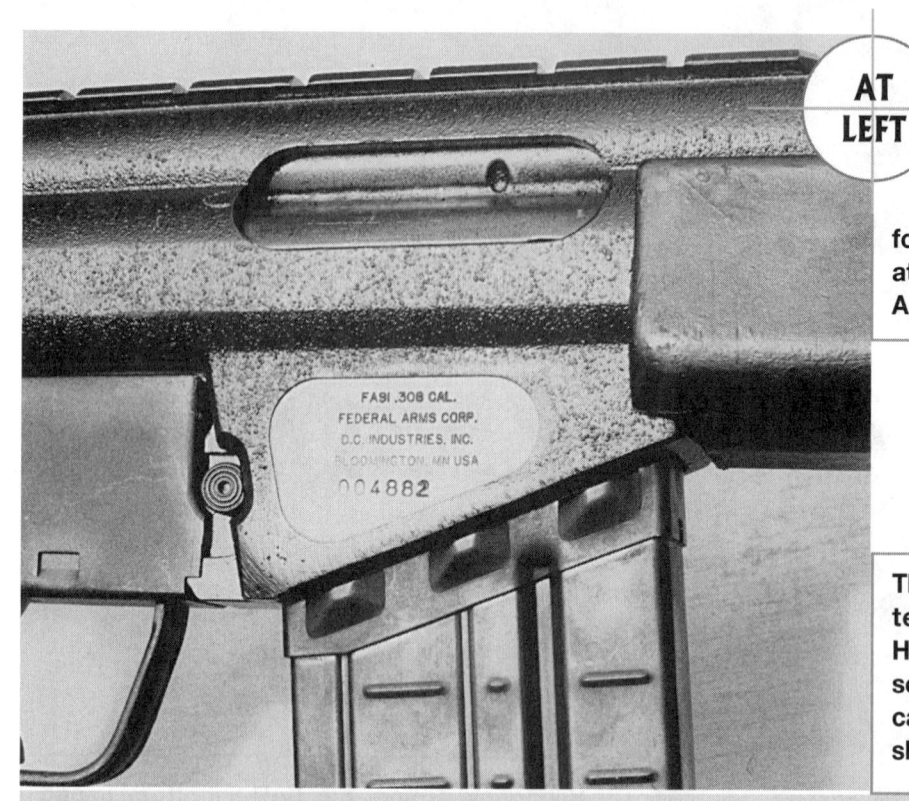

AT LEFT — D.C. Industries (Bloomington, MN) produces the G-3 Millennium Sporter's receiver for both Federal Arms Corporation and Century International Arms.

BELOW — The G-3 Millennium Sporter, like all commercial Heckler & Koch variants, offers semiautomatic fire only. S indicates safe and E indicates one shot for each pull on the trigger

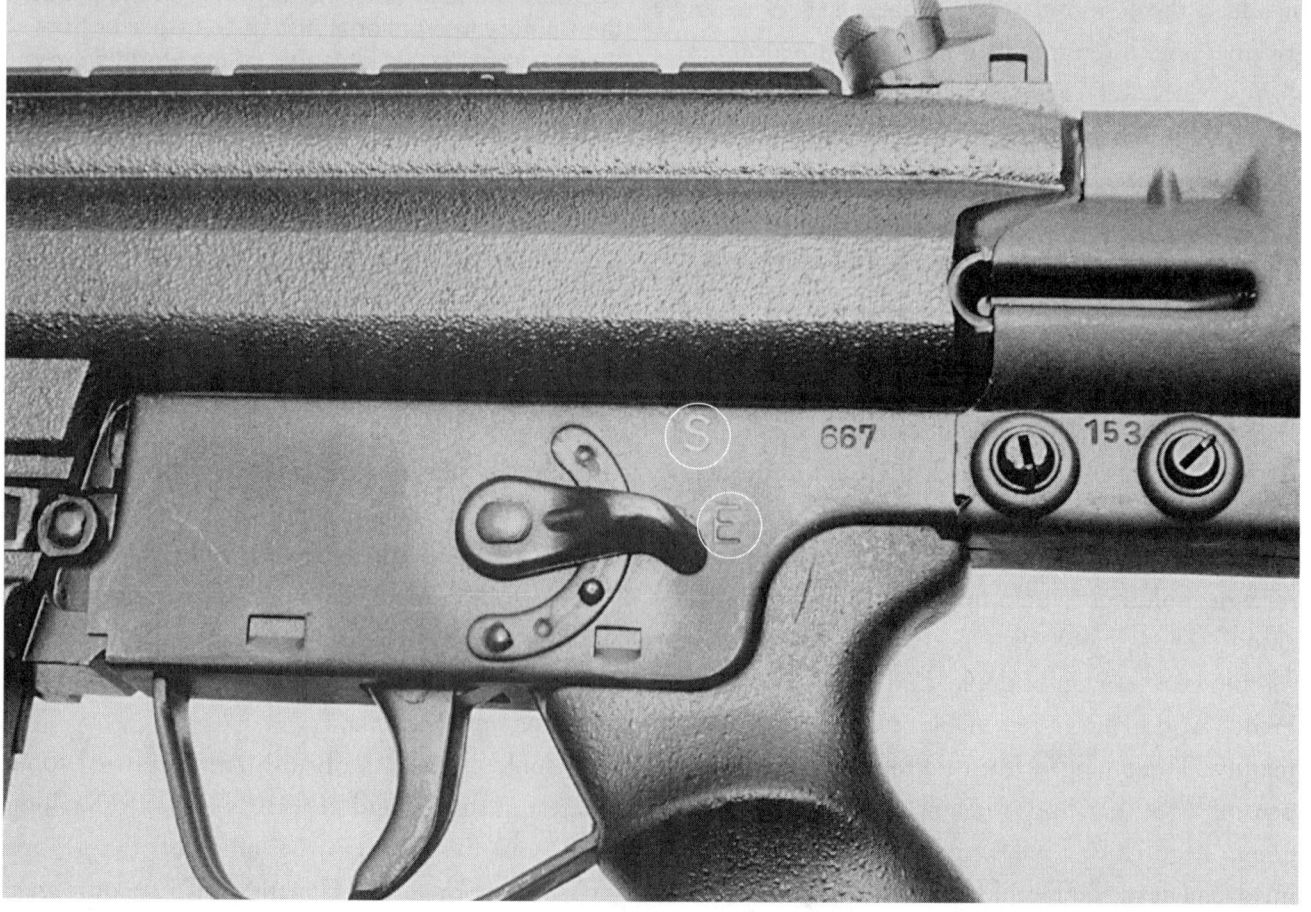

204　Heckler & Koch

The G-3 Millennium Sporter represents the latest semiautomatic-only G3 variant, combining traditional G3 furniture with a newly-manufactured and machined aluminum-alloy receiver.

several 9mm MP5 submachine gun variants. The British were even more intimately involved in the Heckler & Koch story than RSAF's production figures would suggest, as evidenced by the Royal Ordnance plc's acquisition of Heckler & Koch in 1991. As a result, production of the G3 and HK33 continues to this day, although the ultimate fate of this program has yet to be determined.

Greece

In 1930, Greece bought several thousand Mauser 98-type military bolt-action rifles and, following World War II, received 188,000 M1 Garand-type rifles (thanks to U.S. military aid). After replacing some of these aging weapons with Belgian-made FAL and FAL-Para rifles, the Greek army purchased in 1974 a selection of G3A3 and G3A4 rifles. Their purpose was to see if these weapons might serve as an adequate replacement for all the service rifles acquired earlier. The service trials went so well that the Greek government acquired a manufacturing license for both G3A3 (fixed stock) and G3A4 (collapsible stock) models from Heckler & Koch. The Greek licensee for Heckler & Koch products is EBO, for *Elleniki Biomichanika Opion* (meaning "Hellenic [Greek] Arms Industry"). Subsequently, the Greek armed forces ordered 200,000 G3s from EBO, which began delivering G3 rifles to Greek armed forces in 1979. Arrangements were later made to produce the 9mm Parabellum MP5 submachine gun and the 7.62mm HK11 light machine gun for local use and export as well. At this writing, all three guns remain standard Greek service issue.

By the mid-1980s, EBO was well on its way to satisfying Greek military orders and began looking for export customers. Springfield Armory (now Springfield, Inc.) began importing EBO rifles of the

Chapter Seven   **205**

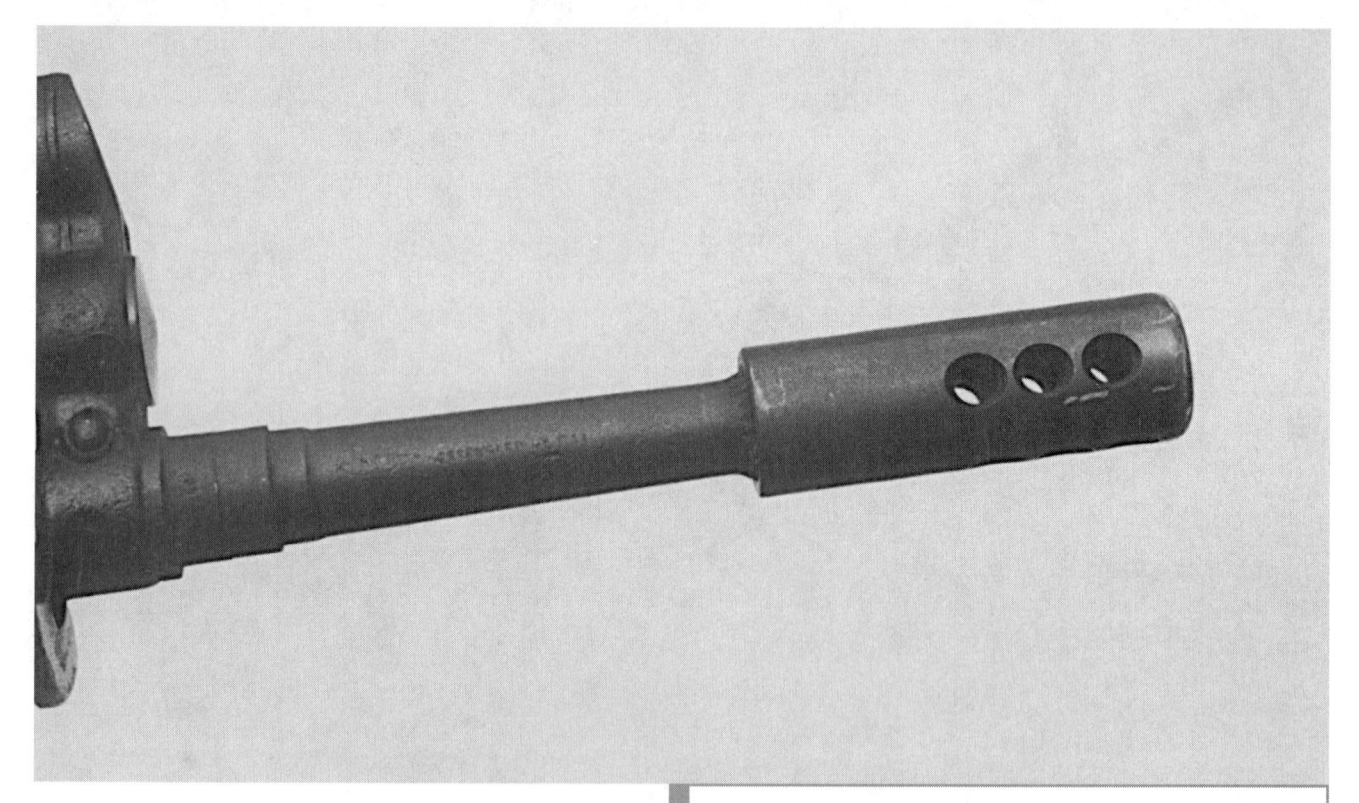

The G-3 Millennium Sporter's muzzle device includes three holes which serve as a muzzle brake. The device is permanently welded to the barrel as shown.

semiautomatic-only G3 type (equivalent to the HK91) into the U.S. beginning in 1985. Until 1989, Springfield called this rifle the SAR-3, assembling SAR-3s at its plant in Geneseo, Illinois, from parts kits supplied by EBO.

Springfield made two distinct SAR-3 subtypes. The SAR-3 Standard Model featured a fixed black plastic stock, similar to the HK91A-2. The SAR-3 Retractable Stock Model was like the HK91A-3, featuring a collapsible twin-strut metal stock. Both rifles had 18-inch barrels and 20-round box magazines.

With its SAR-3, Springfield Armory was able to offer U.S. firearms customers an HK-91-type rifle at a much lower price than a German-made gun from Heckler & Koch's own Oberndorf plant, including complete parts interchangeability and identical handling and performance.

As with Heckler & Koch, Inc. and other importers of military-style rifles limited to semiautomatic fire, Springfield Armory was forced to stop importation of the SAR-3 in 1989 following the U.S. government's order banning the import of rifles with overtly military-style features.

Limited production of the modified SAR-8 began at Geneseo in 1990. Mechanically identical to the HK91 and SAR-3, the SAR-8 featured a thumbhole "sporterized" stock and a fake flash suppressor (a nonfunctional muzzle attachment used solely for looks). In 1992, after it had expanded its automatic pistol product line too ambitiously, the company went out of business. Reorganized as Springfield, Inc. in late 1993, the company resumed sales of the SAR-8, using receivers supplied by EBO.

On November 17, 1997, all import permits on foreign semiautomatic rifles were rescinded by the government until such time as BATF could determine which of these rifles were in fact "suitable for sporting purposes." Since the changes Springfield had made to the SAR-3 in creating the SAR-8 had already received government approval, the company was naturally upset by this decision. In any event, the SAR-8 did not pass government muster and is no longer imported, thus sharing the fate of the SR9 series then imported by Heckler & Koch, Inc. While the loss of U.S. business hurt EBO some, they were still supplying other armed forces and commercial customers with H&K rifles.

Selector markings on EBO-made rifles destined for Greek service include AΣ on top (for safe), BB in the middle (for semiautomatic fire), and BP on the bottom (for automatic fire). Rifle markings for U.S. sales were a white S on top for safe and a red F below for fire.

The Springfield SAR-8 is a well-made and highly accurate semiautomatic rifle. Indeed, it ranks high among the most accurate rifles of any type the author has ever tested (a three-shot group fired from 100 yards grouped as small as 9/10ths of an inch). The SAR-8 shared other, less benign handling characteristics common to rifles based on the G3 design. These included vigorous ejection of spent cartridge casings–about 15-20 feet to the right side and slightly ahead of the shooter–and etched cartridge cases from the fluted firing chamber.

Iran

In 1971, Iran, then ruled by Shah Mohammed Reza Pahlavi, placed a large, lucrative order with Heckler & Koch. The contract called for several hundred thousand G3A3 fixed stock and G3A4 collapsible-stock rifles. The Iranians also purchased a production license allowing them to build a plant in Mosalsalasi capable of producing large numbers of G3-

Springfield Armory, Inc.'s imported its SAR-3 from Greece between 1985 and 1989 in both fixed-stock and collapsible-stock forms (courtesy of Springfield Armory, Inc.)

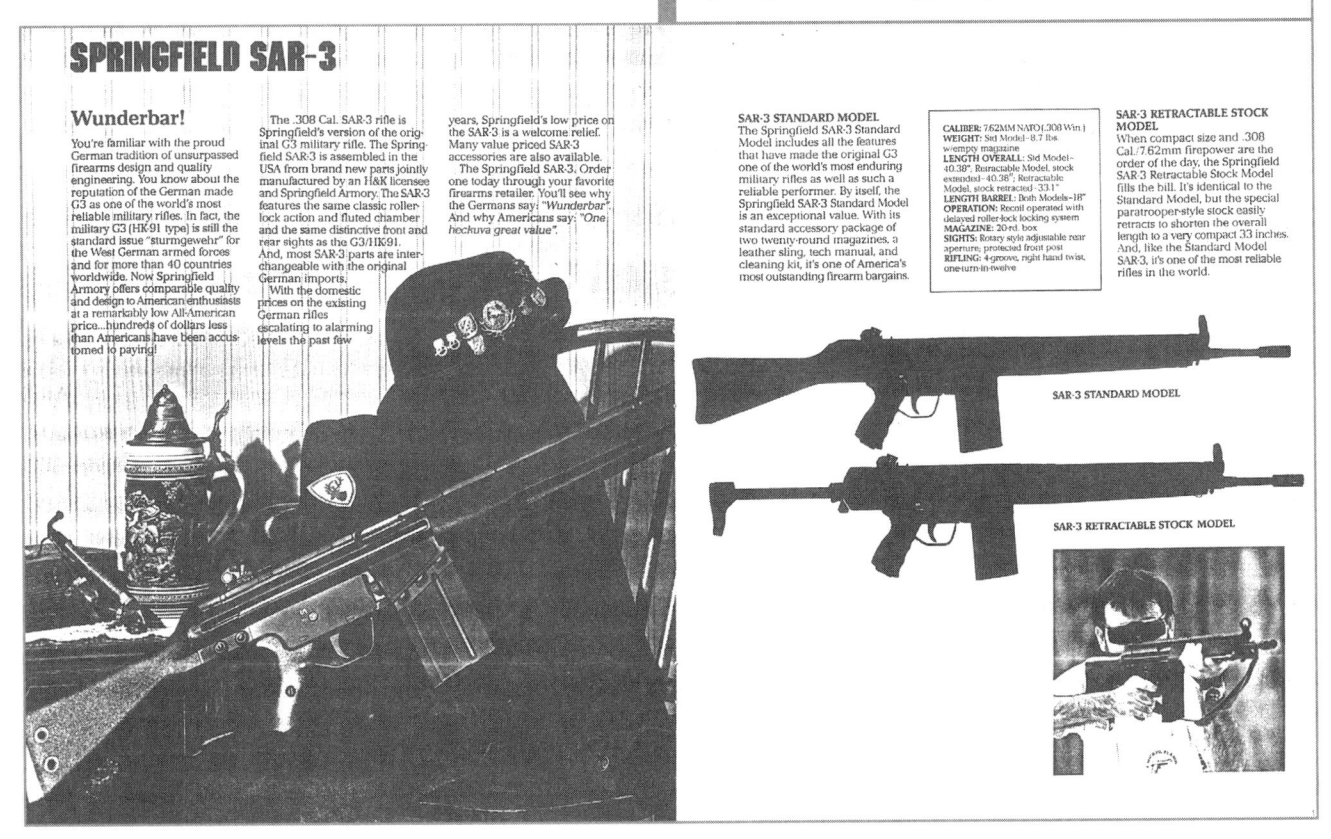

Chapter Seven 207

The G-3 Millennium Sporter's machined aluminum alloy receiver features an integral rail to simplify the mounting of a scope or other aiming devices.

type weapons for its army. For this production at the Mosalsalasi factory, Heckler & Koch developed a G3 variant–the G3A6–especially to Iranian specifications. Before the Islamic Revolution of 1979 and the eight-year war with Iraq that began the following year, the Mosalsalasi factory produced 145,000 of these rifles annually. By 1985, this figure had dropped by two-thirds as the disruptions of war and poor Iranian management took their toll.

Malaysia

Malaysia's armed forces were among the earliest official users of the .223 caliber (5.56x45mm) HK33 rifle. In 1971 Heckler & Koch helped Malaysia set up a factory of its own to produce the HK33 domestically. Total Malaysian HK33 production ultimately reached about 50,000 rifles.

Mexico

Mexico has used Heckler & Koch military long arms extensively. Mexican police forces have been issued the MP5 submachine gun, and the military has carried the G3A3 and G3A4 rifles, the HK53 5.56/.223 caliber submachine gun, and the HK21A1 machine gun. After buying weapons directly from Heckler & Koch, the Mexican authorities decided in 1976 to undertake G3 production (and later the HK21A1) under license.

Norway

In 1964, Norway adopted the fixed-stock G3A3 as the *Automatisk Gevaer 3*, or AG3 (*Automatisk Gevaer* = Automatic Rifle). The country wasted no time tooling up for local production at the *Kongsberg Vapenfabrikk* (*Vapenfabrikk* = "Weapon" or "Arms Factory"). Kongsberg completed its first completely Norwegian-built rifles in December of 1966, with delivery to Norway's armed forces beginning in early 1967.

The earliest examples eliminated the folding operating handle, forcing shooters to insert a finger into a hole and pull the bolt back, much like the M3A1 submachine gun. Obviously, this arrangement proved unsatisfactory because of the G3's stiff recoil spring, just as it had in the much smaller M3A1 some 25 years earlier.

Moreover, it's not something one would want to try in Norway's extremely cold winter, whether wearing a glove, a mitten, or operating barehanded. Not surprisingly, the Norwegians soon reinstituted the standard German arrangement of a folding cocking handle on the rifle's left side. Later, the Kongsberg factory introduced an AG3 with an A4-type collapsible metal stock. Later still, a sniping version with telescopic sight and receiver limited to semiautomatic fire only was produced.

Norway's production of the AG3 has been intermittent and slow, leading the country's armed forces to buy G3s direct from Heckler & Koch from time to time to make up shortfalls. Norway also tested the HK33 rifle but did not proceed further because the small bullet lacked adequate penetration and lethality given the heavy winter clothing likely to be worn in the area. Beginning in 1989, however, Norway did buy MP5 submachine guns from Heckler & Koch to replace its aging World War II MP40 "Schmeisser" sub-machine guns left behind when the Germans surrendered in 1945.

Pakistan

The Pakistani armed forces began ordering G3-type rifles from Heckler & Koch in 1967. A year later, they bought a production license for the G3A2, with local production beginning at a government-owned arms factory in the city of Wah. Production shifted to the G3A3 variant in 1986.

The Pakistan military prefers guns with the broad "tropical" forearm. The furniture is brown

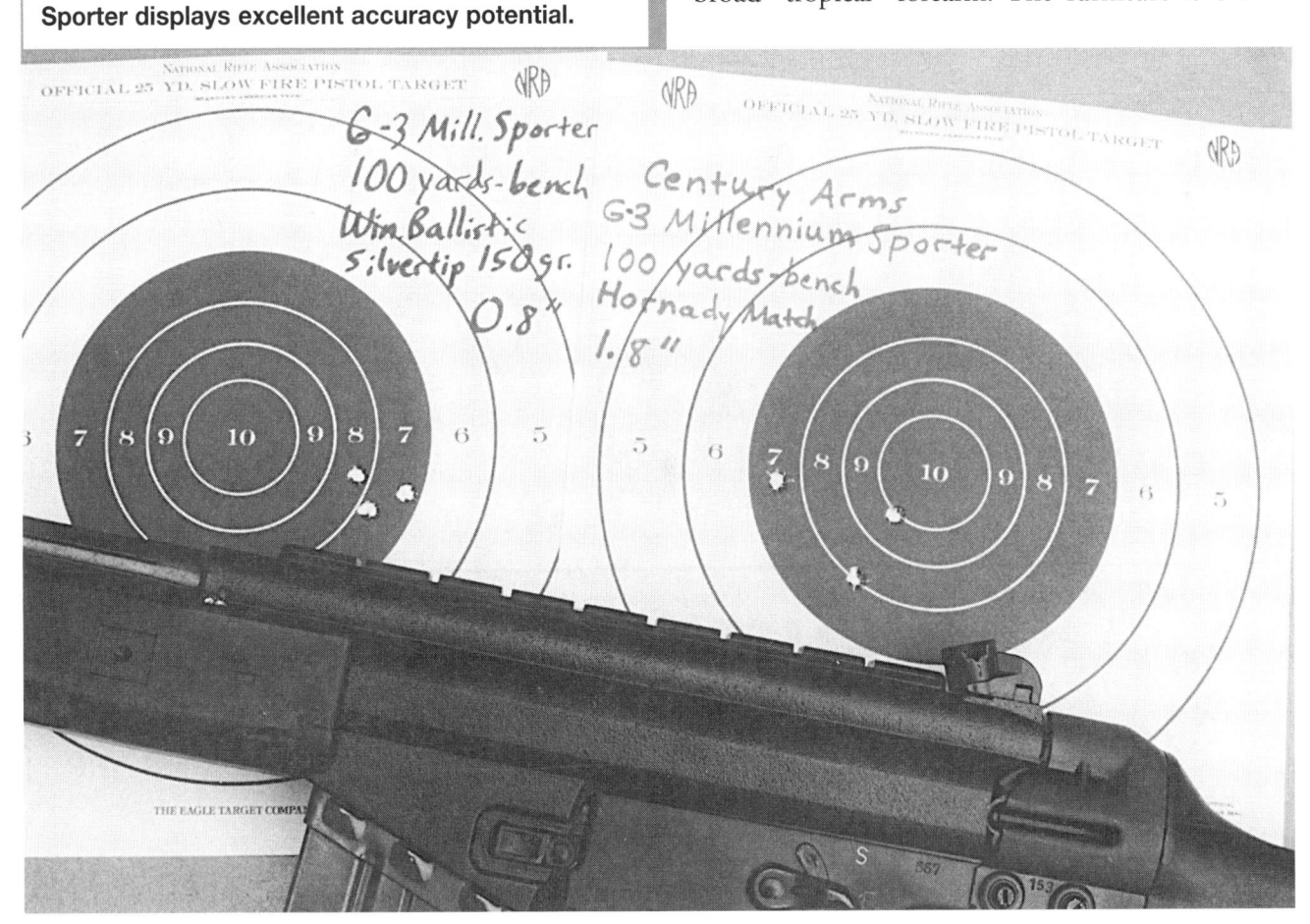

Like other G3-type rifles, the G-3 Millennium Sporter displays excellent accuracy potential.

Chapter Seven **209**

plastic well suited to the arid land. All metal parts have been painted and parkerized. Production continues and the G3A3 remains service issue. Pakistan has advertised its rifle widely and is believed to have made sales to other Asian and Islamic nations. One confirmed sale was that involving older surplus G3A2 rifles to Bangladesh.

Portugal

Portugal became an early convert to the Heckler & Koch system in 1961, when the *Fabrica Military de Braço de Prata*, or FMBP received an order from the West German government for the original G3 rifle. Once this order was completed, FMBP kept on building these rifles with the designation "*Espingarda Automatica Mo. 961.*" In 1963, the FMBP updated its production to the new G3A2 standards,

Above & Below. Although the SAR-8's safety/selector is not ambidextrous, its settings are visible on the receiver's right side. A white S indicates the safe setting, while a red 1 indicates semiautomatic firing mode (one shot for each pull on the trigger).

210 Heckler & Koch

changing its designation to "Mo. 963." Both rifles saw extensive use in Portugal's colonial wars in an unsuccessful effort to keep Angola and Mozambique as her possessions. At any rate, the Mo. 963 remains in service as the country's standard service rifle.

In 1968, FMBP bought a production license from Heckler & Koch for the HK21 machine gun, placing it in service as the M968. In 1985, Portugal bought several hundred HK33 parts kits from Heckler & Koch and assembled them in its FMBP plant for issue to selected troops for service trials and possible adoption. Eventually, the armed forces decided against switching to the smaller .223 caliber and dropped the HK33 project.

FMBP has also offered the Mo. 963 for foreign sales. Some modified Mo. 963-type rifles made in Portugal have new receivers limited to semiautomatic fire. These were imported into the United States in 1997, featuring distinctive jungle-green plastic furniture and the early-style slimline handguard. As with the SAR-8 and SR9 series, U.S. importation of these Portuguese G3 variants ceased in late 1997.

Saudi Arabia

The Kingdom of Saudi Arabia once made extensive use of G3-type rifles, starting in the early 1960s. After acquiring many of these weapons, first from West Germany and then from Great Britain, the Saudis obtained in 1968 a production license from Heckler & Koch. They then built a factory and made G3s for slightly more than a decade. Among its distinctive features was the receiver, whose left side was embellished with crossed scimitars and a palm tree, with some writing in both Arabic and English script.

Production stopped in 1980 in favor of the 5.56mm Steyr AUG, but large numbers of G3s were used to arm Saudi Arabian contingents of the coalition forces operating against Iraq during Operations Desert Shield and Desert Storm (1990-1991). During that period, the Saudis clearly preferred the G3's long-range abilities with the 7.62mm cartridge as opposed to the 5.56mm AUG. Finally, in addition to their own G3 needs, the Saudis supplied G3A3s to North Yemen and the United Arab Emirates.

Sweden

Sweden adopted the G3, which it designated the *Automatkarabin* 4 (Ak-4), in 1963. Resembling the German G3A3 variant, this Swiss rifle featured the standard slimline, rounded handguard. Immediately upon its adoption, the Swedish government bought a production license from Heckler & Koch, setting up two factories for Ak-4 production. Both the privately-owned *Husqvarna Vapenfabrik* ("Weapons Factory") and the government-owned *Carl Gustafs Stadts Geversfactori* ("State Rifle Factory") took up Ak-4 manufacture, delivering their first Ak-4 rifles (built locally) in 1965. By 1971, production was concentrated at the plant in *Eskilstuna* (now called *Forenade Fabriksverken*, or FFV.

Between 1979 and 1982, the Swedes tested 5.56mm/.223 service rifles, including Israeli Galils and Belgian FNCs modified to suit Swedish requirements, particularly with respect to cold-weather operation. Swedish AK-4 production stopped in 1985 in favor of the 5.56mm FN-designed FNC, which Sweden had adopted in a modified version in 1984 as their AK-5. Deliveries began in 1986, the Swedes having passed their Ak-4s on to the reserve and selling off large quantities of Ljungman AGB-42 semiautomatic rifles and the bolt-action Mauser Model 1896, which had been in reserve since the Ak-4 supplanted them.

Chapter Seven 211

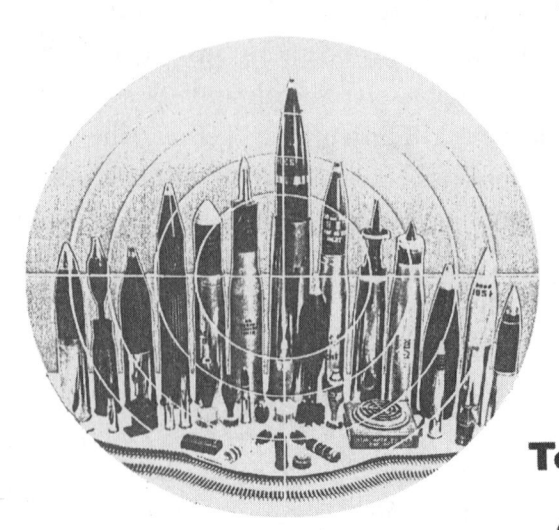

allowed to produce the rifles locally. It took about five years to tool up, with parts manufacture commencing in 1977 and the first guns issued in 1978. The Turkish guns are distinctive in appearance, featuring a collapsible stock. Because they differ so from all other G3s with regard to the stock design, Heckler & Koch gave the G3-type rifle (as ordered by the Turks) a special factory designation: G3A7. In addition to the unusual collapsible stock, the Turkish G3s have a prominent "MKE" marking on the right side of the magazine housing.

Thailand

The Thai armed forces were an early buyer of the .223 caliber (5.56x45mm) HK33 rifle. In 1975 Heckler & Koch helped the Thais set up a local factory to assemble the HK33 from parts imported from Germany. Production stopped after about 30,000 were made.

Pakistan began producing the G3A2 under license in 1968 and from 1986 advertised the G3A3 variant as well as an MP5 clone.

Turkey

Turkey purchased its first fixed-stock G3A3 and collapsible-stock G3A4 rifles from Heckler & Koch around 1972. As a NATO member, Turkey needed a modern rifle in the NATO-standard 7.62mm chambering to replace a hodgepodge of older rifles, most recently 312,00 M1 Garand rifles supplied by the U.S. The Turkish designation for the G3 was "*G3 Otomatic Piyade Tüfegi.*"

With a production license in hand, the *Makina v Kimya Endustrisi* (MKE) factory in Ankara was

United States

With Heckler & Koch's SR9 series and Springfield's, SAR-8 both unavailable in the U.S. from November 1997 on, Century International Arms (St. Albans, VT) took up the challenge of supplying G3-type rifles to the American trade. In early 1999, Century's "G-3 Millennium Sporter" **(photos p. 204-6)**

appeared. Based on the G3A3, with its thumbrest molded into the separate pistol grip and a small-diameter rounded handguard, the G3 Millennium Sporter boasts a new receiver made at the D.C. Industries plant (Blooming-ton, MN) including an integral Weaver-compatible scope rail of the same type developed in the 1970s at Picatinny Arsenal. Made of aluminum alloy machined to shape (in the manner of an M16 receiver), the G-3 Millennium Sporter's receiver is slightly thicker than the stamped sheet steel receiver of the Heckler & Koch G3. The added thickness compared to the original stamped sheet steel receiver makes operating the manual safety more difficult. It probably affects the proper functioning of some accessories as well. The G-3 Millennium Sporter's safety mechanism, modeled after that of early HK91 rifles, offers two positions: push down to fire, marked E (German for "*Einzelfeur*," meaning semiautomatic fire) and up to safe, marked S.

Following the lead of DS Arms, permission was obtained from BATF to add a muzzle device to the FAL spin-off by permanently attaching the device to the muzzle. A welded muzzle brake on the G3 Millennium Sporter adds 2½ inches to the barrel length.

The sighting system on the G-3 Millennium Sporter follows the current Heckler & Koch pattern, including a rotary three-position rear sight, with a front sight featuring a protective hood. The integral Weaver-compatible rail makes scope mounting easy as well,

The G-3 Millennium Sporter takes standard G3-type 20-round magazines. The example tested was a ribbed plastic pattern made in Portugal. The G-3 Millennium Sporter utilizes the less desirable push-button magazine release found in the commercial HK91 rifle, rather than the semi-ambidextrous lever release installed in the original G3. The magazine release pushes in from right to left and, while not great, it is certainly usable. Remember, though, that when inserting any magazine, it must be "rocked" in by first inserting the front portion all the way and then swinging the rear part up until it clicks, much like the AK-47, M14 and FAL magazines.

The G-3 Millennium Sporter used in the test proved highly accurate, producing three-shot 100-yard groups as small as 0.8 inch across and all less than two inches wide at that distance. Any semiautomatic service rifle that can shoot that well is indeed impressive.

Despite the change in receiver dimensions, the rest of this rifle remains faithful to the classic H&K design. The G-3 Millennium Sporter succeeds greatly in offering Heckler & Koch features and performance at a reasonable price.

Conclusion

With production, distribution and use of Heckler & Koch designs occurring on virtually a worldwide basis, it's clear that these designs, particularly the G3, have gained enormous respect. Less expensive to manufacture than its chief rival–FN's excellent FAL–Heckler & Koch's reliable G3 will doubtless show up on the world's battlefields for decades to come. • **H&K**

SPECIFICATIONS: H&K CLONES

	Overall Length (in.)	Barrel Length (in.)	Weight (lbs.)	Caliber	Magazine (rounds)
Springfield SAR-3	40.3	18.0	8.7	7.62mm/.308	20
Springfield SAR-8	40.3	18.0	8.7	7.62mm/.308	20
G-3 Millennium Sporter	40.5*	23.5	7.0	7.62mm/.308	20

*Note: Includes 2.5-inch device, permanently attached

As the new century evolves, combat shotgun design has reached an impasse. For all its faults, including hgh recoil, limited magazine capacity and short range, the 12-gauge shotgun remains a formidable weapon. A variety of relatively inexpensive, well-made and tested shotgun designs already exists. Intensive ammunition development over the past century has created several effective antiperonnel rounds......

Chapter 8

THE SHOTGUN STORY

Although Heckler & Koch has built only one new shotgun over the years, the company has merchandised several shotgun lines quite extensively from other companies, making them an important part of the company's history. This survey will begin by considering Heckler & Koch's own abortive CAW project, followed by the Franchi, Benelli and FABARM shotgun lines, all of which Heckler & Koch has marketed at one time or another. We will also consider the Joint Services Combat Shotgun (JSCS), a Heckler & Koch/Benelli partnership recently accepted by the U.S. Armed forces.

Part 1. The Close Assault Weapon (CAW)

The CAW, an acronym for Close Assault Weapon, first appeared in 1980 as a result of a Joint Services Small Arms (JSSAP) program, which was

The pump-action Mossberg Model 590, introduced in 1979, demonstrates how a combat shotgun can be made from a reliable sporting shotgun. This example lacks the usual perforated sheet metal heat shield around the barrel normally found on these guns.

Chapter Eight 215

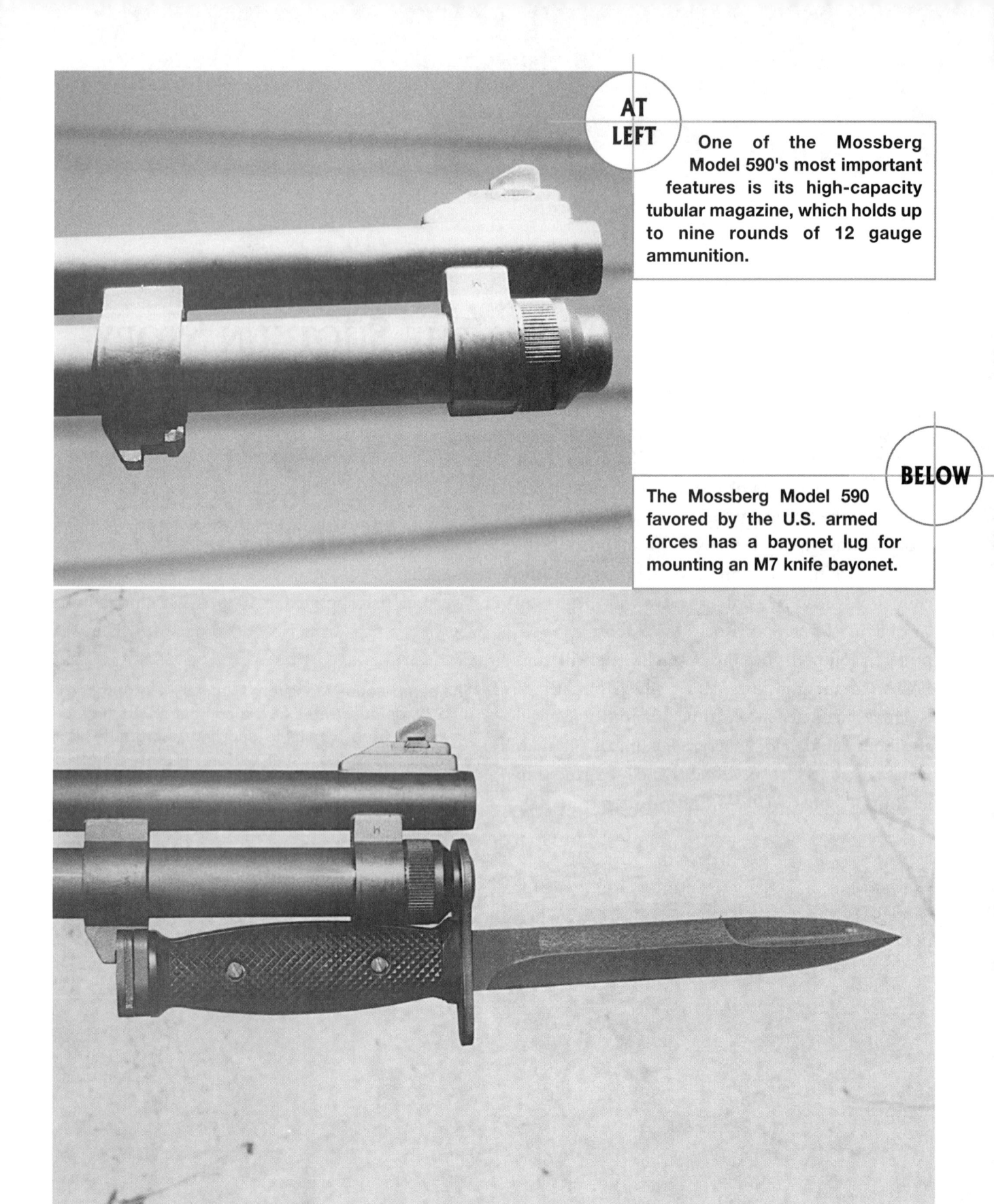

AT LEFT One of the Mossberg Model 590's most important features is its high-capacity tubular magazine, which holds up to nine rounds of 12 gauge ammunition.

BELOW The Mossberg Model 590 favored by the U.S. armed forces has a bayonet lug for mounting an M7 knife bayonet.

AT RIGHT

The fixed rear square notch sight on the M3 Super 90 offers sighting capabilities within the 100-yard distance considered maximum for most shotgun uses. Like the front sight, it includes recesses which the operator may fill with paint if desired.

BELOW

The M3 Super 90's cocked-hammer indicator consists of a small flag next to the triggerguard (marked with a red dot).

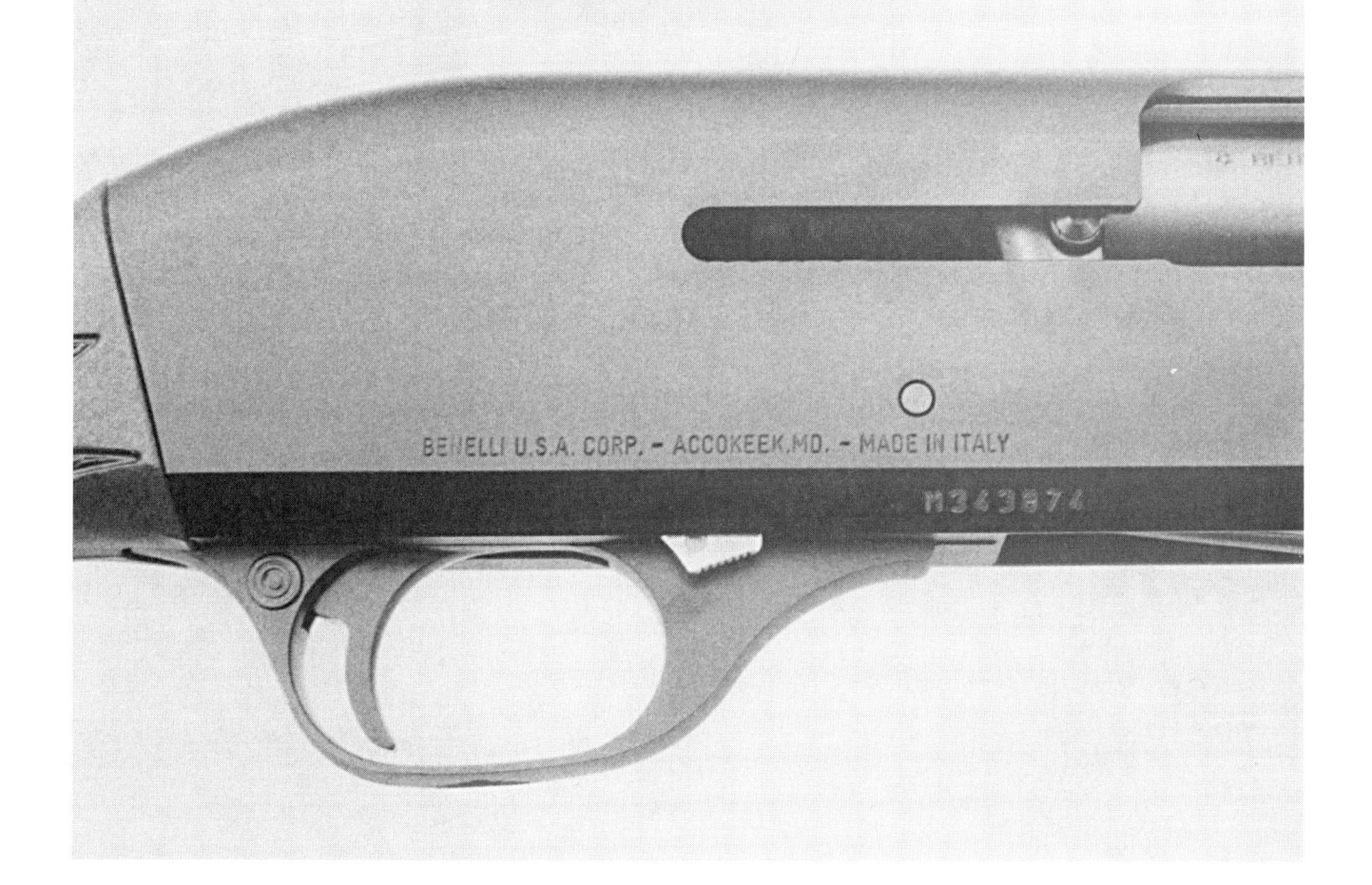

Chapter Eight 217

AT LEFT The M3 Super 90's mode-selection ring and barrel ring are joined by a hook beneath the forearm, enabling the gun to reload by manual pump action.

BELOW The M3 Super 90's mode-selection ring and barrel ring are shown pushed together (but not mechanically joined) by a connecting hook located below the forearm. The gun will reload itself automatically each time it's fired.

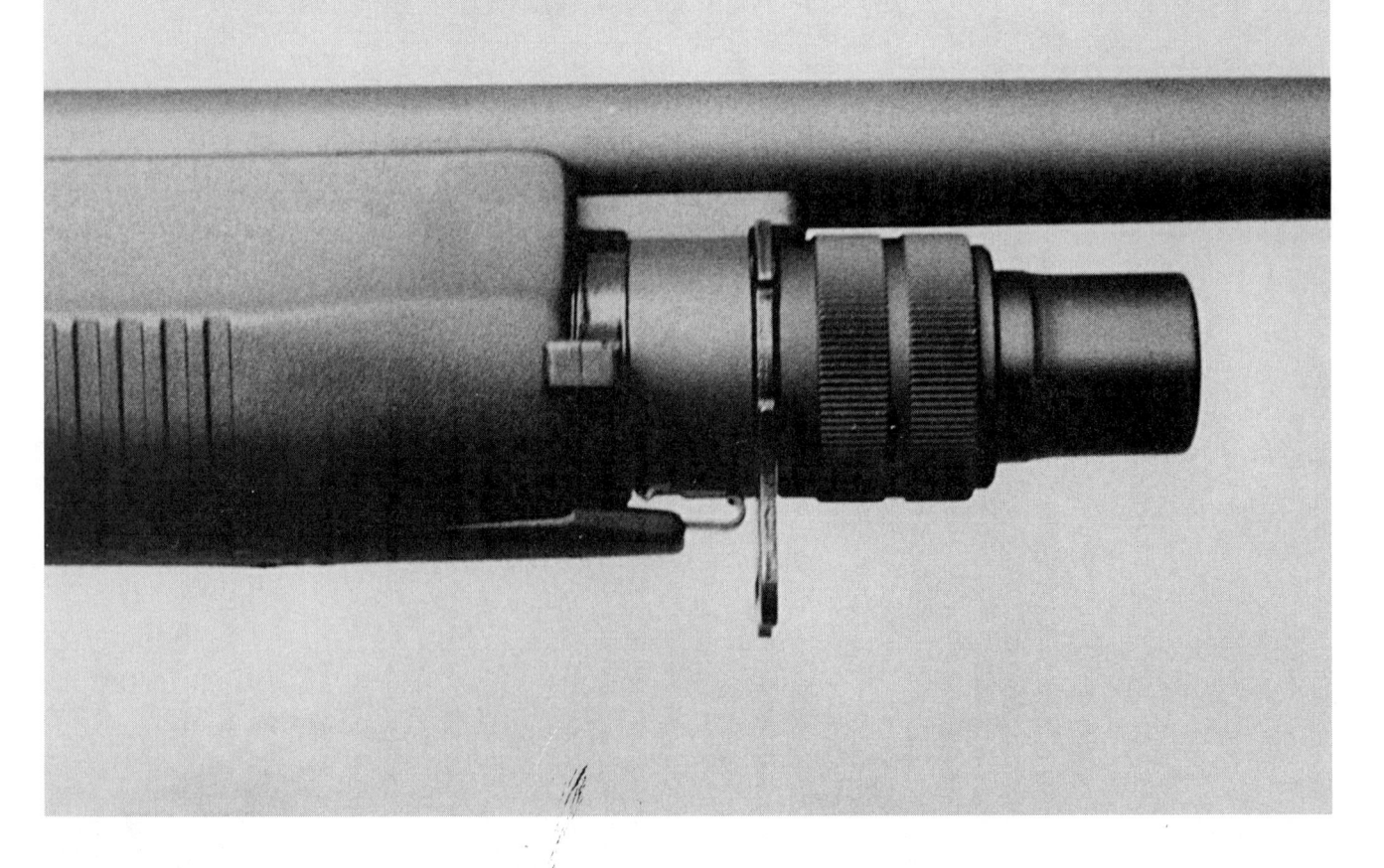

218   Heckler & Koch

Benelli's M3 Super 90 Entry Gun retains the combined semiautomatic and pump action options of Heckler & Koch's original M3 Super 90. This short-barreled (18-inch) model has a reduced-capacity, shortened tubular magazine to match.

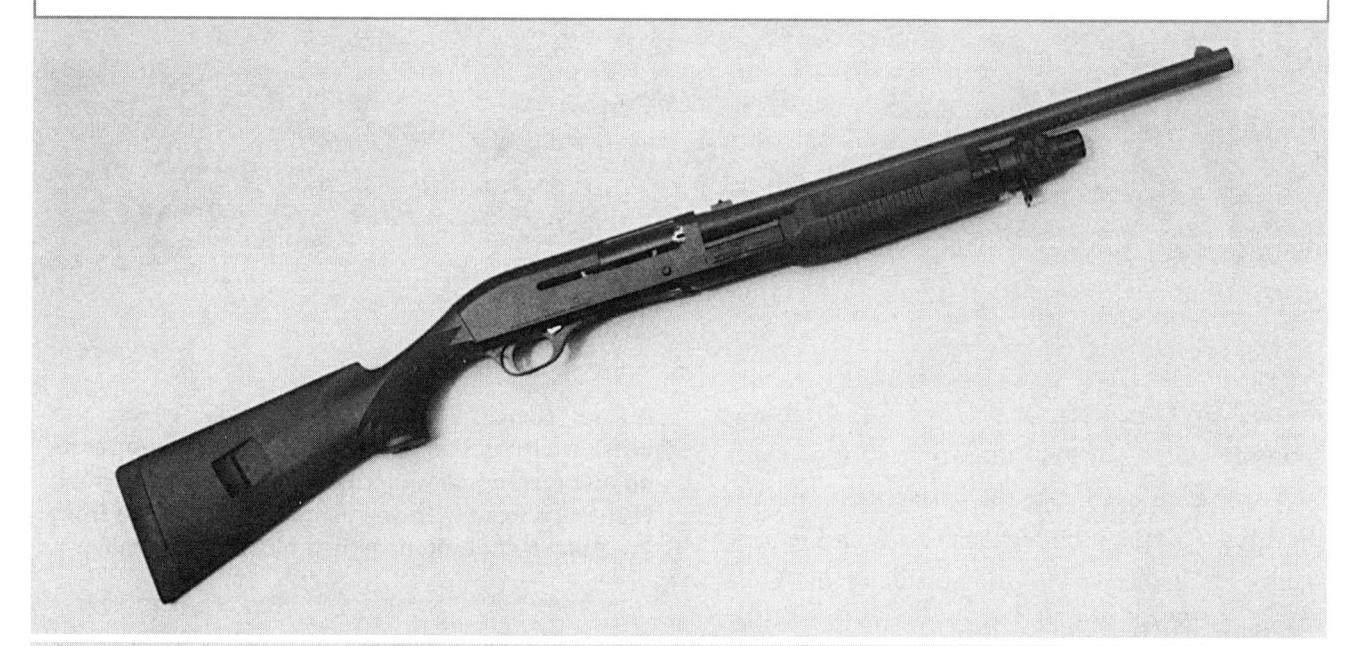

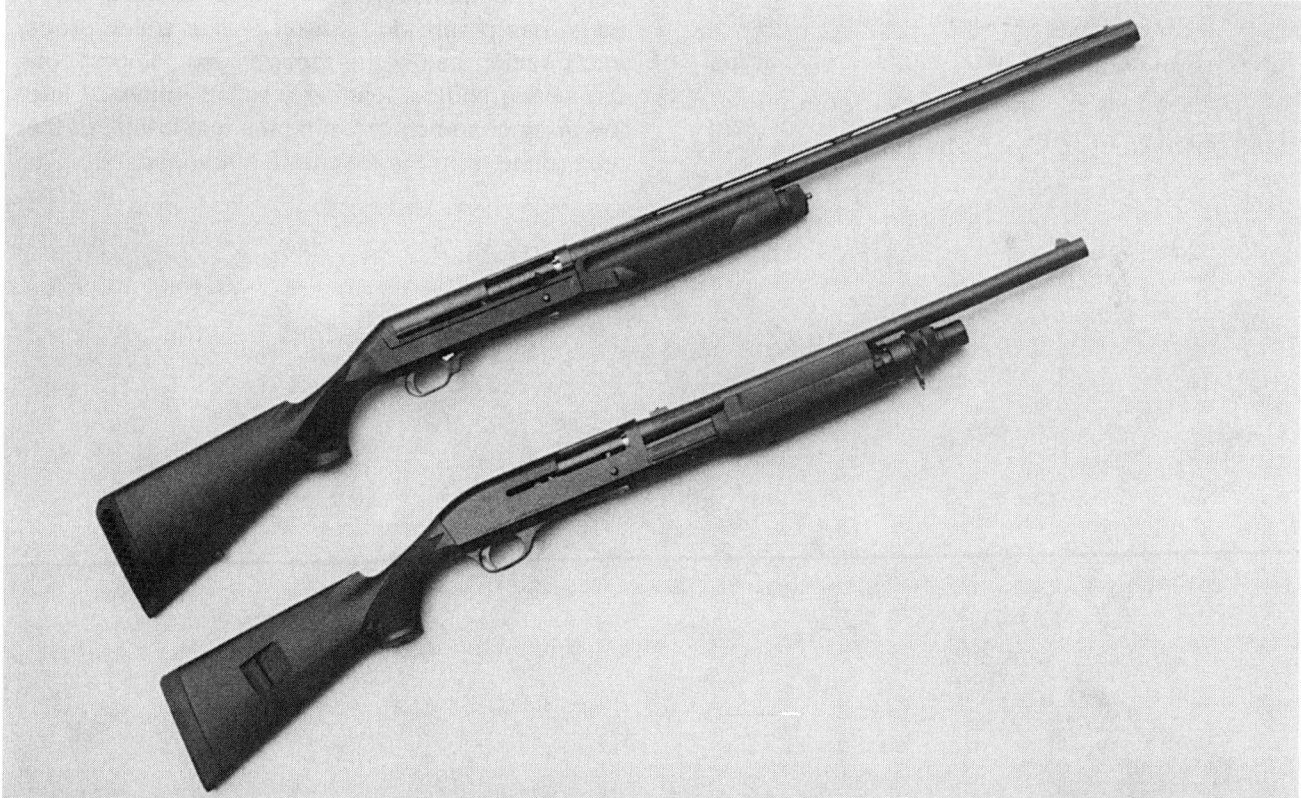

Two of Benelli's most popular shotguns are the semiautomatic Super Black Eagle (top), and the M3 Super 90 (bottom).

Chapter Eight 219

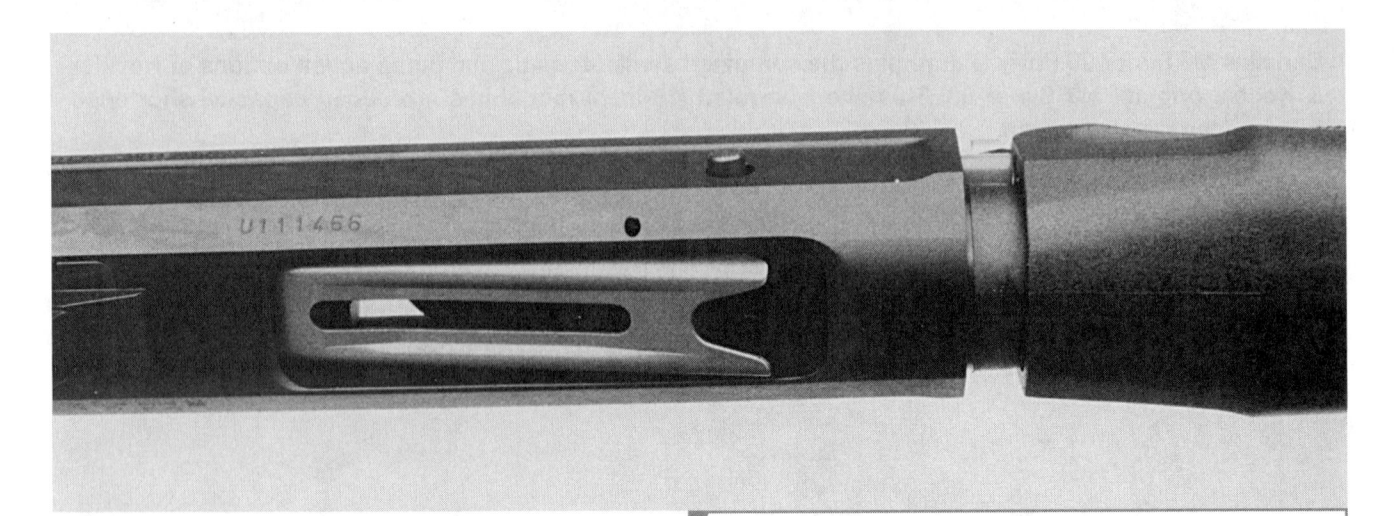

formed in December of 1978 by a committee sponsored jointly by the United States armed forces. Its task was to encourage the development of weapons built to meet the high standards and requirements of all the services. In pursuit of the CAW mandate, JSSAP sought a weapon suitable for use in raids, ambushes, search-and-destroy missions, survival situations, and other close-combat scenarios, both offensive and defensive. Continuing a trend observed in all U.S. Arms designs since World

Above. Benelli's Super Black Eagle, which has been in production since 1991, is a recoil-operated autoloading shotgun. The Benelli system, which features a fixed (non-recoiling) barrel, differs from the Auto-5 shotgun designed by John Browning.

Below. The latest version of Benelli's Super Black Eagle has a cartridge cut-off device which drops into position below the receiver, providing shooters with a choice: loading a round manually into the firing chamber, or letting the gun bring out the next round from the magazine automatically.

AT RIGHT

To determine by sight whether the hammer on this Super Black Eagle is cocked or not, note how the hammer shows through the slot for the cocking handle, indicating the hammer is uncocked.

BELOW

The Super Black Eagle's hammer is cocked and the gun is ready to fire when the hammer does not show through the cocking handle slot, or by noting the small flag protruding from the right side of the triggerguard.

Chapter Eight 221

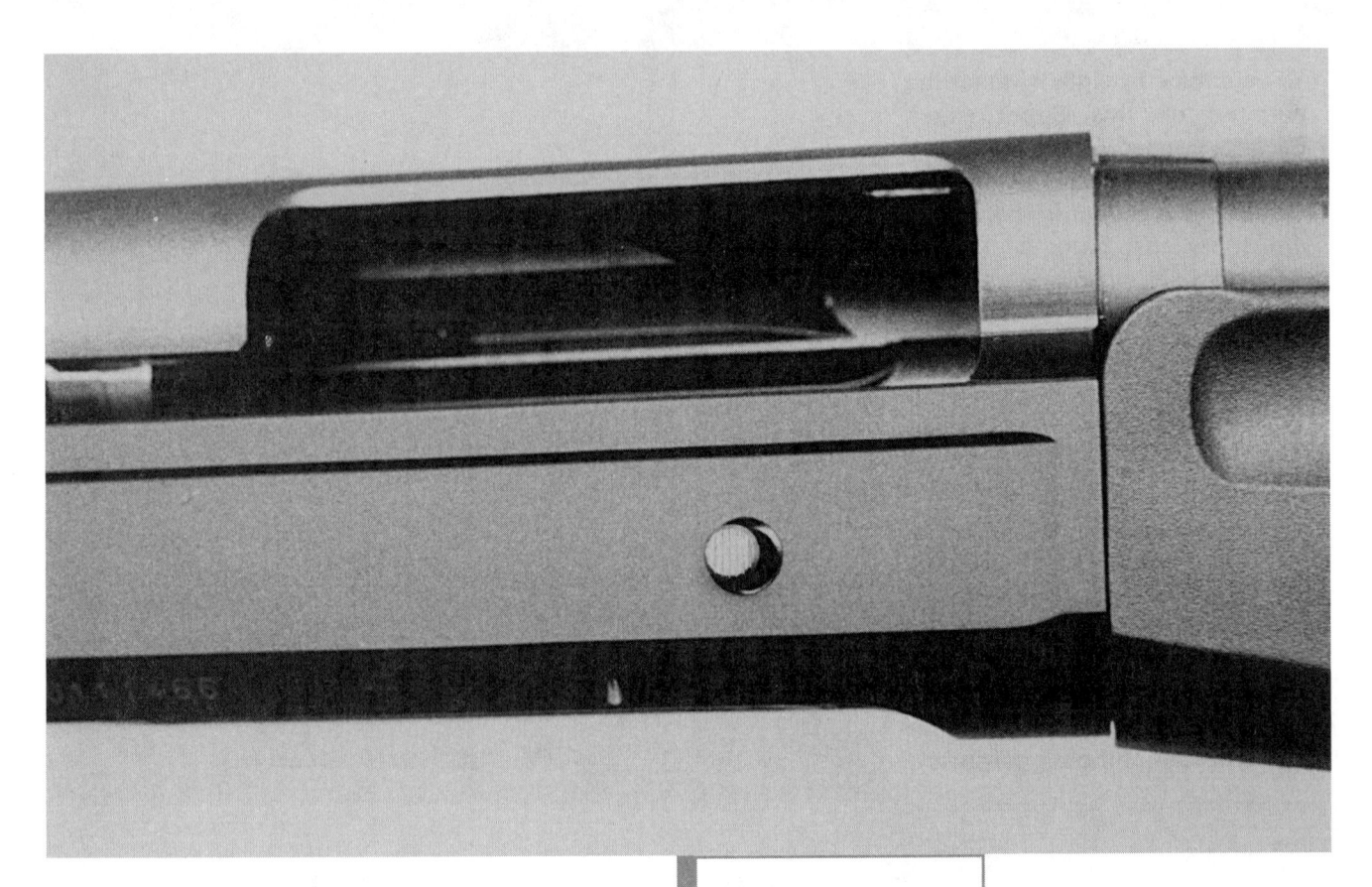

The button shown underneath the ejection port releases the bolt (shown open) so it can unlock and run forward.

War II, JSSAP also sought from the CAW project a greatly improved hit probability over existing small arms.

The CAW shotgun developed by Heckler & Koch was not the first one to be influenced by JSSAP input. That honor went to the Model 590 shotgun which had been offered by the O.F. Mossberg company since 1979. That weapon was militarized in the time-honored American tradition: taking an existing sporting shotgun design (in this case, Mossberg's well-tested Model 500 pump-action) and adding features deemed desirable by the armed forces. These included a parkerized finish, a nine-round tubular magazine under a 20-inch barrel, a perforated sheet-steel handguard around the barrel, a weatherproof synthetic stock, and a mounting lug for the M7 rifle bayonet. The Mossberg Model 590, nicknamed the "Milsgun," remains in U.S. Armed forces service and is also available commercially.

While the Mossberg 590 is a rugged combat shotgun offering effective weather resistance, the JSSAP program managers sought to advance the state of the art beyond the traditional pump action shotgun. In short, for the role of Close Assault Weapon, JSSAP was seeking a revolutionary weapon rather than the continuation of a slow evolution in shotgun design. The CAW mandate was for a weapon that was suitable for both close-range attack and defensive scenarios and roles traditionally reserved for shotguns. But JSSAP's vision called for a weapon more powerful, more reliable and more accurate than any existing shotgun. While recognizing the formidable close-range capabilities of the 12 gauge shotgun, JSSAP sought extended range capability for the CAW, with accuracy and lethality out to 150 meters, about twice the effective range of contemporary 12 gauge shotguns. JSSAP's goal was a shotgun offering improved performance with a significant reduction in recoil, always a problem with shotguns. Moreover, the armed forces demanded a selective-fire capability, something rarely found in a shotgun up to this point.

As we've observed with the advanced G11 military rifle (see Chapter 2), Heckler & Koch realized it lacked the expertise in ammunition research and development to go it alone on a project that broke so much new ground. That said, the company enlisted the aid of Olin, a well-known and highly regarded ammunition manufacturer. Olin's role was to create new ammunition having far greater range, lethality and reliability than the old paper shotshells that had become the industry standard. For the CAW project, Olin performed admirably by developing brass-cased 19.5mm CAW ammunition in three forms. One was a 9mm load firing eight .36-caliber lead balls at a muzzle velocity of 1600 feet per second. Another was a 7mm load firing eight .27-caliber tungsten alloy balls at a muzzle velocity of 1800 feet per second. And finally, there was a flechette (French for "little arrow") load firing 20 steel darts at a muzzle velocity of 3000 feet per second. These three anti-personnel rounds represented a significant increase in combat effectiveness over standard 12-gauge buckshot. Olin also developed longer CAW rounds with anti-armored vehicle and fragmentation loads. Because of their greater length, such rounds didn't fit properly in the CAW magazine; as a result, they had to be loaded individually into the breech. As for versatility and reliability under adverse conditions, these experimental Olin cartridges far surpassed any shotgun ammunition previously developed.

Meanwhile, the hardware aspect of the program was equally successful. Indeed, Heckler & Koch created an impressive weapon worthy of the new Olin cartridges. Its CAW prototype, designed and built in record time, was given a bullpup configuration to reduce overall length. Obviously, the considerable developmental work already invested in the G11 project helped to accelerate the CAW project. Heckler & Koch enclosed the entire weapon in a

Benelli's Super Black Eagle utilizes the innovative Montefeltro rotating bolt system. It allows an extremely high rate of fire--up to five rounds per second--and works with a wide variety of shotgun shells and loads.

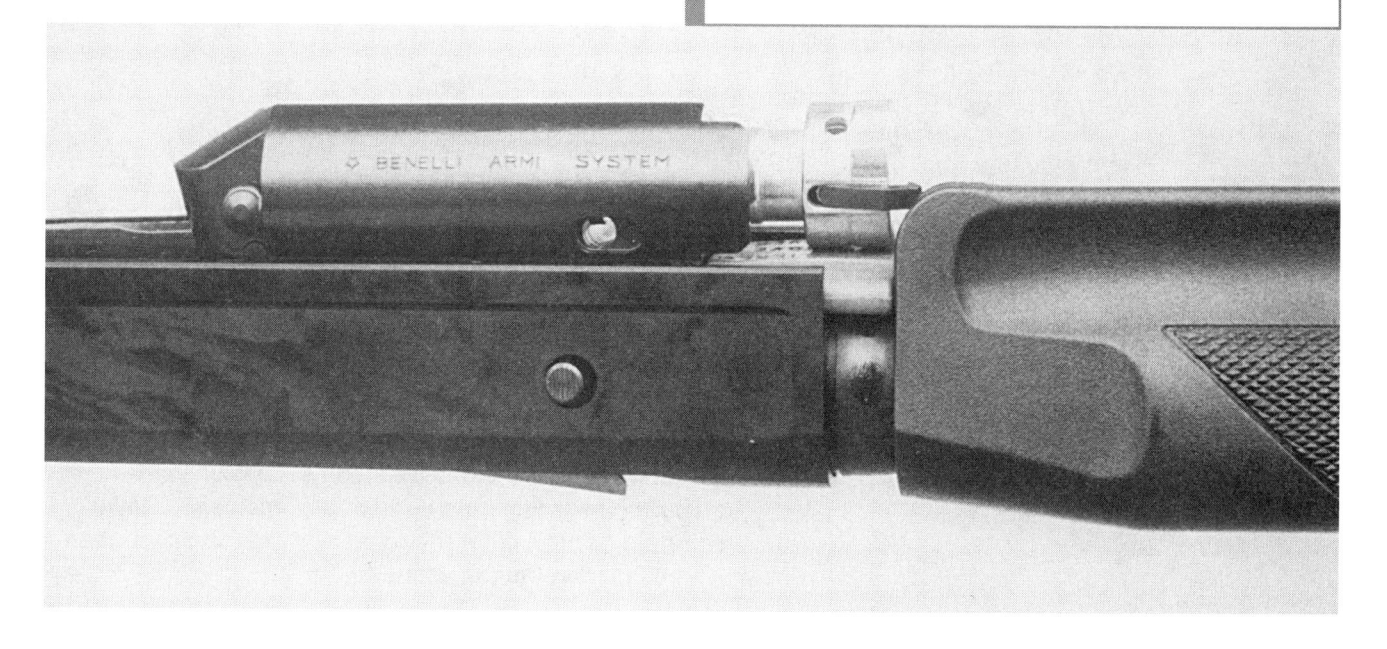

Chapter Eight

The Montefeltro rotating bolt system is a clever mechanism representing the first major advance in a recoil-operated autoloading shotgun design since Browning developed his Auto-5 in the late 1890s.

BELOW

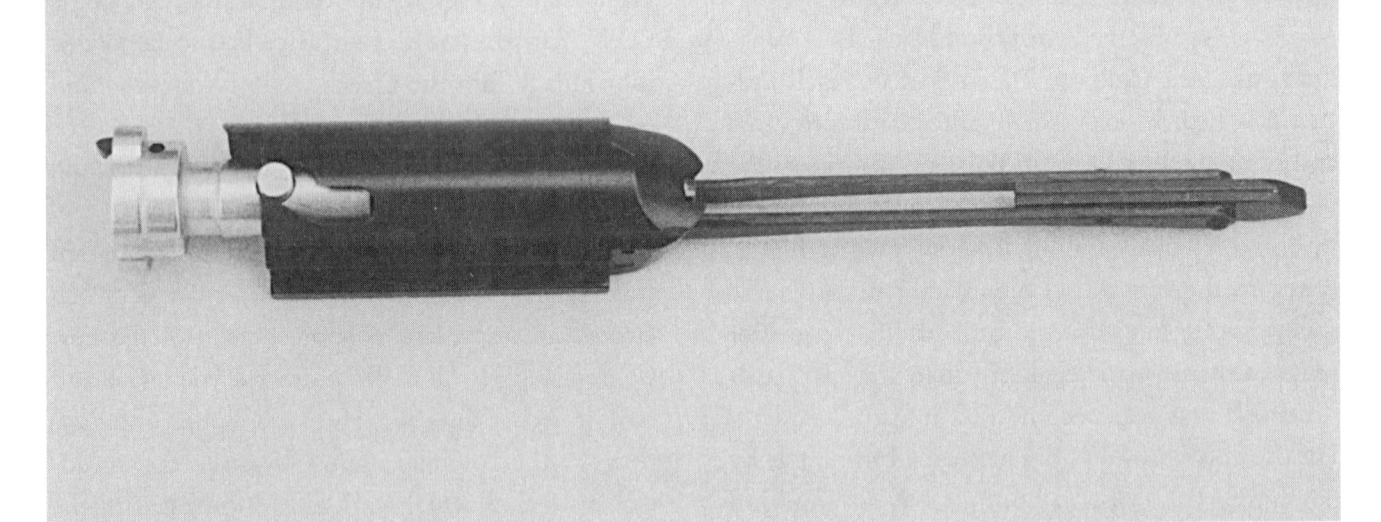

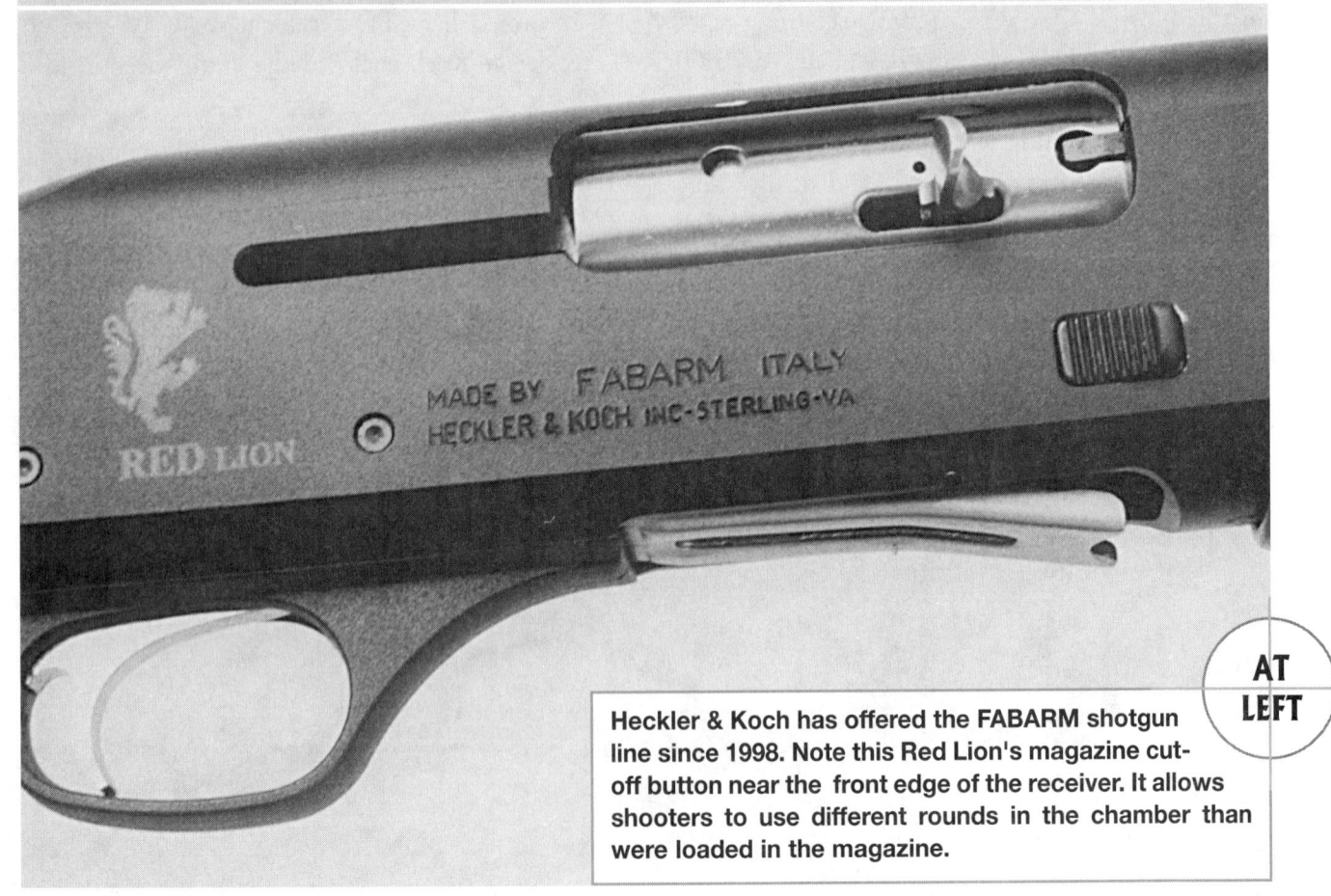

AT LEFT

Heckler & Koch has offered the FABARM shotgun line since 1998. Note this Red Lion's magazine cut-off button near the front edge of the receiver. It allows shooters to use different rounds in the chamber than were loaded in the magazine.

AT RIGHT

The FABARM's Red Lion shotgun disassembles quickly and easily by removing the cap on the forearm and then sliding the forearm off from the front, followed by the barrel, gas piston, cocking handle and bolt. The holes in the forearm cap allow excessive gas to vent harmlessly; they also accept an optional recoil reducing accessory.

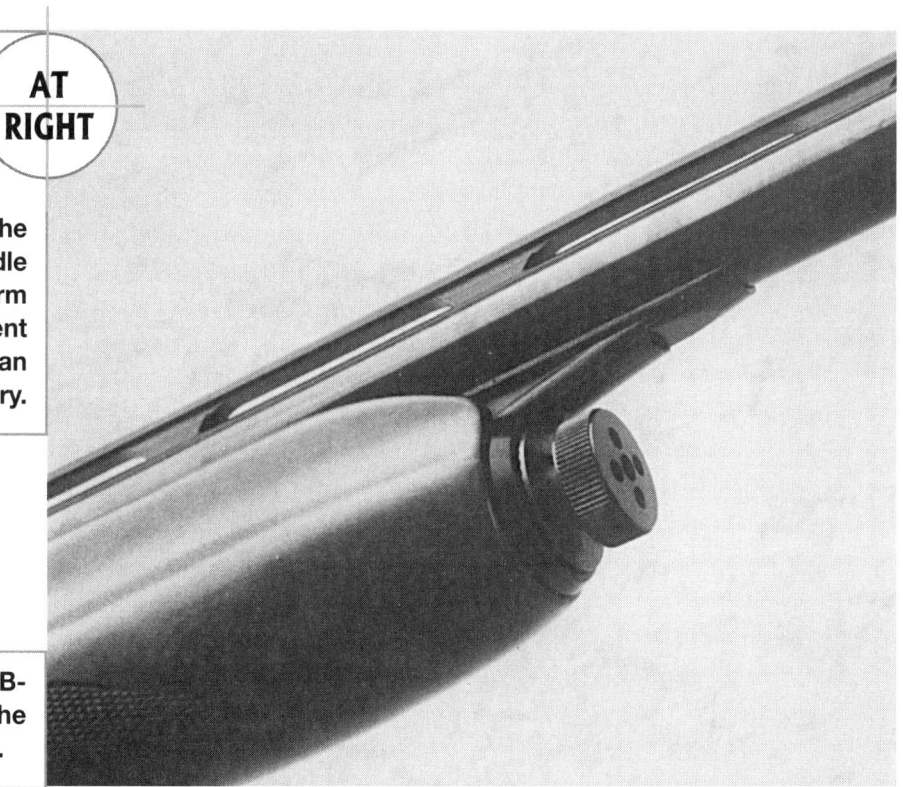

BELOW

The recoil spring on FABARM's Red Lion uses the magazine tube as a guide rod.

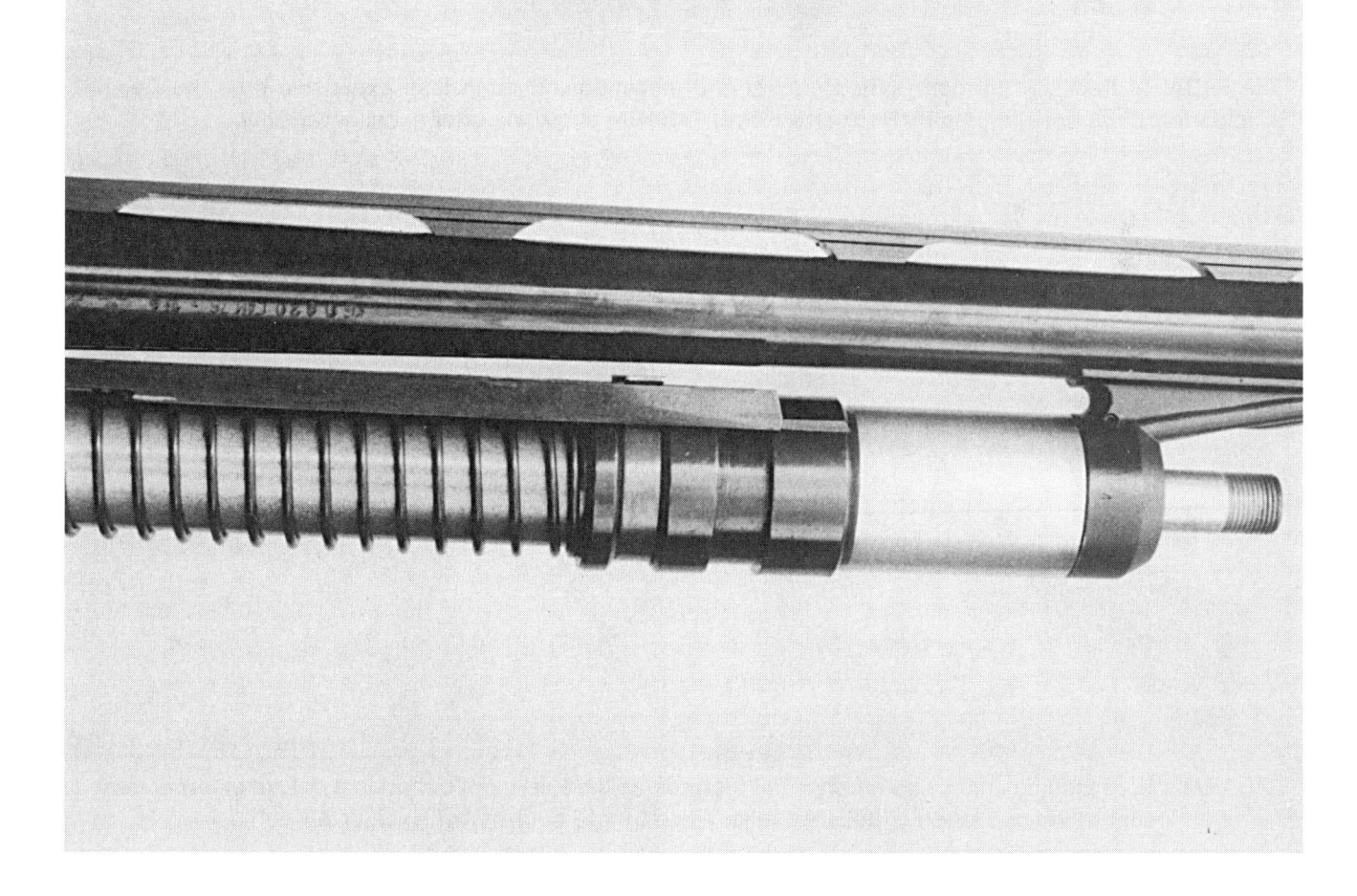

Chapter Eight 225

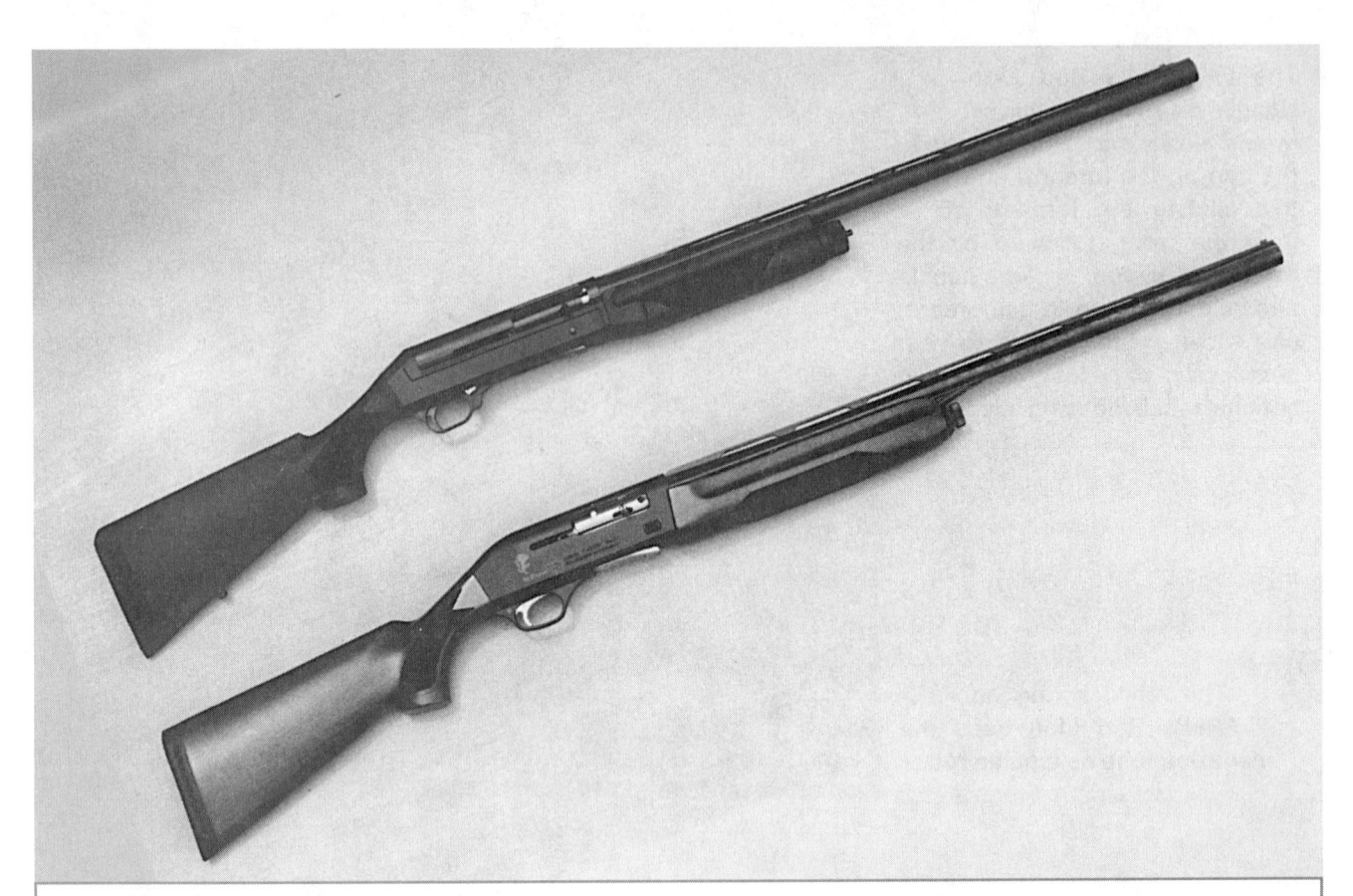

The FABARM Red Lion (bottom) offers quality and innovation. Though less expensive than the Benelli autoloaders (top) once offered by Heckler & Koch, FABARM shotguns offer excellent quality.

FABARM's Gold Lion has the same mechanical features as the Red Lion, but adds a deluxe external treatment, including a grip cap made of polished olive wood (photo courtesy of Heckler & Koch).

sturdy plastic outer casing much like the one used later on the G11 infantry rifle. An M16-style carrying handle atop the casing contained a sight channel for the front and rear sights. Another feature inspired by the M16 was a spring-loaded dust cover over the ejection port, one that popped open when the first shot was fired. A 10-shot box magazine fit underneath the receiver, close to the shooter, who now had the option of either semi-automatic or fully-automatic fire. To help keep recoil and control to manageable dimensions, especially in fully-automatic fire, Heckler & Koch opted for a straight-line stock configuration. Its slightly greater weight--8.8 pounds as opposed to 7.25 pounds for Mossberg's Model 590--also helped control recoil.

In addition to Heckler & Koch, several other manufacturers submitted prototype CAW systems for evaluation. These included Beretta's M3P and Franchi's SPAS-16, both from Italy, and Smith & Wesson's AS. The Italian designs featured a convertible action, giving the shooter a choice of semiautomatic or pump action. Both Franchi and Smith & Wesson entries shared straight-line stock configurations with an integral carrying handle/ sight channel. Clearly, the Heckler & Koch CAW prototype was by far the most advanced weapon submitted for testing in terms of its operating features and capabilities.

Regrettably, even though the CAW project had created what would have made a formidable weapon in close-quarters combat, the U.S. armed forces decided not to buy it. As far as the U.S. military was concerned, the CAW project was effectively dead by 1987. With the withdrawal of U.S. military support, Heckler & Koch soon shelved the project, while Olin did the same with its ammunition. What JSSAP, Heckler & Koch and Olin learned from the CAW project would serve as a kind of springboard to the current Small Arms Master Plan (SAMP) published by the U.S. Army's Infantry School (Fort Benning, GA) in September of 1989. This plan calls for three types of weapons, each providing a revolutionary increase in defensive and offensive firepower for the infantry in the years to come. SAMP's requirements, to be considered as guidelines in advancing the state of the art in weapons design, are as follows:

SAMP's REQUIREMENTS

	Weapon Name	Max. Weight	Effective Range	Comments
Personal Defense Weapon (PDW)	1.5 pounds (to be worn on the body)	Lethality to 50m; hit probability to 100 meters	Penetration of body armor at 50 meters	
Individual Combat Weapon (ICW)	10 pounds fully loaded	Lethality to 500 meters vs. people wearing body armor	Capable of engaging vehicles and slow aircraft; multiple ammo types and advanced aiming apparatus	
Crew-Served Weapon (CSW)	38 pounds in two 19-lb. Loads	2000m vs. personnel; 1000m vs. light armored vehicles	Based on ICW, with commonality of aiming apparatus, munitions and fire control systems	

The **FABARM** Camo Lion automatic shotgun uses the same basic mechanism as the Red Lion and Gold Lion models, but adds a durable camouflage finish that helps conceal shooter's from animals and increases resistance to the elements (photo courtesy of Heckler & Koch).

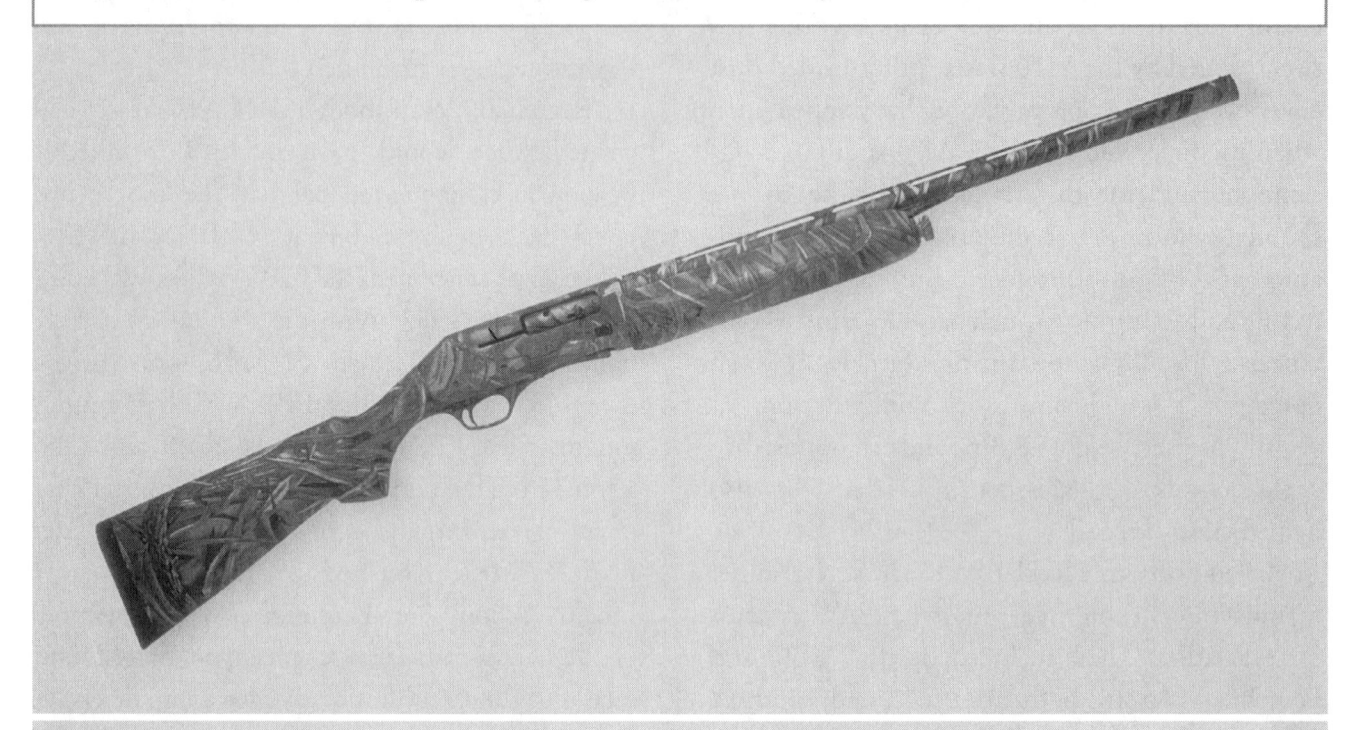

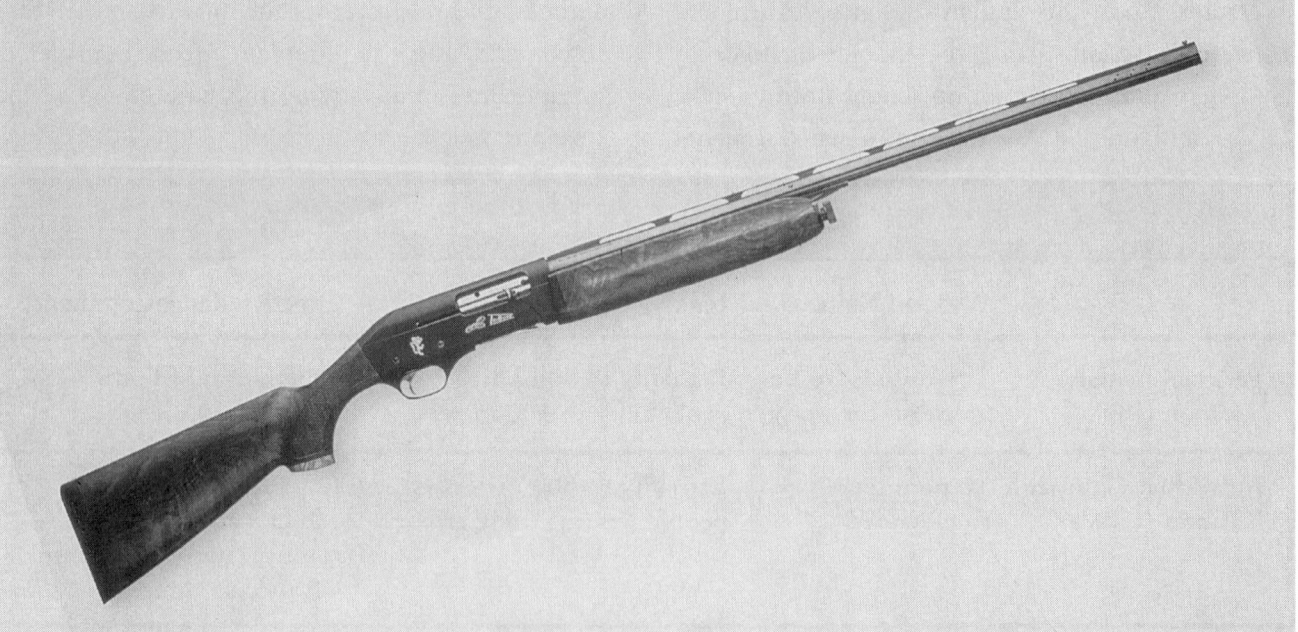

The **FABARM** Sporting Clays Lion combines the well-tested operating mechanism of the Red Lion with a high quality finish, plus an aiming bead halfway down the sighting rib, and a TriBore barrel. A recoil reducing mechanism in the buttstock and a thick leather-covered rubber recoil pad enhance shooter comfort (photo courtesy of Heckler & Koch).

AT RIGHT The manual safety on FABARM FP-6's is pushed to the left (as shown) to fire. Note also the heavy stippling on the black synthetic pistol grip.

BELOW The FABARM FP-6 can take 2 3/4-inch or 3-inch shotshells. Note the manual safety button located on the triggerguard's trailing edge, just behind the trigger.

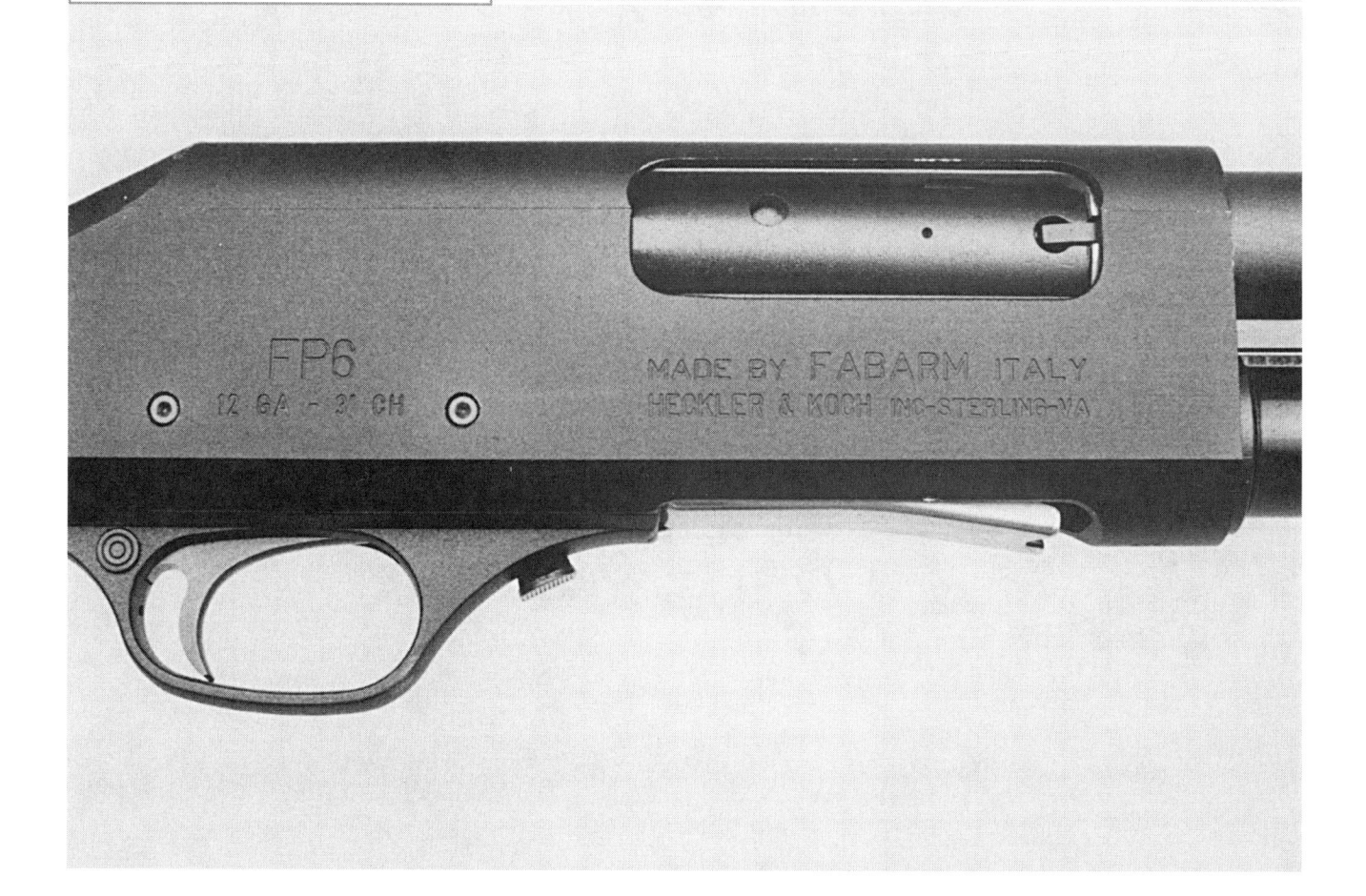

Chapter Eight 229

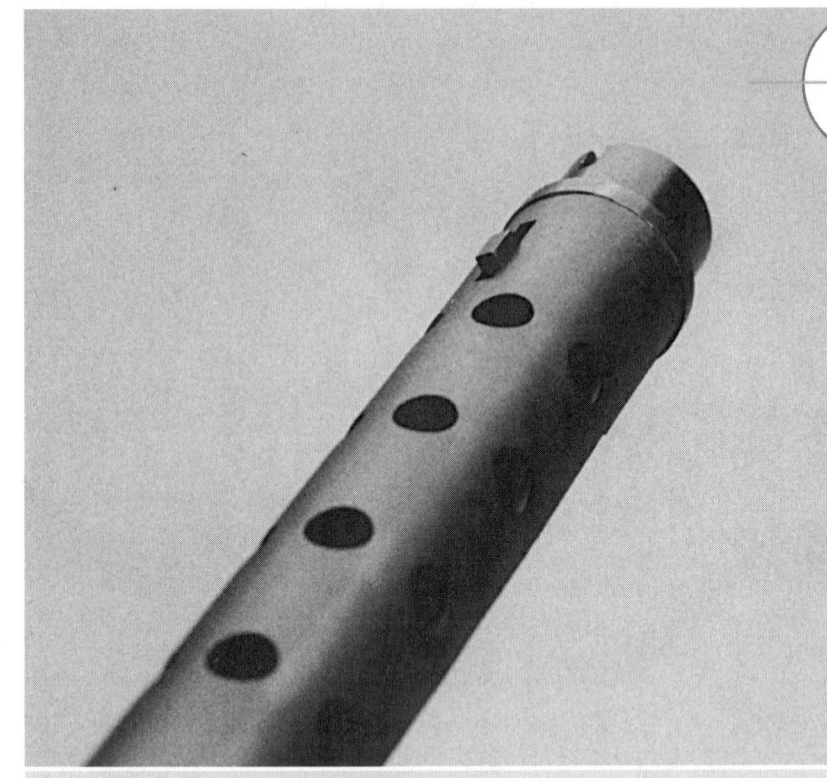

AT LEFT — The FABARM FP-6 needs a more prominent front sight for fast, easy sight acquisition in dangerous environments. The existing front sight barely rises above the perforated sheet steel handguard.

BELOW — The deep ribbing across the pump handle of the FP-6 assures fast, smooth operation, even when heavy gloves are worn.

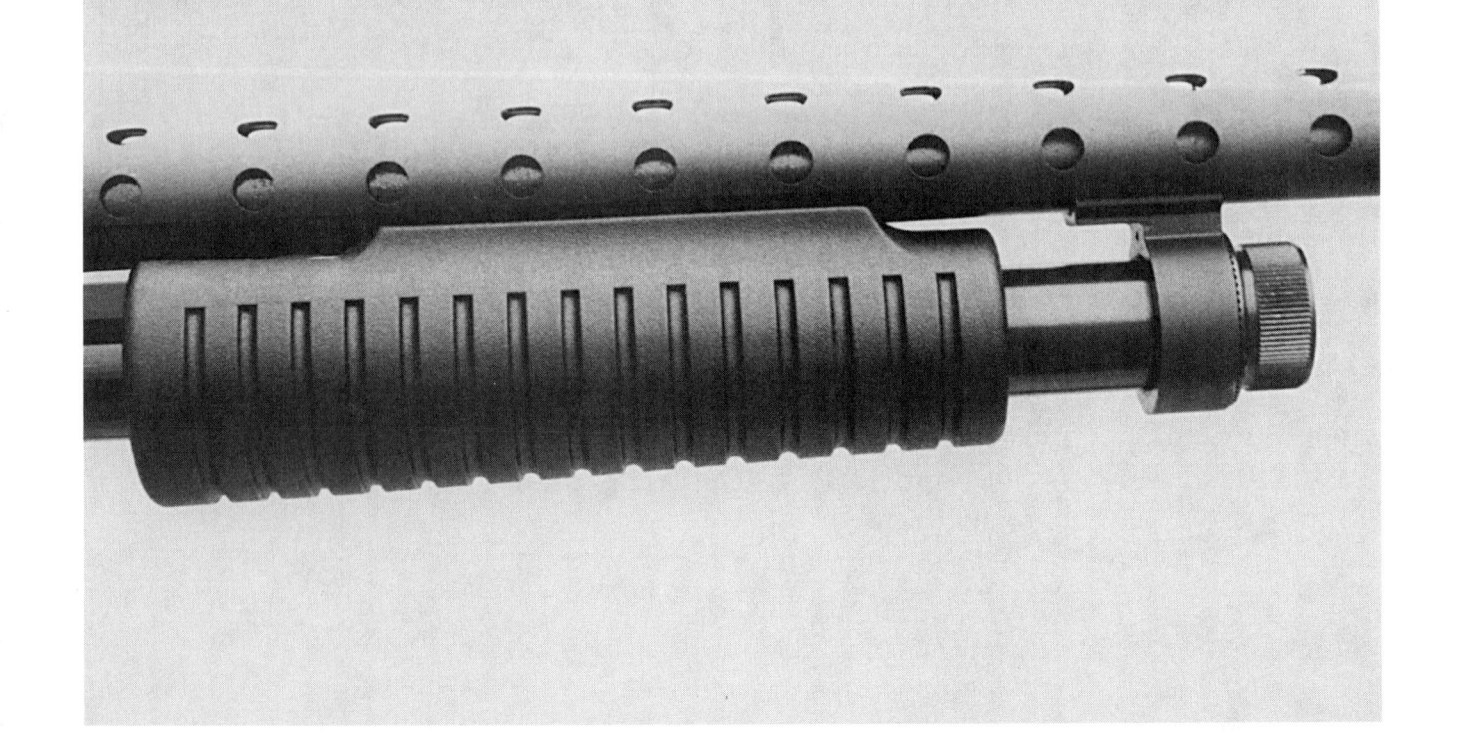

Heckler & Koch

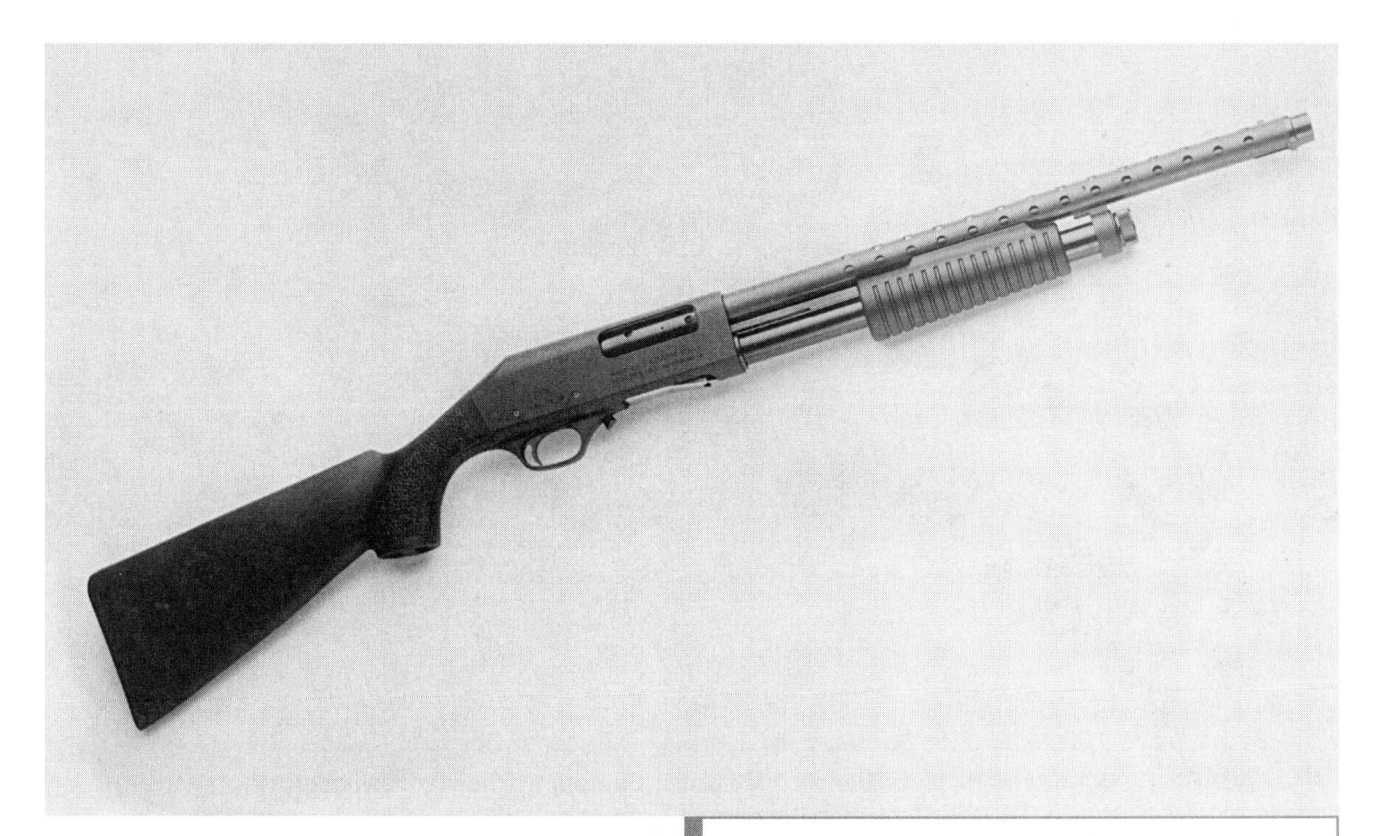

The FABARM FP-6 pump shotgun is a formidable weapon and a valuable addition to Heckler & Koch's law-enforcement product line (photo courtesy of Heckler & Koch).

As the new century evolves, combat shotgun design has reached an impasse. For all its faults, including high recoil, limited magazine capacity and short range, the 12-gauge shotgun remains a formidable weapon. A variety of relatively inexpensive, well-made and tested shotgun designs already exists. Intensive ammunition development over the past century has created several effective antipersonnel rounds, especially in the popular 12 gauge. With shotguns being built with current technology widely distributed and accepted throughout the world, a certain complacency has set in. Gun legislation has also played a role in limiting shotgun development by killing such promising box magazine designs as the Franchi SPAS-15. We cannot, of course, blame this state of affairs on Heckler & Koch, who, along with CAWS, took a significant step forward. As with other H&K projects, this one failed not through any technical shortcoming, but because it was too far ahead of its time.

Part II. Franchi

The Luigi Franchi firm began operations in Brescia, Italy, in 1860. Specializing in shotguns from the start, the company has developed a comprehensive line of products that includes semi-automatic, pump, over-and-under and side-by-side models. Franchi shotguns are famous around the world for their innovative design features, excellent handling characteristics and outstanding quality at a reasonable price.

Heckler & Koch's limited association with Franchi took place in the late 1980s, when West Germany's armed forces were in the market for a shotgun for a variety of reasons. Franchi had earlier made a modified version of its Model 502 semi-automatic shotgun for the West German armed

ABOVE The FABARM FP-6 (bottom) replaces Benelli's M3 Super 90 (top) as the standard pump shotgun in the Heckler & Koch line. The FP-6 lacks the Benelli's selectable action feature, but it compensates by being extraordinarily rugged and appreciably less expensive than the Benelli shotgun.

ABOVE The FABARM FP-6 (bottom), a surprisingly versatile and handy long arm, is slightly less than six inches longer than a U.S. M1 Carbine (top), which is highly regarded for its easy handling.

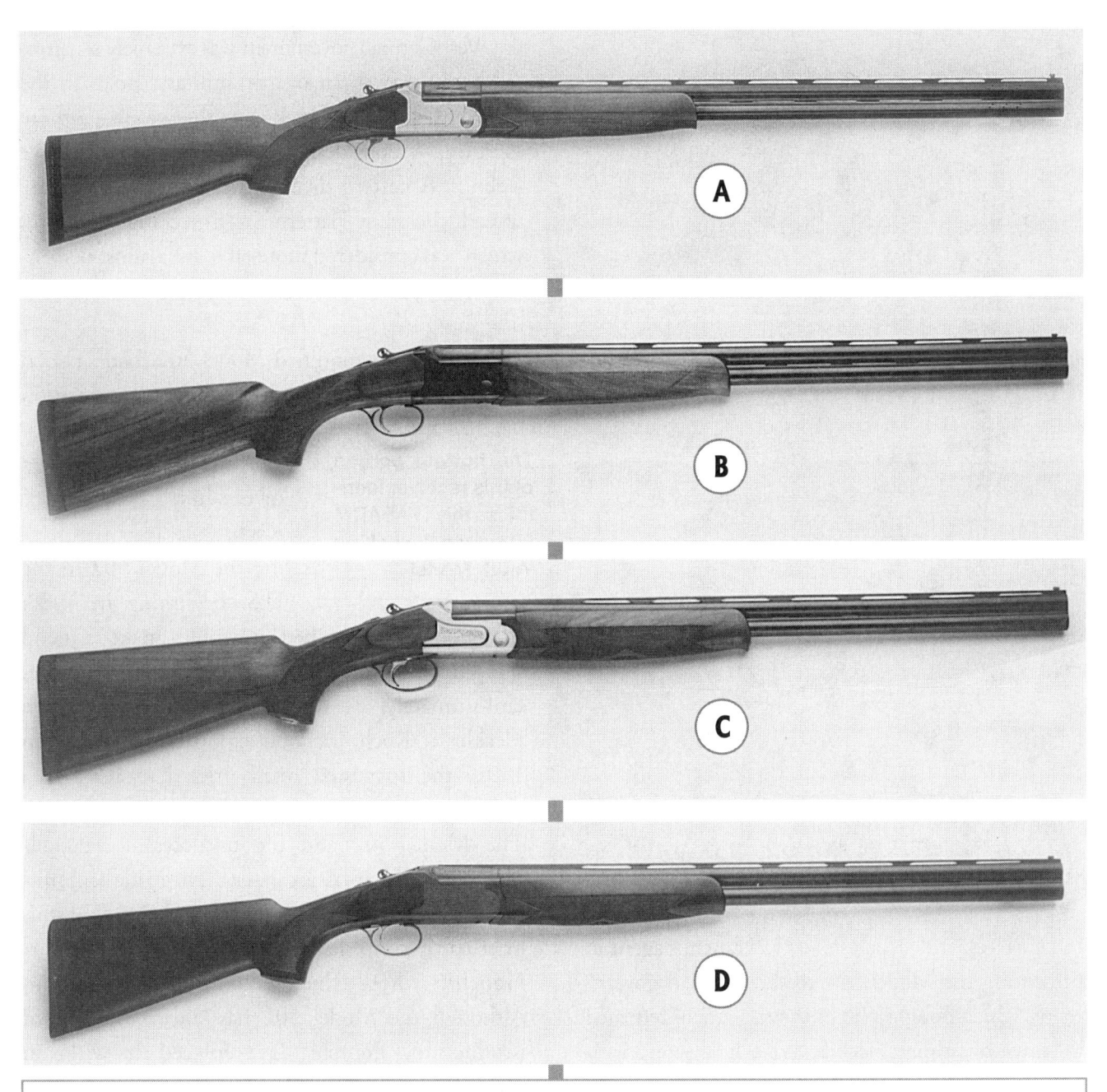

A. The FABARM's Sporting Clays over and under shotgun boasts a hand-cut, checkered forearm and many high-quality internal features, including chrome-lined barrels (photo courtesy of Heckler & Koch).

B. The FABARM Black Lion Competition employs a single trigger that resets by inertia when preparing the second barrel for shooting. The mechanism is fast and reliable (photo courtesy of Heckler & Koch).

C. Like other FABARM shotguns, the Max Lion utilizes rebounding hammers for added safety. In this system, once the firing pin has pierced the primer of a cartridge and fired it, a spring pushes the hammer back and away from the firing chamber (photo courtesy of Heckler & Koch).

D. The FABARM Max Lion is a deluxe over-and-under shotgun that accepts 12- or 20-gauge chambering and features a boxlock action with single selective trigger (photo courtesy of Heckler & Koch).

The bottom portion of this receiver identifies this FABARM 20-gauge Silver Lion Youth Model.

forces. Heckler & Koch served as Franchi's agent in presenting the Model 502 to the German government, which bought 500 of them. Franchi returned the favor by helping Heckler & Koch develop a variant of its G41 .223 caliber service rifle, which met Italian armed forces requirements. This Franchi/Heckler & Koch rifle participated in a competition that ultimately led to adoption of the Beretta Model 70/90 by the Italian army as its service rifle.

As modified for West German military and police use, the Franchi Model 502 differed from the commercial variant because of its sights and matte finish. The stock remained walnut, however, because the West German government was extremely sensitive to shotguns with an overtly military look. To the Germans, a walnut stock gave the weapon a more "sporting" look designed to allay any negative feelings. A pattern diverter attached to the muzzle spread the shot pattern in a rectangular form, which was considered more effective against personnel than the usual round shot pattern of hunting shotguns.

Because the modified Model 502 made a good defensive shotgun, and because its configuration and features did not violate any laws for civilian ownership, Heckler & Koch, Inc. began exporting the Model 502 to the U.S. beginning in 1986. The company reasoned it would make a good shotgun both for police use and for civilian sale. Unfortunately, its price became a factor. When Heckler & Koch, Inc. quit exporting this model in 1991, the suggested retail price had reached a daunting $1,895. Consequently, sales were limited. The Model 502 and the unsuccessful Franchi/Heckler & Koch .223 caliber service rifle (submitted for Italian trials) represented the end of this brief partnership. Its failure, however, has not hurt Franchi, whose line remains in production. Although the Model 502 has since gone out of production, Franchi has replaced it with an improved variant, the Model 612.

Part III. Benelli

Having ceased distribution of Franchi's Model 502 in 1992, Heckler & Koch became U.S. distributor for the highly-regarded Benelli line of Italian shotguns. While sporting shotguns had long been Benelli's specialty, the firm made an attempt in the 1980s at producing Model 121 M1 Police/Military, a variant of the unsuccessful SL-80 series. This model was discontinued in 1985 when Benelli dropped the SL-80 line. The current "Super 90" **(photos p. 217, 218, 219)** line, which was introduced by Benelli in 1986 and remains in production (though no longer handled by Heckler & Koch), is much superior.

Before teaming up with H&K, Benelli had made two attempts at expanding into the military and police market. The first of these forays in the mid-1970s led to the creation of a technically interesting but ultimately abortive submachine gun. The gun worked well, and its ammunition in particular showed considerable merit, but the whole project was too radical to appeal to police and military buyers. The submachine gun market was, and remains, limited at best; besides, Benelli was off in its timing by trying to introduce what would have been a radical new system.

Benelli's next foray into the military/police market occurred in 1976 with its introduction of the B-76 9mm handgun. It, too, was technically interesting. It featured a breech-locking mechanism and toggle conceptually similar to those of the famous Parabellum or "Luger" pistol. Like the Luger, the Benelli pistol boasted a strong operating mechanism. It also had a steep grip angle, which many shooters liked, along with numerous modern features. Benelli even marketed a training version of this pistol in .22 Long Rifle caliber as a means of providing inexpensive shooting practice for the full-powered centerfire model. Unfortunately, Benelli had no success in selling the B-76 to military or police agencies, although modest civilian sales did keep the B-76 in production until 1990.

By 1992, Benelli was ready to team up with a respected manufacturer/distributor with a proven record in military and police sales. A partnership with Heckler & Koch looked attractive; and by the

The FABARM 20-gauge Silver Lion Youth Model has a shortened buttstock for easier handling by shooters of small stature.

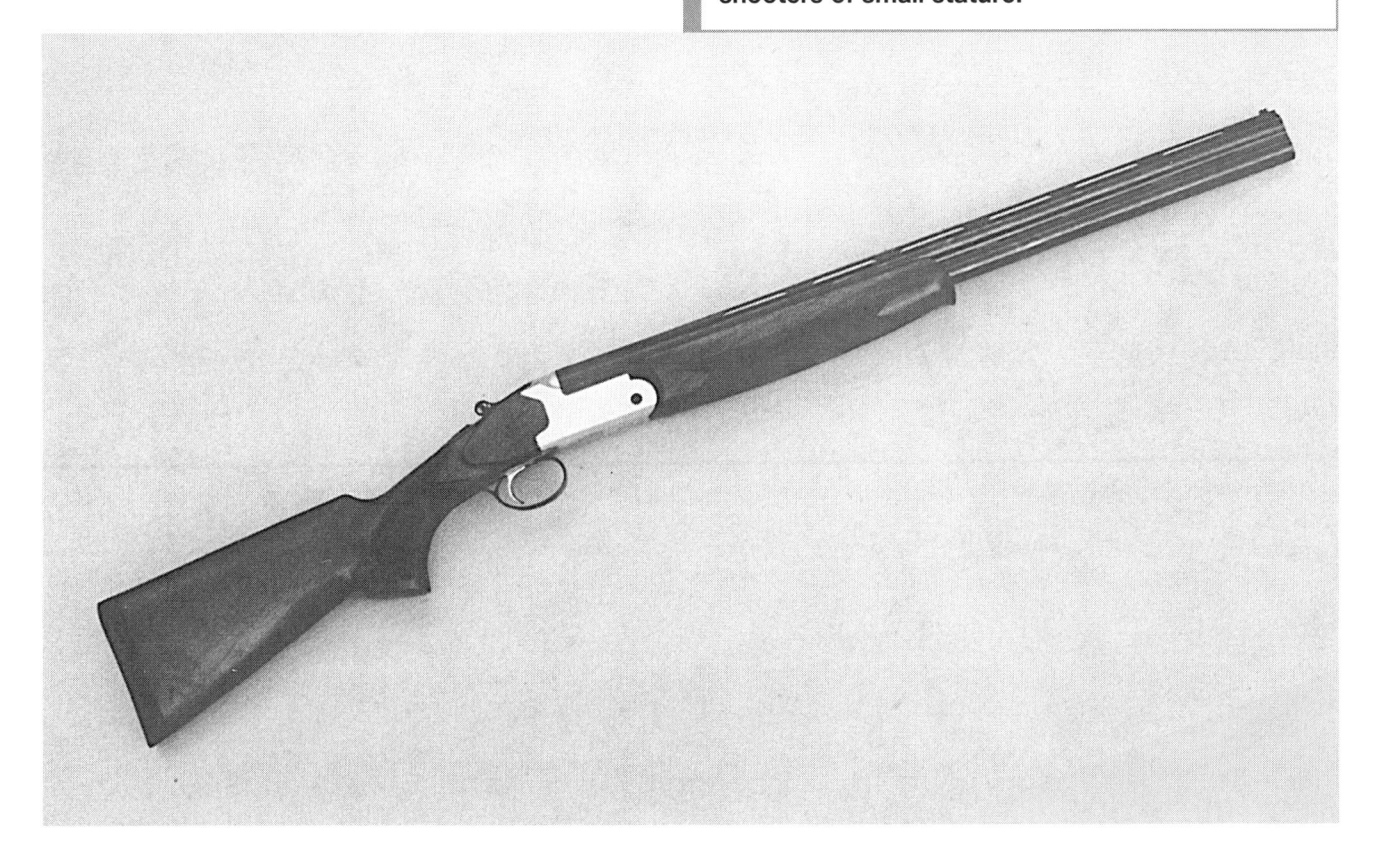

Chapter Eight **235**

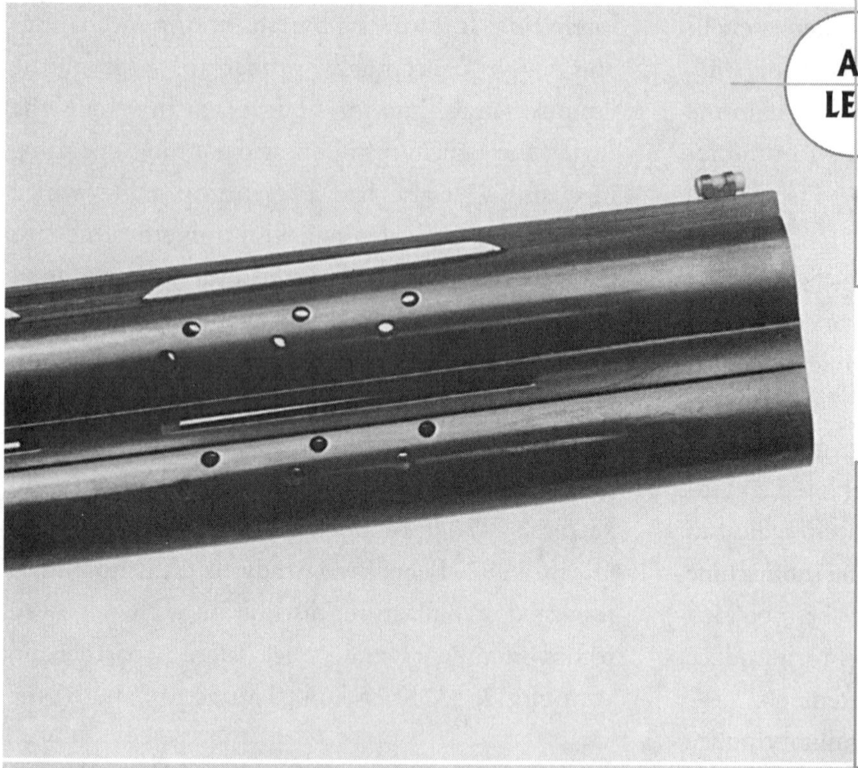

AT LEFT The FABARM Silver Lion Youth Models come standard with barrel porting and the company's impressive TriBore barrel system.

BELOW The FABARM 20-gauge Silver Lion Youth Model features a forged steel receiver, plated and engraved. The 12-gauge model includes a receiver made from lightweight Ergal, an aluminum alloy often found in Beretta handguns.

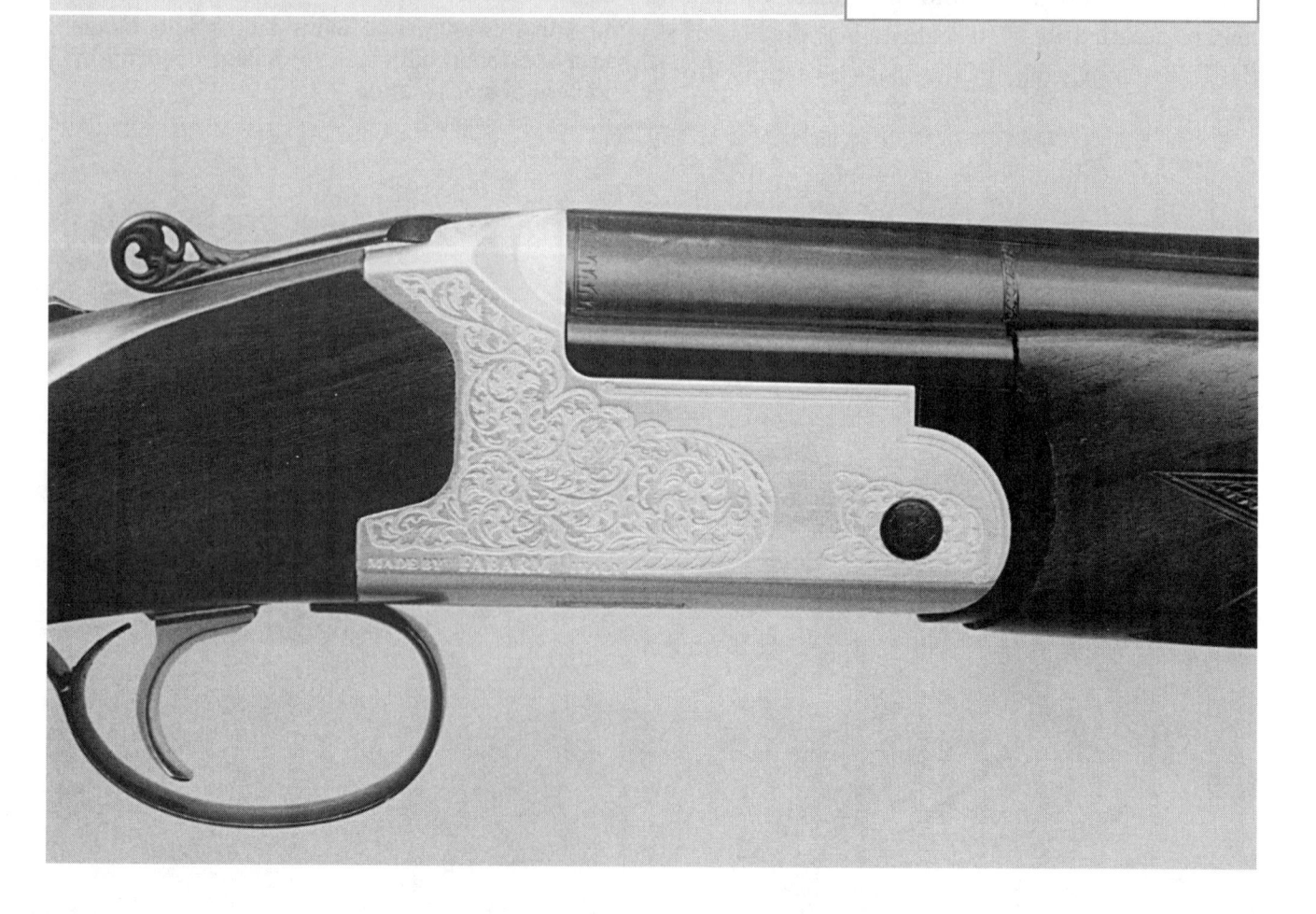

AT RIGHT On this FABARM 20-gauge Silver Lion Youth Model, pushing the barrel selector to the left prepares the bottom barrel for firing, exposing a single dot.

BELOW The controls on FABARM's 20-gauge Silver Lion Youth Model include a sliding tang safety. A manual safety is located inside the trigger selector. In this photo, the top barrel is ready to fire.

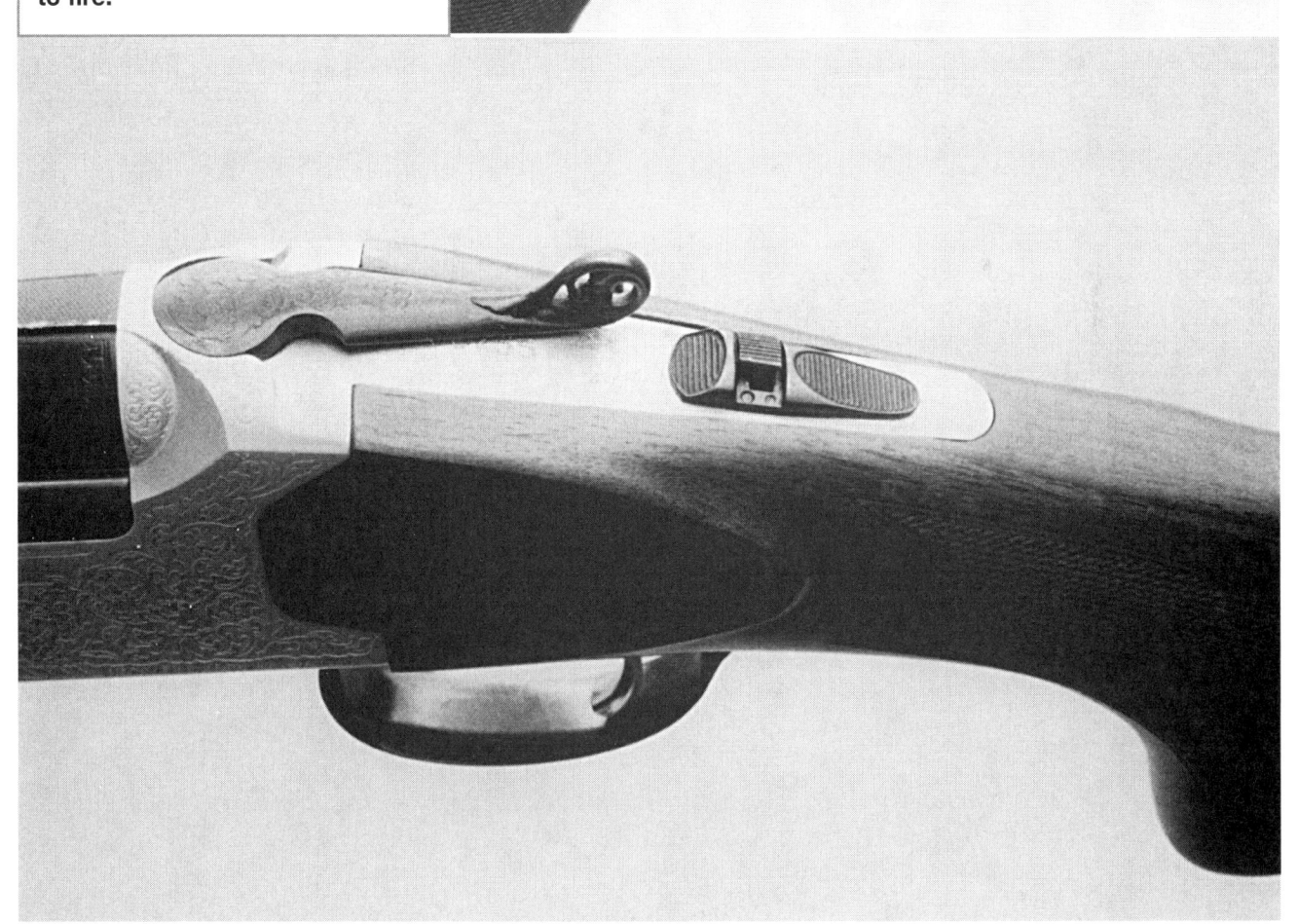

Chapter Eight 237

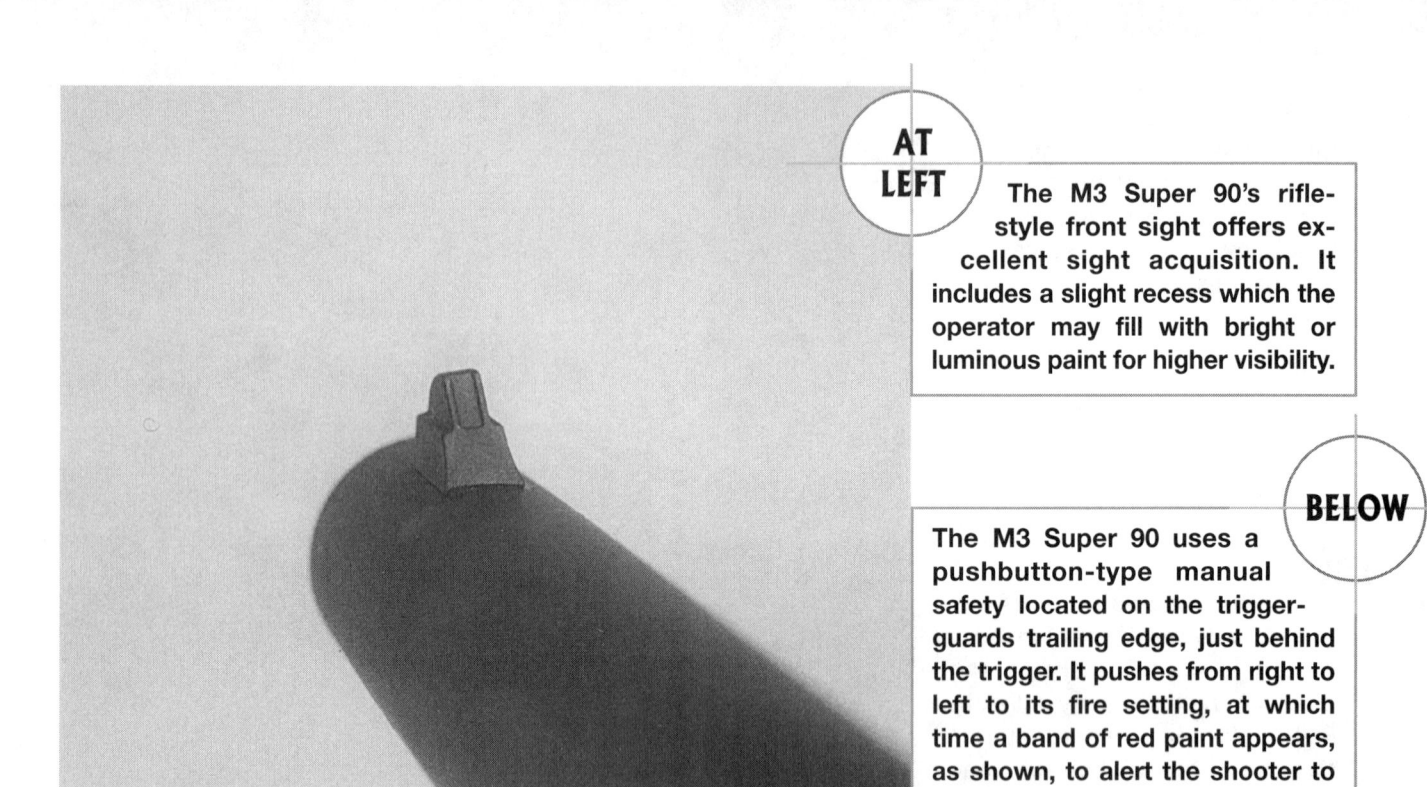

AT LEFT — The M3 Super 90's rifle-style front sight offers excellent sight acquisition. It includes a slight recess which the operator may fill with bright or luminous paint for higher visibility.

BELOW — The M3 Super 90 uses a pushbutton-type manual safety located on the triggerguards trailing edge, just behind the trigger. It pushes from right to left to its fire setting, at which time a band of red paint appears, as shown, to alert the shooter to the gun's ready status.

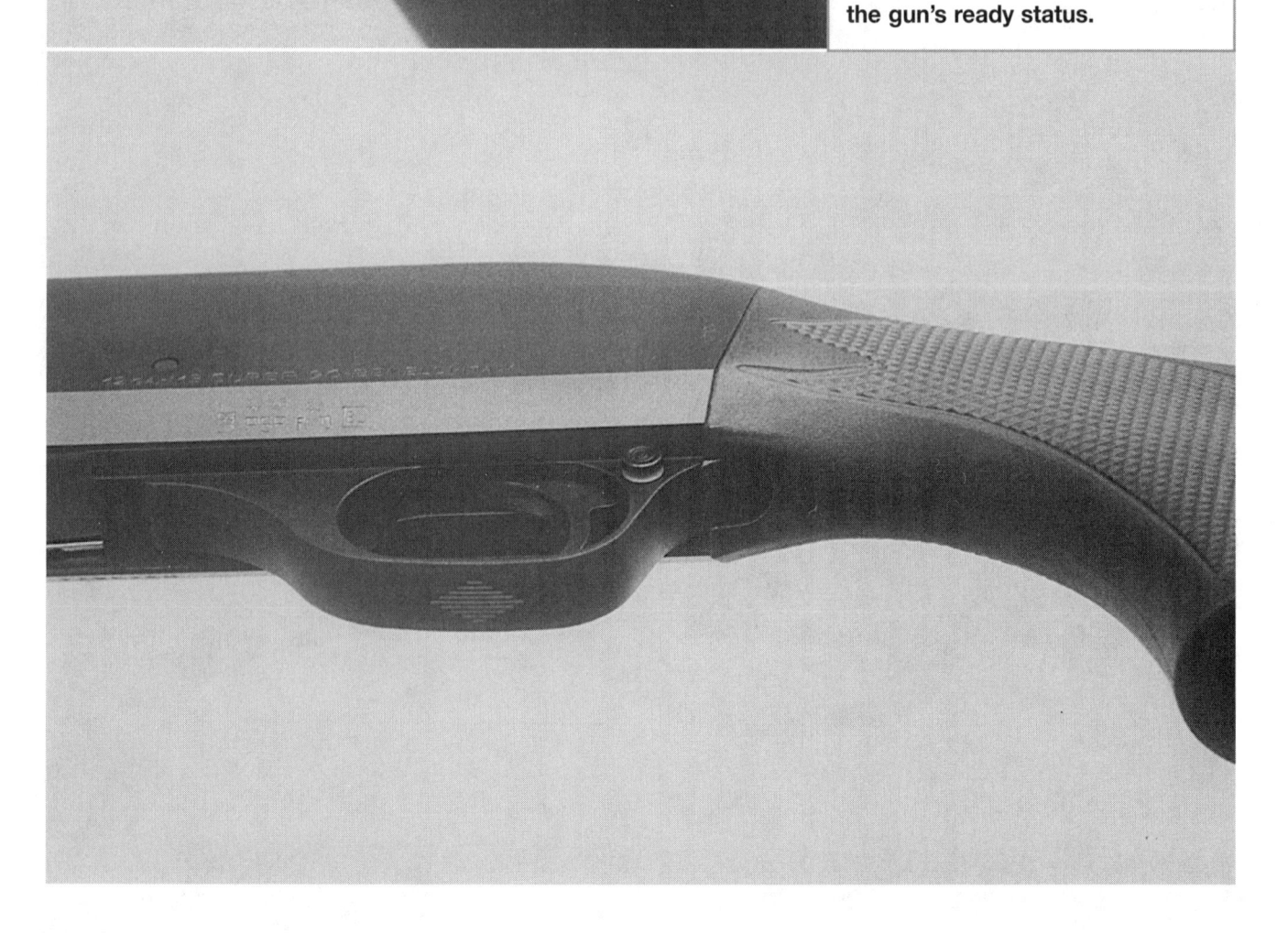

AT RIGHT

Like current Benelli autoloading shotguns, the FABARM Red Lion employs a fiber optic front sight element which amplifies the available light and draws the shooter's eye better than the traditional brass, gold or silver bead used on older shotgun front sights.

BELOW

The FABARM motto is Latin, not Italian. The Red Lion shown uses a pushbutton manual safety on the triggerguard's trailing edge. The safety's direction of travel is reversible to suit right-handed or left-handed shooters.

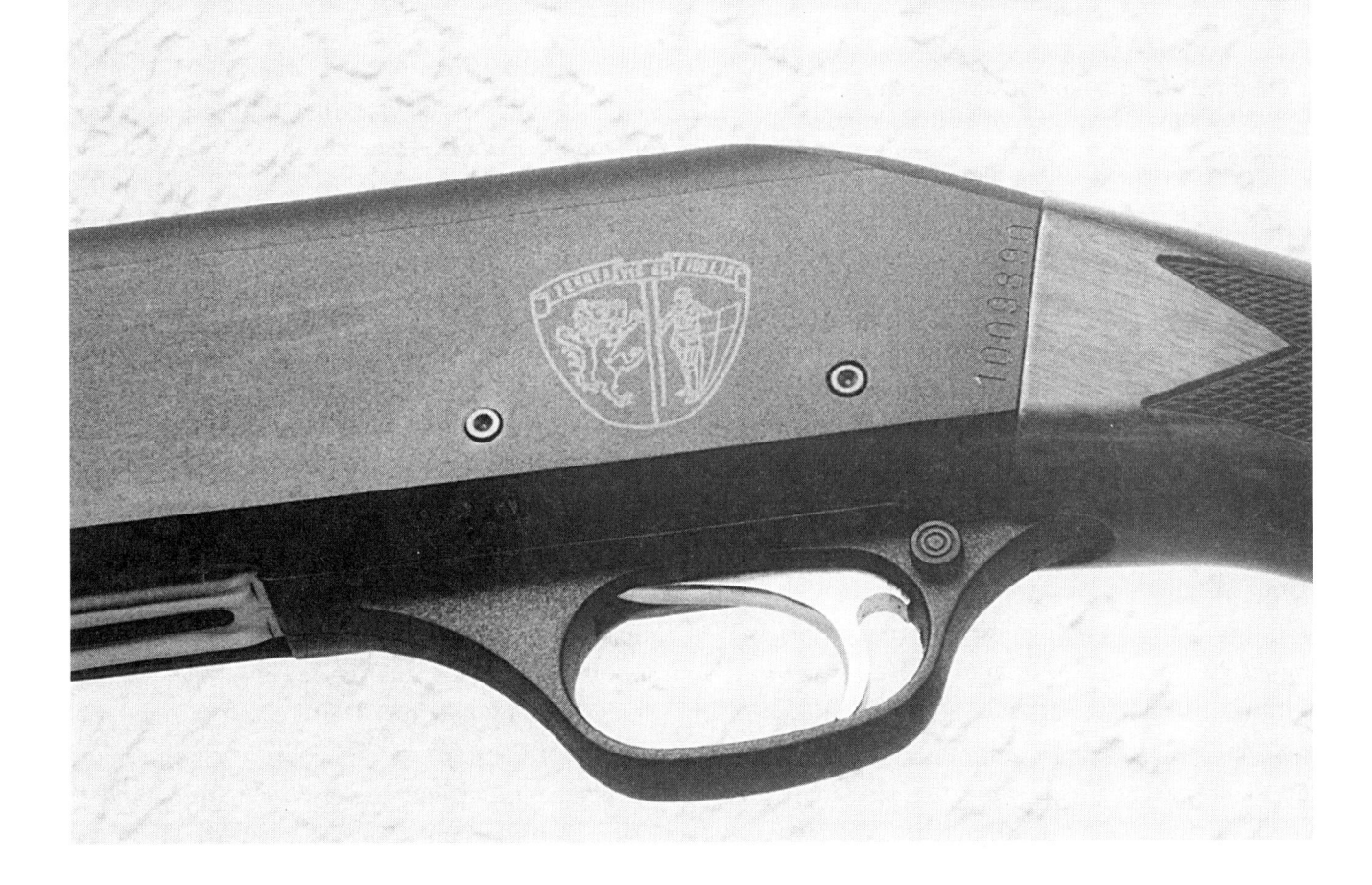

Chapter Eight 239

The FABARM Camo Turkey Lion includes 3.5-inch chambers for accommodating magnum shotshells. A Picatinny-style receiver rail (used to facilitate scope mounting) comes standard. Turkeys are wary and can be taken only at extended ranges (photo courtesy of Heckler & Koch).

same token Heckler & Koch wanted to create a full shotgun line with commercial as well as official potential. Benelli had just such a line, plus a well-established reputation among shotgun connoisseurs. Its M1 Super 90-series shotgun had been in production since 1986, establishing a name for itself as a sturdy, reliable and attractively-priced gun. As such, it made a good match with the Heckler & Koch product line. The first of Benelli's Super 90 series--the M1 Super 90 Slug--went into production in 1986. The M1 Super 90 series went on to become an entire line of multi-purpose shotguns, all sharing a recoil-operating semiautomatic mode of fire, called the Montefeltro rotating bolt.

Strong and reliable, this system is also extremely fast, with rates of fire up to five rounds per second of *semiautomatic* fire, wherein the shooter pulls the trigger once for every shot. While such rates of fire are typical for an automatic pistol or some types of self-loading rifle, they're amazing when fired with a shotgun.

All current Benelli shotguns feature a crossbolt safety at the back edge of the triggerguard which, when pushed from right to left, allows the gun to fire (a red band indicates the safety is in its "fire" setting). A cocking indicator, consisting of a signal flag, is located on the right forward edge of the triggerguard, protruding downward and out of the receiver. When the shotgun is cocked, a red dot appears. The gun's state of readiness can also be determined by checking the slot at the right rear portion of the receiver. The polished hammer rises up behind the firing chamber upon firing and is visible once the gun is uncocked. In the M1 Super

90 Slug, the furniture (stock and forearm) is black fiberglass. Rifle-type sights, a seven-shot magazine and a 19 1/2-inch cylinder bore barrel complete the package. Its modern construction, including an aluminum alloy receiver and chrome-lined barrel, contributes to the shotgun's light weight of only 6.7 pounds.

Other guns in the Super 90 line include the M1 Super 90 Defense, which is similar to the M1 Super 90 Slug except for its pistol-grip stock, which raises the unloaded weight to 7.1 pounds. The M1 Super 90 Entry gun, introduced in 1992, has a 14-inch barrel with a reduced tubular magazine that holds only five rounds (an extension magazine holding the standard seven rounds was also available). Stock options included a pistol grip or the standard buttstock. Because of the gun's short barrel, private citizens who wish to own this model must arrange for its purchase through a Class III federally licensed firearms dealer, as if buying a machine gun.

The M1 Super 90 Tactical, which dates from 1993, has an 18 1/2-inch barrel and offers an option of rifle sights or the increasingly popular ghost ring rear sight. This model comes with three interchangeable choke tubes\improved cylinder, modified and full choke settings--depending on the various missions. The choke tubes screw into the muzzle portion of the barrel and can be interchanged or left in place. Another gun with an 18 ?-inch barrel bore the misleading name of M1 Super 90 Sporting Special, featuring ghost ring sights. It remained in production for only two years (1993-1994).

The M1 Super 90 Field model catered more to the sporting and hunting crowd. Basically, it featured a choice of barrel lengths (21-, 24-, 26- or 28-inch). Early issues featured a black poly-

The FABARM Ultra Mag Lion also includes a 3.5-inch chamber to accommodate magnum shotshells. A black walnut stock ensures better recoil control (photo courtesy of Heckler & Koch).

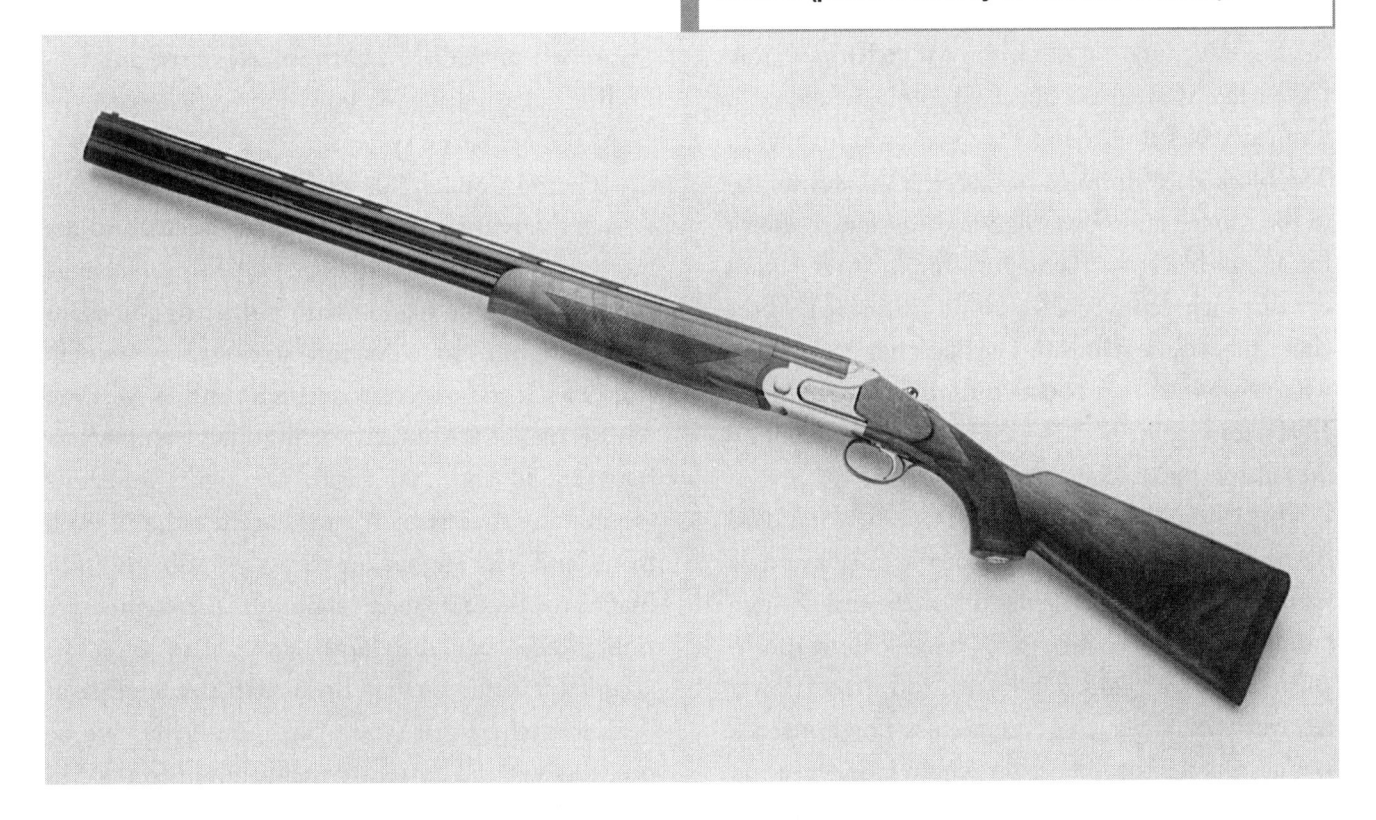

Chapter Eight 241

mer stock and forearm, but from 1994 heavier wooden furniture was standard. A three-shot hunting magazine was also standard, although extended magazines were also available.

The M1 Super 90 Field inspired a whole array of similar field guns. The Montefeltro Super 90 Standard Hunter, introduced in 1988, was originally in 12 gauge, but later became the first gun in the line to be offered in a 20-gauge option. Buyers had a choice of four barrel lengths and a hardwood stock and forearm. Magazine capacity was five rounds. The Montefeltro Turkey Gun was similar but with only a 24-inch barrel option (with three choke tubes) and satin-finished furniture. It was in production for only one year (1989). The Montefeltro Uplander followed the same design as the Turkey Gun, but offered a choice of 21- or 24-inch barrels. It was discontinued in 1992. The Montefeltro Slug Gun, which was designed for deer hunting, featured rifle-style sights and a 19-inch barrel. Like the Uplander, it was dropped in 1992.

In 1995, Benelli decided to bring out a top-of-the-line 20 gauge based on the Montefeltro action. Called the Montefeltro Super 90 Limited Edition, it featured a nickel-plated receiver with gold highlights. The Black Eagle **(photos p. 220-4, 248)** was similar to the Montefeltro Super 90 Standard Hunter, except for its all-black synthetic furniture. Barrel length options included 21-, 24-, 26- or 28 inches. Three choke tubes came standard. The Black Eagle Slug Gun, which remained in production for only a year (1990-1991), featured a rifled 24-inch barrel and a mount on the receiver for attaching a telescopic sight.

In 1991, Benelli changed from the Standard Black Eagle configuration to the Black Eagle Competition Model, which offered 26- and 28-inch barrel lengths, five choke tubes, a self-loading mechanism setup (for light trap loads), and a fancy lower receiver with silver embellishments. The buttstock was adjustable, too. Those for whom money was no object could opt for the Executive Series Black Eagle in three grades. Benelli's Super Black Eagle was capable of taking 3?-inch shotshells. The company has improved the Montefeltro action over the years to make it more versatile and able to handle all 12-gauge loads. It's available in polished blued, satin, engraved and Realtree Camo finishes.

The M3 Super 90 **(photo p. 238)** also introduced in 1989 along with the Black Eagle, differs from previous Benelli offerings with a choice of operating systems. Simply by turning a ring placed at the front of the forearm (below the barrel), a shooter had a choice between a pump action or the Montefeltro rotating bolt system (same as the M1 Super 90 series covered above). The inspiration for the convertible operating mode found on the M3 Super 90 came from Franchi's SPAS-12 military/police shotgun, the first production shotgun that could be changed at will from semiautomatic to pump action and back again. It made its debut in 1984 and was enormously successful. Shooters should know, however, that Benelli's M3 Super 90 improves considerably, both in easy of use and reliability with lighter loads, when joined with the SPAS-12 operating system.

The M3 Super 90 features a set of rifle-style sights, the rear sight being a square notch and the front a thick, sturdy blade. The former can be moved from side to side with a drift to adjust for windage, but no elevation setting is provided, nor was it considered necessary on a weapon whose maximum effective range falls somewhere between 50 and 100 yards. No sight protectors (sometimes nicknamed "ears") are fitted, but both front and rear sights are heavily built and not likely to be damaged. Though the sights are unmarked, they are large enough to offer an acceptable sight picture on a man-sized target at distances where this type of weapon is likely to be used. As with all current Benelli shotguns, the M3

Super 90 features a crossbolt safety on the rear edge of the triggerguard (see above for additional specifications and features).

In light of its intended role, the M3 Super 90 has a 3-inch firing chamber for use with either 2-inch or 3-inch shotgun shells. This model can also fire slugs although the barrel is not rifled for them. Normal magazine capacity is seven rounds. With appropriate adapters, the M3 Super 90 can fire other ordnance, such as smoke and tear-gas grenades. Heckler & Koch marketed the M3 Super 90 in fixed stock or folding stock variants, with both configurations offering a separate pistol grip. The current M3 Super 90, which is sold independently by Benelli U.S.A. has a fixed rifle-type stock with abbreviated pistol grip.

An early Benelli M3 Super 90 Entry Gun appears on the right, along with a Beretta Model 1201 recoil-operated semiautomatic shotgun to the left. Note the Benelli is equipped with the optional pistol-grip stock, a useful feature that among other things allows the shooter to fire the gun one-handed in an emergency.

Heckler & Koch, Inc. and Benelli severed their business relationship in 1998. A new firm--Benelli U.S.A.--in association with Beretta U.S.A. (Accokeek, Maryland), now imports Benelli shotguns into the United States.

Part IV. FABARM

Upon discontinuing its association with Benelli in 1998, Heckler & Koch decided to pick up the FABARM (*Fabbrica Bresciana Armi S.p.A.*) shotgun line. Also Italian-made, it offers a wider product line than Benelli and at lower prices. Founded in 1900, the company began business with the manufacture of double-barreled sporting shotguns, both over-and-under and side-by-side. After World War II, FABARM expanded and developed a range of pump action and semiautomatic models. In time, its reputation grew until, by the early 1990s, the FABARM shotgun line had become one of the most successful in Europe.

Previous importers of the FABARM line into the U.S. Included Beeman Precision Arms of Santa Rosa, CA (until 1986), St. Lawrence Sales of Lake Orion, MI (1988-1990), and Ithaca Acquisition Corporation, Kings Ferry, NY (1993-1998). From 1990 to 1993, the FABARM line was virtually unavailable in America. Thus, its current partnership with Heckler & Koch, Inc. can only benefit FABARM, which until recent years had been little known in the U.S.A. Having FABARM on board also helped Heckler & Koch, too, since they had severed their relationship with Benelli.

FABARM shotguns display a combination of innovative design and quality workmanship. One particularly innovative touch is the "Tribore" system

Chapter Eight 243

Use Enough Gun.

The **Heym .600 Nitro Express** is the largest caliber bolt action rifle produced. Shooting a 900 grain bullet at 1,980 feet per second, the .600 Nitro is definitely "enough gun" for hunting the most dangerous game.

A specially designed box magazine, made from solid steel, holds the cartridges secure from recoil damage, preventing deformed bullets and overpressure cartridges. In .416 Rigby, the magazine holds five cartridges, plus one in the chamber.

Barrels of **Heym Express** rifles are made of special Krupp steel, the same tough steel used in cannon barrels. Cold-hammer forging on CNC machinery ensures that all barrels are produced to exact tolerances for greater accuracy. And after stringent accuracy testing, all Heym rifles are then proof fired by the German government.

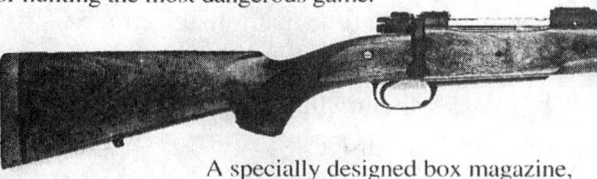

The modern magnum Mauser-type action is machined from a solid block of steel and guarantees the strength needed to handle heavy-hitting cartridges like .600 Nitro Express. A crisp Timney trigger is standard. **Heym Express** rifles are available in a variety of big game chamberings, including .338 Lapua, .375 H&H, .378 Weatherby, .460 Weatherby, .416 Rigby, .450 Ackley, .500 Nitro Express, and .500 A-Square.

For an elite hunting arm built to the legendary standards of men like Robert Ruark, choose a **Heym Express** rifle.

HEYM
A hunting tradition you can stake your life on.

HECKLER & KOCH offered the Heym rifle line until 1993. The Magnum Express series rifles were the tip of the line in power, features and price tag, the .600 Nitro Express cartridge offering a power level sufficient for the most dangerous game (courtesy of Heckler & Koch).

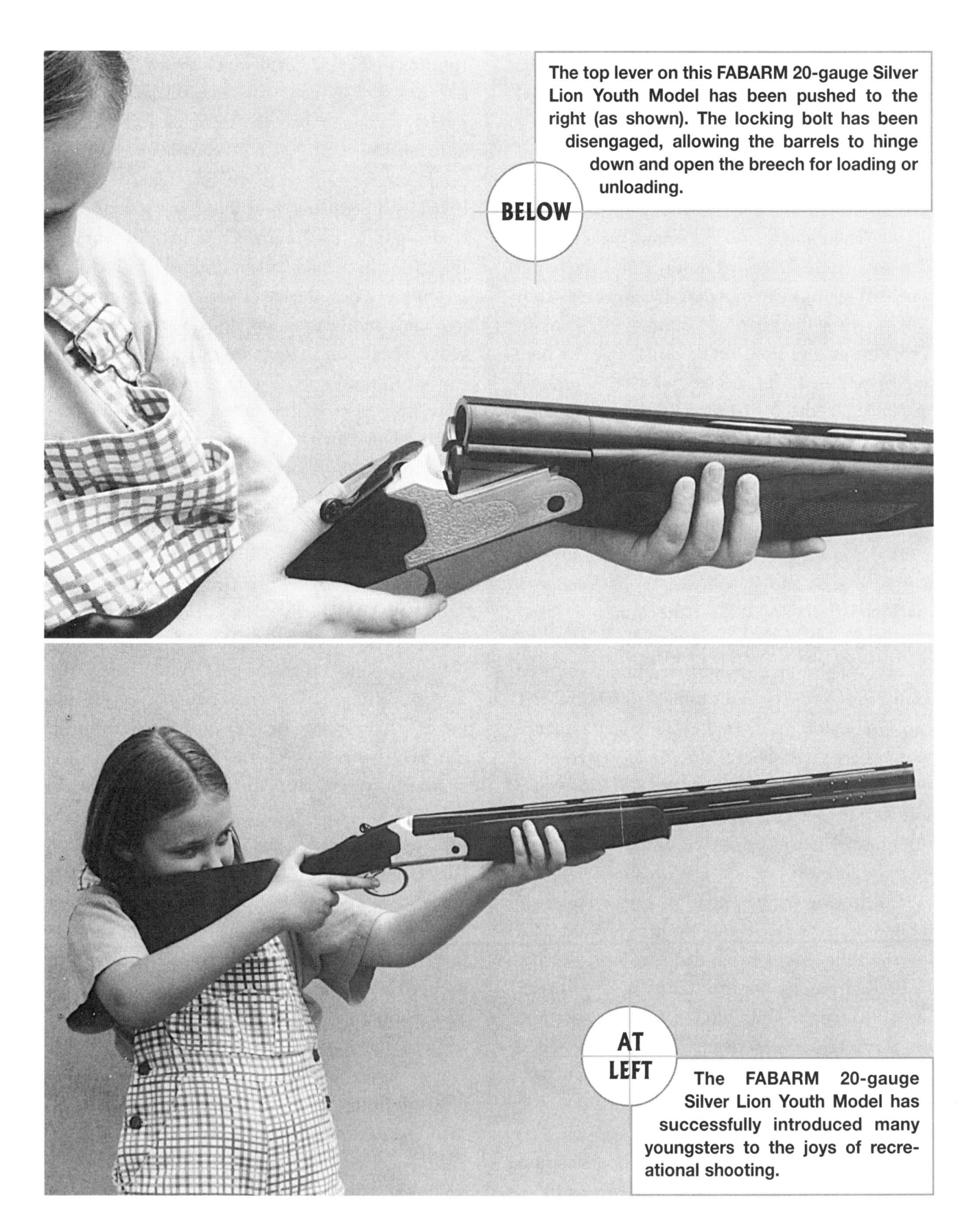

BELOW — The top lever on this FABARM 20-gauge Silver Lion Youth Model has been pushed to the right (as shown). The locking bolt has been disengaged, allowing the barrels to hinge down and open the breech for loading or unloading.

AT LEFT — The FABARM 20-gauge Silver Lion Youth Model has successfully introduced many youngsters to the joys of recreational shooting.

Chapter Eight 245

on which their shotgun barrels are built. As the name suggests, these barrels (available as an option) feature three "regions" or areas. Starting nearest the receiver, the first region is slightly overbored at 18.8mm (.74 inch) and a little wider than usual. The intent was to reduce felt recoil without giving up shot-column velocity. The second region, called the "first choke," occurs midway down the barrel where it gradually constricts (chokes) the shot column to a diameter of 18.4mm (.724 inch). The shot pattern now has the usual cylinder bore appearance and the velocity of the column is increased. In the final region, nearest the muzzle, FABARM shotgun barrels employ a choke system, with the last two inches or so reverting to a cylinder bore once again.

FABARM's "Red Lion" (**photos p. 224-6, 239**) is a gas-operated auto-loading shotgun with a fixed ejector and is lightweight. Its receiver is machined from Ergal, the same aluminum alloy perfected by Beretta in the 1950s for making the frames of lightweight automatic pistols. The Red Lion offers 24-, 26- and 28-inch barrels and five choke tubes for maximum flexibility in accordance with a particular shooter's needs or target situation. For a 12-gauge shotgun, the Red Lion offers soft recoil to begin with, then adds optional features that reduce recoil, including a device that fits over the forearm cap and another that fits in the buttstock. The manual safety is a crossbolt type located at the rear edge of the triggerguard, and is reversible for left-handed shooters. Other FABARM autoloading shotguns in the "Lion" series include the Gold Lion, the Camo Lion and the Sporting Clays Lion. Among their best shared features is a recoil pad at the end of the buttstock offering an excellent non-skid design that stays put on the shoulder.

One of the best-selling pump action shotguns currently available in Europe is FABARM's FP-6, (**photos p. 229-32, 249**) which shares many internal parts with the company's semiautomatic "Lion" series. Twin action bars and interchangeable chokes are available. Four major FP-6 variants have been produced in recent years, the first being a 20-inch barrel with perforated heat shield and a small front blade sight. Its fixed buttstock is made of synthetic material. The second variant utilizes a 14-inch barrel without a heat shield, a Picatinny rail for mounting lights and laser-aiming devices at the back end of the receiver, and a front sight that folds out of the way when not in use. Because of its short barrel, a Class III licensed dealer must process all paper work when selling this model to a private U.S. citizen. The third FP-6 variant features a 20-inch smooth barrel, a Picatinny rail and a flip-up front sight. The fourth variant is the same as the third except for a folding stock made of heavy-gauge wire, plus a pistol grip.

The FABARM FP-6 was a major purchase by France's *Gendarmerie Nationale*, which speaks volumes about this model (the French rarely buy foreign weapons). For France to buy a shotgun made in Italy, it must be truly superior. Its future in the U.S. personal defense and policy markets appears bright indeed. FABARM continues to make over-and-under shotgun models in the Lion series, including the Black Lion, Max Lion and Sporting Clays Competition (**photos p. 228, 233-5**). All are made with top-quality wooden stocks and forends featuring hand-cut checkering. Barrels are chrome-lined for added durability, with five choke tubes supplied as standard. Porting and Tribore boring are available barrel options, as are inertia-type single triggers. Rebounding hammers add to the safety aspects of these o/u shotguns, extending as they do into the firing chamber at the moment of firing, then withdrawing away from the chamber.

In an effort to get young people involved in the shooting sports, FABARM produces two Youth

The FABARM Classic Lion Grade I features a three-inch chamber; oil-finished European walnut furniture, a boxlock action, and chrome-lined chambers and bores (photo courtesy of Heckler & Koch).

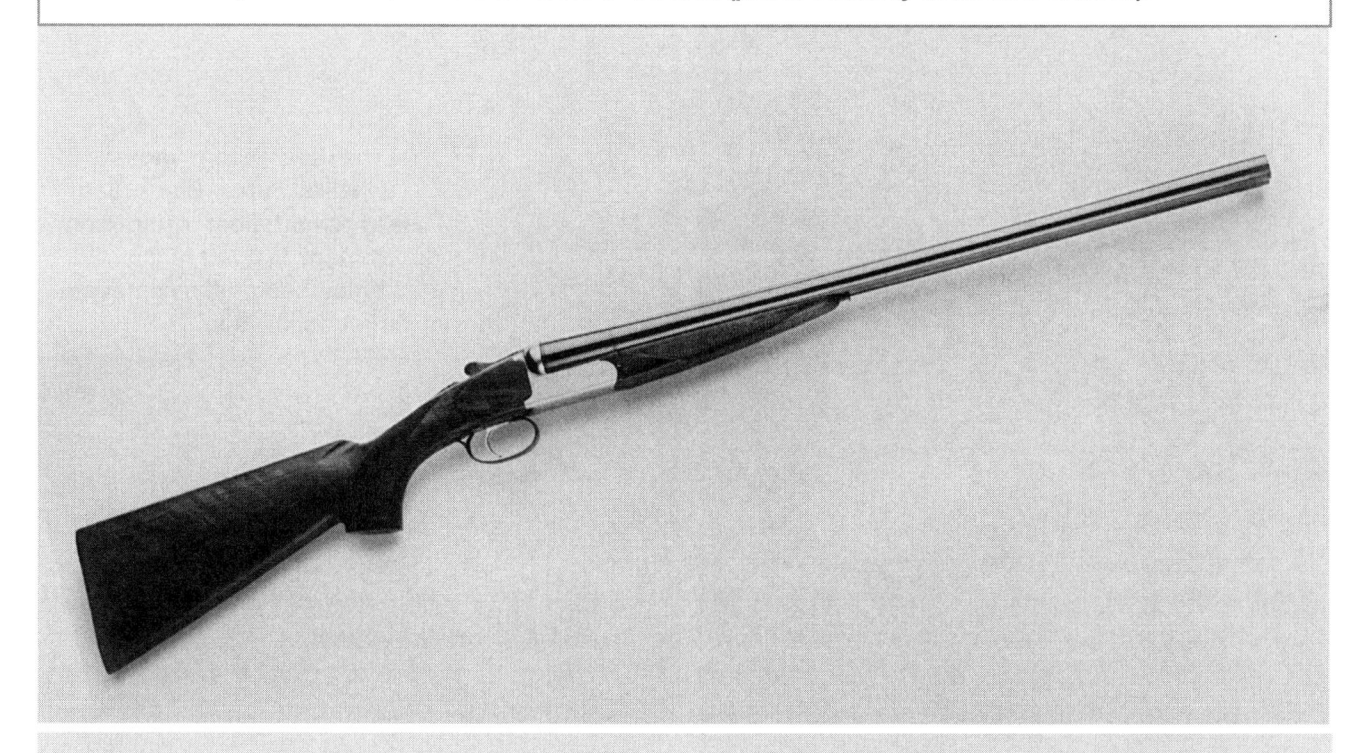

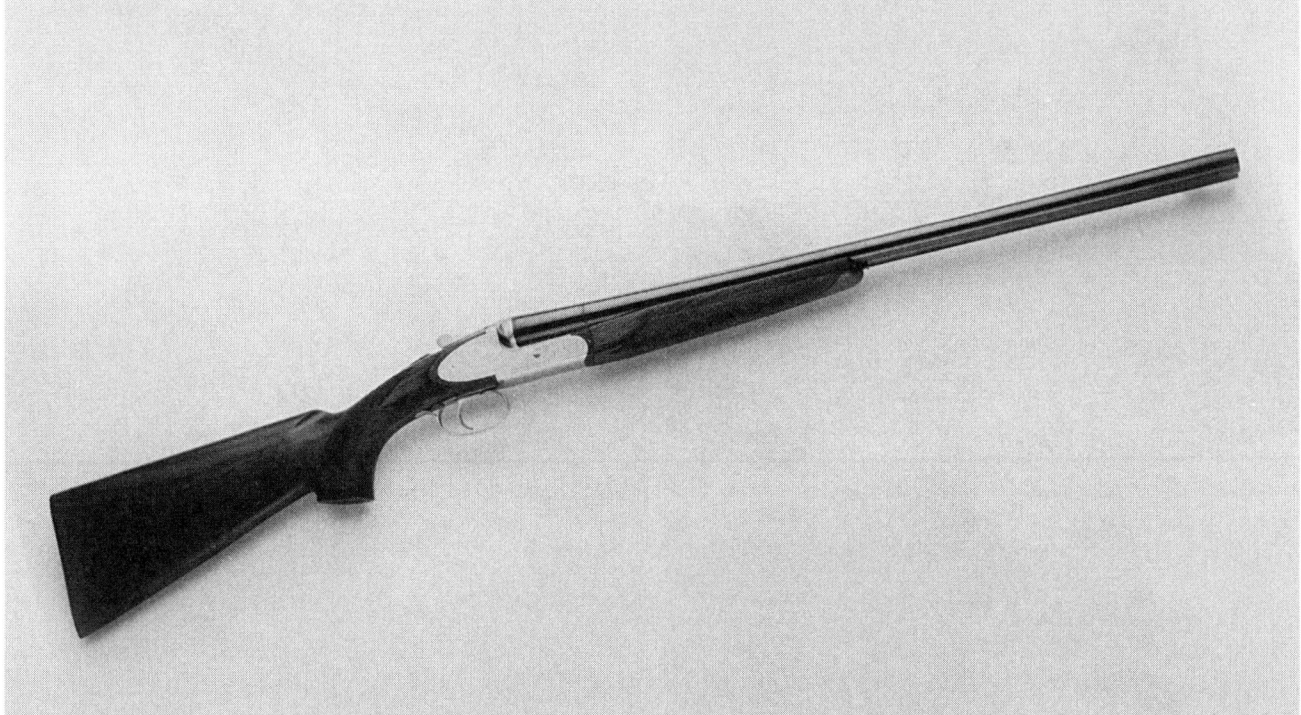

The FABARM Classic Lion Grade II includes a sidelock action with attractive removable sideplates (silver-plated and engraved with game scenes) (photo courtesy of Heckler & Koch)

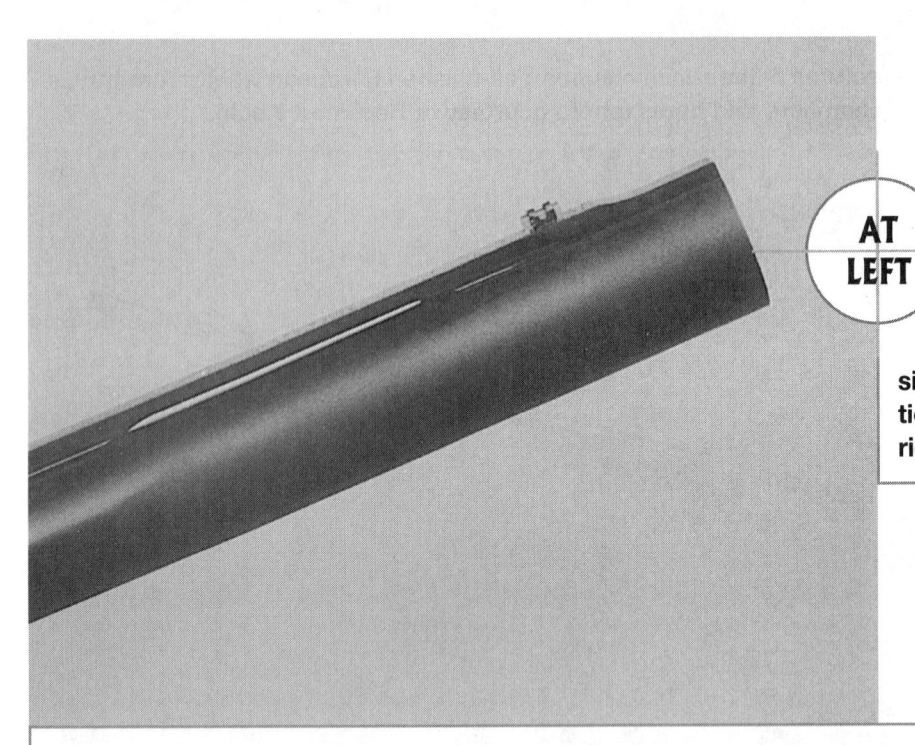

AT LEFT The most recent variants of Benelli's Super Black Eagle use a bright fiber optic front sight element, instead of the traditional brass bead, allowing superior target acquisition.

BELOW Benelli's Super Black Eagle disassembles as shown for cleaning and easier storage.

AT RIGHT The FABARM Silver Lion Youth Models come standard with an additional aiming bead midway down the sighting rib.

BELOW The FP-6 uses a perforated sheet steel handguard around the barrel proper, a feature favored by many military and police organizations.

Chapter Eight 249

Model (**photos p. 236-7, 245, 249**) o/u shotguns in 12 and 20 gauge. Most FABARM 12-gauge shotguns have 3-inch chambers, but three of the company's o/u models feature 3 1/2-inch chambers, allowing shooters to use all types of 12-gauge shotshells. These models are the Camo Turkey (**photo p. 240**) with Picatinny receiver rail, the Ultra Mag Lion with blackened walnut furniture (for superior recoil control), and the Ultra Camo Mag Lion (**photo p. 241**). The company still makes two striking side-by-side, double-barreled shotguns in the Classic Lion series. Both feature chrome-lined barrels with five choke tubes and 3-inch firing chambers. Standard barrel length is 26 inches (28-inch barrels are available on special order), with shooters controlling both barrels with a single trigger. The Classic Lion Grade I has a traditional boxlock design, while the Classic Lion Grade II is a sidelock with removable sideplates. Both guns feature polished receivers with attractive engraving. The combination of polished blued barrels, oil-finished walnut furniture and receivers in the white is most attractive--a far cry from the somber G3, and yet both continue to play important roles in the Heckler & Koch story.

Part V. The Joint Services Combat Shotgun (JSCS)/M1014

The U.S. armed forces still employ a wide collection of shotguns, including the militarized "*Trench*" models, festooned with such mil-spec features as ventilated handguards and bayonet lugs. "*Riot*" guns, on the other hand, are durable and reliable "off-the-shelf" sporting-type shotguns. Trench models are usually found in the front lines, while the riot models are generally used for rear-echelon duties, such as training and prisoner escort. Standards are obviously higher for trench shotguns than for the riot models.

Shotguns used by the U.S. military date back to the Winchester Model 97 designed by John Browning. Widely issued in both World Wars, the Model 97 also saw limited combat action as late as the Vietnam War. A 12 gauge, pump-action repeating shotgun, its tubular magazine is located beneath the barrel. Aside from its exposed hammer, the Model 97 served as a pattern for most of the guns that followed it into service. The U.S. Army also issued a few thousand Model 10 pump action 12 gauge shotguns made by Remington during World War I. This weapon operated much like the Model 97 but featured a hammerless receiver instead of an exposed hammer. During World War II, Winchester's Model 12--another hammerless design--supplemented the Model 97. Other pump action shotguns issued to U.S. military forces since World War I include the Ithaca Model 37, the Remington Model 31, the Stevens Models 520 and 620, the Savage/Stevens Model 77E, and the Remington Model 870. More recently, Mossberg's Model 590 has seen wide use in military service along with commercial-type Mossberg Model 500s.

The pump-action repeating shotgun has many advocates in the armed forces, but many military shooters prefer the self-loading type, largely because, under stress, shooters sometime fail to cycle the gun's action with sufficient vigor to reload the mechanism. This phenomenon, known as "short stroking," can jam a shotgun tight and put it out of action at critical moments. With few exceptions, self-loading shotguns are made in a semiautomatic configuration (rather than selective fire) because of the heavy recoil from the 12 gauge round. Semiautomatic shotguns issued to the U.S. military since the 1930s have included the Remington Model 11 (a close copy of Browning's Auto-5) and the Savage Model 720. These guns, having proved a disappointment in arduous front-line service, saw relatively little military service following World War II and were ultimately replaced by the pump-action guns described above.

By the late 1990s, the multiplicity of shotgun types was viewed by U.S. Armed forces as a burden, allowing military personnel the luxury of choosing from among several different firearms, a process not normally considered efficacious by most military organizations, which think in terms of high volume buying, stocking spare parts and standardizing training. Whatever its efficiencies, Mossberg's Model 590 offered little in the way of design advancement over the aged Winchester Model 97. Both are pump-action guns employing tubular magazines and firing the same ammunition. The armed forces saw room for improvement, however, and as a result the Joint Services Small Arms Program (JSSAP) returned to one of its earliest projects: the creation of a versatile, modernized shotgun design that would appeal to all branches of the U.S. Armed forces, including the Army, Navy, Marine Corps, Air Force and Coast Guard.

Accordingly, JSSAP directed the U.S. Army Armaments Research Development and Engineering Center (ARDEC) to select a new shotgun. Soon after, the Joint Services Combat Shotgun (JSCS) committee considered five competing shotgun designs. On February 9, 1999, Heckler & Koch was declared winner of the "Base Year," or first-phase, contract calling for submission of 20 shotguns, called the M1014, for

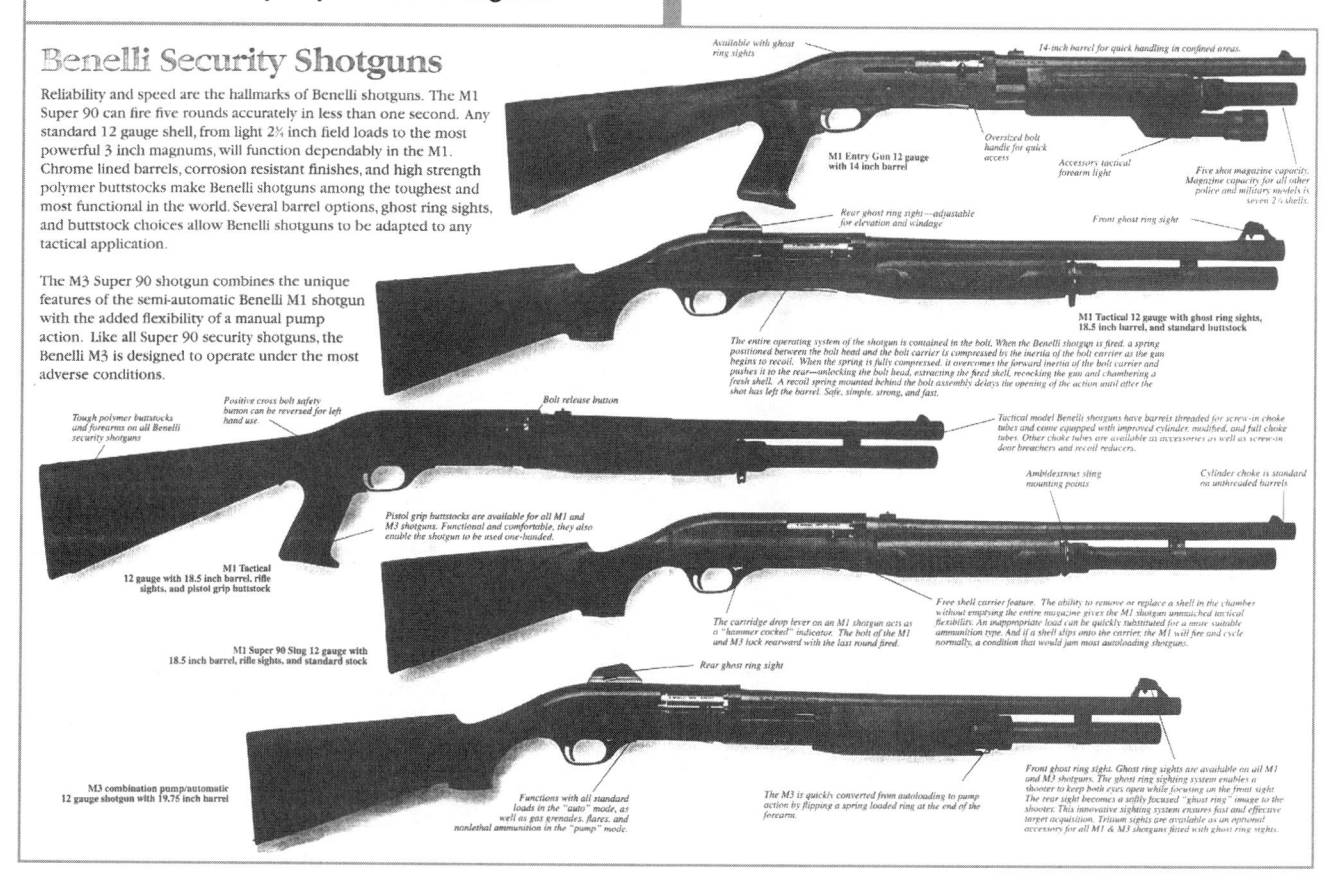

> **A 1994 advertisement from Heckler & Koch's military and police division shows an assortment of Benelli M1 Super 90 semiautomatic and M3 Super 90 semiautomatic/pump tactical shotguns.**

Chapter Eight 251

Ghost-ring rear sights, as shown here on a Mossberg Model 590, have become highly favored on fighting shotguns since their popularization by Colonel Jeff Cooper in the late 1980s. A number of Benelli shotguns formerly carried by Heckler & Koch also included this useful feature.

Technical Feasibility Testing. The tests began in April, 1999, at the Aberdeen Proving Ground in Maryland. On February 10, 2000, the U.S. Marine Corps announced its satisfaction with Heckler & Koch's M1014, formally requesting production of 3,977 guns in the first year. On May 12, 2000, Heckler & Koch won a production contract valued at $2.8 million covering four years, with delivery beginning in September of 2000 and quantities set at a rate of 500 shotguns per month thereafter. Additional M1014 shipments were made in 2000 (U.S. Army) and 2001 (Coast Guard), with others scheduled in 2002 (Coast Guard) and 2003 (U.S. Navy).

With Benelli producing the M1014 combat shotgun for Heckler & Koch, the former partnership between these two companies has been restored. Having learned from past mistakes, the Marine Corps insisted that the M1014's self-loading mechanism be made especially rugged and reliable. Benelli addressed these concerns by creating a new gas-operating system featuring dual gas ports, pistons and cylinders for a more reliable operation ("redundancy" as the military calls it). Heckler & Koch calls this new mechanism its "Auto Regulating Gas Operated" system, or ARGO. This system uses surplus propellant gas to flush the system with each shot, a self-cleaning feature that reduces maintenance requirements to a minimum.

The rot-proof polymer furniture and collapsible stock on the M1014 add to its versatility. With the stock extended, the shotgun measures 39.8 inches in length, and with the stock closed its length is reduced to 34.9 inches. Unloaded, the M1014 weighs 8.4 pounds. The rear sight, with its Ghost Ring configuration, is demonstrably one of the best types of its kind for rapid target acquisition. The front sight is a sturdy post, but without a protective hood. A scope rail enables shooters to mount accessory aiming devices on the receiver in front of the rear sight. Aside from these features, as mandated by the military, the receiver, barrel, pistol grip and magazine clearly reveal the M1014's Benelli ancestry.

To make this shotgun as versatile as possible, it's equipped with a three-inch chamber, which means it can use either 2 1/2-inch or 3-inch 12 gauge shells. With the former, the M1014's tubular magazine holds up to seven rounds; and with three-inch shells it holds six rounds. Two additional rounds--one in the firing chamber and one on the magazine carrier--enable the M1014 to carry up to nine rounds. To hold down costs, JSSAP decided to eliminate development of specialized ammunition, which had been a cornerstone of the ill-fated CAWS project. Not having this ammo proved less disadvantageous than one might think, since manufacturers have spent decades refining the 12 gauge shotgun shell. With several types available, shooters were free to adapt their shotguns to different missions. The choice of a tubular magazine feed for the M1014 unfortunately proved a missed opportunity in updating the design of combat shotguns. A detachable box magazine would have allowed much faster reloading and safer unloading than is possible with a tubular magazine. For these reasons, firearms manufacturers had abandoned tubular magazines for military rifles by the early 1900s in favor of the detachable box magazine. Nevertheless, the M1014 has outperformed any of the militarized shotguns that preceded it into U.S. Armed Forces service.

With the military's adoption of the M1014, the Heckler & Koch shotgun story has come full circle, starting with the CAWS. Heckler & Koch has, at last, a military shotgun design in production. • **H&K**

SPECIFICATIONS: H&K SHOTGUNS

Model	Mfr*	Action	OAL (in.)	Barrel (in.)	Weight (lbs.)	Gauge	Magazine
M3 Super 90	BN	Pump/SA	41	19.75	7.9	12	7 rd tube
Super Black Eagle	BN	Semiauto	49.6	28	7.3	12	3 rd tube
M1 Super 90 Field	BN	Semiauto	49.5	28	7.4	12	3 rd tube
FP-6	FA	Pump	41.25	20	6.7	12	5 rd tube
Red Lion	FA	Semiauto	49.5	28	7	12	2 rd tube
Silver Lion Youth	FA	O&U	44.6	24	6	20	2-rd capacity
Classic Lion	FA	S&S	47.6	26	7	12	2-rd capacity

*Note: Manufacturer's code: BN=Benelli, FA=FABARM

Chapter Eight 253

1950

Fifty years of Heckler & Koch Firearms Fabarm Shotguns. Firearms Safety Begins With You. Read and follow all safety information in the operator's manual. Store all firearms in a safe and secure location. Keep firearms away from children. Always be a safe shooter.

2000

Appendix A

50 Years Of Leading Through Technology

1950

In the closing days of December 1949, three forward-looking engineers–Edmund Heckler, Theodor Koch and Alex Seidel–establish the engineering firm that later becomes HK.

The traditional center of German gunmaking enterprises, the small Black Forest village of Oberndorf becomes the home of Heckler & Koch GmbH in the winter of 1949-50.

256 Heckler & Koch

> Within a few short years of its founding, HK engineering innovation was apparent in the first firearm it developed: the G3 rifle. Used by the military in more than fifty nations, some three million G3 rifles have been produced.

1960

Appendix A 257

H&K

1960

Adopted by the German military in 1959, the G3 uses the unique delayed-locked roller bolt system; an operating system widely hailed today for its strength, reliability, and low recoil. Although more than forty years old, the G3 is still in general use throughout the world. The G3 led to the development of many other HK firearms and influenced advancements by a generation of firearms designers.

In the aftermath of general discouragement following World War II, the new engineering firm founded by Heckler, Koch and Seidel helps rebuild a nation destroyed by war. In the beginning, the company manufactures precision components for domestic and industrial sewing machines. Their range of products soon expands to include the design and manufacture of gauges and specialized tooling.

H&K

1970

In the mid-1960s, Heckler & Koch adapted the basic G3 design and operating system into a variety of other popular calibers–the most famous being the 9mm "HK," better known as the MP5. The MP5 (Machine Pistole 5) was adopted by the West German police and military and, within a few short years, by many of the world's special operations units. A variety of models were added in the past thirty years and the MP5, in all its models and configurations, is still the preeminent arm of its class.

HK came to the USA in 1976 when Heckler & Koch, Inc. was established in Arlington, Virginia, to serve the U.S. military, law enforcement and civilian markets. HK firearms like the semi-automatic HK91 .308 were especially popular with American shooters who wanted a tough and highly accurate rifle.

1970

1980

The breakthrough technology pioneered by HK on the B11 & Advanced Combat Rifle (both used "caseless ammunition") was thoroughly tested and validated in the 1980s. It was not adopted for political reasons related to the end of the Cold War.

1980

Despite restrictions placed on the importation of advanced semi-automatic rifles by the U.S. government in 1989, redesigned HK rifles like the HK911 and SR9 continue to find favor with American sportsmen.

During the 1980s and '90s, the precision accuracy found on the HK91 and its related variants—the SR9T, the SR9TC and PSG1—enabled target shooters to achieve performance unmatched in semi-automatic rifles.

262 Heckler & Koch

H&K

1990

During the earyl 1990s, Heckler & Koch develops the Mark 23 for U.S. Special Operations Command using much of the technology and engineering knowledge gained in creating the USP.

Appendix A 263

1990

Heckler & Koch is a key player in the firearms technology of the 21st century. Partnered with Alliance Techsystems and five other international firms, HK helps in the development of the OICW (Objective Individual Combat Weapon) for the U.S. military.

In 1999, HK introduced the Lock-Out Safety Device, a simple and effective way to lock a gun's action. The Lock-Out is now a standard feature on all HK USP-type and Mark 23 pistols.

H&K

2000

The year 1999 marks the first time since World War II that German soldiers are in combat. Using the newly developed Heckler & Koch G36 5.56mm rifle, German army units fight in support of human rights and social justice during NATO's ground deployment in Kosovo.

Appendix A 265

H&K

FABARM SHOTGUN SPECIFICATIONS

Description & Article Number	Gauge (Chamber)	Operation	Magazine Capacity*	Barrel Length/Type	Overall Length	Weight (in pounds)	Choke	Receiver Finish	Stock	Sights	Length of Pull	Drop at Heel	Drop at Comb
Red Lion Mark II #14120MK	12 (3 in.)	semi-automatic gas operated	2	24 in./TriBore	44.25 in.	7	C,IC,M,IM,F**	matte	gloss walnut	red front bar	14.58 in. 370mm	1.58 in. 40mm	2.44 in. 62mm
Red Lion Mark II #16120MK	12 (3 in.)	semi-automatic gas operated	2	26 in./TriBore	46.25 in.	7.1	C,IC,M,IM,F**	matte	gloss walnut	red front bar	14.58 in. 370mm	1.58 in. 40mm	2.44 in. 62mm
Red Lion Mark II #18120MK	12 (3 in.)	semi-automatic gas operated	2	28 in./TriBore	48.25 in.	7.2	C,IC,M,IM,F**	matte	gloss walnut	red front bar	14.58 in. 370mm	1.58 in. 40mm	2.44 in. 62mm
Gold Lion Mark II #14220MK	12 (3 in.)	semi-automatic gas operated	2	24 in./TriBore	44.25 in.	6.9	C,IC,M,IM,F**	matte	oil finished walnut with olive grip cap	red front bar	14.58 in. 370mm	1.58 in. 40mm	2.44 in. 62mm
Gold Lion Mark II #16220MK	12 (3 in.)	semi-automatic gas operated	2	26 in./TriBore	46.25 in.	7	C,IC,M,IM,F**	matte	oil finished walnut with olive grip cap	red front bar	14.58 in. 370mm	1.58 in. 40mm	2.44 in. 62mm
Gold Lion Mark II #18220MK	12 (3 in.)	semi-automatic gas operated	2	28 in./TriBore	48.25 in.	7.2	C,IC,M,IM,F**	matte	oil finished walnut with olive grip cap	red front bar	14.58 in. 370mm	1.58 in. 40mm	2.44 in. 62mm
Sporting Clays Lion #18220SC	12 (3 in.)	semi-automatic gas operated	2	28 in./TriBore	48.25 in.	7.2	C,IC,M,IM,F**	matte	oil finished walnut with olive grip cap	red front bar	14.58 in. 370mm	1.58 in. 40mm	2.44 in. 62mm
Sporting Clays Extra #18220EX	12 (3 in.)	semi-automatic gas operated	2	28 in./TriBore	49.50 in.	7.2	C,IC,M,IM,F,LM,LF** competition chokes	carbon fiber	oil finished walnut with olive grip cap	red front bar	14.58 in. 370mm	1.58 in. 40mm	2.44 in. 62mm
Sporting Clays Extra #13220EX	12 (3 in.)	semi-automatic gas operated	2	30 in./TriBore	51 in.	7.3	C,IC,M,IM,F,LM,LF** competition chokes	carbon fiber	oil finished walnut with olive grip cap	red front bar	14.58 in. 370mm	1.58 in. 40mm	2.44 in. 62mm
Camo Lion #14120C	12 (3 in.)	semi-automatic gas operated	2	24 in./TriBore	44.25 in.	7	C,IC,M,IM,F**	camo	camo covered walnut	red front bar	14.58 in. 370mm	1.58 in. 40mm	2.44 in. 62mm
Camo Lion #16120C	12 (3 in.)	semi-automatic gas operated	2	26 in./TriBore	46.25 in.	7.1	C,IC,M,IM,F**	camo	camo covered walnut	red front bar	14.58 in. 370mm	1.58 in. 40mm	2.44 in. 62mm
Camo Lion #18120C	12 (3 in.)	semi-automatic gas operated	2	28 in./TriBore	48.25 in.	7.2	C,IC,M,IM,F**	camo	camo covered walnut	red front bar	14.58 in. 370mm	1.58 in. 40mm	2.44 in. 62mm
FP6 #40621HS	12 (3 in.)	pump action	5	20 in./TriBore	41.20 in.	6.7	cylinder, barrel threaded for chokes	black protective	polymer	flip-up front & Picatinny rail	14.58 in. 370mm	1.58 in. 40mm	2.44 in. 62mm
FP6 Carbon Fiber Coated #40621CF	12 (3 in.)	pump action	5	20 in./TriBore	41.2 in.	6.5	cylinder, barrel threaded for chokes	carbon fiber	polymer	blade front	14.58 in. 370mm	1.58 in. 40mm	2.44 in. 62mm
FP6 Entry #40821T	12 (3 in.)	pump action	5	14 in.	33.75 in.	6.4	cylinder	matte	polymer	flip-up front & Picatinny rail	14.58 in. 370mm	1.58 in. 40mm	2.44 in. 62mm
Monotrap #79300MT	12 (2¾ in.)	single barrel	n/a	30 in./TriBore	48.50 in.	6	M,IM,F** competition chokes	matte	oil finished walnut	red front bar	14.58 in. 370mm	1.58 in. 40mm	2.44 in. 62mm
Max Lion #26320TB	12 (3 in.)	over-&-under	n/a	26 in./TriBore	43.25 in.	7.4	C,IC,M,IM,F**	silver	walnut	red front bar	14.58 in. 370mm	2.29 in. 58mm	1.50 in. 38mm
Max Lion #28320TB	12 (3 in.)	over-&-under	n/a	28 in./TriBore	45.25 in.	7.6	C,IC,M,IM,F**	silver	walnut	red front bar	14.58 in. 370mm	2.29 in. 58mm	1.50 in. 38mm
Max Lion #23320TB	12 (3 in.)	over-&-under	n/a	30 in./TriBore	47.25 in.	7.8	C,IC,M,IM,F**	silver	walnut	red front bar	14.58 in. 370mm	2.29 in. 58mm	1.50 in. 38mm
Max Lion 20 Gauge #26300TB	20 (3 in.)	over-&-under	n/a	26 in./TriBore	43.25 in.	6.8	C,IC,M,IM,F**	silver	walnut	red front bar	14.58 in. 370mm	2.29 in. 58mm	1.50 in. 38mm
Max Lion 20 Gauge #28300TB	20 (3 in.)	over-&-under	n/a	28 in./TriBore	45.25 in.	7	C,IC,M,IM,F**	silver	walnut	red front bar	14.58 in. 370mm	2.29 in. 58mm	1.50 in. 38mm
Max Lion Light #24320LT	12 (3 in.)	over-&-under	n/a	24 in./TriBore	42.5 in.	7.2	C,IC,M,IM,F**	silver	walnut	red front bar	14.58 in. 370mm	2.29 in. 58mm	1.50 in. 38mm
Max Lion Light 20 Gauge #24300LT	20 (3 in.)	over-&-under	n/a	24 in./TriBore	42.5 in.	7	C,IC,M,IM,F**	silver	walnut	red front bar	14.58 in. 370mm	2.29 in. 58mm	1.50 in. 38mm
Sporting Clays Competition #23720	12 (3 in.)	over-&-under	n/a	30 in./TriBore	48.5 in.	7.8	C,IC,M,IM,F**	silver	deluxe walnut	red front bar	14.58 in. 370mm	2.29 in. 58mm	1.50 in. 38mm
Sporting Clays Comp. 20 Ga. #28700	20 (3 in.)	over-&-under	n/a	28 in./TriBore	45.3 in.	7	C,IC,M,IM,F**	silver	deluxe walnut	red front bar	14.50 in. 368mm	2.17 in. 55mm	1.38 in. 35mm
Sporting Clays Comp. Extra #23720EX	12 (3 in.)	over-&-under	n/a	30 in./TriBore	48.5 in.	7.8	C,IC,M,IM,F,SS-F,SS-M**	silver	deluxe walnut	red front bar	14.58 in. 370mm	2.29 in. 58mm	1.50 in. 38mm
Sporting Clays Comp. Extra #28720EX	12 (3 in.)	over-&-under	n/a	28 in./TriBore	46.5 in.	7.8	C,IC,M,IM,F,SS-F,SS-M**	silver	deluxe walnut	red front bar	14.58 in. 370mm	2.29 in. 58mm	1.50 in. 38mm
Silver Lion #26520TB	12 (3 in.)	over-&-under	n/a	26 in./TriBore	43.25 in.	7.2	C,IC,M,IM,F**	silver	walnut	red front bar	14.50 in. 368mm	2.29 in. 38mm	1.50 in. 58mm
Silver Lion #28520TB	12 (3 in.)	over-&-under	n/a	28 in./TriBore	45.25 in.	7.5	C,IC,M,IM,F**	silver	walnut	red front bar	14.50 in. 368mm	2.29 in. 38mm	1.50 in. 58mm
Silver Lion #23520TB	12 (3 in.)	over-&-under	n/a	30 in./TriBore	47.25 in.	7.7	C,IC,M,IM,F**	silver	walnut	red front bar	14.50 in. 368mm	2.29 in. 38mm	1.50 in. 58mm
Silver Lion 20 Gauge #26500TB	20 (3 in.)	over-&-under	n/a	26 in./TriBore	43.25 in.	6.8	C,IC,M,IM,F**	silver	walnut	red front bar	14.50 in. 368mm	2.17 in. 55mm	1.38 in. 35mm
Silver Lion 20 Gauge #28500TB	20 (3 in.)	over-&-under	n/a	28 in./TriBore	45.25 in.	7.1	C,IC,M,IM,F**	silver	walnut	red front bar	14.50 in. 368mm	2.17 in. 55mm	1.38 in. 35mm
Silver Lion Cub 20 #24500Y	20 (3 in.)	over-&-under	n/a	24 in./TriBore	39.45 in.	6	C,IC,M,IM,F**	silver	walnut	red front bar	12.50 in. 318mm	2.17 in. 55mm	1.38 in. 35mm
Camo Turkey #50520C	12 (3.5 in.)	over-&-under	n/a	20 in./TriBore	37.2 in.	7.5	ported chokes ultra full	camo	camo covered walnut	front bar & Picatinny rail	14.50 in. 368mm	2.29 in. 58mm	1.50 in. 38mm
Ultra Mag Lion #58520TB	12 (3.5 in.)	over-&-under	n/a	28 in./TriBore	47.3 in.	7.9	C,IC,M,IM,F,SS-F,SS-M**	black	black colored walnut	red front bar	14.50 in. 368mm	2.29 in. 58mm	1.50 in. 38mm
Ultra Camo Mag Lion #58520C	12 (3.5 in.)	over-&-under	n/a	28 in./TriBore	47.3 in.	7.9	C,IC,M,IM,F,SS-F,SS-M**	camo	camo covered walnut	red front bar	14.50 in. 368mm	2.29 in. 58mm	1.50 in. 38mm
Super Light Lion #64520TB	12 (3 in.)	over-&-under	n/a	24 in./TriBore	41.25 in.	6.5	C,IC,M,IM,F**	black	walnut	red front bar	14.50 in. 368mm	2.29 in. 58mm	1.50 in. 38mm
Super Light Lion Cub #64520Y	12 (3 in.)	over-&-under	n/a	24 in./TriBore	39.3 in.	6	C,IC,M,IM,F**	black	walnut	red front bar	12.50 in. 318mm	2.29 in. 58mm	1.50 in. 38mm
Classic Lion Grade I #38520TB	12 (3 in.)	side-by-side	n/a	28 in./TriBore	46.5 in.	7	C,IC,M,IM,F**	silver	walnut	red front bar	14.58 in. 370mm	2.29 in. 58mm	1.50 in. 38mm
Classic Lion Grade I #33520TB	12 (3 in.)	side-by-side	n/a	30 in./TriBore	48.5 in.	7.1	C,IC,M,IM,F**	silver	walnut	red front bar	14.58 in. 370mm	2.29 in. 58mm	1.50 in. 38mm
Classic Lion Grade II #38320TB	12 (3 in.)	side-by-side	n/a	28 in./TriBore	46.5 in.	7.2	C,IC,M,IM,F**	silver	walnut	red front bar	14.58 in. 370mm	2.29 in. 58mm	1.50 in. 38mm
Classic Lion Grade II #33320TB	12 (3 in.)	side-by-side	n/a	30 in./TriBore	48.5 in.	7.3	C,IC,M,IM,F**	silver	walnut	red front bar	14.58 in. 370mm	2.29 in. 58mm	1.50 in. 38mm

*Magazine capacity given for 2.75 inch shells, size variations among some brands may result in less capacity. **Cylinder, Improved Cylinder, Modified, Improved Modified, Full, Light Modified, Light Full
SS-F (Steel Shot -Full) SS-M (Steel Shot -Modified) Specifications & models subject to change without notice.

H&K

PISTOL & RIFLE SPECIFICATIONS

HK PISTOL SPECIFICATIONS

Description & Article Number	Caliber	Operating System	Magazine Capacity*	Sights	Barrel Length	Overall Length	Weight (in pounds.)	Height	Grips/Stock
USP9 709001	9mm	short recoil, modified Browning action	10	3-dot	4.25 in.	7.64 in.	1.66	5.35 in.	polymer frame & integral grips
USP9 (stainless steel) 709021	9mm	short recoil, modified Browning action	10	3-dot	4.25 in.	7.64 in.	1.66	5.35 in.	polymer frame & integral grips
USP40 704001	.40 S&W	short recoil, modified Browning action	10	3-dot	4.25 in.	7.64 in.	1.74	5.35 in.	polymer frame & integral grips
USP40 (stainless steel) 704021	.40 S&W	short recoil, modified Browning action	10	3-dot	4.25 in.	7.64 in.	1.74	5.35 in.	polymer frame & integral grips
USP45 704501	.45 ACP	short recoil, modified Browning action	10	3-dot	4.41 in.	7.87 in.	1.90	5.55 in.	polymer frame & integral grips
USP45 (stainless steel) 704521	.45 ACP	short recoil, modified Browning action	10	3-dot	4.41 in.	7.87 in.	1.90	5.55 in.	polymer frame & integral grips
USP9 Compact 709031	9mm	short recoil, modified Browning action	10	3-dot	3.58 in.	6.81 in.	1.60	5.00 in.	polymer frame & integral grips
USP357 Compact 702357	.357 SIG	short recoil, modified Browning action	10	3-dot	3.58 in.	6.81 in.	1.60	5.00 in.	polymer frame & integral grips
USP9 Compact (ss) 709041	9mm	short recoil, modified Browning action	10	3-dot	3.58 in.	6.81 in.	1.60	5.00 in.	polymer frame & integral grips
USP40 Compact 704031	.40 S&W	short recoil, modified Browning action	10	3-dot	3.58 in.	6.81 in.	1.70	5.00 in.	polymer frame & integral grips
USP40 Compact (ss) 704041	.40 S&W	short recoil, modified Browning action	10	3-dot	3.58 in.	6.81 in.	1.70	5.00 in.	polymer frame & integral grips
USP45 Compact 704531	.45 ACP	short recoil, modified Browning action	8	3-dot	3.80 in.	7.09 in.	1.75	5.06 in.	polymer frame & integral grips
USP45 Compact (ss) 704561	.45 ACP	short recoil, modified Browning action	8	3-dot	3.80 in.	7.09 in.	1.75	5.06 in.	polymer frame & integral grips
USP45 Tactical 704501T	.45 ACP	short recoil, modified Browning action	10	adjustable target	5.08 in.	8.64 in.	2.24	5.90 in.	polymer frame & integral grips
USP45 Expert 704580	.45 ACP	short recoil, modified Browning action	10	adjustable target	5.20 in.	8.74 in.	2.30	5.90 in.	polymer frame & integral grips
Mark 23 723001	.45 ACP	short recoil, modified Browning action	10	3-dot	5.87 in.	9.65 in.	2.66	5.90 in.	polymer frame & integral grips
P7M8 045002	9mm	blowback operated, gas retarded	8	3-dot	4.13 in.	6.73 in.	1.75	5.04 in.	plastic grips & steel frame

HK RIFLE SPECIFICATIONS

Description & Article Number	Caliber	Operating System	Magazine Capacity*	Sights	Barrel Length	Overall Length	Weight (in pounds.)	Height	Grips/Stock
USC 701445	.45 ACP	blowback	10	adjustable	16 in.	35.43 in.	6	9.75 in.	polymer receiver & integral grips
SL8-1 701578	.223	gas operated, short stroke piston, rotary locking bolt	10	adjustable	20.80 in.	38.58 in.	8.6	9.84 in.	polymer receiver steel frame

* Civilian magazine capacities subject to limits imposed by the 1994 Crime Bill. Specifications, models, and pricing subject to change without notice. (ss) stainless steel

Appendix A 267

The U.S. affiliate of the world famous firearms manufacturer Heckler & Koch, GmbH of Oberndorf, Germany, HK, Inc. is the U.S. distributor of a wide range of technologically advanced fire-arms for the defense, law enforcement, and sporting markets. In addition to renowned HK handguns like the USP, P7, Mark 23, and the MP5 and UMP family of submachine guns. Heckler & Koch is the exclusive American distributor for FABARM shotguns of Italy.

Appendix B

A Sampling Of Current H&K Products

USC .45 ACP CARBINE

Derived from the HK UMP, the USC is a civilian utility carbine that uses the classic hard-hitting .45 ACP cartridge. Matched with the ultra-reliable blowback operating system, the HK USC is a radical departure from tradtional firearms designs.

Extensive use of the same durable, reinforced polymers used on HK's new line of military and police arms ensures light weight and durability. And the highest grade of weapons steel is used where it matters—in the cold hammer forged target barrel and the solidly-constructed bolt mechanism.

User ergonomics are not sacrificed. The skeletonized buttstock is topped with a comfortable rubber cheek rest and recoil pad. The web of the pistol grip is open for a comfortable shooting handhold. Hard points located on the top and front of the receiver make attachment of optional Picatinny rails easy, allowing almost any kind of sighting system or accessory to be mounted.

USC .45 utility carbine joins the HK SL8-1 .223 rifle as new age firearms made almost entirely of high strength polymers.

USC Carbine (shown with accessory forearm and upper-receiver Picatinny rails with Aimpoint red dot reflex sight)

Appendix B

SL8-1 .223 RIFLE

This new rifle—the HK SL8-1—is constructed almost entirely of a reinforced cabon-fiber polymer. Based on the current combat-tested German Army G36 rifle, the SL8-1 uses a proven short stroke, piston-actuated gas operating system, well known for simplicity and reliability.

Designed and engineered to deliver exceptional shooting performance, the SL8-1 is already a favorite among European rifle shooters, due in large part to the many modular sighting systems available. These include extended and short Picatinny rail mounts with open sights, a 1.5 power scope with an integral carry handle, and a dual optical system that combines a 3 power scope with an electronic red dot sight. The ergonomic lines of the HK SL8-1 are functional and modern, giving the SL8-1 the look and feel of a 21st century firearm.

FIELD PUMP 12 GAUGE
with 28-inch barrel

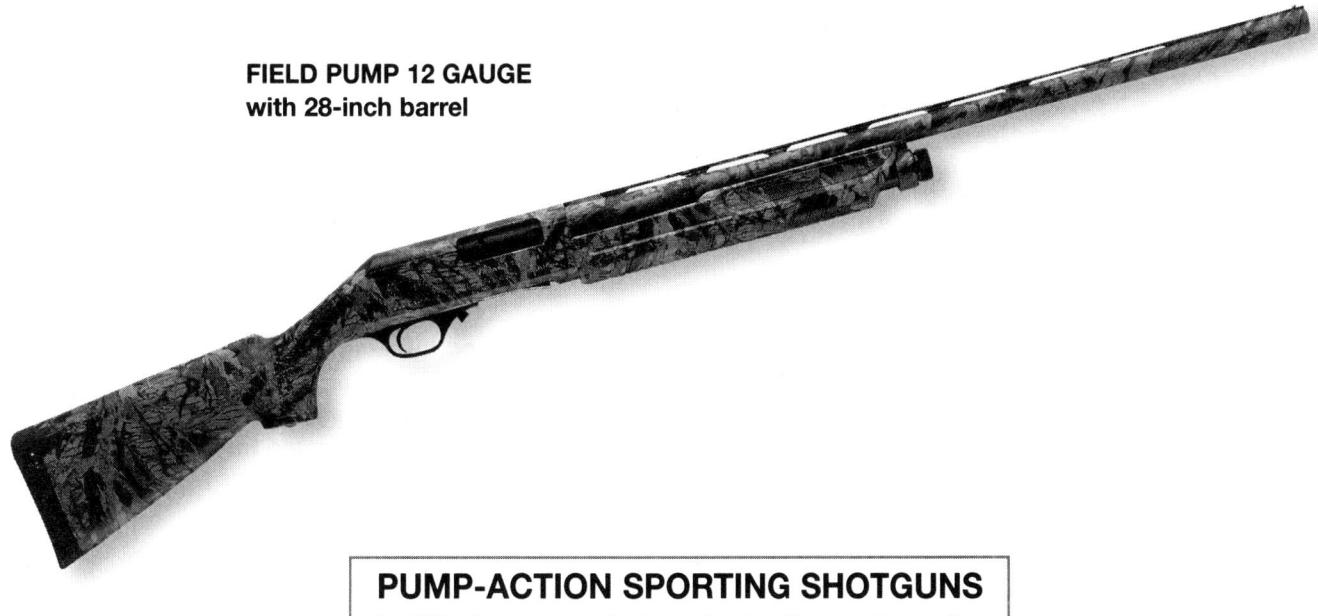

PUMP-ACTION SPORTING SHOTGUNS
A utilitarian pump shotgun for hunting and sporting use, the FABARM Field and Camo Field models combine the reliability of the FP Series security shotguns with the qualities of the popular FABARM semi-automatics. This manually operated shotgun alternative to the dime-a-dozen scatter guns is protected by a lifetime warranty!

CAMO FIELD PUMP 12 GAUGE
with 28-inch barrel

USP45 TACTICAL

An enhanced version of the USP45, the Tactical is designed for users who need the features found on the Mark 23, but in a smaller and more affordable pistol. The USP45 Tactical pistol approaches the precision found on the Mark 23 by adding an extended threaded barrel with a rubber O-ring, match trigger with adjustable trigger stop, and adjustable target-type sights.

USP EXPERT

Using the common lineage of the USP and developed in conjuction with internationally renowned pistol shooters, the USP Expert achieves the highest levels of accuracy by combining features of the USP Tactical and Mark 23 pistols with a new longer slide design. The result is a USP well suited to a wide variety of tactical shooting scenarios.

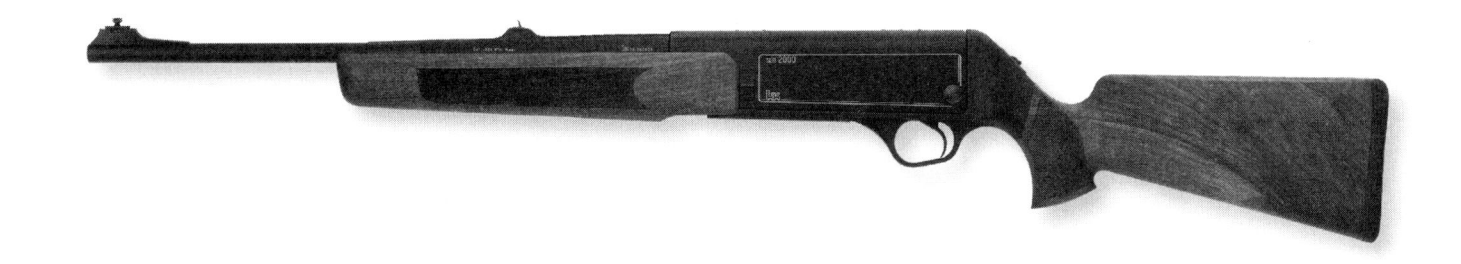

SLB 2000 .30-06 RIFLE

The SLB 2000 represents the ultimate achievement in the design and manufacture of a modern semi-automatic hunting rifle. By combining high strength materials with HK's famous metallurgy. Heckler & Koch engineers have wedded the practical ergonomics of a modern high tech firearm with traditional rifle sophistication. The SLB 2000 uses a proven gas operating system that is extremely robust. The same bolt system can handle a wide array of popular international hunting cartridges (.308, .30-06, 7x64mm, 9.3x62mm) when barrel conversion is called for. The exaggerated shape and angle of the pistol grip make accurate shooting easier and more natural than traditional hunting rifles.

The SLB 2000 uses a simple and robust short stroke, piston-actuated gas operating system and is completely modular.

Appendix B

**USP9 COMPACT 9MM
STAINLESS MODEL**

HK USP COMPACT

The HK USP Compact is a small frame pistol capable of firing the most powerful cartridges in 9mm, .40 S&W, .357 SIG, and .45 ACP. Based on the full-size USP models, these handy pistols combine compact size with optimum effective shooting performance.

USP Compacts are smaller and lighter than large frame USPs. The reduction in trigger reach and grip circumference increases concealability and enhances shooting ergonomics. Unlike some sub-compact semiautomatic pistols that use a difficult to shoot "two-finger grip" frame, the USP Compact uses a narrow, full-hand grip frame with a choice of interchangeable extended or flush-fitting magazine floorplates. This makes the pistol easy to shoot without sacrificing concealability. Like their large frame predecessors, USP Compacts are designed with the demanding needs of the American shooter in mind. Using a modified linkless Browning-type action, the USP Compact is built to take the punishment of high energy +P loads.

To reduce the length of the slide and barrel on the USP Compact, the mechanical recoil reduction system found on large frame USPs has been replaced by a specially designed flat compression spirng contained in the captive recoil spring assembly by a polymer absorber bushing. Service life is engineered to exceed 20,000 rounds.

MAX LION 12 GAUGE

MAX LION 20-GAUGE

MAX LION LIGHT 12-GAUGE

SPORTING CLAYS COMPETITION LION EXTRA

OVER-&-UNDER SHOTGUNS

Recognized in Europe and throughout the world as affordable, high quality competition and hunting shotguns, these arms have been unavailable in North America until very recently.

These fine shotguns are distinguished by their elegant styling and sophisticated engineering; yet they are no less devoted to performance, utility, and reliability in the field. FABARM over-&-under shotguns are practical, multi-functional sporting arms and covered by a Lifetime Warranty.

The high grade Nickel-Chromium-Molybdenum receiver is machined from a block forging using CNC tooling. Barrels are made by the innovative FABARM process of deep drilling and honing of premium steel barrel stock. Thanks to the patented TriBore Barrel System, each FABARM over-&-under shotgun achieves superior shot patterning and less felt recoil—with no decrease in shot velocity.

Using the right balance of advanced engineering technology and old world craftsmanship also leads to the creation of functional artwork.

G36K 5.56MM CARBINE

G36 COMMANDO 5.56MM SHORT CARBINE

HK G36 WEAPON SYSTEM

The G36 is a modular weapon system in caliber 5.56x45mm NATO (.223 Remington). It is constructed almost entirely of a tough carbon fiber-reinforced polymer material and uses a simple, clean shooting, self-regulating gas system. The G36 thus offers a lightweight weapon that delivers high performance with extremely low maintenance. The barrel of the G36 can be exchanged to create a rifle, short carbine, carbine, or light support variant using the same common receiver. Tested and currently in service with German and Spanish Armed Forces (including the new NATO Rapid Reaction Force), the G36 is available to U.S. law enforcement and military customers.

**HK/BENELLI M1014
COMBAT SHOTGUN
(RIGHT SIDE VIEW,
STOCK COLLAPSED)**

**HK/BENELLI M1014
COMBAT SHOTGUN
(LEFT SIDE VIEW,
STOCK COLLAPSED)**

CLASSIC LION (ENGLISH) GRADE I 12 GAUGE with 28-inch barrels (also available with 26 and 30-inch barrels)

CLASSIC LION GRADE II 12 gauge with 28-inch barrels (also available with 30-inch barrels)

SIDE-BY-SIDE SHOTGUNS

The Classic Lion shotguns are made from the finest materials by **FABARM**'s most accomplished craftsmen. A truly functional work of art, a **FABARM** side-by-side shotgun uses strong monoblock barrel construction and four separate lugs instead of two, elminating any lateral weakness. The Grade I (English) is a tradtional boxlock design; the Grade II has removable side plates—and both accept the widest range of chokes. A mixture of the modern and the old world, **FABARM** Classic Lion doubles are ageless in artistry and performance.

HK PDW
(Personal Defense Weapon)
4.6mm x 30mm

Appendix B 281

MARK 23 .45 ACP

HK MARK 23

The HK Mark 23 Caliber .45 ACP pistol gives shooters match grade accuracy equal to that of the finest cusom made handguns—yet it exceeds the most stringent operational requirements ever demanded of a combat shotgun.

The Mark 23 provides this accuracy without the need for hand-fitted parts common in custom-built match pistols costing thousands of dollars more.

A thoroughly tested handgun, the MK23/Mark 23 project originated in 1991 when HK began developing it for the U.S. Special Operations Command, the organization that directs the activities of America's elite military units, including the Navy SEALs and the Army Special Forces.

The first HK MK 23 pistols were delivered to the U.S. Special Operations Command in 1996 for operational deployment, making the MK 23 the first caliber .45 ACP pistol to enter American military service since the venerable Government Model 1911A1.

Index

A
AAI Corporation, 97
Aberdeen Proving Grounds, 168, 252
Advanced Combat Rifle (ACR) testing, 95, 97
Advanced Development Objective, 165
AG3, 208, 209
Aiming Point Projector, 189, 194
AK-4, 211
AK-47, 88, 91, 118, 213
AKM, 88
Alliant Techsystems, Hopkins, Minnesota, 100
Ameli, 163
American Defense Preparedness Association, 96
American Expeditionary Force (AEF), 181
APC, 147
ARGO (Auto Regulating Gas Operated) system, 252
Armalite
  AR-15/M16, 98
  AR-18, 98
  /Colt CAR-15, 76
Australia, 163

B
Baden-Württemberg, 34
Bahrain, 76, 130
Bangladesh, 76, 159, 210
Bayern (Bavaria), 34
Bayonets, 189, 190, 192, 194, 197
Beeman Precision Arms, Santa Rosa, California, 243
Belgium, 130, 163, 172
Benelli, 167, 215
  B-76 9mm handgun, 235
  Black Eagle series, 219-223, 242, 248, 253
  M1 Super 90, 240-242, 251, 253
  M3 Super 90, 217-219, 232, 238, 242-243, 251, 253
  M1014, 252-253
  Model 121 M1 Police/Military, 234-235
  Montefeltro system, 242
Benelli U.S.A., 243
Beretta
  Model 9, 146, 168
  Model 38/42, 126
  Model 70/90, 234
  Model 92, 12, 41
  Model 92F, 52, 143
  Model 92S-1, 44, 45
  Model 1201, 243
  Model 1934, 36
  Model AR70/90, 87
  Model M3P, 227
  Model PM-12, 130
  Model PM-125, 137
Beretta U.S.A., 243
BFA (Blank Firing Attachment), 182, 197
Bipods, 170, 172
Bolivia, 76, 159
Brazil, 79, 80, 130, 136
Bren gun, 172
British Aerospace, 101
Browning, 57
  Auto-5 shotgun, 220, 224, 251
  BAR, 159, 163-164, 172
  High Power, 12, 13, 19, 145
  M1917 and 1919, 116, 163, 173
  Model 1918 Automatic Rifle, 116
Browning, John, 250
Brunei, 76, 159
BTU (Universal Bullet Trap), 183-184
Bullpup rifles, 117-119
Burma (Myanmar), 76, 199, 200, 202
Burundi, 76

C
Cameroons, 159
Canada, 76, 130, 141, 163
Carcano Model 28 TS, 182
Caseless ammunition, 92-95
CAW (Close Assault Weapon), 101, 215, 220, 222-223, 227, 230, 253
Century International Arms, St. Albans, Vermont, 204, 212
  L1A1 Sporter, 203
CETME (Centro de Estudios Técnicos de Materiales Especiales), 67-69, 89, 92, 163
Chad, 68, 76

Chartered Industries, 163
Chauchat Model 1915 machine rifle, 181
Chile, 80, 130
Choate Machine and Tool Corporation, 142
Ciener rimfire conversion kits, 12
Colombia, 76, 113, 159
Colt, 101, 168
  ACR, 97
  CAR 15, 76, 189
  Double Eagle, 54-57
  M1911A1/Government Model, 13, 19, 41, 46, 54, 59, 186
  Match Target HBAR, 121
  Model 231, 147-148
  Model 1911, 10, 12, 150
  9mm submachine gun, 145
  SM177E "Commando," 73
  Stainless Steel Pistol (Model SSP), 44
Congolese Republic, 68
Contraves Brashear Company, Pittsburgh, Pennsylvania, 101
Cooper, Jeff, 252
Cyprus, 76
CZ, 40
Czech vz 52, 14
Czech vz 58, 88

D

D.C. Industries, Bloomington, Minnesota, 204, 212
Delta Force, 168
Denmark, 68, 76, 130
Djibouti, 68, 76
Dominican Republic, 68, 76
DS Arms, 213
DUX Model 53, 123, 126
DWM, 13
Dynamit Nobel, 94, 95, 100

E

EBO (Elleniki Biomichanika Opion), 205-207
EFL (Emergency Flare Launcher), 175-176, 180
El Salvador, 76, 80, 130
Eltro-Zeiss image-intensifying sight, 193
Energa rifle grenade, 181, 190
Enfield Model 1917, 116
Equatorial Guinea, 68
Ethiopia, 76

F

FABARM (Fabbrica Bresciana Armi S.p.A.), 215, 224-226, 243, 245-247, 249-250
  Black Lion, 246
  Black Lion Competition, 233
  Camo Lion, 228, 246
  Camo Turkey Lion, 240, 250
  Classic Lion series, 247, 250, 253
  FP-6, 229-232, 246, 249, 253
  Gold Lion, 226, 246
  Max Lion, 233, 246
  Red Lion, 224-226, 239, 246, 253

  Silver Lion Youth Model, 234-237, 245, 249, 253
  Sporting Clays Competition, 246
  Sporting Clays Lion, 228, 233, 246
  Ultra Camo Mag Lion, 250
  Ultra Mag Lion, 241, 250
Fabrique Nationale (FN), 84, 101, 126, 166, 168, 203
  double-action (FN DA), 44
  FAL, 64-67, 70, 73, 79, 91, 92, 117-118, 196, 199, 205, 213
  Fast Action, 44
  High Power, 19, 44
  Minimi, 163, 168
  Model 1910, 10
  NAG, 172
  SAFN rifle, 65
FALO, 172
FAMAS, 84, 118, 203
FBI (Federal Bureau of Investigation), 124, 132
Federal Arms Corporation, 204
Flare projectors, 175-176, 180
FMBP (Fabrica Military de Braço de Prata), 210
FN (*see*) Fabrique Nationale (FN))
Ford Aerospace and Communications Corporation, 168
Foreign Legion, 203
FPW (Firing Port Weapon), 144, 146-147
France, 130, 136, 199, 202-203, 246
Franchi, Luigi, SpA, 87, 215
  Model 502, 231, 234
  Model 612, 234
  SPAS-12, 242
  SPAS-16, 227

G

G1, 64, 66
G6, 170
G8, 159, 166
G8A1, 166
G41, 63, 191
G43, 63, 65
Gabon, 76, 202
Gal, Uziel, 126
Ghana, 76, 80, 130, 203
GIAT, 203
GIGN (Groupement d'Intervention de la Gendarmerie Nationale), 136
Glock
  Model 17, 48, 56
  Model 18, 142
  Model 26, 142
Golden State Arms, Pasadena, California, 103, 104
GPMGs (general-purpose machine guns), 154, 172
GR6, 170
Great Britain, 76, 87, 130, 136, 142, 145, 146, 199, 203, 205
Greece, 39, 77, 130, 159, 200, 205-207
Grenade launchers, 174, 179, 181-184, 186, 187, 190-191, 195
GrP (Grenade Pistol), 187
GSG-9 (Grenshutz-gruppe-9), 34, 136, 141, 142, 170, 193, 194
Guatemala, 68
Guyana, 77

H

Hague Convention, The, 26
Haiti, 77
Handguards, 183, 184, 193, 196-197
Handguns, 7-61
Harrington & Richardson, 13
Heckler & Koch (*see also* Benelli; FABARM)
    G3, 7, 11, 14, 32, 46, 62, 64, 66-83, 85-89, 91-93, 97,
       99-102, 105, 108, 111, 113, 117, 127, 129, 132, 139, 145,
       154-157, 159, 163, 164, 172, 175, 181, 182, 187, 191, 193,
       196, 197, 199, 200, 202, 203, 205, 210-213
    G3A1, 71-72
    G3A2, 72, 103, 210, 212
    G3A3, 66, 72, 74, 202, 203, 205, 207-213
    G3A4, 72-74, 203, 205, 207
    G3A6, 208
    G3K, 73, 117
    G3KA4, 72
    G-3 Millennium Sporter, 201, 204-206, 208, 209, 212, 213
    G3SG1, 74, 77-78
    G3 Zf, 77, 78
    G11, 84, 86, 90, 92-97, 100, 101, 170, 223, 227
    G36, 93, 96-98, 100, 119, 121, 171
    G36K, 171
    G41, 86-88, 101, 145, 196
    G41A2, 86
    G41A3, 86
    G41 INKAS, 87, 193-194
    G41K, 86, 87
    G41 TGS, 86
    G41 Zf, 87
    GeA4, 208, 212
    GR3, 87-88
    GR3CA2, 88
    GR3CA3, 88
    GR3KC, 88
    GR3KS, 88
    GR3SA2, 88
    GR3SA3, 88
    HK4, 7, 10-13, 37
    HK11 series, 88, 159, 166, 170, 173
    HK12, 88, 170
    HK13 series, 160, 170, 173
    HK21 series, 88, 153, 155-159, 160, 164, 170, 172-173, 175,
       191, 200, 211
    HK21A1, 153-156, 161, 162, 165, 166, 168, 169, 208
    HK21E, 155-158, 180
    HK22, 88
    HK22A1, 170
    HK23 series, 160, 163, 170, 173, 191
    HK23A1, 168
    HK23E, 163, 170
    HK32, 88
    HK32A1, 88
    HK32A2, 88
    HK32A3, 88
    HK33 series, 74, 79-80, 82, 84, 85, 87-89, 92, 104, 106, 109,
       110, 113, 181, 182, 196, 197, 200, 203, 205, 211
    HK33A2, 77, 80, 81, 82
    HK33A3, 80
    HK33E series, 80-82
    HK33K, 80, 82, 86, 87
    HK33KA1, 86
    HK33 SG1, 82
    HK33 Zf, 82
    HK36, 92
    HK41, 82-87
    HK53, 80, 117, 144-146, 151, 208
    HK69, 187
    HK79, 86
    HK91, 46, 74, 85, 102, 104, 105, 107-108, 110, 121, 196,
       206, 213
    HK91A2, 103, 105
    HK91A3, 105
    HK93, 108, 109-110, 121
    HK93A2, 106
    HK93A3, 108
    HK94, 109, 110, 112, 121, 196
    HK94A2, 112
    HK94A3, 110, 112
    HK270, 114-115
    HK300, 115-116, 121
    HK630, 114, 121
    HK770, 112-114, 116, 121
    HK940, 115-117, 121
    HK940K, 116, 117
    Mark 23, 17, 23, 33-35, 42, 43, 45-61, 195
    M911, 107
    M1014, 167, 251-253
    MP4SD, 135, 136
    MP5, 110, 112, 127-132, 141, 142, 144, 145, 147, 148, 151,
       175, 191, 200, 209
    MP5A1, 129
    MP5A2, 123, 129
    MP5A3, 126, 129, 149
    MP5A4PT, 148
    MP5A5PT, 148
    MP5K, 28, 36, 46, 47, 125, 134-141, 149, 151
    MP5KA1, 135, 138-139
    MP5KA4, 133, 139
    MP5KA5, 139
    MP5K-PDW, 138-143
    MP5PT series, 148
    MP5SD, 124, 125, 130-132, 134-137, 141, 145, 197
    MPSSD1, 151
    MP5SF, 132
    MP55D3, 149
    MP55D5, 149
    MP5/10, 124, 127, 128, 132-133
    MP5/40, 129, 133-134
    MSG 3, 79
    MSG 90, 79, 100, 106, 108, 180
    P2A1 flare pistol, 176, 180, 186
    P7, 20, 21, 24-27, 47, 175, 195
    P7A13, 29, 30

P7K3, 16, 28, 37
P7K7, 37
P7M7, 31, 38
P7M8, 25-27, 36-39
P7M10, 17, 37
P7M13, 25, 27, 30, 37, 39, 46
P7M45, 38
P7PSP, 25, 38
P9/P9S series, 11, 12-15, 32, 44-45, 47, 118-20, 127
PSG-1, 78-79, 100, 107-109, 180
PSP/P7, 8-10, 12, 15, 18, 19, 27, 29-32, 34, 36-41
SABR, 100-101
69A1 grenade launcher, 180
SL-6, 111, 113, 121
SL-7, 111-113, 121
SL-8, 118, 119
SL8-1, 98, 120-121
SP89, 36-39, 46-47, 61
SR9, 102, 104-108, 121, 211, 212
  TGS (Tactical Group System), 186, 187, 190
  UMP45, 147, 148, 150-151
  USP9, 23, 48
  USP9 Compact, 42, 48, 57, 60
  USP40, 22, 40, 48, 59
  USP40 Compact, 50, 51
  USP45, 22, 42, 48, 55, 56, 58, 70
  USP Expert, 49
  USP Match, 49
  USPO, 16
  USP series, 35, 47-52, 61, 195
  USP Tactical, 48-49
  VP70, 14, 20-21, 25-28, 44-45, 56
  VP70M, 26
  VP70Z, 26
  Aiming Point Projector, 189, 194
  BASR, 119-120
  CAW (Close Assault Weapon), 101, 215,
    220, 222-223, 227, 230, 253
  EFL (Emergency Flare Launcher), 175-176, 180
  handguards, 183, 184, 193, 196-197
   multipurpose sling, 177-178, 191, 196
   triggerguards, 188, 197
Heckler & Koch, Inc., 104, 107, 110, 112, 119, 234, 243
Heritage Stealth, 32
Heym, Friedrich Wilhelm, 120
Heym, F.W. GmbH, 120
Heym Express, 120
Heym rifle, 244
Honduras, 130, 136
Hong Kong, 130
HTIP (High Temperature Ignition Propellant), 95

I

Iceland, 130
Indonesia, 77
Ingram Model 10, 150
INKAS system, 87, 193-194

Insight Technologies, 58
Iran, 77, 130, 200, 207-208
Ireland, 80, 146
Israel, 126
Italy, 87, 130, 136, 163, 234
Ithaca Acquisition Corporation, Kings Ferry, New York, 243
Ithaca Model 37, 250
Ivory Coast, 77, 202

J

Japan, 130
Japanese Type II machine gun, 170
Johnson, Melvin, 112
Joint Services Combat Shotgun (JSCS), 215, 250-253
Joint Services Small Arms Program (JSSAP), 41, 45, 215, 220, 222-223, 227, 251, 253
Jordan, 77, 159

K

Kampfpistole "Battle Pistol," 183
Kästner, Günter, 93
Kenya, 77, 130, 159, 203
Ketterer, Dieter, 93
Knight's Armament Company, Vero Beach, Florida, 45, 54, 57
Kuwait, 130, 136

L

L85A1, 118
LAM (Laser Aiming Module), 58
Lebanon, 77, 80, 202, 203
Lebel Model 1886 rifle, 181
Libya, 77
Ljungman (AGB-42), 65, 211
Lower Saxony, 34
Luxembourg, 130

M

M1, 165
M1 Carbine, 232
M1 Garand rifle, 63-65, 71, 116, 163, 197, 205, 212
M1 Thompson, 163
M2 Carbine, 163
M3, 150, 208
M3A1 "Grease Guns," 148
M3 submachine gun, 163
M4 Carbine, 73
M7, 182
M9, 29, 39, 41, 42, 44-46, 52, 53, 143
M11, 52, 53
M14, 83, 91, 92, 163, 164, 174, 197, 213
M14Volksgewehr VG1-5, 32
M15, 163, 172
M16, 73, 76, 79, 98, 145, 187, 213, 227
M16A1, 83-85, 184, 186, 195, 197
M16A2, 80, 89, 97, 141
M16/AR-15, 133, 146
M60, 162-164, 172, 173, 183

M79 grenade launcher, 174, 179, 183, 184, 186, 187
M193, 84, 165, 168
M196, 168
M203 grenade launcher, 89, 184, 186, 187, 195
MG3, 154-155, 172
MG34, 154, 173
MG42, 154, 163
Machine guns, 79, 88, 152-173
Magnum Express series, 244
Malawi, 77
Malaysia, 77, 80, 159, 208
Manufacture Nationale d'Armes de Saint-Etienne (MAS), 202-203
Manurhin, 12, 13, 202
Maremont Corporation, 168
Mars Equipment Corporation, Chicago, Illinois, 69
MAT-49, 129
Mauritania, 68, 77, 202
Mauser-Werke, 67, 101
  Model 98, 63, 120, 197
  Model 1896, 211
  Model HSc, 7, 10, 12, 13
  Model HsP, 307
Maxim machine gun, 154
Mean Rounds Between Stoppages (MRBS), 27, 44-46
Mecar Company, 183-184, 190
Mexico, 77, 130, 146, 159
Micro-Uzi, 28
MICV (Mechanized Infantry Combat Vehicle), 146-147
Military rifles, 63-101
Mitch Rosen Extraordinary Gunleather, 39-40
Möller, Tilo, 93
Montefeltro rotating bolt system, 223, 224, 240, 242
Morocco, 77, 130, 159, 202
Mossberg, O.F., Company Model 500, 215, 216, 222
Model 590, 215, 216, 222, 227, 250-252
MP-38, 130
MP-40, 130, 137, 209
Multipurpose sling, 177-178, 191, 196
Munich Olympic Games (1972), 29, 126

N
NATO (*see* North Atlantic Treaty Organization)
Nazi Germany, 63, 66, 67, 83, 126
Netherlands, 80, 130, 136
New Zealand, 130
Niedersachsen, 34
Niger, 77, 130, 159, 202
Nigeria, 77, 130, 159, 203
NOCS (Nucleo Operativo Centrale di Sicurezza), 136
North Atlantic Treaty Organization (NATO), 41, 64, 65, 67, 72, 79, 82-85, 87, 93, 95, 97, 98, 155, 163, 164, 212
  Army Armaments Group, 83
  Small Arms Test Control Commission, 83
Norway, 68, 77, 130, 200, 208-209

O
OICW (Objective Individual Combat Weapon), 100
Olin cartridges, 223, 227
Operations Desert Shield and Desert Storm, 211

P
Pakistan, 68, 77, 130, 200, 209-210, 212
Parabellum ("Luger"), 10, 13, 235
Paraguay, 77
Peru, 77
Philippines, 77
Phillips Elektro-Spezial BM-8028, 193
Picatinny Arsenal, 212
Portugal, 68, 77, 80, 200, 210-211
PPSh-41, 130
PSO-1 telescopic sight, 192

Q
Qatar, 130, 159, 203

R
Rall, Dieter, 96
Remington
  Model 10, 250
  Model 11, 250
  Model 31, 250
  Model 700, 120
  Model 870, 250
Rodman Laboratory, 268
Rosen, Mitchell, 39-40
Royal Ordnance plc, 101, 205
Royal Small Arms Factory (RSAF), 203, 205
RPD machine gun, 88, 164
RPK machine gun, 88, 164, 172
Ruger, 40

S
SABR (Selectable Assault Battle Rifle), 100-101
S.A.C.O., 104
St. Lawrence Sales, Lake Orion, Michigan, 243
SAMP (Small Arms Master Plan), 227
S*A*T*S*, 119
Saudi Arabia, 77, 130, 136, 211
Sauer Model 38H, 15
Savage Model 720, 251
Savage/Stevens Model 77E, 250
SAW (Small Arms Weapons Study) program, 163-166, 168
Seidel, Alex, 7
Senegal, 80, 146, 159, 202
Shotguns, 214-253
SIG
Model 540, 203
  Model 550, 98
  P210, 39 P210 9mm Parabellum, 12
  P225, 12, 30
  P228, 52
  P239, 48
Sights, 191-195
Singapore, 130, 136
SKS, 88
Smith & Wesson, 45
AS (Smith & Wesson), 227

Index   **287**

Model 459A, 44
Model 638 Bodyguard, 19
Sniper rifles, 77-79, 82, 87, 159
Somalia, 77
South Africa, 77
Spain, 80, 130
Special Air Services (SAS), 76, 87, 136, 142, 146, 203
Sporting rifles, 103-121
Springfield Armory, 205
  Model 1903, 116
  SAR-3, 198, 199, 206, 207, 213
  SAR-8, 198-203, 207, 210-213
Sri Lanka, 130, 159
"Starlight" scope, 193
Star Model 28, 44, 45
Sten, 130
Sterling submachine gun, 129, 130
Stevens Models 520 and 620, 250
Steyr GmbH, 97
  AUG rifle, 87, 118, 170, 211
  Model GB, 32
StG45/CETME/G3 series, 152, 155
Stoner, Eugene, 98
Submachine guns, 122-151
Sudan, 77, 130, 159
Sudayev Model PPS43, 123
SVD nipper rifle, 192
SVT-38, 65
SVT-40 "Tokarev," 65
SWAT teams, 137, 190, 195
Sweden, 68, 77, 156, 159, 200, 211
Switzerland, 80, 130

T

Tanzania, 77, 80, 203
Taurus, 40, 41
TGS (Tactical Group System), 186, 187, 190
Thailand, 80, 130
Thompson, 130, 145, 148, 150, 163
Togo, 77
Tomark Industries, 119
TRADOC (U.S. Army's Training and Doctrine Command), 166
Triggerguards, 188, 197
Tripods, 170, 172
Turkey, 77, 130, 200, 212

U

Uganda, 77, 159
Ultimax, 163
United Arab Emirates, 77, 146, 163
United States, 27, 33, 37-39, 41, 42, 44, 46, 49, 51, 58, 77, 80, 82-83, 97, 100, 108, 110, 130, 134, 136, 141, 146-148, 156, 163-166, 168, 187, 215, 250-252
United States Army Armaments Research Development and Engineering Center (ARDEC), 251

United States Bureau of Alcohol, Tobacco and Firearms (BATF), 37, 47, 104, 198, 206, 213
United States Drug Enforcement Agency (DEA), 50-51, 145
United States Navy SEALS, 19, 58, 77, 80, 89, 92, 137, 141
United States Navy's Naval Weapons Support Center, 141
United States Navy Surface Warfare Center, Crane, Indiana, 56, 58
United States Special Forces, 73, 77
Upper Volta, 202
Uruguay, 130, 136
USRAC, 203
USSOCOM (Special Operations Command), 52, 54-56, 58
UTL (Universal Tactical Light), 58
Uzi submachine gun, 126, 130

V

"Vampir" unit, 192
Vekktor pistol, 32
Venezuela, 130, 136
Vietnam War, 79, 84, 163, 164, 174, 179, 183, 184, 250
Vivens-Bessières (V-B) grenade launcher, 181

W

Walther
  MPL/MPK series, 126
  P1, 18, 30
  P5, 12, 30
  P38 series, 10-12, 15, 18, 19, 30, 36, 202
  P88/P99 series, 39
  PP/PPK series, 10, 12, 15, 29
  PP Super, 31
  Wk361 "Modell Heer," 182
West Germany, 12, 18, 19, 29-31, 34, 63, 66, 69, 71, 72, 79, 84, 86, 90, 92, 93, 95, 96, 122, 126, 127, 129, 136, 142, 157, 159, 194, 202
Winchester
  Model 12, 250
  Model 97, 250, 251
Wössner, Ernst, 93

X

XM9, 29, 39, 41, 42, 44-46, 56
XM231, 147
XM723, 146
XM777, 84

Y

Yugoslavia, 130

Z

Zaire, 77, 130, 203
Zambia, 77, 130, 203
Zimbabwe, 77